SOMETHING beautiful
A NOVEL

KAIT WEAVER-SMITH

Copyright © 2023 by Kait Weaver-Smith

All rights reserved. No part of this publication may be reproduced, stored or transmitted in any form or by any means, electronic, mechanical, photocopying, recording, scanning, or otherwise without written permission from the publisher. It is illegal to copy this book, post it to a website, or distribute it by any other means without permission.

This novel is entirely a work of fiction. The names, characters and incidents portrayed in it are the work of the author's imagination. Any resemblance to actual persons, living or dead, events or localities is entirely coincidental.

First edition

To Nick

Thank you for being my something beautiful.

"Find someone who grows flowers in the darkest parts of you."

- Zach Bryan

Content Warning

Something Beautiful addresses sensitive themes that may be distressing to some individuals. The narrative delves into the profound emotional landscape of spousal death, grief, and the intricate journey of healing. There is also brief mention of suicide. Additionally, please be advised that the book contains sexually explicit material. We understand the importance of self-care and respecting personal boundaries, so if you find any of these themes distressing, we recommend exercising discretion or considering whether this book aligns with your current emotional well-being. If you have concerns or need support, don't hesitate to reach out to appropriate resources. Your well-being is our priority.

SOMETHING *beautiful*

THE OFFICIAL PLAYLIST

Spotify

Apple Music

Contents

Chapter 1	1
Chapter 2	5
Chapter 3	11
Chapter 4	23
Chapter 5	33
Chapter 6	42
Chapter 7	47
Chapter 8	56
Chapter 9	61
Chapter 10	67
Chapter 11	75
Chapter 12	80
Chapter 13	88
Chapter 14	96
Chapter 15	101
Chapter 16	109
Chapter 17	119
Chapter 18	129
Chapter 19	140
Chapter 20	152
Chapter 21	158
Chapter 22	164
Chapter 23	171
Chapter 24	181
Chapter 25	189
Chapter 26	201

Chapter 27	214
Chapter 28	224
Chapter 29	236
Chapter 30	247
Chapter 31	257
Chapter 32	268
Chapter 33	277
Chapter 34	282
Chapter 35	290
Chapter 36	296
Chapter 37	303
Chapter 38	309
Chapter 39	318
Chapter 40	324
Chapter 41	332
Chapter 42	337
Chapter 43	342
Chapter 44	347
Chapter 45	356
Chapter 46	366
Chapter 47	376
Chapter 48	384
Chapter 49	389
Chapter 50	395
Epilogue	405

Chapter 1

Olivia

"Marry me."

The theoretical record player in my mind scratched to a stop, and the ambient noise of our Saturday in bed dissipated. The hum of our air conditioner and the laughter from the sitcom playing on the TV—gone, making it painfully obvious how fast my heart was thumping in my chest.

I gaped at Liam, the dumbfounded look on my face challenging the relaxed expression on his.

Married? This man was out of his mind.

He chuckled softly, pulling my body closer to his. "Marry me."

"Oh. Okay," I managed to say, my voice tinged with disbelief. "So, I didn't imagine that."

"No, Livie, you didn't." His lips stretched into that lopsided grin that I loved so much, and the swarm of butterflies in my stomach swooped into my chest, making my pulse flutter.

He was being serious.

"Liam, *what?* We're eighteen."

"And I've wanted to marry you since we were sixteen."

"Everyone will think I'm pregnant."

"Are you?"

I huffed, torn between the urge to laugh and the weight of the situation. "No! Maybe. I don't know! *No!* That's not the point!" I sat up, yanking the comforter up over my bare chest. "What is– Why are you— What is happening right now?"

There was no way that he was seriously asking me to marry him.

We were way too young. Our high school graduation was two months ago. We were only living in this house because his parents lent us the money for the down payment. Of course, I loved him with my whole heart, and there was no doubt in my mind that he was my forever person, but eighteen was entirely too young to get married... *Right?*

Evergreen, Wyoming was home to two thousand nosy-ass people. The whispers and speculation about why we were rushing things would fly through this town before the ink on our marriage certificate dried.

"I love you," Liam said, his voice soft but persistent. "I want to spend the rest of my life with you. I don't care what anyone else thinks. This town can talk all it wants, but it won't change how I feel."

My lips parted with a sharp breath as I struggled to collect my thoughts. The answer should be easy. It was easy. But did he not worry about what others would say?

Liam chuckled at the shocked look on my face. "Come here. *Please.*"

I fell back into his arms, my gaze locked onto the man I loved. His green eyes flickered with amusement.

"You okay?"

I somehow managed a weak nod.

"Olivia, babe. Listen." He softly caressed my cheek, his thumb tracing the length of my cheekbone. "I love you. I wasn't kidding, and I'd marry you right now if you wanted. But if it's not what you want, I'll wait. I'm planning on spending the rest of my life with you. Whether it's next month, next year, or fuck– the next decade that we get married, I don't care. I'll wait."

His lips ghosted over mine. "I mean it. There's no rush. I don't know. When you know, you know, right?" He paused, a hint of vulnerability in his eyes, as he swallowed hard. "I know. I've *known.* You, this– *Us.* It's for life. Whether you have a ring on your finger or not."

Liam's conviction didn't waver with my silence.

An amused smile tugged at his lips. "I was just thinking, who doesn't love gifts and a big party?"

I let out a watery laugh, snuggling closer to his bare chest as my eyes flooded with tears. "You mean it?" It felt silly to ask the question. I didn't need to.

Liam never said anything he didn't truly mean, especially when it came to his feelings about me.

I'd never met someone so confident in himself and his emotions. He told me two weeks after our first date that he was falling in love with me. Two weeks later, he told me he was, in fact, head over heels. He didn't expect me to say it back; he made that very clear, but the second he so confidently said, 'I'm in love with you,' the words flew out of my mouth almost instantly. *Of course,* I loved him. How could I not?

"About the gifts and the party?" He shrugged and cracked a smile when I reached over and slapped his shoulder. "Of course, I mean it. I've never been so sure about anything."

"We're eighteen."

His lips twitched as he held back a smile. "Correct."

"My mother will throw a fit."

He ran his tongue over his teeth, considering my words before replying, "Also correct."

I pulled away just enough to meet his gaze, "Okay, yeah. Yes."

A slow smile spread across his face. "Are you sure?" His grin faltered for a moment. "I don't want you to feel pressured; there's no pressure. Truly. We can–"

I cut him off with a kiss, one that bloomed something so beautiful and warm in my chest. Liam's hand settled on my lower back as he pulled me closer. "I mean it, I'm so sure. I want to marry you, Liam Brooks."

He rolled away from me, rummaging through his discarded clothes before sitting up and facing me. "I was planning on doing this in a much more romantic way."

Liam smiled, rolling his shoulders as he unclasped his hands and presented me with a tiny black box. "Olivia Claire, will you marry me?"

I laughed, shaking my head in disbelief. "How long have you been carrying that around?"

"Can you answer my question first?" he demanded, quirking an eyebrow.

"Yes!" I answered, throwing my arms around his neck. His shoulders relaxed, his arms winding around my waist.

His lips grazed my throat, leaving a gentle kiss that sent my pulse fluttering. "I love you."

"I love you, too, Li."

That boyish, lopsided grin was back when he pulled away. My heart tugged at the way his hands trembled when he reached for mine.

Tears welled in my eyes as a beautiful solitaire ring slid into place on my left ring finger. "When did you get this?"

Liam chuckled, toying with the ring as he looked down with nothing but pure adoration in his eyes. "The week after graduation," He answered truthfully. "I had a whole thing planned. There's even a custom fortune cookie hidden in the closet. Thought we could add it to the collection. But I couldn't wait."

"You were going to propose to me with a fortune cookie?"

His cheeks flushed an adorable shade of pink, and *god,* I wanted a picture of this moment. "I just— You know, it's how I asked you to prom. And we've saved all of them ever since. I thought it would be… cute." Liam's thumb traced the curve of my bottom lip.

"It would've been perfect; *this* was perfect. Everything with you will always be perfect," I reassured.

He tilted my chin and caught my lips in a gentle kiss. "You are my forever person, Olivia."

Chapter 2

Olivia

Ten Years Later

"Mommy?" Kennedy's soft, sleepy voice ripped through my daydream, snapping me back into reality.

I stood up straight and cleared my throat, swiping at the tears on my cheeks. "Shit." I turned off the faucet, pulled the plug, and let the water drain. I'd been so lost in my thoughts that the sink had overflowed.

"Yes, honey?" I asked, clearing my throat again, hoping to lessen the strain pulling my vocal cords taut.

Kennedy giggled from behind me, her little foot splashing in the small puddle dripping onto the linoleum. "You kind of made a mess."

"Yeah, I did, didn't I?" I smiled at her amusement, snagging one of the rags from the oven door to clean up the mess.

She stared at me with those big, green eyes—Liam's eyes— and smiled wide before kicking a little splash of water my way.

I was so jealous of her innocence.

Even after I tried my hardest to explain what happened with Liam, the next day, she was… fine. She said she understood that Daddy wasn't coming home and that she'd miss him. And that was it.

I longed for that kind of acceptance.

To miss him occasionally instead of constantly. To ache briefly when I was reminded that he was no longer here instead of spending my days treading water and gasping for air.

It'd been a year. A year and two months.

Even after moving across the country from Evergreen, Wyoming, to the small town of Rose Hill, Delaware, I couldn't escape the constant pain.

I couldn't breathe in Evergreen. It was already suffocating enough when I was happy, and driving past that fucking red light *every single day* was too much. *One* person was holding me to that tiny town in the middle of Wyoming, and now that he was gone, so was I.

The decision to leave was sudden and impulsive, and it pissed everyone off. But two weeks ago, when I drove past that intersection to get Kennedy from preschool, the shimmer of a broken headlight on the side of the road taunted me, and I knew it was time to go. No one would help me. After so many months of screaming into the void, I did what was best for my daughter and me.

I gave her a little splash back, smiling at the belly laugh that shook her body. She stomped in the water again, splattering droplets onto the cabinets and my shirt, making me laugh, too.

After wiping up the mess, I scooped her into my arms and held her close, resting her on my hip. It wouldn't be long until she no longer let me hold her like this. My heart broke a little at the thought.

My index finger poked into her ribs, another smile forming on my lips when she threw her head back, laughing.

"I thought I put you to bed, missy?"

She shrugged, snuggling her little face into the crook of my neck. "I wasn't tired."

I laughed and shook my head knowing she was knocked out before her head hit the pillow over an hour ago.

I walked toward her new bedroom, maneuvering around the still-packed boxes in the hallway, ignoring the sense of inadequacy that settled in my chest.

If Liam were here, these would've been unpacked and recycled the day we moved in.

But instead, they sat in the hallway, slowly being unpacked when the need for an item inside arose. It was the best I could do right now.

I carried Kennedy into her room, gently setting her on the bed after pulling the covers back. She wasted no time climbing in and yanking the blanket to her chin.

"Mommy?"

"Yeah, baby?"

Smoothing down the fabric of her princess blanket, I gently tucked her in. It wasn't until I leaned in to kiss her forehead that I saw the tears in her eyes and the quiver in her lip.

"What's wrong?"

She sniffled, shrugging her shoulders. "I kind of wish Daddy was here to tuck me in instead."

If this were a year ago, that comment would've hurt in a different way. I would've tucked her in, called Liam while he was on his night shift at the hospital, and jokingly vented about how she loves him so much more than she loves me.

But I understood it now.

I would give *anything* for Liam to be the one tucking her into bed right now.

I took a deep breath, brushing her honey-blonde hair out of her face. "I know, baby. Me, too." The struggle to remain composed and strong while holding back tears was a fight I would lose. "I miss daddy, too."

"But he's not coming, right?" She asked softly, her voice breaking.

My lips pinched together as hot tears pricked at the backs of my eyes. I was so close to losing my composure. "No, honey. He's not. Remember what we talked about?"

I brushed my fingers through her hair again, her little eyelids fluttering with exhaustion.

"Daddy got hurt," she replied sleepily.

"Right. Daddy was in an accident, and he got hurt. You feel this?" I lifted her hand to my heart, allowing her to feel the steady rhythm thumping against her tiny palm.

She nodded.

"Well, when people are big and strong like me, you, and Daddy, our heartbeat means that we're alive. Right? And when Daddy was in his accident, his heart stopped beating. So instead of living here with us, he lives up here." I lifted my finger and tapped on her temple.

Her eyes widened, and I couldn't help but laugh. "He lives in *my brain?*"

"Your memories, Ken. Tell me, when you think of Daddy, do you see him in your mind?"

Kennedy closed her eyes real tight and nodded excitedly. "I do!"

"I see him in my memories, too. I see him holding my hand or lifting you onto his shoulders." I inhaled a shaky breath, taking a second to collect myself.

"So, whenever you miss him, you just close your eyes real tight, and he's right there. He'll *always* be right there. And if you ever feel like he's not, come find me, and we'll look at every picture we can find."

She smiled again, sleep slowly taking over, and again, I found myself jealous of her innocence.

I waited a minute until her breathing evened out, battling a storm of emotions the entire time.

This apartment was entirely too small. I couldn't lose it here. I couldn't grieve how I needed to in an apartment with walls composed of paper mache. As quietly as possible, I pushed through her bedroom door and contemplated my next move.

A sob ripped through my body, my hand immediately slapping over my mouth to muffle the noise. I made a beeline for the front door and threw it open, stepping into the carpeted hallway.

My knees gave out, and I hit the floor, letting my grief consume me in a way that it hadn't since that police officer showed up at my door. How could it still hurt so much? It'd been *over a year.*

How could I raise Kennedy to be strong and independent when I could barely get out of bed in the morning?

I leaned back against the apartment door and brought my knees to my chest. Every tear that I've held inside since we drove into Rose Hill streamed out of me as I sobbed on the floor.

How was this fair? What did I do to deserve this? What did Liam do to deserve this?

I was tired of not having the answers, tired of screaming questions into the void. Tired of begging for a reprieve that wouldn't come.

There was no one here to hold me together anymore. So I finally let it all go.

I cried. I cried until my legs fell asleep from the awkward angle I sat in. I cried until my throat was scratchy and raw, my chest aching from the sobs that had been trying to tear it in two.

I cried so hard that I missed the sound of my neighbor's door shutting and heavy footfalls coming to a stop in front of me.

"Are you okay?"

Oh my god.

My face flushed bright red as I scrambled to my feet, reaching for the door handle to escape this nightmare. "Oh, god. This is embarrassing. I'm so sorry." I pushed on the handle, and as if this night couldn't get any worse, it *fucking stuck.*

Something between a groan and a whimper left my lips. This was mortifying. And pathetic.

"I mean, I was just– Are you okay?" He asked again. It sounded as if he was trying to soften his voice, almost like he was uncomfortable with trying to comfort me. Even with the rough tone, there was still a genuine sincerity behind his words. Not just a mindless question asked out of obligation for the stranger losing her shit in the hallway.

At this point, Ken was bound to wake up. If my sobbing hadn't already scared her out of bed, my shoulder ramming into the old wooden door surely would've done the trick.

Finally, the handle loosened, and I shoved my way in, avoiding the eyes of this kind stranger.

"I'm okay. Sorry if I woke you or disturbed you." I swung the apartment door shut as soon as I cleared the threshold, hurrying inside and burying my face in my hands. *Oh god...*

If this place were anything like Evergreen, within two days, everyone would know about the pathetic girl in Rose Hill Apartments with a face as red as a fucking fire engine.

I groaned quietly again, throwing my head back against the wall.

Holding my breath, I waited for any indication that my meltdown stirred Kennedy from her sleep, but the apartment was quiet.

Too quiet.

And for just a moment, the mortification was gone, and the grief took over once again.

Little moments like this hurt the most.

The quiet in my life would never again be filled with faint footsteps and low whistles as Liam made his way through the house. I would never hear his laugh again. I would never see him smile again. He would never kiss the freckle on my wrist before he left for work at night.

The quiet of knowing that he was at work and coming home soon was so different from the quiet of knowing he would never walk through the door again.

The little moments that meant so much, that I remembered so vividly, would eventually fade in my mind as I grew older without my husband. Liam would be a ghost of the person I once knew and loved, and I would be living off of the memories we made instead of creating new ones.

We would never reach thirty together. I would never see his hair gray or the smile lines form around his eyes.

How was any of this fair?

I swiped at the drying tears on my cheeks, stopping in the bathroom to blow my nose before I opened the door to my new bedroom.

It was so small. So small and empty.

My queen-sized bed had been shoved into the corner just to fit in the room, and the boxes stacked against the wall thankfully covered the ugly yellow paint. A dresser from our old house was shoved into another corner, and that was all.

It smelled stale and nothing like the home I was used to. Nothing like *him*.

With no energy left to rifle through box after box for pajamas, I pulled back the covers and climbed underneath in jeans and a t-shirt.

I pinched my eyes shut and used the heel of my palm to massage the ache that lingered in my chest, wishing I could do *something* to ease the pain.

Anything.

Even if I could only have *one* day of being able to breathe normally, I'd take it.

Chapter 3

Olivia

As if I didn't embarrass myself enough last night, Kennedy woke me up this morning at six-thirty for a simple breakfast of eggs and toast, and I was already doing a horrible job.

It was a blessing and a curse that every little thing reminded me of Liam.

He would be getting home from work around this time, already in the kitchen whipping up something for the three of us. Liam was the true cook of the family. I was all too happy to sit on the bar stool and watch him roll up his sleeves and work his magic.

But instead, I got myself up and changed into a pair of leggings and one of Liam's band shirts. He had a massive amount of Pink Floyd merch for someone who never listened to their music. If I let my imagination take over, I could still smell his body soap and cologne.

I was in the middle of toasting some bread when a light knock sounded on my door. My stomach instantly dropped, thinking that amid my meltdown, someone called and complained to the landlord.

I couldn't get evicted already. We had nowhere to go. There was no way I could go back to Wyoming and face Deb or my parents. I could already hear their condescending tones while they gloated about being right. Maybe that wasn't the best reason for staying away, but it was going to work for now.

After turning the burner down, I wiped my hands with a rag and made my way over to the front door, easing it open just enough to get a view of the stranger standing on the other side.

"Hi?" I questioned, my brows furrowing together. She definitely wasn't my landlord.

Her dark copper hair was pulled up into a perfect messy bun, like the kind of bun you spend years trying to perfect only to do it on a random Wednesday while you're getting ready for bed. The stranger smiled awkwardly, wrinkling her nose like she hated the idea of human interaction before noon as much as I did.

She was pretty. Her face was short and round with defined cheekbones and a smattering of freckles. Her hazel eyes looked tired, dark circles underneath covered up by concealer.

"Hi." She let out an awkward laugh. "I know this is really weird, and I apologize in advance... But my brother is nothing if not persistent. My name is Avery; I live across the hall." She motioned vaguely to the hallway with her elbow, both her hands carrying coffee cups. "My brother said he saw you in the hallway last night when he was leaving, and you seemed... upset. He didn't wanna bother you, but he made me promise to check on you this morning."

I could feel my face heat with embarrassment– *Correction. My whole body* was beet red. As if it wasn't mortifying enough that one person saw me like that, he turned around and told his sister. Though it was sort of comforting that she didn't look put off by some lady prone to having complete mental breakdowns living across the hall from her. Must run in the family.

The less comforting thought: the whole town had to know by now. "Oh god. That's humiliating." I laughed nervously, though all I wanted to do was crawl into a hole and wither away. "I'm sorry if I woke you guys up. I have a four-year-old and I just needed a minute."

She shook her head. "Here, I got this for you." Her hand extended in my direction, freshly manicured nails wrapped around the white cup. "No need to apologize; I get it. I just wanted to make sure you were okay."

I smiled gently. This was the same small-town hospitality I was used to. "You know–" I paused and let out a humorless laugh. "I'm not. But I hope to be soon." I took a second, swallowing the knot in my throat.

Again, if this place were anything like Evergreen, if I didn't give her an explanation of what was going on, wild accusations and rumors would float around, slowly getting back to me.

"I'm recently widowed. I'm not from here, I'm sure you know that. And I have a 4-year-old who can't wrap her head around death, and I guess I can't either because I never thought I'd have to explain it to her alone." My nose burned with emotion, and tears formed in my eyes.

"I'm sorry. I don't mean to unload on you." I stopped what had the potential to be a long ramble she probably didn't want to hear that early in the morning, but I at least shared why we moved. Maybe now, no one would form their own conclusions about why I ended up in a small town in Delaware with no husband and a child.

Gossip was the bread and butter of any small town. When we got married at the courthouse ten years ago, everyone assumed I was eighteen and pregnant. Then it was cancer. Because why else would someone get married so young? It took people a long time to come to terms with the fact that Liam and I were simply in love.

Avery smiled at me, a sad smile that I knew all too well. One that was void of happiness but not warmth. One that was usually given in lieu of words, because what can really be said in a situation like this? I got it from everyone at the funeral.

Who was I kidding? I'd gotten it from everyone almost every day from the day Liam died until I packed our shit to move a year later.

"Don't apologize… I'm sorry, it sounds like you're going through a lot."

I nodded slowly at the understatement. "Yeah… A lot of changes in what feels like not a lot of time. But I needed a fresh start." Kennedy laughed somewhere in the living room, and I amended my statement. "*We* needed a fresh start."

She sipped her coffee, her cherry red nail tapping against the cup in thought. There was some knowing look in her eyes, her lips twisting to the side like she wanted to say something but didn't want to cross a line.

Were there any lines at this point that someone hadn't crossed? Something about losing a loved one just ripped the filters out of people's minds. It was like a free-for-all of shitty comments and well-wishes. If I heard 'everything happens for a reason' from one more person, I was going to lose it.

"Well," Avery paused, clearing her throat. "I know I'm just a stranger, but I'm here if you ever need to talk. I have a five-year-old. Eleanor. Nellie. She's with my mom this weekend, but normally, she's running around my apartment like a bat out of hell. So if you ever need a sitter or just someone for your little one to play with, we're just right across the hall." She smiled, gesturing to the door across the hall and two doors down. "Also, if it makes you feel any better, you're not the only one losing it in the hallway. These walls are thin, kids are never asleep when you think they are. Sometimes you need a good cry." Something passed over her expression, something tortured and knowing. I wasn't sure what it meant, but it gave me hope that maybe my breakdown was confined to the halls of this building instead of circulating through a game of small-town telephone.

"Thank you, Avery. For the coffee, too." I smiled back at her, unsure if I would take her up on her offer. But it wouldn't hurt to have a friend to know that maybe I wasn't the only one sorting through a clusterfuck of emotions. "Oh, I'm Olivia, and my daughter is Kennedy, by the way."

"It was really nice meeting you, Olivia. I look forward to meeting little Kennedy. And again, if you ever need to talk or if you ever need anything in general, I'm just a knock away! Even if you two just need a tour of the town." She waved and walked toward her apartment door.

I started to return to my apartment, then whipped around right as she opened her door. "Is anyone hiring?"

Avery turned back around, a pensive look on her face while she pondered my question. "Kent Automotive. I hear they might be looking for a receptionist or assistant of some kind. Someone to help keep the shop in order outside of working on cars."

"I know nothing about cars." I let out a small laugh, hoping she might offer something else.

But instead, she just shrugged. "I'm sure you'll do fine. Just... give them a call. Or swing by. The shop is just up the road. Let him know I sent you over. It's family-owned."

"Great, thanks. I'll check it out." I offered Avery a small wave as she disappeared into her apartment, then turned and walked back into mine.

I closed the door, sipping the coffee she handed me. It was bitter. It screamed 'small town.' A small town that lacked any coffee shop that wasn't attached to a gas station or a diner.

Smiling to myself, I made my way back to the kitchen, cursing under my breath when I found the egg on the stove burnt to a crisp.

This was why Liam did all the cooking.

I scraped off what I could into the trash and started on another one.

It was six-thirty in the morning, and I had already made a friend and would hopefully have a job by the end of the day. Kennedy started at her new pre-k on Monday, so I would just have to get through this weekend, and then hopefully, with the distraction of a steady job, I could breathe a little.

***

We strolled down the sidewalk on the way to the body shop, Kennedy skipping a little further ahead in her wool tights and long sleeve dress. I took out my phone to snap some pictures and send them to my family, trying to prove to Deb and my mom that we were happy. But ultimately, I decided against it.

If I sent a picture now, Deb would look up the temperature in Rose Hill and scold me for letting Kennedy leave the house like this. My parents, on the other hand, wouldn't even acknowledge the text. Jackson, my brother, would at least make an empty promise to call soon. But I knew it would never come.

It was hot and sticky, and while the temperature didn't differ too much from Evergreen, the air was different. I'd lived next to trails and mountains my entire life. Rose Hill was a small, rural town. Not that Evergreen wasn't, but the two had different definitions of rural.

Evergreen smelled like my childhood and days of playing in the rain, climbing trees, and getting lost in nearby trails.

Rose Hill smelled of rich soil, humidity, and unfamiliarity. It was also significantly smaller than our hometown, and I didn't think I realized just how much smaller until I pulled my car into the small gravel parking lot for the lone apartment complex in the town.

From town edge to town edge, Rose Hill was thirty-eight square miles. And most of it was corn fields, a large pond, and "downtown" Rose Hill: a tiny town hall building, the diner, Kent Automotive, a general store, a few small eccentric shops we hadn't explored yet, and a bookstore. Almost all of the houses were spread out behind the fields and tucked into heavily wooded areas along the outskirts of town. No one here had close neighbors.

I knew it would take me a while to settle in and feel comfortable, but right now, everything was strange and so vastly different from Evergreen.

Not that it was bad. It was just different. A good palate cleanser, I suppose.

We neared Kent Automotive, and my stomach twisted nervously. When I quit my job after Kennedy was born, I didn't plan on ever having another one. She *was* my job.

Without Liam, I didn't have a steady income. I'd already used most of the savings we'd built up to pay six months of rent upfront. And thanks to the disapproving voice of my mother-in-law that now lived in my head, I was constantly reminded of the fact that I needed to do *something* now that I was a single mother.

I could try and pass the blame off on Deb as much as I wanted, but truth be told, this was just as much something I needed to prove to myself as everyone else.

After taking a few deep breaths, Kennedy looked up at me with curious eyes. "What are we doing here?"

I wiped my sweaty palms against my jeans and tried to will the nerves away. It was just a job. More than likely, I wouldn't even need to know anything about cars. I could just sit and answer the phone, right? Easy.

"Mommy is gonna try and get a job," I answered, pushing the negative thoughts out of my brain.

There was no reason to psych myself out now. I didn't have another option, either. I *had* to work, and if this were the only place hiring, it would have to do.

Kennedy reached up to take my hand, tugging it softly. "Come on, it's hot. Can I get a milkshake when we're done getting a job?" she asked, eyeing the diner a few doors down.

I smiled down at her and shook my head. "Such a sweet tooth! But maybe later. It's still really early. Too early for sweets."

She sighed in response, the hopeful look on her face falling. I squeezed her hand and took another breath. Answering phones. That was all.

I pushed the door open, the bell overhead chiming to alert the small, empty lobby of my arrival. The rich smell of motor oil and gasoline filled my nostrils as I entered the room.

The one working overhead light flickered every couple of seconds like something out of a horror movie, shedding just a little light on the worn-down shop. The floor was scuffed and dirty with a clear path of what I could only assume was oil, starting at the front door and disappearing behind the old paneled desk. A couple of plaques on the walls named Kent Automotive the number-one shop in Rose Hill for four years running.

Was this town even big enough for more than one shop?

The walls, which I think started with a fresh coat of white paint, were now yellowing from lack of care or fumes. Or maybe both.

"You really wanna work here, Mommy?"

"Kennedy, shh!"

"It's dirty," she replied, her nose scrunching up while she surveyed the room.

She wasn't wrong. But I didn't need my only job opportunity in this tiny town stripped away before it was even offered because Kennedy didn't have a filter.

"Maybe I can clean it up." I shrugged, tugging her toward the desk just a few feet away. I tapped on the bell, but it, too, had fallen victim to the neglect of this tiny shop. Clearing my throat, I shifted nervously, peering around the desk to see if I could spot anyone toward the back.

"I don't think anyone works here," Ken whispered, stretching on her tiptoes to peer over the desk.

Just as I began to think the same thing, the front door whipped open so quickly that I half expected the glass to shatter when it connected with the drywall. I watched the large man step through the threshold, balancing a to-go box and two coffees in his hands while he used his foot to kick the door open wider.

He looked up from the floor, his hazel eyes meeting mine, and a brief look of surprise flashed over his features. "You here to get a car fixed?" the stranger asked, his gravelly voice breaking up the silence that filled the room.

For a second, I couldn't speak as I took him in. I'd been in love with Liam since high school and had never so much as looked at another man with interest since, but this stranger that stood in front of me was making it *impossible* not to.

He stood well over six feet tall, broad shoulders stretching out the plain gray t-shirt that hugged him like a second skin. The soft waves of his brunette hair were combed back and out of his face, and a light dusting of stubble lined his cheeks and jaw, shaping out the strong cut of his jawline.

My eyes swept over his face, a tinge of guilt digging at my chest when I admitted to myself just how handsome he was.

It felt wrong to admire someone else's beauty like this. Despite being extremely aware of the fact that Liam was dead and I was technically a single woman, I was still very much in love with him. And when in love with another person, ogling handsome strangers is typically noted on the 'don't' list.

The dim light from the lobby cast shadows over his muscular build, his biceps flexing against the thin material of his shirt while he adjusted his hold on the items in his hands. He was almost as dingy as the shop. Oil and god knows what else caked his hands and stained his clothes. There was even a smudge of black under his eye, like he was gearing up for the Super Bowl.

The blush slowly creeping up my neck made it very clear how aware I was that the question he asked still remained unanswered, but one look at him and the English language was lost to me.

Kennedy had it under control.

She cleared her throat, her tiny hand still wrapped in mine. "I'm Kennedy. We're here to get a job."

The corner of his mouth twitched as he held back a smile and stepped further into the room, the glass door swinging shut behind him. "Really? Both of you?"

Ken nodded, her shoulders pushed back and her head held high.

I peeled my eyes away from this man as he crossed the small room, also painfully aware that they'd lingered on him for a minute too long.

He stepped around the counter, setting his white plastic bag and two cups of coffee on top. "Well, I only have one to offer. So... you or her," he told Kennedy, quirking an eyebrow as he lifted one of the coffees to his lips and took a small sip.

She mulled it over for a second, releasing my hand so her index finger could tap against her chin. "I think maybe her. I don't think I can go to preschool and fix cars."

Sweet lord, this child.

I stifled a laugh, massaging my forehead with my fingers while this man entertained her train of thought.

"I was thinking the same thing."

Kennedy shrugged, her hands slapping against her thighs. "Maybe next year."

Another small smile formed on his lips. "Maybe." His eyes jumped from Kennedy's to mine. "So. A job?"

The nerves were back. And once again, they had nothing to do with the man standing before me.

"A job," I confirmed, wringing my hands together since I no longer had the comfort of holding my daughter's. Bored of the conversation, she strolled to the small trophy case and eyed the several plaques behind the glass doors. "I uh– Well, I don't know anything about cars," I laughed nervously, rocking back on my heels. "In fact, I haven't had a job in four years."

I let my gaze drift over to Kennedy and added, "But things have... changed, and I need something. My neighbor, Avery, sent me over. Said you might need some receptionist or shop assistant help? I used to work in an office before I had Kennedy. I– I know a lot about bookkeeping, and I'm good at organization... And cleaning," I added quietly, strongly resisting the urge to let my eyes wander over the grime caked on the floors, countertops... and basically every surface in this place.

I hated cleaning. *Loathed it.* Procrastination was my best friend when it came to household chores. But this? This was the perfect distraction. With Kennedy off to school in just a couple of days, I would be home alone in that shitty, stale apartment with nothing to do but unpack and wallow in my own grief.

Given the option of crying over one of Liam's old t-shirts for the five-hundredth time or cleaning someone else's floors, I would gladly choose the floors. I caved and let my eyes sweep over the shop again, taking in the job I had ahead of me. If there were as much to do as I thought there was, there would be little to no time for my mind to wander.

No time to mull over what-ifs. No time to realize just how unhappy or broken

I was.

When he died, it felt like most of me died with him, and there was no patching up the holes or stitching myself back together. I needed to figure out who this new, broken version of me was.

A person tossed into the middle of the unforgiving sea of grief, treading water and begging for reprieve.

"You got a name?" His eyebrow remained hitched, and the soft thud of the coffee cup on the counter brought my attention to the gold band on his left ring finger.

He was married.

Relief washed over me like a bucket of cold water, and I fucking hated it. Because for the first time since high school, I allowed myself to look twice at a man who wasn't my husband, and the guilt I had felt earlier increased tenfold. Whether I wanted to admit it or not, that gold band was my saving grace.

That gold band meant the line had already been drawn for me, and I wouldn't have to battle the storm of grief, guilt, and attraction that brewed within me. There was no room for temptation. Because he was married.

Sure, I was in need of a distraction, but not *that* kind of distraction.

I cleared my throat, scrubbing a hand down my face in hopes of making the blush burning at my skin less noticeable, but I was almost sure I brought more attention to it. "Olivia," I answered.

He grunted in response, toying with the lid of his coffee cup. "I can't offer much more than minimum wage. Garage is open nine to five, Monday to Friday," he said. His eyes shifted to where Kennedy stood, who, despite being unable to read, was currently enthralled by a framed newspaper article. "I'm assuming you'll need after-school help with the kid. Avery brings Nellie around three. She hangs out until Ave gets off of work. Your daughter is more than welcome, too, if your husband isn't around to help." His eyes flicked to the ring still on my finger before meeting my gaze again.

I really needed to stop wearing it so people would stop bringing it up. But that felt so... Final. And I couldn't bring myself to do it.

"Oh." I stared at him, my lips parted in surprise. "Are you sure?"

I couldn't tell if he either had no idea how helpful that option was or if he knew and wasn't planning on bringing any attention to it. I had no idea that when Avery said it was family-owned, she meant her and her husband.

And now I felt guilty because Avery had been so friendly to me this morning, and here I was drooling over her husband.

"Wouldn't offer it if I wasn't."

Fair. I would add 'conversational skills' to the list of things this place needed, but I was assuming that wasn't included on the list of job duties.

"Thank you," I breathed, overcome with a wave of emotion. This moment was the closest I'd gotten to happy tears in a long time. It felt good to finally get a win. "Does that– uh– Do I have a job then?"

He grabbed a pen from a plastic solo cup on the counter and began scribbling something onto a notepad in front of him, seemingly done with this conversation. "Yup."

This felt very anticlimactic.

Not that I was expecting confetti and a bottle of champagne, but an unenthusiastic 'yup' with no eye contact? *Come on.*

I pursed my lips, rocking back on my heels again. "Okay. Uh– When do I start?"

"Monday."

"Okay. Monday works," I nodded slowly, my eyes shifting nervously around the shop. "Okay, I'll um– I suppose I'll see you Monday." I turned to drag Kennedy away from her newspaper article, then realized he had never introduced himself. "Do *you* have a name?"

He spared a glance in my direction before looking back at the paper in front of him. "Noah."

"Okay, Noah. Thank you. See you Monday."

All I got was a nod and some kind of caveman grunt in response, so I took that as my cue to leave.

Don't get me wrong, the band on his finger was enough to tell me he's not available. But the blatant disinterest would've done the trick if his hand had stayed concealed behind his coffee. No matter, I didn't have to be friends with him. I came here for a job, and I got one.

I rushed over to Kennedy, grabbed her by the shoulders, and attempted to lead her out of Kent Automotive without another word. But of course, Ken couldn't stand for that. She was Liam's child after all. The Brooks in her always needed the last word.

"Oh, Mom! I have to ask him a question!"

I froze, just a few steps from freedom, and narrowed my eyes at my daughter. Part of me wanted to say "Fine." But the other part of me had no clue what was going to come out of her mouth ninety-nine percent of the time.

Noah stood up straight, tucking the pen behind his right ear, and crossed his large arms over his chest. "Ask away."

"Will my mom have to cook for you?"

"No," he answered, a hint of a smile on his lips. At least *someone* found her entertaining.

Kennedy's whole body seemed to relax. "Oh, that's good. She burned my eggs this morning. You do *not* want her to cook for you."

My cheeks burned a deep shade of pink. Though, technically, she wasn't wrong. I *did* burn her eggs this morning, and he certainly did not want me cooking for him.

I could count on both hands the number of times I've had to cook something on a stovetop in the past ten years. So I was a little rusty?!

"Okay, that's enough out of you," I said as I clamped my hand over her mouth, ignoring her when she stuck her tongue out against my palm. "Say goodbye to Mr. Kent!"

He stifled another laugh when she mumbled "Goodbye, Mr. Kent!" from behind my hand.

"Goodbye, Kennedy."

She grinned against my palm as I ushered her out of the door. Despite her announcing my cooking skills (or lack thereof) to my new boss, I left the auto shop with a huge weight lifted from my shoulders. Sure, it was just some receptionist work, and sure, I wouldn't be making a ton of money. But I was doing it. I was figuring this out.

All I had to do was get through the weekend.

One more weekend to let my mind and body mourn, and on Monday, I'd have a brand new project to occupy my mind, and then maybe, just maybe, I wouldn't feel so desperate for a breath of fresh air.

I could do this.

Chapter 4

Noah

I watched Olivia and Kennedy disappear out of the door, dragging my eyes away and back to the invoice sitting on my desk when the door swung shut.

She didn't recognize me. And she asked me for a job.

When I asked Avery to run her some coffee this morning, I should've known she wouldn't be satisfied with *just* that. Of course, my little sister had to meddle and give the girl a damn job. I had a feeling I knew what Ave's motives were, too, and that left a sour taste in my mouth. With the amount of meddling she'd been doing lately, I was starting to regret forcing myself back into everyday life in Rose Hill. I had been perfectly fine in that cabin surrounded by nothing but trees.

After Adeline died, every single thing in this town became nothing but an ugly reminder of the grief and guilt that threatened to buckle my knees every damn day.

I didn't have it in me to sell our house. Instead, I bought a cabin on the outskirts of town and lost myself in the wilderness. Addie's life insurance wasn't much, but it covered a life of solitude just fine. If I needed money, I'd come and live out of the garage for a week or two, earn my keep, and then disappear once more. And for three years, I was happy. Or at least whatever kind of happy someone with a vast, gaping hole in their chest could be. Numb might've been a better term to describe whatever the hell I was feeling.

Regardless, I was surviving, which was just about the only option I had since

I killed my wife. I didn't deserve anything more.

And then an incessantly sassy and demanding five-year-old showed up at my doorstep with her mother and begged me to come back. A visit to my parents once a year and the occasional video chat weren't enough.

I could sense everyone's worry; I even understood it. I lived in a secluded cabin, my beard was insanely grown out, and I was living off of microwave meals and cheap beer.

Avery did the one thing she could to get me to come back: she shoved Nellie in my face.

I stood there in my five-hundred-square-foot cabin and was berated by a four-year-old until I finally caved and agreed that the lifestyle I was living wasn't sustainable. I didn't have many weaknesses. But Nellie was one of them, and the second those hazel eyes filled with tears and the words 'I need my uncle Noah' came out of her mouth, I knew I was at her mercy.

It had been a year since then. A year since I had to face everything that I'd been hiding from and about nine months since my father's heart attack forced me to run the shop alone. I could feel the stares. Shit, I could see them. That's why my food from the diner was always "to-go" and why I never spent more than twenty minutes in a place with more than five people. I was pretty sure this tiny little town invented the saying 'if you give an inch, they take a mile,' because if I even so much as smiled politely in someone's direction, it invited them over, and I'd have to suffer through yet another conversation about my dead wife.

I wish that I could remember her as everyone else did. Her smile, her laugh, that long black hair that was always perfectly curled... it was all tainted now. They weren't there that night. These people might've grown up with us, but they didn't love her as I did. Sure, they might have mourned her loss, but they weren't drowning in it like I was. They didn't cause her death. I did. Every time I tried to focus on the good, the bad came back, rearing its ugly head, and I was sucked under by a riptide of grief.

I wanted to remember her laugh, but all I heard was her crying my name as we hung upside down, still buckled into our seats and barely hanging on to consciousness.

I wanted to remember her smile and the way my heart would skip a beat every time it was pointed in my direction, but all I saw was the blood painted on her lips as she cried in pain.

God, that hair. I wanted to remember what it felt like in my hands and how it smelled like peaches and summertime, but even that was stained red in my mind and so fucking painful to think about.

Yet every time I made eye contact with someone in public and offered the smallest of smiles, even after four years, the same few things were said. "How are you holding up?", "I just miss her so much," "This too shall pass," and "At least she's in a better place."

So I buried the person I used to be with my wife and reinvented myself as the town grump. I fixed cars, kept to myself, and shoved everything down until the pain was just bearable enough to get through the day.

I'd always had a love for cars. Any mechanic would probably say the same thing. For me, what started as the innocent curiosity of a bored, clueless kid being hauled into work with his dad every day over the summer quickly shifted into an obsession. The challenge, the satisfaction of solving something easy or complicated with my own two hands and knowledge of the machine sitting in front of me... No feeling could beat it.

I did a good job avoiding basically every other problem in my life. Getting under the hood of someone's car and figuring out why they brought it in the first place was the only source of conflict resolution in my life. Plus, for the most part, I didn't *have* to interact with people. The diner was just a couple buildings down, and no one liked to hang out in the dingy lobby of my shop with an equally dingy mechanic grumbling to himself in the garage.

Emoting was for the birds. And that mindset had been expressed to my sister many times, which was why I suspected her sending Olivia here wasn't completely innocent. Avery was meddling. *Again.*

I pinched the bridge of my nose, dug into the pocket of my jeans for my phone, and dialed my sister's number.

Her voice was muffled when she picked up. "I can't hear you, Ave. How many times have we talked about this? Move your finger." I chuckled, taking a sip of the black coffee sitting in front of me and waiting for her to sort her shit out.

There was more shuffling on the other end of the line before Avery spoke up again. "Hello. Good morning to you, brother. In case you forgot, your niece is the spawn of Satan in the morning. My finger placement on a damn cell phone is the least of my worries." She ended her sentence in a whisper like Nellie was just waiting to overhear this conversation.

"Shouldn't she be at school?" I asked, checking the clock on the wall. It was almost nine. She should definitely be at school.

"Listen here, Noah Kent. I don't need your back-sass this morning either. You come over here and tell her it's time to leave, and there's no time to sort through three loads of laundry to find her Peppa Pig socks."

I smiled, listening to Nellie whine in the background about how her day was ruined. She had used that same voice on me many times. She might only be five, but the kid's got emotional manipulation down pat.

"Ave, why did you send the neighbor here?"

She clicked her tongue while contemplating her answer. "You need a receptionist."

I rolled my eyes. Her answer was a partial truth, and she knew it. "I don't *need* a receptionist. I'm doing just fine."

"Your Google reviews say you don't answer your phone."

"I have one Google review, and it's from Sheila."

"I know. And it's two stars because you don't answer your office phone."

My eyes slid over to the black landline sitting on the desk, covered in a layer of dust. I chose not to let her know that I had unplugged it over a month ago. People in this town didn't call to get their cars fixed. They called to talk about Addie, and I was not interested in doing that during business hours (or any hours, really) with anyone but my sister.

"You're meddling, Avery."

She scoffed, her keys jingling in the background as she finally coaxed Nellie out of the house. "I am not! I talked to her this morning, she needed a job, and you need an employee. You're overthinking things."

My first instinct was to argue, but I knew this was one I couldn't win. We'd only done it a thousand times in the past year. She'd "introduce me" to someone I already knew with a hopeful smile that I absolutely obliterated every single time. I was not interested in dating. I wasn't interested in moving on. I knew everyone in this town, and Addie was the only one for me.

"She's married," I stated firmly.

I heard Avery take a breath as she closed her car door. "She– Well..." she paused to clear her throat. "It's not my business to tell."

What did that even mean? My sister was the queen of cryptic messages, and I had wasted too many years trying to figure them out. Either she gave me a straight answer, or I wasn't interested. And I was very much not interested in deciphering this one. "Okay, well, she's still married."

She sighed. "Look, I gotta run. Just– Please give her a chance. She really needs a friend right now."

"And *I* have to be that?"

"I didn't say that, you grump. Just take it easy on her. That's all."

Avery knew what she was doing. Saying *just enough* for my curiosity to grow without giving me any real answers. She was obviously new to town, she had a kid, and apparently, whether or not she was married was up in the air despite the rings on her finger. Not to mention the breakdown I had interrupted.

"Fine."

I could feel her rolling her eyes. "Was that too much to ask?"

I grunted in response, looking at the sticky note that had my jobs for the day scribbled onto it. Wallace needed his brake pads changed, Amanda needed an alignment, and Carson Jr. needed an oil change. Pretty easy Friday if you asked me.

"Hey, I'm taking Nell to mom and dad's tonight. You should go for dinner."

Going to my parent's house tonight would derail the plans I already had set in my mind: watching some shitty sitcom while I downed a pack of beer. Not to mention the way my Ma would steal worried glances all night, and my Dad would gripe about my appearance. I knew it was just him projecting his own thoughts and fears about his recent health scare onto me, but it was still hard to listen to. "Are *you* going?"

"Uh–" she paused, "Not tonight, I'm getting dinner a couple of towns over with... someone."

My eyebrows shot up, her hesitation piquing my interest. "Avery Kent. Are you going on a date?" She hardly ever corrected me on her last name anymore.

Technically, she never changed it back to Kent, but I refused to acknowledge the presence of that asshole anywhere in her life or Nellie's. As far as I was concerned, her last name was Kent.

I laughed at her flustered state, incoherent words sputtering out of her mouth while she tried to come up with a lie.

"I don't– Noah, that is– Why don't you just mind your own business?" she huffed. I could practically hear the blood rushing to her cheeks.

Normally, even the prospect of her meeting someone would kick my older-brother-protective-instinct into overdrive, but it had been a long few years for Avery.

Derek, her ex, was in and out of their lives for two years after Nellie was born, originally telling Avery he wanted nothing to do with her or the baby. But then he 'came around to the idea' and tried to be involved, only leaving her more exhausted and emotionally scarred when he started selling off her belongings for money.

I was happy to hear she was putting herself out there again. Derek officially terminated his rights after the divorce was finalized and hadn't shown back up since I paid him a pretty penny to disappear. She needed someone.

I took another sip of coffee while she rattled off more jumbled nonsense about why I should mind my own business before I cut her off. "Ave, I'm happy for you. I'm glad you're going out. You need it."

There was radio silence from her end of the phone for a few moments, and I thought we might have a sweet, endearing, brother-sister moment. Should've known better than that. "What the hell is that supposed to mean? 'I need it'? I'm perfectly capable of handling my own and going out when I want. Jesus Christ, *I need it.*" She scoffed, then continued mumbling under her breath as she started the car.

"I gotta go, asshole," Avery laughed softly. "If you went to the diner this morning, I hope your food is cold. Love you."

Chuckling, I pocketed my phone, snagged my to-go box from the counter, and headed toward the garage to start my day.

***

Monday rolled around entirely too soon, and my whole weekend was a blur of microwavable chicken nuggets and cheap beer from the convenience store. Against my better judgment, I did end up going to dinner with Nellie Friday night and left as quickly as I could, not being able to stand the way my mom's eyes filled with tears every time she looked at me or the way my dad kept reminding me that my fast metabolism wasn't going to last much longer.

I was thirty-four, for Christ's sake. The last thing I wanted or needed was my parents nagging at me the way that they did. If I wanted to spend the rest of my life chugging beer and getting fat, that's my prerogative. I knew I sounded like a damn teenager, but Avery nagged enough for all of them.

Just like I'd done every morning before work, I made a quick stop by the diner to grab something to eat, keeping my head down with a deep frown and stiff posture. Completely unapproachable. To everyone… Except Barb.

Barb was exactly the kind of woman you'd picture working in a small-town diner in a place like Rose Hill. She approached the counter from the opposite side, a cigarette tucked behind her ear, her pink lipstick just a shade too bright, thick black eyeliner under the waterline instead of on it. Her hair always reminded me of Dolly Parton. Sky-high, blonde, and curled.

I was used to the diner coming to a halt whenever I walked in, but it didn't make it any easier or any less embarrassing. There were always a few moments of awkward silence, followed by quiet whispers and not-so-subtle staring, but the second Barb grinned at me and called out my name like a long-lost friend, the diner snapped out of its catatonic state, immediately returning to their conversations. The small room was filled with the noises of people talking and eating, silverware scraping against plates, mugs, and glasses being set down and picked up from the tables.

Spectacle over. For now.

"Noah Kent." She beamed up at me, resting her elbows on the counter. "The usual?"

I nodded, offering a small, appreciative smile. "Thank you."

"Scrambled eggs, two sausage links, two pieces of wheat toast, and two coffees coming right up, baby." She rapped her knuckles against the counter before turning and disappearing into the kitchen.

I avoided looking around the diner, knowing that the second my gaze landed on someone, I'd get that stupid fucking half smile accompanied by furrowed brows and a head tilt that says 'Wow, that poor man.' So I swiveled away from the counter and leaned back on my elbows facing the front door, just in time to see Olivia pass by with what looked like her body weight in plastic bags from the convenience store.

I watched her struggle for probably a second too long, one of the bags slipping from her grip and falling to the sidewalk. She took a deep breath and pursed her lips, her eyes flickering from the ground to the direction she was heading. It was eight-thirty, so a little early for her to be heading into the shop, but I wasn't sure where else she would be going. The apartment complex was in the opposite direction.

"You gonna help her or just keep standing there useless?"

I kept my back turned to Barb and rolled my eyes, pushing off of the counter and walking out of the diner. Olivia turned to face me, her blue eyes widening almost comically.

"Oh– Hi."

I didn't give myself a chance to really look at her when she came in Friday. Sure, I saw her. Blonde hair, blue eyes. Seemingly average. But that was under the broken, dim light in the shop, and now that I stood with her face just inches from mine, I found myself guilt-ridden over how stunning she was.

She had a slim face with high cheekbones; her nose dotted with freckles and flushed a light shade of pink. Olivia pulled her bottom lip between her teeth, and my eyes fell to track the movement. She was beautiful.

My chest tightened at the revelation. It felt so fucking wrong.

Tearing my eyes away, I snagged the lost bag off of the sidewalk and stood up straight, eyeing the rest of them in her hands. I could feel Barb's eyes burning a hole into my back. My wife might've been dead, and I might've been *extremely* out of practice in the dating arena, but I still knew how to act like a damn gentleman.

"Can I– um– Here, let me help you." I reached down, grabbing the rest of the bags out of her hands. "Are you... Going to the shop with all of this?"

She swallowed, a slow blush crawling up her neck and painting her cheeks a darker shade of pink. The kind of pink that graced the sky during a perfect sunset and made the freckles on her neck stick out even more. Her fingers flexed as she tried to get some blood circulating through her hands again. "Uh– yes."

I eyed the bags, my brows furrowing. There were at least fifteen bags full of cleaning and office supplies. Did she buy all of this for the shop?

"I hope I didn't overstep. I uh– I stopped by the corner store and just got some stuff I thought I could use to clean up a bit and maybe organize. You know, get those pens out of the solo cup." She paused, chuckling nervously. It was almost cute how flustered she was. She palmed the back of her neck, "I'm sorry, this was so out of pocket. I shouldn't have–"

"It's fine." I didn't mean for my interruption to sound like a bark coming from a dog backed into a corner, but my social skills still had room to improve. I cleared my throat. "You shouldn't have spent your own money. There's petty cash in the shop. Just give me the receipt, and I'll reimburse you."

"Oh, you don't have to. I mean, you didn't ask for it or anything. I was just going to call it my treat." She shrugged her shoulders, a nervous smile spreading across her lips.

I didn't like owing people things. I especially didn't like the way my ribs seemed to shrink wrap around my lungs at the hopeful yet nervous look on her face. Olivia reminded me a little of Avery. She seemed to carry the weight of the world on her shoulders while giving no indication that it was slowing her down in the slightest.

I admired my sister for that.

But this feeling for Olivia didn't stop at just admiration. It pulled me to her. I didn't know her or her situation, but the tiredness I could see behind her eyes ignited an ember of protectiveness that hadn't burned since Adeline was alive, and I wasn't sure what to do with that besides feel guilty.

"I'll pay you back," I muttered under my breath, already feeling guilty at my tone. Avery insisted Olivia needed a friend right now, and I was sure my unnecessary grumpiness would only add to whatever stress brought her to Rose Hill in the first place. I rolled my shoulders to shake off whatever feeling this was and started toward my shop. She and Avery would be fast friends, and I had no intention of letting Avery assume that I was going soft for some disinfectant wipes and a pencil holder.

She would take that and run, I just knew it. Once that happened, I'd never be able to escape her meddling.

I shifted the bags to my left hand, digging into my pocket to grab my key, and Olivia was still standing in front of the diner. Even from here, I could see the blush in her cheeks, and her brows pinched together.

Dammit. Now I needed to apologize.

I didn't have to be her friend, but I wouldn't be able to sleep at night knowing I put that look on her face.

Chapter 5

Olivia

I stood on the sidewalk outside of the diner, watching Noah as he walked toward the shop with my haul from the convenience store in his hands, a tinge of guilt burrowing into my chest. He said I didn't overstep, but the deep-set frown on his lips led me to believe otherwise. I couldn't help but feel as if I'd done something wrong.

I realized now that it was extremely possible I offended him. I was so lost in the reverie of finally having a distraction that I didn't stop to think that showing up on my first day with bags full of cleaning and office supplies might rub him the wrong way.

And now I felt like shit. My cheeks burned with embarrassment as I watched him make his way into the shop, transferring the bags to his left hand and digging into his pocket for his keys.

Great.

The first day on the new job, and I'd already managed to piss off my boss.

The glass door of the diner swung open as Noah made his way inside the shop, and my feet stayed cemented to the sidewalk.

"Here."

My head swiveled to the door as an older woman with bleached blonde hair extended a bag with a to-go box in my direction, two cups of coffee cradled in her other hand.

"For Noah."

"Oh, right." I glanced back toward the shop and then reached out, taking his food and coffee. "Thanks."

Rose Hill-Dolly-Parton shot a wink in my direction before slipping back into the diner, the glass door swinging shut behind her.

I knew that I should move. I also knew that Noah was waiting for me to walk into the shop. But the nerves of starting a new job and the uncertainty of where I currently stood with my new boss were swirling around in my chest and seemed to have super glued me in place.

I wasn't entirely sure how long I stood in front of the diner, but poofy, bleached hair made its way into my peripheral after a while. Her arms crossed over her chest as she followed my gaze to the shop.

Bubble gum popped and smacked in her mouth.

"He's all bark and no bite," she said, snapping her gum in her mouth again.

I was inclined to believe her, especially after his interactions with Kennedy. Unfortunately for me, Kennedy was at school, and I didn't have the privilege of using my four-year-old as a buffer between the two of us.

"I think I offended him."

She snorted out a laugh, shifting her weight so she was leaning against the open door. "Noah Kent? He don't get offended easily. I think you're fine, honey." She jerked her chin toward the direction I should be walking in. "Whatcha got in those bags anywho?"

"Cleaning supplies," I replied, scrunching my nose as our interaction replayed in my head.

I *definitely* offended him.

I finally tore my eyes away from Noah's shop and met her gaze, the corners of her eyes crinkling as she grinned. "I've been telling them to clean that shop since his daddy owned it." She plucked the cigarette from behind her ear and popped it into her mouth. "I think I like you."

I couldn't stop the small grin that tugged at the corners of my mouth. Finally, I read the name tag on her chest.

Barb.

She rested the unlit cigarette between the index and middle finger of her left hand, neon pink nails shaped to a pointy tip aimed toward the morning sky. She seemed to be doing everything with that cigarette but smoking it. "What's your name, darling?"

"Olivia."

Barb caught the door with her hip, stretching her hand out to me. "Barb." She gestured vaguely to her name tag. "But I'm guessin' you caught onto that already."

Extending my hand in her direction, I met her halfway, her slender fingers wrapping around me with a grip that took me by surprise.

My dad would've been impressed.

I shook off the subtle ache building behind my breastbone at the thought of my father and Wyoming and plastered on a smile that might've been a little too telling of my fake enthusiasm. Though, I had a hard time letting myself feel any sort of guilt about it.

I was entirely too nervous about what awaited just up the street to concern myself with feigned excitement for strangers on the street. Don't get me wrong, I was looking forward to getting to know this town and the people in it. I was still holding out hope that it would supply the reprieve I'd been searching for, but in that moment, I just couldn't find it in me to concentrate on anything other than the nerves.

Still, I threw a grin her way, thankful that my acting skills had improved tenfold over the past few months. "It's really nice to meet you, Barb."

She pulled away and leaned against the door again. "So what brings you and that cute little girl to this small town?"

I knew this question was coming sooner rather than later and I definitely wasn't surprised that she knew I had a daughter despite this being our first interaction. Small Town 101: *Figure Out Why The Hell A Stranger Has Invaded Our Town.* Because if my assumptions were correct, my being here had already circulated through town. If everyone here knew that we were new and nobody here had a connection to us, the conspiracies were without a doubt circling just as fast.

Even knowing this was undoubtedly the next question she was going to ask, I couldn't stop the sweat that beaded at my hairline. I hated answering that question.

My clothes were itchy. The denim of my jeans started clinging to my skin uncomfortably, and the high-neck blouse I threw on this morning tightened, suffocating me.

I scratched at the material, clearing my throat and readying myself for the pity. "My husband passed. I'm just here for a fresh start. I grew up in a small town and thought maybe I could figure out how to breathe again in a new one."

The same sad but knowing look that Avery had at my doorstep Friday flashed across Barb's face, her eyes flickering to the shop down the street, then back to me. I wished that I could decipher the meaning behind it. But that's the funny thing about small towns. Everyone is always so desperate to unravel the secrets of any newcomer, yet equally determined to protect their own. The answer to whatever this look was meant to portray wouldn't come easily to me.

"I'm really sorry to hear that." The raspy edge to her voice softened with her eyes.

The door to Kent Automotive opened, the soft chime of the bell carrying down the quiet street. Both Barb and I turned our attention to Noah, who poked his head out of the doorway, his food and coffee still in my hands.

Now I was nervous that not only had I managed to offend him before nine in the morning, but I was also holding his food hostage, and I had no clue how long my feet had been cemented to this sidewalk outside the diner. His food was probably cold, and I was probably late for my first day.

Barb watched me as I watched Noah striding toward us with cool, confident steps, a key chain spinning around his index finger. A man of his size had no business moving with such ease.

I hated how he pulled my attention, but something told me this was nothing new regarding Noah Kent. His seemingly reserved nature led me to believe he didn't enjoy being the center of attention, but Noah was the kind of person that when he entered a room, you almost couldn't help but drink him in.

Everything about him, even the way he effortlessly swung that keychain around his finger, commanded the attention of any innocent bystander. He was an anomaly, someone to break up the everyday routine of a small town like Rose Hill.

And as fascinating as I found him, I didn't want to be so pulled in by the way his dark jeans hugged his thighs or the dark snake tattoo that started at his wrist and disappeared under the sleeve of his black t-shirt, only to peek out again at the collar. I didn't come to this town with the hopes of moving on or finding someone else. I wanted to grieve and figure out who the hell this empty, broken shell of a human was supposed to be without my husband by my side, and try to be the best mother that I could be to Kennedy.

Not that Noah would be the person that I find or move on with.

Because he was married. To my kind, sweet neighbor.

And I was not interested.

Barb pulled me from my thoughts, clearing her throat but keeping her voice low. "Be patient with that boy. He's– Well, he's not the easiest person to get to know. Just give him time, you'll see he's not such a grump."

I hadn't gotten the impression from Noah that he was a grump, per se. He was sweet to Kennedy and entertained every out-of-pocket thought that ran unfiltered from her brain straight to her mouth. He offered to let her stay at the shop after school until closing. He gave me a job. He didn't seem to be a man of many emotions– or words– but my first instinct wasn't to label him as a grump. Maybe closed off or uninterested in forming any sort of genuine connection with someone. Though, I suppose Barb would know better than me.

He came to a stop in front of me, his eyes dropping to the food and coffee in my hands as he cleared his throat. "So, my shop's dirty *and* you're stealing my breakfast?"

I stood there for a moment, my mouth gaping like a fish out of water. "Oh, no! No, I was just–"

"Olivia, no," Noah cut me off with something that was supposed to be a smile, but it resembled more of a grimace. "That was a joke in case it didn't land."

He cleared his throat and palmed the back of his neck nervously.

Oh.

A joke. See. Grumpy people don't joke.

I closed my mouth and swallowed hard, trying to recover from the small jump in my heart rate.

I let out a breathy laugh and lifted my shoulder in a shrug, tipping my chin up to meet his eyes, those amber irises swimming with amusement. "Ah, well.

Figured I'd need all the sustenance I could get to make a dent in that oil path from the front door to the garage door. Kennedy vouched for my cooking. Clearly, that won't cut it."

The corner of his mouth twitched, but he refused to let his smile grow. "Why don't you grab something to eat? Barb, add it to my tab."

"Oh, no. You don't–"

"Did you eat this morning?"

"I– Well–" I sighed, using my thumb to scratch my eyebrow.

The answer was no. I hadn't eaten this morning. I packed a small lunch, and I would be fine until then. A large part of it had to do with all the nerves twisting around in my stomach, but I didn't want to share that part with him.

Noah tilted his head and raised his eyebrows as if to say *see?* And reached over, grabbing his food and coffee from my hands. He jerked his chin toward the diner. "Go. Grab something to eat. Barb," he paused to look at her, "please make sure it's added to my tab. Don't let her pay."

Barb winked and disappeared back into the diner, and I tried to ignore the way my heart fluttered in response to his concern because it didn't mean anything. It was my overactive, hopeless romantic brain making something out of nothing because when was the last time someone took care of me? When was the last time someone asked me if I had eaten anything?

"Go," he urged gently. His eyes lingered on me for just a second longer than I'd anticipated, causing my breath to hitch in my throat.

"Okay," I nodded, fleeing into the diner before he could spot the way my cheeks warmed.

Ten minutes later, Barb was sliding a Styrofoam container into my hands. "You're gonna do just fine over there. Promise."

"Thank you," I responded shyly, swiping my food and coffee from the counter.

"Oh, and grab one of those on your way out." She pointed to the door. "I accidentally ordered two thousand instead of two hundred, so I'm trying to get rid of them."

I turned and followed the direction she was pointing in, my eyes landing on a crystal bowl filled to the brim with fortune cookies. My steps faltered, and the breath in my lungs trembled out of me.

Fortune cookies.

The sight of them hit me like a bittersweet wave, memories of Liam flooding back.

"You okay?" Barb asked. "You look like you've seen a ghost."

"Yeah," I breathed, looking back at her with a small smile. "I just— I have a thing with fortune cookies."

"Oh," she responded, her brow furrowing a tad before she shrugged with a bright grin. "Well, take as many as you want."

I approached the bowl, and a strange mix of grief and gratitude enveloped me as I gently balanced my takeout container on the edge of the little table.

My hands shook a little as I reached into the bowl to pull one out. I ripped at the plastic and cracked it open, holding my breath as I slid the paper out.

Embrace the winds of change.

My heart skipped a beat as I read the words, my breath catching in my throat on the exhale. The corners of my eyes pricked with tears. I wasn't typically one to believe in superstitions; that was more Liam's thing. But I couldn't ignore this weird little coincidence. All weekend, I'd been battling with my nerves. I was terrified of starting this new job, nervous for Kennedy's first day at a new pre-k. My brain was a broken washing machine stuck in a constant spin cycle of negativity. Until now.

I always told Kennedy that he was with us no matter what. Maybe this was his way of trying to convince me that was the truth.

I jumped when Barb's cheerful voice broke through my reverie. "Find a good one?"

I nodded, a grateful smile tugging at the corners of my lips. "Yeah, it's perfect."

Folding it and tucking it into my pocket, I grabbed my food, walked out of the diner, and headed toward Kent Automotive.

I'd spent most of the day Saturday staring at a lot of packed boxes, wishing they'd magically put themselves away. I knew that a huge weight would be lifted from my shoulders if I could just get myself to sort through them, but after several hours of just staring, I just decided it wasn't in the cards for me. We'd spent our Sunday at the park after a trip to the convenience store for all the supplies that waited for me at Noah's shop, and when I'd put Kennedy to bed last night and asked her if she was happy, she said yes.

That and the phone call I'd shared with my best friend, Gia, whispered something to my soul that told me I'd done the right thing. Gia was the only person who stood by my side when I packed everything to leave. She knew how good this would be for me. For us. She understood. And from across the country, she still supported my decision.

I took one more deep breath before pushing through the glass door and stepping inside the shop. Noah stood behind the counter, glancing up from whatever he was scribbling down when the bell chimed quietly.

"Did you pay?"

"No. But technically, I don't think you did either." He nodded, smiling softly. "Sounds about right."

The door shut behind me as I walked further into the shop, letting my eyes do a subtle scan of the room. My memory was a lot kinder to this place than I'd realized. My work was cut out for me, and that didn't even factor in the actual job I was supposed to be doing.

The white linoleum tiles were dirty and scuffed with grime, oil drips, and something that was making the heels of my flats stick as I walked. Even the dark wood on the paneling that covered the desk was a shade darker than it should be. Every corner housed a cobweb, and the floor-to-ceiling windows in the front were blanketed with dust.

My eyes finished their journey around the room and landed on Noah again, who was staring at me with his eyebrow cocked.

"Subtlety doesn't seem to be a strong suit of yours," he mumbled, returning his attention to the sticky note on the desk as I approached, dropping my food and coffee onto the counter.

Shit.

I loathed the way that all of my thoughts and feelings were so easily exposed by the blush on my cheeks. Ever since I was Kennedy's age, whatever I was feeling was displayed on my face for all to see, and I hated it. I couldn't get away with anything.

Case in point: this interaction. I *thought* I was being subtle. But my face was so damn readable that even Noah could tell I was judging the hell out of this place.

And now he could tell just how mortified I was that I'd been caught.

"Sorry," I winced, scrunching my nose as I looked up at him. "I don't mean any offense. Just... planning my day."

Noah dipped his chin, rifling through some papers until he found what he was looking for. "Just fill this out first so I can get you on payroll, and then we'll go over the–" he paused, gesturing vaguely to the mess that covered the desk, "system."

The corner of his mouth twitched just a little when I snorted a laugh. "It's been only me for a while now. So... it worked. But I'll explain what I have going on and then fall in line with whatever you figure out. Sound good?"

I smiled softly, the tension melting from my shoulders as I relaxed.

Noah Kent was a quiet man who possessed a lot of traits I'd yet to learn. But I could confidently say being a grump was not one of them.

Chapter 6

Olivia

This place was a mess.

I was pretty sure Noah was doing almost all of this work for free at this point, or he was just an extremely forgetful person and never sent invoices.

The phone was unplugged, there wasn't a single piece of technology for tracking customers or invoices, and there wasn't even a calendar. Just a stack of sticky notes that he jotted shit down on as people came in.

There was a lot that needed to change.

As much as my fingers itched to start cleaning the layers of grime coating the inside of this building, I started with the desk. The red solo cup that once housed an assortment of pens from some bank in Wilmington was now trash, and a new black mesh pencil cup sat in its place.

I dug through random filing cabinets and desk drawers until I found the things I needed for invoicing, and immediately started copying all of Noah's notes from the randomly placed sticky notes to the carbon copy invoice sheets I'd found. Now, both Noah and the customer would have a copy of all the work that was done. I organized those into the manila folders I'd purchased for him so he knew what was outstanding and what had already been paid. Once that was done, I grabbed the desk calendar from one of the convenience store bags and copied down every last appointment or note that was sticking to the desk.

The desk was sparkling clean and *visible* by noon, and when I took a step back to admire everything I had accomplished, I basked in the warmth of the pride that washed through my body. I couldn't wait for Noah to see. If only I could get myself to organize the apartment like this.

The next thing I needed to do was organize the bottom drawer of the desk.

Noah had left to grab us lunch at the diner, and despite my protests, it was his treat. I'd made him walk from the garage and past the desk with his eyes covered so he wouldn't see the progress I made until I was finished. He'd been gone for about twenty minutes, and now that I was done, I was anxious for him to return.

With only one more thing to do before the desk could be considered done, I knelt down in front of the bottom drawer and pulled it open, the mechanism groaning in protest. It sounded like it hadn't been opened in years.

I pulled out a couple of larger envelopes, each addressed to Noah with a return address that said 'Rose Hill Funeral Home.' This felt wrong. Something told me there was a reason this drawer was difficult to open.

Setting the envelopes off to the side, I kept digging. It wasn't my intention to go through any of Noah's personal belongings. I just wanted to clear out and organize this drawer and then it could go back to being sealed shut for the next however many years.

There was a lot of junk. Some paper clips, a stapler, a tape dispenser, and some extra pens. But the one thing that caught my attention was a picture. I picked it up gently, the top corner sticking to the bottom of the drawer like it hadn't been touched in a while.

It was Noah. He was younger, probably by ten years or so with a giant grin plastered to his face. I ignored the way my stomach fluttered at the sight of it. So far, I'd only gotten a little glimpse of his smiles, though they seemed reserved for Kennedy and her nonsense. I don't think my knees would be able to withstand the devastation of this smile if it were directed at me. His dark brown hair was longer, curling at the nape of his neck, but still brushed back and out of his face; his eyes were the same sweet shade of honey, though they were happier in this picture. They weren't so haunted and tired.

A *beautiful* woman who wasn't Avery was attached to his side.

Long, black hair draped over her shoulders and hung down almost to her waist. She had striking blue eyes and a smile that lit up her entire face. Beautiful wasn't a good enough term to describe her. Her left hand was placed over Noah's chest, a shiny diamond ring perched on her ring finger.

Did this mean he was married before Avery?

If that was the case, it made sense why this picture was shoved into the bottom drawer and seemingly forgotten. Though, I couldn't help but wonder why he didn't just throw it away.

I flipped the picture over and saw their names scribbled in the corner.

Adeline and Noah, 2009

Adeline.

I couldn't put my finger on why, but Adeline seemed like such a fitting name for someone so beautiful.

The front door kicked open, the bells chiming and signaling Noah's return. I felt like I'd been caught with my hand in the cookie jar, the picture falling from my grip and floating to the ground when I jumped in surprise.

I grabbed it and stood just as he made his way to the desk, dropping a to-go container in front of me.

"The special was a turkey melt with cheddar and spinach, hope you like turkey."

I nodded, "Thank you, yeah. That sounds great." I offered a small smile then lifted the picture and held it out toward him. "I uh– I found this when I was cleaning the drawer. I wasn't sure what to do with it."

Noah's face blanched, his jaw tightening as his eyes jumped from mine down to the picture extended in his direction. Obviously, there were some kind of negative feelings associated with whoever this person was.

"I'm sorry, Noah. I wasn't trying to—"

He snatched the picture from my grip and shoved it into his back pocket, then without a word, grabbed his to-go box from on top of mine and stomped past me to the garage, leaving me standing behind the desk confused and riddled with guilt.

The next couple hours went by slowly. Noah didn't come back out of the garage. I could hear the sound of tools and the heavy footfalls of his boots as he walked around, a car engine turning over every once in a while and the garage door opening to the back alleyway, but that was it.

I felt horrible about what happened earlier, though I was still unsure of what I did. I should've kept that picture at the bottom of the drawer and left it at that.

Once the clock hit two-thirty, I needed to walk over to Kennedy's school, Rosy Cheeks Pre-K, and pick her up.

I followed the dirty footprints and oil drips from the desk and back to the garage, pushing the swinging doors open. My nose was immediately assaulted with the smell of the garage, the faint fumes that had permeated through the building and into the lobby were extremely faint compared to being back there.

My eyes wandered the room; the concrete floors were just as stained as the front, but compared to the lobby and desk area, the garage was surprisingly clean. It wasn't anything special, just a sealed concrete floor with walls composed of what looked like concrete blocks painted an off-white color. I wasn't familiar with any of the larger equipment that sat on the far side of the garage, but the several red tool chests lining the wall next to me were spotless, and not a single tool was out of place.

Noah was bent over, his upper half disappearing under the hood of an old Cadillac. I stepped just a little closer and watched him work, the bicep of his right arm straining against the fabric of his t-shirt as he used some kind of wrench to tighten something under the hood. My eyes followed the curve of his spine and landed right on his ass. Despite the guilt that gnawed at my chest, I let myself admire the man and the perfect, rounded muscles under those tight jeans.

He shifted his weight slightly, grunting as he gripped the wrench tighter in his hand and put more body weight behind whatever he was working on, my skin flamed as I imagined those grunts in a completely different scenario. That picture being painted in my brain felt so wrong for so many reasons.

"Jesus, Olivia," I whispered, closing my eyes for a second and shaking my head.

I didn't think he could hear me over the country music playing softly in the background, but he stood abruptly, turning to look at me and proving me wrong.

"Did you say something?"

The flush in my cheeks deepened. "No, sorry. I just— I have to go grab Kennedy."

Noah's eyes flickered to the clock before looking back at me. "Just flip the sign so people know you're coming back in a minute."

Without waiting for a response, he gave me his back and turned his attention to the car.

I closed my eyes and sighed, unsure of whether or not I should say anything about the picture. My gut said no. But did I listen to it? Of course not.

"Noah, about the picture—"

"It's fine, Olivia. Just— it's fine." He rested his hands on the metal frame of the car, his chin falling to his chest, his back to me the whole time.

I longed to know what was eating him up about this picture. I wished he would let me apologize for upsetting him. But instead, I turned and made my way back up front, accepting that he didn't want to talk about it. Not that I blamed him. I was a stranger. His employee. Nothing more.

I hated being an outsider. Not knowing anything about the people I called my neighbors was a foreign feeling. I was used to knowing everything about everyone, just like the people here did about each other. But now, I was the one they gossiped about. I was the one who didn't belong. And I hated it.

Chapter 7

Noah

The bell above the door chimed as Olivia left the building, and all the tension I'd been holding in since that picture landed in my hand seemed to come to a head. I pushed away from the car I was working on, throwing the wrench in my hand across the room. It hit the concrete wall and bounced off, clattering against the floor.

It'd been two years since I'd seen a picture of Addie. Two years since I let myself see the way that she was before, instead of torturing myself with the last images of her that were seared into my brain.

I should've told her to leave that drawer alone. I should've remembered that I left that picture in there when the funeral home dropped off the paperwork from her services.

But I didn't. And now that picture of her was burning a hole in my pocket.

I didn't want to look at it. I didn't want to remember what we looked like all those years ago, so happy and in love. It hurt too much.

Pacing the length of the garage, I contemplated pulling it out. I could give myself just one last look at the woman I loved and the man I used to be. Did I deserve it? No. But it was the sweetest, most addicting drug, and I craved that high. The high of seeing her so happy and in love, that ring sparkling on her finger. There was nothing like it and I would torture myself with it over and over again, even knowing the low that came after would knock the air from my lungs.

I hadn't given myself the privilege of looking at her for two years now.

It's the longest I've been clean.

But today I had one glimpse. One tiny hit and I was sucked back in.

Cursing under my breath, I pulled the picture from my pocket, my breath hitching in my throat. God, we were so happy. And so young. I remember this afternoon like it was yesterday and not almost thirteen years ago. It was July Fourth weekend; we drove forty-five minutes to Lake Warman and spent the whole day with our families, burning under the hot summer sun. Addie's face was sun-kissed, her black hair curled and falling down her back.

It was the day I proposed. We were twenty-one, she was home from Boston University for the summer, and I'd stuck around, studying anything and everything that had to do with the shop. We all knew I was going to take it over one day. I'd asked for her parents' blessing the night before and was given my grandmother's ring; everything was perfect.

We got married the summer after she graduated from BU, and I had six wonderful years with Addie before she was ripped from this world. It wasn't long enough. We didn't have enough time together. She didn't have enough time on this Earth.

I stared at the picture until it blurred, then blinked the unshed tears away and walked over to one of the tool cabinets, gently placing it in the back and shutting the drawer.

I sniffed right as the door chimed, then cleared my throat and pushed through the garage doors, making my way toward the front. Avery always dropped Nellie off here after school, and she'd spend the afternoon doing her homework at the desk in the back. I'd drop her off at the apartment on my way home and save Avery from making another trip. It was a little distracting, but my sister needed the help, and I loved having Nellie around. She talked almost as much as Kennedy did.

I heard Avery's voice carry through the hallway, Olivia's laugh following closely behind whatever she'd said.

"Are you sure? It's really no bother at all."

Olivia shrugged, smiling softly at Avery. "We live in the same building, and they clearly love each other–" she gestured toward their daughters, who were now sitting in the corner, giggling to themselves. "I'm happy to walk her over here so you don't have to leave work."

"Then it's a deal." Avery smiled, her eyes flickering over to me for a second as I leaned against the wall in the hallway. "Olivia here is going to bring Nellie to the shop with her so I don't have to leave or eat a late lunch."

"That's nice," I responded quietly, crossing my arms over my chest.

And like I wasn't even in the room, Avery and Olivia continued their conversation without missing a beat. I knew those two would hit it off. Unfortunately for me.

I disappeared back into the garage, grabbing the wrench from the ground and getting back to work on Carla's transmission. After a few minutes, the garage doors swung open, and Avery walked through with her eyebrow cocked. I sighed, looking over at my sister, unsure if I had the energy for whatever fight she was getting ready to pick.

She walked up next to me, resting her hip against the car. "What happened?"

I scratched my forehead with my thumb, undoubtedly leaving behind some kind of oil mark. "What do you mean?"

"Don't play stupid. It doesn't suit you."

Rolling my eyes, I dropped my wrench on the tray off to the side and faced Avery. "Can you at least elaborate?"

She lowered her voice and said, "With Olivia? She thinks you're mad at her."

I fucking knew they were going to be friends. Day one and they were already talking about me.

Avery rolled her eyes at my lack of response. "Seriously. What happened? How did she manage to piss you off?"

"She didn't piss me off," I sighed again, running my fingers through my hair. "I just– She found a picture of Addie. I wasn't expecting it, and it caught me off guard. That's all."

Her features softened, her small hand resting on my forearm. "I'm sorry, honey. That's– I can't even imagine. I'm sorry."

I shrugged, not interested in talking about it. There was a time and place for talking about shit like this, and the garage during business hours wasn't it.

"You wanna talk about it? About her?"

"No," I snapped, almost instantly regretting my tone. I knew she was only trying to help. I knew she didn't deserve it, but fuck. I was tired of people bringing her up.

"Fine. You should–" She paused, sighing and letting her gaze drift to the garage doors before looking back over at me. "Get to know her, Noah. You might have more in common than you think."

With that, she turned and left me alone in the garage with nothing but the sound of the doors swinging shut behind her. I hated the cryptic messages. Couldn't she just tell me why she was pushing so hard for us to get to know one another? Hadn't she considered the fact that I didn't want to get to know her?

I combed my fingers through my hair, the gold band on my finger catching in the light. Avery's words echoed through my brain.

You might have more in common than you think.

As I stared at my ring, Olivia's wedding rings, her breakdown outside of her apartment, and the dark circles under her eyes flashed through my mind. Was it possible that the same tragedy that had ripped my life apart was what drove her to Rose Hill?

I needed Avery or Olivia to offer up the answer to that question. There was no way in hell I was asking her myself.

For the next forty-five minutes, I dove into the Cadillac, losing myself under the hood. It was easy to forget the things that kept me up at night when I was working. Normally, Nellie was back here talking my ear off about what she did at school, and whatever project I was working on took twice as long as it normally did. Though, I shouldn't complain. After all, I was the one who offered to let her stay here until Avery got off of work in the first place.

I wiped my hands on the rag in my back pocket just as Nellie and Kennedy scurried through the doors, Olivia following closely behind.

"Sorry, I told them to stay up front. Come on, girls." Olivia gripped their shoulders, trying but failing to usher them back toward the front.

I waved her off. "Don't worry about it. Nell has a desk in the corner she sits at. Kennedy is welcome to sit back here with her, too. She normally just works on her homework until it's time to go."

She hesitated, tucking a strand of blonde hair behind her ear. "Are you sure?"

"Wouldn't offer if I wasn't."

Olivia smiled softly. "Right." She bent down to get eye level with Kennedy, cupping her chin gently. "Behave. Listen to Mr. Kent. If he tells you to come up front, you come up front. 'Kay?"

Kennedy smiled, nodding her head eagerly. "Yes, Mommy."

"I'll be up front. Holler if you need me." Olivia rubbed her palms against her jeans awkwardly before turning and disappearing through the swinging doors once more.

Kennedy eyed me curiously for a moment before Nellie grabbed her sleeve and pulled her toward the desk in the corner. The two of them immediately dove into the coloring supplies I kept on hand for her. I turned my attention back to the car in my garage, finishing up with the transmission while the girls were distracted because I knew it wouldn't last long. Thankfully, they had each other to talk to, and Nellie wasn't perched on a stool next to me asking if unicorns lived in the woods at the edge of town or if tortoises had feelings.

I'd just finished and lowered the hood when Olivia's raised voice carried through the shop. I glanced over at the girls, who were too distracted by their own laughter to realize that anything had changed. After wiping my hands clean, I tossed the dirty rag off to the side and made my way toward the front of the shop. There weren't a ton of people I could picture her getting into it with, but I would bet my next paycheck it was Sheila complaining about the fucking phone again.

I pushed through the swinging doors, coming to a halt right before the lobby when I realized she was talking to someone on her cell phone.

"He'd be disappointed in *me?*" Olivia scoffed and let out a sarcastic laugh, running a hand through her hair. "Debra, I will *not* be having this conversation with you again. The only person he would be disappointed in is you for talking to me like this. *He's dead.* I'm so sorry that you lost your son— I am— but I'm hurting, too. He was my *husband,* Deb. He was the father of my child. Liam would want me to be happy. If he would've seen me a month ago, he would've been the first person to tell me to leave. You know this. I couldn't–" she paused, her voice cracking. "I couldn't be there. I couldn't breathe. I couldn't *live.* I needed to leave. For me and for Kennedy. I hope one day you can see that. I have to go."

I stood frozen in the hallway as she ended the call, the sound of her voice breaking echoed through my mind and it seemed to crack my chest wide open. She tossed her phone onto the counter and let out a frustrated groan. I could hear every emotion within the deep, controlling breaths she was taking as she attempted to hold everything in. She gripped the edge of the front desk, her back to me as she took another breath, exhaling slowly as her head hung between her shoulders.

Avery and her stupid cryptic messages were starting to make sense. She wasn't meddling because she was trying to set me up with her. She was meddling because she thought we could both benefit from bonding over our shared tragedies. I wasn't sure if that was better or worse. Olivia had lost her husband and the father of her daughter and moved to Rose Hill as an escape. Funny how one person's solitude is another's personal hell.

Avery could push us together all she wanted, but the pain that I experienced when losing Addie wasn't comparable to Olivia losing her husband. It was just me and Addie. We didn't have kids. I didn't have to put on a brave face and keep it together for anyone besides my mother.

The first two years after she died, it was a struggle for me to even keep myself fed and alive. I couldn't imagine grappling with the overwhelming loss of someone I'd imagined spending my life with on top of caring for a child. It would've destroyed me.

Our situations weren't comparable because I wouldn't survive Olivia's, and she was doing so much more than that.

I lost my wife and shut down.

Whatever light I had burning inside of me when she was here was snuffed out the second Addie took her last breath, and I'd done absolutely nothing to revive it.

Olivia was strong. I could see it. I could *feel* it. I was a coward compared to her.

I couldn't pinpoint where the feeling of protectiveness that washed over me came from, but I could see the defeat rolling off her shoulders in waves with every breath she took. Olivia was hanging on by an extremely thin thread.

This Debra person was taking a knife to whatever was left of it, seemingly unapologetic about what would happen when it finally snapped.

It took an embarrassing amount of willpower to keep my feet planted on the linoleum tile. I wanted nothing more than to stomp over, snatch her phone off of the counter, and block Debra's number from her phone.

I didn't even have time to process the ridiculousness behind that thought and how many lines it would be crossing before Olivia was pushing away from the counter, turning and coming face to face with me. She gasped, and my jaw clenched when I realized she was crying. Her face was red and splotchy, a couple of stray tears slipping down her cheeks. I fucking hated that she was crying again.

I hated even more that I couldn't help.

She was broken, and there was no sense in attempting to put her back together when I was still trying to figure it out myself.

Olivia opened her mouth, and I just knew the first thing she was going to do was apologize. I raised my hand to stop her. "If you apologize right now, I think I'm gonna have to fire you."

She stared at me with wide eyes, her chin quivering as her eyes filled with tears.

"Fucking Christ," I mumbled, scrubbing a hand down my face. I was on a fucking roll today. "Just another shitty joke, sorry. I guess I'm not as funny as I think I am."

I hated tears. I never knew what to do. I couldn't even handle Nellie's tears, and she was a child. The second those little eyes flooded, I folded like a cheap lawn chair and gave her whatever the hell she wanted, and the damn kid used it to her advantage.

Olivia let out a small whimper, and my stomach clenched at the sound. She was so close to losing it, and I didn't have the slightest clue what to do.

"I was kidding, I swear."

She nodded, quickly wiping away a couple of tears that slipped down her cheeks.

I swallowed the lump in my throat, spearing my fingers through my hair.

Ah, fuck.

With slow, tentative steps, I closed the distance between the two of us, her warm vanilla scent filling my nostrils as my arms wrapped around her shoulders. I pulled her to my chest and hugged her tight, unsure of how many lines I was crossing but ignoring the awkward tension that hung in the air around us. Neither of us knew what the hell I was doing.

Her arms stayed glued to her sides as she sniffled. "You're hugging me?" she murmured, her voice muffled by my chest.

"I think so. I don't hug people often, but I don't think the concept has changed." I started to pull away, but her arms wrapped around my middle, keeping me in place.

"Just– One more second," she whispered, "Please."

The tension melted from our bodies as we relaxed into the hug we both clearly needed. While it might've started out a little awkward, it was hard to ignore the way she fit so perfectly against me. Her cheek was pressed against my chest, my chin rested easily just on top of her head. I wasn't typically one for metaphors and cliches, but something about having Olivia in my arms like this healed a piece of my broken soul. The storm that'd been raging inside of me for the past four years was finally muted by a simple hug from a woman I knew almost nothing about. One simple hug and I was determined to change that.

I wanted to know her. I wanted to be the one offering her hugs and shitty jokes when she was on the verge of breaking down. I wanted to figure her out. She carried so much on her shoulders and even with my own burdens to bear, I wanted to alleviate the weight of whatever she was struggling with.

This newfound desire to protect and take care of Olivia brought on a slew of confusing feelings that I just couldn't make sense of. Especially when Adeline crossed my mind.

Before I could stop it, my body tensed as my mind caught up with us. My arms were wrapped around another woman, and her hands were on me. My wedding band seemed to burn around my finger. Almost as abruptly as the embrace started, Olivia's spine straightened like she'd also just realized what the hell was going on, and she pulled away, her arms dropping to her sides as she took a few generous steps away from me.

"Sorry," I mumbled, shaking my head. "I thought maybe you needed a friend."

She swiped at her cheeks, clearing away a few stray tears. "I did. Thank you."

I cleared my throat, palming the back of my neck. The awkward tension was definitely back. "Okay. Well. I gotta– will you call Carla and let her know her car is done?"

"Sure." Her voice was low, that familiar flush of pink sweeping up her neck and painting her cheeks. "I'll do it now."

Without anything left to say, I turned and made my way back to the garage, leaving the confusing feelings and guilt behind me.

Chapter 8

Olivia

I was right about Kent Automotive being the distraction I desperately needed.

After two weeks of nonstop scrubbing, dusting, and sweeping, there were muscles in my body I didn't even know existed screaming for me to take a break. But I knew I couldn't. The second I stopped, and my attention was no longer captivated by bleach and rubber gloves, it would be taken over by Liam. Liam and the fact that I had no clue what I was doing.

So I did whatever I could to occupy my thoughts every second of every day.

When I was at work, I had Noah and the busyness of the shop to pull my thoughts elsewhere. When I got home, each and every thought from the time we stepped through the doorway to Kennedy lying down in bed revolved around her. But once she was asleep and I was alone with my thoughts, my last conversation with Deb would just play on a constant loop through my mind.

It was like her voice had taken over my inner monologue, and instead of reminding myself that I was capable and strong, I just heard her telling me that I was failing my husband and daughter. I heard her telling me I was selfish. I heard the disappointment that intertwined with the venom in her voice. We'd never been super close, but this wedge between us was still confusing and hurtful.

So I cleaned.

Even after the lobby was spotless, I cleaned. Even after Noah told me I didn't have to keep cleaning, I cleaned. He didn't know that I'd made two more trips to the convenience store to load up on more cleaning supplies because I'd already used up everything from the first trip. It was easy enough to sneak them in after he'd given me a key to the shop.

I'd swing by the diner every morning for a coffee and a fortune cookie and then make my way over to the shop, hiding all the new supplies with the old ones so Noah wouldn't get suspicious.

We still hadn't talked about the picture or the hug after my phone call with Deb. I wasn't sure if we needed to. He was married after all. I didn't want there to be any sort of misconstrued intentions or Avery to be upset that she'd essentially gotten me a job and I was hanging all over her husband for comfort because my mother-in-law was determined to drive me insane.

That was part of the reason I'd also been avoiding her invitation to breakfast before work. I didn't think I could look her in the face after checking out Noah's ass.

I kept to my offer and was still picking up both Kennedy and Nellie after school and escorting them back to the shop where they would hang out in the garage with Noah until we all walked home. Their friendship was another reason I couldn't afford to fuck anything up.

It had only been two weeks, but Kennedy was settling into this new town so well. She was getting along with everyone at school and even better, her teacher said she was thriving in class. She was happy and excited to go to school every morning. In Evergreen, it was hard to get her to look forward to school. Almost every morning, I was met with a tantrum and tears while dragging her out the door. Now, Kennedy was waking up before dawn and yanking me out the door every morning.

I was exhausted. I couldn't sleep through the night, my cooking hadn't improved since we moved in so Ken got all the good stuff while I settled for the cut-off burnt bits. And while Deb hadn't stopped calling, there was nothing but radio silence from my parents.

Eventually, I settled on letting Ken answer the phone so she could talk to her grandmother and I didn't have to subject myself to another round in the ring with Deb.

There was already enough self-doubt and disappointment clouding my mind. I didn't need any of her input to pull me in deeper.

"Shit." I sat back on my heels, wiping the sweat from my forehead. My phone alarm was blaring from where it sat on the desk, bringing a welcome disruption to my thoughts. Staring at the clock in disbelief, I pushed myself up off the floor I was scrubbing for the third time in a week and walked over to silence my phone.

There was one stubborn splotch of *something* that I couldn't get up from the tile, but I was becoming determined.

I slid off the yellow rubber gloves and dropped them onto the counter, silencing the alarm and trying to figure out how the fuck it was already two-thirty. I'd been running into this problem all week. I'd drop Kennedy off at Rosy Cheeks, swear that I'd only clocked in two hours at work, and then my alarm would be pulling me from whatever surface I was deep-cleaning at the time, telling me that six hours had actually gone by and I needed to get the girls from school.

I made my way back to the garage and pushed the swinging doors open, searching for Noah to let him know I was heading out. I followed the sound of the socket wrench, spotting him on a creeper, and stretched out under a car. His arms were extended over his head, lifting his shirt to expose the hard muscles under that signature black t-shirt. The sight of him and the way my heart seemed to skip a full beat did absolutely nothing to ease the guilt that had been eating me alive.

My mind kept trying to convince me that it was okay to see someone else as attractive, despite the fact that my heart still belonged to Liam.

On top of that, there was Avery. She was amazing. And so sweet. And the only person in this town that had gone out of their way to befriend me, and I was the asshole daydreaming about what the muscles that belonged to her *husband* would feel like under my hands.

I shook the image from my thoughts, clearing my throat so Noah would know he had company. "I'm gonna run and grab the girls. Be right back."

Regardless of how much time I spent with him, I still wasn't used to his method of communication, which typically consisted of one-word answers or grunting. So, while I didn't necessarily care for it, I wasn't surprised when all I got in return was a barely audible "'Kay."

The distant chirping of birds and my tennis shoes against the pavement were the only sounds that accompanied me on my short walk. My t-shirt clung to my skin, the sweat from cleaning mixing with the sheen building from the summer sun beating down on me. August was revealing itself to be a brutal month.

After my fourth day at Kent Automotive, I'd asked Noah if it was okay for me to dress down on the days that I would be cleaning, to which he responded: "You can wear your pajamas. I don't give a fuck."

So, I traded my blouses and jeans for leggings and t-shirts so I wouldn't feel so guilty about leaving permanent sweat stains on all of my nice shirts.

I was even more grateful for casual clothes now that the humidity was at an all-time high.

I smiled when I approached the school, Nellie and Kennedy had their arms locked together as they skipped down the sidewalk toward where I waited. It'd been such a hard year, and seeing her with such a careless smile on her face filled my chest with a warmth that rivaled the temperature of the summer air.

She and Nellie had become fast friends and were practically joined at the hip. They'd been begging every night for the past week to have a sleepover, and now that it was finally the weekend, Avery offered to keep Kennedy overnight tonight so I could have some time alone.

I wasn't sure how to tell her that alone time was the absolute last thing I wanted or needed. But Kennedy was looking forward to it, so I would endure one night alone with my haunted thoughts if it put a smile on her face.

They giggled as they approached, Kennedy leaning over to whisper something into Nellie's ear which elicited another fit of high-pitched giggles.

"Hi, Mommy!"

I squatted down to pull my little girl into a hug, but she and Nellie held onto each other, so I snagged them both, giggles and all, and hugged them to my body. "Hello, cuties!" Kennedy squirmed away from my kiss on the cheek, and for the first time today, a genuine smile spread across my lips.

Picking her up from school was the best part of my day. Seeing her smile and listening to her little laughs float through the air filled the hole in my chest little by little each day.

"Come on, let's go to the diner and get some milkshakes. Barb says you guys owe her a drawing, too."

I grinned when they squealed, following quickly behind as they tore down the street. These were the moments I loved so much. I took out my phone and snapped a picture of Kennedy and Nellie to send to my family. I knew that I probably wouldn't hear anything in return, but at least they couldn't say I didn't try.

I wasn't sure if I'd ever be happy again, but Kennedy was, and that was all that mattered to me.

Chapter 9

Noah

"How do you know the moon *isn't* made out of cheese?"

I looked down at my niece, remnants of her chocolate milkshake outlining her mouth as she stared up at me with arched brows.

I blew out a slow breath, my cheeks puffing as I considered my answer. Because truthfully, I didn't fucking know. Logically, I knew that the moon wasn't made out of cheese. Unfortunately, logic wasn't a sound argument when it came to Nell, and I couldn't tell her *exactly* what the moon was made out of, so it might as well be made out of cheese.

I was hungover, running on little to no sleep, and hadn't had a sip of water since seven this morning. I was in no mood to field questions from Nellie as she worked her way through another existential crisis.

Turning back to the truck, I shrugged. "I don't know, Nell. I really don't. The moon *could* be made out of cheese. I have no way of proving or disproving your theory."

Seemingly thrilled with that answer, she turned and skipped back to her desk in the corner of the garage, sliding onto the bench next to Kennedy. I watched as she described something to Kennedy, flailing her arms around and talking with her hands. That was something else she'd picked up from Avery. The copper hair was a dead giveaway that she was her daughter, but Nellie was just a little Avery. They walked the same, and they talked the same, and they both stuck their tongue out to the side when they were concentrating too hard.

However, given her father, taking after Avery was better than the alternative. Derek was an idiot for a lot of reasons. But missing out on this little girl's life was definitely in the top three.

My phone alarm blared, and I wiped my hands on a semi-clean cloth, tossing it into the pile of rags that needed to be washed. If I didn't set an alarm every day, I'd work until well past midnight, forget to eat, and spend the night on the bench in the back.

I'd noticed over the past couple weeks that Olivia was the same way.

Normally, I'd be impressed with that kind of work ethic, but I knew firsthand that it was a distraction. She was doing everything she could to keep her mind off her husband. It'd been two weeks since I overheard that conversation with her and her mother-in-law, and neither of us had brought it up.

We didn't talk about her husband. We didn't talk about the hug or the tears or the way the lobby was the cleanest it'd been in years, and she was still scrubbing.

The conversations we shared were surface-level at best, but every once in a while, I'd be able to coax a small smile or a laugh out of her. I bit my tongue every time the urge to ask her how she was *really* doing and if she was eating and sleeping enough clawed its way up my throat. However, it was mostly selfish on my part because I knew if she were honest with me, I wouldn't be able to stomach the answer.

Before I could tell the girls it was time to go, Olivia was pushing through the garage doors, tucking her phone into her pocket, fresh tears sitting on her waterline. My body stilled, and my jaw clenched. She was one shitty phone call away from me taking her phone and blocking Debra's number. I couldn't give a shit how many personal and professional lines that would be crossing.

There was no way for me to know if it was actually Debra who called or texted her, but I'd only seen her look like *this* one other time, and that told me all I needed to know.

I shook my head, stepping in front of her to block the girls' view before they noticed she was crying. "Go. Take a second to yourself. I'll bring them up front."

Her shoulders sagged as she nodded, turning on her heels and disappearing into the bathroom at the end of the hall.

I'd heard horror stories about people interacting with their in-laws, but I was thankful that wasn't the case for me. I knew that Stacy and Dan loved me. I knew that I was welcome at their house any time I wanted to drop by. I tried to convince myself that all those years ago when I pulled away, they didn't want to see me. But I knew it was really *me* who wasn't able to interact with *them* because of the memories that would resurface.

I couldn't look at Stacy without seeing Addie. I couldn't be in their house without picturing her walking through the hallways or sitting on the couch in the living room.

I thought I was protecting them, but in the end, I was trying to protect myself.

I had a vague idea of what Olivia was going through and I could see it tearing her down day by day. She'd only worked here for two weeks and already I'd noticed a change.

She looked thin. The kind of thin that comes without effort or intention. Her cheeks were sunken in, and the bags under her eyes were becoming more prominent with every passing day. Whatever life she had left within her was being poured into these conversations with Debra and preserving Kennedy's innocence.

There was a nagging pull in my chest that told me she needed help. I was stuck between overstepping and doing what I thought was the right thing to do. If the roles were reversed and Addie was the one who survived, I'd want someone to look out for her. I'd want someone to make sure she was eating and sleeping and protected.

Olivia didn't have anyone here. There was no one to help her, and while yes, she was an adult, I knew with an unfortunate familiarity the slippery slope she was on. She was grieving and giving everything she had to her daughter, and you can't pour from an empty cup. If the best I could do was offer a shoulder to lean on or a good meal every once in a while, I'd do it.

I turned to the girls. "Alright, ladies. Closing time."

They squealed, pushing away from the desk and gathering their backpacks from the floor. Avery told me they were having a sleepover tonight at her place, and from the looks of it, they were anxious to get home.

A few minutes later, we were gathered in the lobby when Olivia pushed out of the bathroom. The splotchy redness had faded into a light pink, and the small, appreciative smile that spread across her face was a lot more genuine than the one she'd plastered on when walking into the garage.

"Ready?"

She nodded and tucked a loose strand of blonde hair behind her ear, taking another deep breath as her eyes stayed locked on Kennedy. Whatever conversation she had with Debra wasn't a good one; it was written all over her face and the way her shoulders had deflated significantly since I'd seen her an hour or so ago. Her daughter being away from her was the last thing she needed tonight, but I also knew that with how excited Ken was for this sleepover, Olivia wouldn't be the one to tell her no.

I swiped my keys from the counter and waited for Olivia and the girls to walk out the front door before switching the lights off and following closely behind. After locking up, we made a pit stop by the diner so the girls could drop their drawing off to Barb, and then we made our way down the street. I watched Olivia the whole time we walked to Rose Hill Apartments as she laughed half-heartedly at Kennedy's jokes and stared blankly ahead. She had this lost, vacant look in her eyes and I had no idea what to do to bring her back.

Lost in thought, she missed the bump in the sidewalk we overstepped every single day, tripping and falling forward. I grabbed her elbow to keep her upright, stopping for a second while she gathered her thoughts.

"What's going on?" I asked, keeping my voice low so the girls wouldn't overhear.

She swallowed, sweeping her gaze over to Kennedy before letting it find me again. Those deep, ocean-blue eyes filled with tears before she took a staggering breath and blinked them away. "I can't talk about it." Her voice was barely a whisper over the call of the cicadas.

My throat tightened as an uneasy feeling settled deep in my gut. I could feel Kennedy's and Nellie's eyes on us, so I released my grip on her elbow and let her keep her secrets for now. The tightness in my chest wouldn't let me leave it alone for good. She needed to talk about it eventually, and even though my sister had so lovingly pointed out several times in the past year that my social skills needed some work, I had no issue seeing the clear difference between when someone needed a push and when it was just best to back away.

The closer we got to the apartment, the more her body language changed. Her arms clung tightly around her middle like she was the only thing holding herself together and fuck if my chest didn't burn in response.

Every August twenty-fifth, I'd close the shop, get something from the diner for dinner, and chase it down with a fifth of whiskey. I'd lose myself in the burn of the alcohol, trying to forget that Addie wasn't here for yet another birthday.

But when we finally made it to their apartment and walked up the paved pathway that led to the front door, and Olivia let out a deep sigh, I knew my plans had changed.

I knew the second I left and drove home, my thoughts would be pulled to Olivia. I'd grab my dinner from the diner, head home, and find myself wondering if she was eating anything or if she was drinking to forget that no one was going to be there to comfort her or dry her tears.

Again, my thoughts drifted to what would have happened to Addie if the roles had been reversed. Would she be struggling to hold it together? Would she be okay or would her grief consume her in the same way Olivia's grief had? Would there be someone there to pick up the pieces of her broken heart?

Would she let herself look twice at another man on the street?

Would she allow herself to fall in love again, or would she torture herself with the what-ifs until she was drowning in the ruthless sea of what could have been?

I wished I could say these questions had never filtered through my mind, but I found myself more and more curious about the way she would be handling my loss since Olivia came into town.

If I gave into this pull that tugged at my chest and drew me to her, would I be doing a disservice to my late wife?

I hung back as we reached the front door. If this were any other day, I'd walk them inside, only leaving once doors were shut and locks were in place. But not tonight. Tonight, I was anxious to numb the sting in my chest thinking about Olivia being left alone.

She looked back at me, her blue eyes finding mine. The sun was setting in the sky behind her, casting a beautiful contrast of pink and burnt orange on the profile of her face, outlining the soft curve of her lips.

Her brows dipped marginally as I continued my perusal of her face, trying to wrap my head around how someone so beautiful could be filled with so much sadness.

I felt another pinch in my chest.

Since she'd moved to Rose Hill, I'd only seen her eyes reflect such a deep and all-consuming sadness. I wanted to know what it would take to slowly fill them with life again.

I wanted to hear a genuine laugh and see a genuine smile. I wondered if her smile would reveal a shallow dimple on her cheek. If her laugh sounded as soft and gentle as her voice or if it would be loud and commanding.

I didn't want to see this version of Olivia anymore. The one that was surviving. I wanted to see the happy version of her. The one who laughed carelessly and smiled freely. I craved the version of her that would be thriving in this tiny town.

I let out a shaky breath, once again flustered by the way she so unintentionally invaded my thoughts.

"You coming?" she asked softly, the soft dip of her brows forming a small crease in her forehead.

Clearing my throat, I shook my head. "No. Not tonight. I'm gonna head back to the shop for a little bit."

Olivia's eyes searched mine for a moment before she nodded and reached for the door, ushering the girls inside.

In just a few minutes, Kennedy would be dragged over to Avery's apartment by the handles of her overnight bag, and Olivia would be left alone in hers, replaying her conversation with Debra over and over again. Over the past two weeks, I'd watched the light in Olivia's eyes slowly fade. I'd watched the weight melt off of her, and the bags under her eyes grow deeper and deeper. There was no one in Rose Hill to throw her the lifeline she so desperately needed, and I couldn't stop thinking about it.

Chapter 10

Olivia

I didn't want to be alone.

I couldn't *stand* being alone.

But I couldn't let my own grief hold Kennedy back from living the happy life she deserved. Even though my arms ached to hold her against me and stroke her hair while she told me about her day.

The air rushed out of my lungs the second the door swung shut, Kennedy disappearing across the hall with Avery and Nellie. I fought to catch my breath as my ribs seemed to shrink in my chest. Every raw emotion I'd been holding back since that text from Deb started to claw its way up my throat, burning a path like cheap whiskey.

The thought of spending a night alone in this apartment felt paralyzing.

I had the night to myself. I should have been walking around the apartment and unpacking what was left of the moving boxes. I should have been blasting some pop song by an artist I'd never heard of and dancing my way around the kitchen with a glass of wine. But instead, I stood in the hallway, staring at the old wooden door for so long that my eyes went blurry, and my back began to ache from standing still.

My eyes stayed fixed on the wooden door, searching and staring like the deep brown grain and years of wear and tear held the solution to the numbness spreading through my body like a dense fog. It wasn't until my phone vibrated in my pocket that I allowed myself to look away.

I opened the text from Avery, tears rushing to my eyes almost instantly Kennedy looked so happy.

It was a picture of her and Nellie, already spread out on the floor with an assortment of coloring books, a huge smile stretched across both of their faces. A small amount of the tension that'd been all but burying me alive melted from the base of my spine.

My thumb pressed down against the Live Photo, two high-pitched giggles filling the empty space in the apartment as they each colored their own page from one coloring book.

I blew out a breath, one full of relief. One that wavered less around the edges than every other breath I'd taken in the past year. The tightness in my chest loosened by one tiny notch, the smile on my daughter's face justifying every rash decision made to get me from Evergreen to Rose Hill.

I wiped at the tear that slipped down my cheek, savoring the feeling and the emotions that brought me to the first happy tear in over a year. It felt silly. I'd seen Kennedy smile plenty in the past year, even more in the past few weeks since our move. But after the text I got from Deb, I needed this. I needed a sign that I wasn't the person she was making me out to be.

Sliding my phone back into my pocket, I blew out another slow, controlled breath, smiling on the exhale. Whether Avery knew it or not, that one picture changed the trajectory of my entire night.

My stomach grumbled, and the cup of ramen I'd been planning on boiling water for crept into my mind. Every other night, I at least attempted to teach myself how to cook for Kennedy's sake, and the poor girl put on a brave face every single time. Tonight, I knew she was eating well, and it was time for me to do the same.

I shoved my feet back into my dirty tennis shoes and swiped my keys from the kitchen counter, ultimately deciding that tonight, I could treat myself to something from the diner.

The sun had already begun its descent, just barely kissing the fields in the distance. I gave myself a second to stop and take it in. It was so easy to become lost in my own mind and let simple things like enjoying a sunset seep through the cracks. While I stood there, soaking in the deep golden hue that was cast over the trees surrounding the complex, I let myself enjoy the beauty of something so ordinary. There was a slight crimson haze dancing around the edges of the leaves that were stirred by the soft summer breeze, a select few already fading from bright green to a deep yellow, a subtle promise from fall that the brutal summer sun was soon to be a thing of the past.

I took a deep breath of summer air, exhaled through my nose, and turned on my heels, making it approximately half a step before walking into a human wall by the name of Noah Kent.

Large hands reached out to grip my biceps, steadying me as I reared back. "Noah," I said his name with the same breath forced out of my lungs from smacking into him.

His hands dropped to his sides, but the heat from his palms still radiated on my skin. Like most days, Noah was all hard lines and stoic features, the only movement coming from the way the sunset flickered through his eyes, a beautiful mixture of whiskey and honey.

"Olivia," he said my name in a whisper like he was testing the weight of it on his tongue. "I'm sorry, I said your name a few times. I thought maybe you heard me."

"Oh." I shook my head, slightly embarrassed that a sunset had the ability to make me completely unaware of my surroundings.

As if reading my thoughts, Noah fixed his gaze over the top of my head, squinting slightly at the sun as it dipped into the horizon. "S'pretty tonight."

His eyes were thoughtful and soft, reflecting a sadness that bordered on nostalgia. I could tell from the faraway look in his eyes that Noah was somewhere else in his mind.

I turned, following his eye line past the trees and settling on the cornfield that swayed in the wind. The harsh reds softened to burnt orange the longer we stood there, and dusk quickly settled over this small town. We might have moved across the country, but even moments like this still held a certain familiarity.

The roads were still quiet, the cicadas still calling out as the birds sang their last songs of the night. The few people meandering down the streets were still unhurried but not buried so deep within their own conversations that they couldn't lift a hand to say hello.

What I couldn't understand was how living in the tiny town I called home often felt like being buried alive, but leaving and settling into a town somehow smaller had given me the first lungful of fresh air in years.

I think part of it was starting over in a town that didn't know Liam. I was sure everyone knew to a certain extent why I was living in Rose Hill, but I didn't feel this overwhelming pressure to be a certain way while existing in public.

I could smile without thinking I didn't look sad enough, or be sad without assuming someone was judging me for *still* grieving the loss of my husband. I could just feel the way that I felt and move about my day. The last thing that someone should feel while working through such a horrible loss was judgment that they weren't doing it the textbook way and every time I ran into someone in Evergreen, I couldn't help but feel like whatever I did was wrong.

I was too happy or too sad. I was moving on too quickly or not fast enough while everyone else around me suffered no repercussions for how they chose to grieve.

"What are you thinking about?" Noah asked quietly from beside me.

I considered my answer, finally settling on a simplified version of the truth. "Grieving a big loss in a small town. Maybe just grief in general. I don't know."

He made a thoughtful noise in the back of his throat, shoving his hands into his pockets. "What about it?"

I swallowed, trying to make sense of the words and emotions swirling through my brain to give him the not-so-simplified truth. "That it doesn't make sense at first." My eyes shifted from the setting sun and focused on the trees and the way they danced in the wind. "The sun still rises every morning despite the overwhelming dread inside of you. You're forced to face the sun and wonder how it can still shine so bright without the person you loved here to enjoy it. The birds are still chirping. People are still mowing their lawns. It's why grieving in the same town you lost them in is so impossible. These people that you've known your whole life will find you in the grocery store with tears in their eyes, grieving the death of *your* person. Twenty minutes later, you're still stuck on their words while they're scolding the grocery store clerk for putting their eggs at the bottom of the bag."

"You—" Noah blew out a breath, letting out a small chuckle. "You got all of that from a sunset?"

I think in any other scenario with any other person, I would have assumed they were making fun of me. But right now, I appreciated the levity he'd brought to such a heavy spiral of emotions.

I laughed, nudging my elbow into his side. "Hey, you were getting something from it, too. I could see it." I wagged my index finger around in the general direction of my eyes, arching a brow in his direction.

"Yeah," he breathed, his small smile weakening a tad at the edges.

"What are *you* thinking about?" I countered, returning my gaze to the horizon to give him some privacy while he mulled over my question.

Noah freed his hands from his pockets, running his palms over the side of his thighs, still looking straight ahead. "Well, a few things. You—" he paused to clear his throat, "You seem better than... earlier."

I kept my eyes focused straight ahead but fought a grin at the way he shifted nervously in my peripheral. I honestly wasn't sure how much he actually wanted to know, but given Gia wasn't available for our end-of-the-week vent session tonight, Noah would have to do. "I never know if I'm doing the right thing. Just— like in general, I guess? I thought moving from Wyoming would be the best decision for both of us because all I really want is to be a good mom, and while living in Evergreen... I couldn't be a good mom. I wasn't—" I shook my head, trying to forget how desperate and broken I was just a month or so ago. My stomach churned thinking about it. "It was bad. After a year of being stuck in the same rut, I knew something had to change. I don't know, maybe the move didn't have to be so drastic, but I needed to leave. Moving to Rose Hill felt like such a good choice at the time. We got settled, and I finally feel like the page had turned after a year of reading the same words over and over again."

I felt Noah's eyes shift over to me.

"I'm just trying to do my best, and my mother-in-law is hellbent on making me out to be the villain, and maybe I am in her story, but not in mine."

Silence fell over the conversation, but I could feel Noah's eyes burning a hole into the side of my face. I could hear the question he so desperately wanted to ask on the tip of his tongue.

I sighed and offered him the answer. "She texted me today. I've been ignoring her for the past couple weeks. I let Ken talk to her, of course, but I refuse to engage with someone who does nothing but tear me down." I paused, clearing my throat and working past the burn spreading through my nose. "She's not been the nicest to me since we moved, but she's never been cruel. Today... Today, she was cruel, and I— Well, she believes I'm unfit to be a mother and—"

Closing my eyes, I tried to refocus the panic eating away at my chest and remember the picture Avery sent me, Kennedy's wide smile and loud laughter bringing a small smile to my lips despite the tear that escaped. I brushed it away and shook my head, refusing to let her venomous words hold my thoughts captive for another moment.

I spared a glance at Noah.

His expression was tight, jaw clenched, and eyes hard. I could see his pulse hammering an erratic beat in the vein on his neck. Noah took a deep, controlled breath, combing his hair back with his fingers. "She's wrong."

My throat tightened as I tore my eyes away from him and squeezed them shut, hot tears pricking behind my eyelids.

"The smile on that little girl's face and the way she laughs without a freakin' care in the world is enough to prove that she is *wrong*."

I knew Debra was wrong. I *knew* it. Deep down, past all of the self-doubt and insecurities, I knew I was a good mother. But something in the conviction of Noah's voice solidified what little confidence I had in myself.

I'd known this man for two weeks, and if he could see it so clearly, how couldn't she?

"Liv?"

Liv.

Everyone at home called me Livie. I didn't particularly like it, but it started when I was a child and just kind of stuck around.

I liked that Noah called me Liv. It was short and to the point, like most conversations I'd held with the man. It was fitting.

One tiny little nickname, and I felt my heart rate kick up a notch, my stomach fluttering to life. I *really* needed to get ahold of whatever physical reaction my body had to Noah. Avery flashed through my mind, and the reminder of his wife and child sitting upstairs with my daughter so I could have a night alone was like a bucket of ice water dropped over my head.

My face must've had some kind of reaction to that sobering chain of thoughts because when I opened my eyes, Noah's eyes were full of concern, a shallow line forming between his brows.

"Did I say something wrong?"

I shook my head, wishing I could convey to him *just* how much I needed to hear the things that he said. "No, I— I'm sorry. Thank you. I— It's easy to forget the good things about yourself when you hear nothing but negativity. Thank you." I hoped he could read the sincerity in my eyes.

He nodded, nothing more than a subtle dip of his chin before refocusing on the sun.

Following his lead, I looked back to the sunset, watching as the first half of the sun disappeared into the cornfield. "What's the second thing?"

He made a small grunting noise, and I resisted the urge to roll my eyes.

"You said there were a few things you were thinking about. What's the second thing?"

Noah sighed, rocking back on his heels. "My wife."

I wanted to question the sigh and the way he breathed his words with such resignation. But I didn't. I felt like I needed to defend her. Like he needed to know how lucky he was to have someone like Avery in his life. I toyed with a piece of hair that hung over my shoulder, twisting it between my fingers. "Avery is great."

Noah made a choked sound, coughing a few times as his face twisted up. "Excuse me?!" He questioned through a cough, sucking in a deep breath before coughing it out again.

"What?"

His eyes widened comically, a huge grin spreading across his lips. I didn't even have time to fall victim to the devastation of his smile before he leveled me with a roaring laugh, throwing his head back and filling my ears with the sweet sound.

My heart did another little kickflip in my chest, and I cursed at the traitorous movement.

Though I couldn't focus on it for long because I really wanted to understand... what the fuck was so funny?

"Noah, what— Did I miss something?"

My question triggered another round of laughter, Noah falling forward, his palms catching on his knees.

I stood there on the sidewalk, smiling softly as someone walked across the street, staring at him like he was losing it.

He stood, my breath catching when I laid eyes on his smile again. My mind was focused on pink lips, perfectly straight teeth, and the dimple peeking out from under his stubble as his smile grew. "Avery?" He huffed out another laugh, clearly not fazed by my confusion. "Avery," he repeated, chuckling and running his fingers through his hair as he looked over at the apartment complex and then back to me.

I was frozen, my eyes wide and brows furrowed with confusion. "Avery?"

"Liv." He sighed, his eyes shimmering with amusement. "Avery is my *sister.*"

Chapter 11

Olivia

WHAT?!

My head jerked back as my mouth dropped open, my face twisting with confusion.

His sister?

How the fuck could I have misread that situation so badly?

I lifted a hand and pointed it at the apartment building. *"Avery?"* I questioned dumbly. "This Avery? *Avery?* The Avery that got me this job? She's not your *wife?*"

Noah barked out a laugh, shaking his head. "No! Avery is my sister."

"Nellie isn't your daughter?"

He shook his head again, "Niece." No wonder I never heard her call him dad.

"But you— You walk us home. You go into the apartment!" My mind could not wrap itself around this newfound information.

"Yeah, I walk you guys home, then hang out for an hour or so. I always go home," he paused, *"My* home," he clarified. "Avery has me cook for them every once in a while, so sometimes I'll do that. But I don't stay."

"I—" I stopped talking, blowing out a slow breath. "Your sister?"

Noah pinched his lips together to hold back a smile. "Take as long as you need."

His sister.

There was a tiny amount of relief that swept through my body, replacing the guilt that I harbored for checking out Noah thinking he was married to Avery. Granted, he was still married, so I shouldn't have been checking him out at all. But a small amount of the guilt that'd been eating me alive eased, knowing that I could finally take Avery up on her offer for coffee in the morning and not want to throw up because I'd eyed Noah's ass in those dark wash jeans one too many times.

My mind was reeling. From finding out that Avery and Noah weren't married, from the whiplash of this conversation. I don't think I'd ever felt so many different emotions in one conversation before.

Noah's hands clamped down on my shoulders, squeezing gently as he grinned. Fuck if that dimple wasn't begging to be traced by my thumb. "You thought I was married to my sister?"

My hands slapped against my thighs. "Well, I didn't know she was your sister! I thought you were married to a wonderful woman named Avery who told me that Kent Automotive was family-owned and hiring. Why didn't either of you tell me?!"

He released his grip on my shoulders, scrubbing a hand down his face. "God, Avery is gonna get a kick out of this."

My eyes bugged. "No! You can't tell her!" I needed my mortification to stay between the two of us. Though the flicker of mischief in his eyes told me that wasn't a part of his plan.

Noah let out a thoughtful sigh. "My sister. Wow. This whole time."

"It's only been two weeks," I mumbled under my breath, rolling my eyes. Though, I did kind of understand the humor behind that. I'd spent two fucking weeks so lost in my own head that I didn't realize Avery and Noah were *siblings.*

And then it hit me.

I could feel the blood draining from my face, the conversation I'd had with Avery the morning she brought me coffee played through my mind. Slapping my hand against my face, I groaned and took a couple of steps back from Noah.

"*You're* the brother that caught me sobbing and covered in snot in the hallway."

He flattened his lips in a poor attempt to hold back his smile. "I wasn't going to bring up the snot."

"Noah!" I groaned again. The blood that had drained from my face rushed back in, my cheeks burning as I recalled how mortified I was that night. I was so concerned with getting back into the apartment that I hadn't even paid attention to the kind stranger who checked on me.

Although, that might have been a good thing. Because if I had known that it was Noah in the hallway that night, I would've walked right back out of Kent Automotive the second I laid eyes on him.

"Do you know how many times I've walked up to Avery's door and found her crumpled on the floor? You needed a minute, Liv. There's nothing to be embarrassed about." His rough voice was surprisingly gentle, the playful edge to his eyes shifting to something deeper.

"You have a lot going on right now. Don't let yourself be embarrassed about something like grief. Healing from this kind of loss isn't linear. You're going to have really powerful highs and unbearably painful lows. The only way to get over it is to go through it. And if that means crying in the hallway to make sure your daughter doesn't overhear, then cry in the hallway."

I stared at Noah, soaking in the truth of his words. There was something so validating about what he was saying. All this time, I'd felt crazy for the roller coaster of emotions I was battling every single day. I was confused by the way my mood would change so easily and how everyone else seemed to be doing just fine while I was slowly succumbing to a dark cloud of grief.

I also couldn't shake the feeling that Noah wasn't just saying all of this to make me feel better. The conviction behind his words had me wondering if maybe he could relate to the situation I was in.

"Thank you," I whispered, swallowing past the knot forming in my throat.

The corner of his mouth lifted and returned to that small, sad, but knowing smile that made me want to figure him out. I respected the fact that he kept to himself, but that didn't stop me from wondering what happened to dim the light in his eyes so much.

"Don't thank me. Just— give yourself a little credit."

"Eh," I shrugged and smiled up at him, "I'll do my best. But I make no promises."

"Then I'll be there to remind you when you need it."

Both of us seemed a little shocked by his words, but I boxed them up in my brain and stored them for a rainy day. Noah was a moody, brooding introvert.

Not even he could deny that. But he was also proving himself to be sweet, gentle, and kind.

"Thank you, Noah. There's a lot I feel like I need to thank you for, but just—thank you."

I wasn't sure what I expected. A shrug, a dismissive wave. Maybe a grunt that resembled someone being sucker-punched in the gut.

I did not expect the words that came out of his mouth next or the lack of explanation that followed.

"Today is my wife's birthday."

"Oh."

The man had just made his first personal confession, and the only thing I could muster up was *oh.*

His gaze jumped from mine, focusing on something over my head. The sadness in his eyes was so familiar, and my stomach dipped and rolled like I was flying over a speed bump in the road. Noah's Adam's apple bobbed as he swallowed, trying to school the pained look that flashed over his hardened expression, and my heart *broke* for him.

I could *feel* it. I *knew* it. This grief existed within every fiber of my being, it coursed through my veins and weaved itself into every aspect of my life and I was watching it unfold in front of me. I was seeing it through a new lens.

I was seeing it tear this man that I had only ever known as stoic and impassive to shreds from the inside out.

He was hurting.

He'd built this wall to keep everyone aside from Avery and his niece out, but it was cracking under the pressure. Tiny little fissures that he probably once assumed were harmless had started letting his grief seep through, and soon, it would be too much.

"How old would she have been today?" The question was out of my mouth before I could even stop to consider that I was crossing a line.

His gaze snapped to mine and my stomach dropped, an apology balancing on the tip of my tongue until he answered. "Thirty-four. She would've been thirty-four."

"I'm really sorry, Noah. *God.* This pain— I wouldn't wish it on anyone."

He let out a sardonic laugh, his eyes focusing on something over my head again. "I deserve every second of it."

"Noah," I rasped, his confession spearing through my chest.

"Liv." My name was a soft plea as it fell from his lips. He didn't want me to ask any questions or offer up my condolences.

I wasn't sure what to say or do, and suddenly I found myself resonating with the people who always seemed to put their foot in their mouth and say the wrong thing when in the presence of someone grieving or hurt.

It was a stupid question, but I asked it anyway. "Are you okay?"

His answer was simple, but the meaning behind it was anything but. "No." Before Noah, I had no idea that a small, two-letter word had the potential to shatter my heart like it just did. There was no question or uncertainty laced into his answer; he was so sure in his response, and I had no idea what to do.

He clearly didn't want any more attention brought to the matter, so I used the only other thing I had in my arsenal.

"I was gonna go get dinner at the diner. Barb promised me a milkshake. Would you wanna— Do you wanna go?"

Amber irises melted into warm honey as he lowered his gaze back to mine. I could see the conflict playing out behind his eyes. "I—" Noah paused, his fingers stabbing through already disheveled hair.

My eyes fell to the sidewalk, preparing myself for the pang of disappointment. He already told me he had things to handle at the shop, and based on the mood I'd been in all day, why would he want to spend the night entertaining me?

My head snapped up at the low "Sure" that fell from his lips.

I swear there was a tiny twitch at the corner of his mouth from the shock on my face. "Yeah?"

His chin dipped once in acknowledgment, and he stepped aside, sweeping his arm out in front of him. "After you."

Chapter 12

Noah

Liv and I walked to the diner in a calm, comforting silence. I felt her glance up at me once or twice, but for the most part, we kept our eyes trained straight ahead. Except for when her hand brushed against mine. Only then did I look down to see that pretty shade of pink rush to her cheeks. Any lingering tension from our conversation in front of the apartment complex seemed to melt away. But there was a war raging inside my head, indecision and guilt battling it out to what seemed like the death.

I shouldn't be following her to the diner. I shouldn't be spending *this* night doing everything in my power to make her smile.

Honestly, I couldn't believe that I told her about Addie so soon. But the second those blue eyes locked onto mine, I was ready to spill every single thought I'd ever kept to myself.

It was supposed to be a night where I drank and screamed to the skies about the unfairness of the hand I'd been dealt. Instead, I was making sure Liv got a warm meal and something to distract her from the negativity that was swirling around in her head. Maybe I was subconsciously looking for a distraction from mine, too.

I couldn't decide if it was too soon to be so captivated and tempted by another woman. And whenever I thought about the comfort of Liv's touch or the softness of her eyes, the guilt that would consume me threatened to buckle my knees.

She was slowly wiggling her way under my skin and into my heart, and I thought I was trying *so* hard to fight it. But here I was, holding the door open for her as we walked into the diner.

Barb walked through the swinging doors that led to the kitchen with her back to us and her arms full of plates. "Welcome, welcome! Take a—" She turned around, and the words died on her tongue as her eyes flitted back and forth between Liv and me. She schooled the look of shock on her face and replaced it with a coy smile while she cleared her throat. "Hey, you two. Take a seat wherever."

Liv's cheeks flushed again as the diner came to a stop. Drinks and forks were suspended in mid-air, and the usual roar of the dinnertime rush dropped to a quiet hum as curious eyes fell on us. It was easy to ignore this kind of reaction when I was the only one affected by the weird tension.

Before I could offer a way out, Barb stepped out from behind the counter and cleared her throat. "The hell is wrong with you people? Ain't you ever seen two co-workers eating food together? Y'all don't stare at Eddie and Harvey like this."

Eddie and Harvey were the two retired men who sat at Barb's counter all day and night, talking her ear off because they had nothing better to do. Did I think they technically counted as co-workers? No. But I was thankful for her intervention anyway.

Just like that, the spell was broken, and the nosy-ass residents of Rose Hill went back to their dinners. Barb threw a wink over her shoulder before she started dropping plates onto tables.

"Sorry," I murmured. "The people in this town have a weird fascination with widowed spouses, apparently."

Liv snorted and nudged me with her hip. "Maybe they're just not used to seeing you with a friend." She started toward the table in the back, and I smothered the small smile that tugged at my mouth by dragging a hand down my face and followed quickly behind.

* * *

"It's been kind of weird eating with someone who doesn't need to be constantly reminded to chew with their mouth closed," Liv mused before taking the last bite of her burger.

"That could be arranged. If it would make you feel more at home." I cocked my brow at her and popped a fry into my mouth, narrowly dodging the one she tossed in my direction.

Talking with Liv was a lot easier than I thought it would be. I was thankful we avoided the topic of our spouses, our conversation revolving more around Kennedy and how the hell she got the impression that Avery was my wife and not my sister. As much as I didn't want to admit it, I needed this just as much as she did. I'd spent a lot of time stuck in the past and ignoring the fact that life seemed to continue on with or without Addie.

There wasn't a conversation in the world that would be able to take away the guilt that festered inside of me, but it was nice to be able to think about something else, even for just an hour.

I cleared my throat and toyed with the paper napkin in my lap. "So, what's your favorite thing about Rose Hill so far?"

Her head tilted from side to side as she mulled over her answer. "The privacy, maybe."

My chin dropped, eyebrows arched to the sky as I pinned her with a look of disbelief. *"Privacy?* In this town? No such thing."

Liv's laugh was gentle and light, stirring something in my chest that I hadn't felt in a long time.

"Listen," she started, sitting up and resting her forearms on the table. "No one I've encountered here is as nosy as the people in Evergreen. Trust me. Here, unless something directly affects them, they mind their own. Everyone's been friendly and taken the time to introduce themselves, but that's as far as their curiosity goes."

There was a flicker of something sobering in her eyes as she shifted in her seat. "Here... I can just *exist*. There's no pressure to answer questions I'd rather keep to myself or a need to prove myself. It's just refreshing."

I made a thoughtful noise in the back of my throat, a bittersweet feeling swirling in my chest. "I'm glad you're given that courtesy."

Liv's gaze moved to mine; her lips turned up in a melancholy smile. "I'm sorry that you're not."

I waved her off, but her words struck deep. I wasn't awarded that same level of privacy. My grief was broadcast around town and whispered about every time I made an appearance. The way she talked about Evergreen was the same way I felt here in Rose Hill.

I wanted to get back to just existing here. I wanted the whispers and the stares to stop and for people to quit looking at me like I was some kind of wounded puppy. But I guess if I wanted that to happen, I had to stop looking like one.

Barb sidled up to the table with a small smile, leaning her arm against the top of the booth. "You two gonna hang out here all night?"

The sun had disappeared into the horizon some time ago, but we both lost track of just how long we'd been sitting here. My eyes swept over the diner, and to my surprise, we were the only two left. "Jesus, Barb. Why didn't you come get us sooner?"

"Hey, I'm not complaining. It's nice to have someone aside from Eddie and Harvey hanging around after hours." She winked and tossed a rag over her shoulder. "No rush to head out. Just wanted to check on ya."

Liv dug into her purse to get her card, but I knew better than that. No one in my family had paid for food here in years, and we certainly weren't starting tonight. Barb and my grandma were old friends, and ever since she passed, she'd refused to let us pay. Just like I knew she would, Barb waved her off when Liv lifted a card in her direction.

"You ain't payin'."

I smiled at Liv and eased out of the booth, dropping a kiss on Barb's cheek. "Thank you for a lovely evening. See you tomorrow for breakfast."

"Oh, come on, Barb!" Liv thrust her card out again. "I haven't paid for a single meal since I stepped foot in this town. You gotta let me pay for something."

Barb shook her head and patted my arm. "Make sure she gets home alright?"

"Yes, ma'am."

Liv gave me an exasperated look before rolling her eyes, shoving her card back into her purse, and sliding out of the booth. "Thank you, Barb." She finally relented, her exasperation giving way to a soft smile.

We said our goodbyes and made our way to the front door, Liv stopping by the bowl of fortune cookies to snag one. It struck me the second the door shut behind us that I wasn't relieved by the prospect of going home. The thought of sitting in front of my TV with a six-pack of beer wasn't nearly as enticing as the company of the woman walking beside me.

I walked back to the shop alone and was struck by the silence upon entering through the front door. I'd planned on spending the night drowning my sorrows, but my feet carried me back out, seemingly on autopilot, in the direction of Liv's apartment. I walked out and saw her standing at the end of the street, her head tilted as she watched the sun lower beneath the fields.

I wasn't sure what her plan was for the night, but I knew I wanted to be part of it.

"Come on, let's get you home." My hand fell to the small of her back, almost out of instinct, as I maneuvered her to the inside of the sidewalk. I could feel the heat of her skin against my palm, and I tried to control the wild thoughts that spiraled through my mind about just how soft it would feel under my fingers. *Because that would be ridiculous.* Before I could do something stupid that would more than likely freak us both out, I clenched my jaw and took a shaky breath, my hand dropping back to my side.

Despite the impending threat of fall, the night air was still hot and sticky. It was dark and so quiet that the sound of our shoes against the pavement seemed to echo off the surrounding buildings.

There was a dog barking in the distance, a soft beat pouring through the speakers of someone's radio. The silence we shared was always comforting, but this time, my curiosity got the best of me.

I glanced over when the plastic of her fortune cookie crinkled and ripped. She cracked the cookie and pulled the little slip of paper out.

Her eyes swept over the text twice, her face flushing with a subtle shake of her head. She stuffed the paper into her pocket and extended half the cookie in my direction.

"What's your deal with those things anyway?" I asked, taking it from her hand

and popping it into my mouth.

"They were my husband's thing. Somewhere, there's a tiny little shoe box filled with a bunch of little fortunes that he collected while we were together." She looked over at me with a wistful smile. "It kind of just felt like a sign. We moved, and I've been questioning everything ever since. My first day at a new job, Kennedy's first day at a new preschool, and Barb gets a giant order of fortune cookies the night before?"

She shrugged. "I've never been superstitious, but it felt like a sign. Like I was gonna be okay."

I hummed, smiling softly. "What does this one say?"

Liv pulled it out of her pocket. "Release the butterflies of worry; sometimes, the simplest path leads to the grandest adventures."

My brow quirked. "Do you think that means anything?"

"I guess it's a reminder not to overthink things," she mused, gazing into the distance. "Liam used to say I had a tendency to analyze every little detail. Maybe this cookie is telling me to let go a bit, embrace the uncertainty."

"Maybe," I responded.

The breeze played with her hair as we walked and I asked the next thing that popped into my mind. "How the hell did you end up in Rose Hill? Was that a fortune cookie, too? It seems... random."

Liv laughed, tucking her hair behind her ear. "It wasn't, but it's equally as stupid. I was reading a book to Ken one night, and the character lived on Rose Hill Lane. It was this beautiful little street in the book with lots of flowers, and everyone was illustrated so happily. I wish I knew why I felt the need to fixate on it, but it was all such a blur, I really don't remember my thought process."

She shook her head. "At some point, I did an internet search for Rose Hill. There was a movie. Someone famous who died years ago. And then a little article about a small town called Rose Hill, Delaware. I remember clicking on the website and thinking it looked *just* like her book. Everyone in the pictures was smiling; the flowers were bright, and the sun was shining. I thought it looked like somewhere I could be happy. I know that was a stretch, but it just felt so real. Less than a week later, my house was packed and on the market, our apartment was rented, and a cross-country road trip with a four-year-old was planned."

I blew out a slow breath in amazement. "Wow. I'm not sure what I was expecting, but I don't think it was that."

Her smile was soft when she looked over at me. "I wish it were more exciting, but... That's the truth. That's how we got here."

I'd gotten all these little pieces of her through overheard phone calls and a talkative four-year-old, and I should've been satisfied. For someone who merely worked at the desk in my shop, I knew her enough.

But all these little scraps only piqued my interest more. I wanted to sift through them and fit them all together like pieces of a puzzle and figure out exactly who Olivia Brooks was.

I realized how extremely hypocritical that was of me. But I wasn't ready to lose her interest yet. There was something soft in the way she looked at me, but I knew the second she learned about the things I was responsible for, it would disappear.

"Do you regret it?" I asked quietly.

She contemplated her answer, her lips twisting from left to right like she was rolling the words over her tongue before speaking them out loud.

"No," she answered. "I think it's complicated, but I don't regret it."

We were quiet for another moment as we neared the apartment complex. Our steps had slowed drastically since we left the diner, and I wasn't sure who initiated it, but I was thankful for the few extra moments alone.

"I think after we graduated from high school, I knew I didn't want to stay in Evergreen my whole life. I still don't think I could handle the culture shock of moving to a city larger than like five thousand people, but I'd always longed for a change of scenery."

Liv let out a wistful sigh. "It was something that Liam couldn't understand. He was adamant about remaining in Wyoming and raising our daughter on the same street we'd both lived on growing up, enrolling her in the same schools and taking her to the same small diner. But I always needed something different. Not necessarily more. Just different."

She paused, and my stomach slowly sank to my feet as I realized that Rose Hill could lack what she was looking for. Before I would even be able to explain how just looking into her eyes made me feel so much more alive than I had in years, she could be gone.

We came to a stop in front of the apartment complex, and her eyes swept over the empty street and long shadows cast by the street lamps. "I got that when I moved to Rose Hill."

That sentence shouldn't have offered as much relief as it did. But the confirmation that she got what she was searching for was like a soothing balm to an open wound. Selfishly, on my end, it meant I wasn't losing her quite yet.

Liv's teeth sank into her bottom lip, her hands wringing together at her waist. "It's not just the place that makes a difference, ya know." Her elbow gently nudged my side. "It's the people, too. So... thank you."

Thankfully, we came to a stop on a sliver of the sidewalk that the street lamps couldn't quite reach, and she didn't notice the blood that rushed to my cheeks. It felt wrong to say 'you're welcome' and accept her thanks because, truthfully, I hadn't done anything extraordinary. I think we just recognized something broken in each other that made it easy for us to connect.

"You're welcome," I mumbled, the flames beneath my skin burning hotter.

Liv's lips eased into a smile. She glanced at the door and then back at me. "Um—Do you wanna come in? I think I have a dusty bottle of whiskey somewhere."

My heart thudded in my chest, and I knew I should've said no. I should've turned around and gone home and upheld the same tradition I participated in for the past four years: drinking alone. But then her brows dipped together, and I could see the little shimmer of disappointment in her eyes. The word "sure" came tumbling out of my mouth for the second time tonight.

Chapter 13

Noah

"Do you see how long that nose hair is?"

"It's like... As long as my pinky!"

The only thing that stopped me from rolling my eyes was the intensity of the headache pounding behind them. My stomach churned as I took a deep breath, the girls squealing and running away.

The high-pitched noise went straight to the ache behind my eyes and I groaned.

If the girls were here... That meant I ended up staying at Liv's.

I had a vague recollection of last night and the one glass of whiskey that led to many, *many* more. I massaged my temples and took another deep breath to calm the waves of nausea that rolled through me.

God, I had to get home.

I just needed to hold back the puke until I muttered goodbye and made it out the door. There was a hedge outside calling my name.

Slowly, I peeled my eyes open. I couldn't decide what was more painful. The sunlight coming in through the window or how blinking felt like an ice pick to the brain. This was why I normally avoided liquor. Whiskey hangovers put me out of commission for at least two days, but I couldn't say no to Liv. I just couldn't.

One glass of whiskey led to another, and soon we were humming along to Taylor Swift while unpacking boxes in her living room. I vaguely remember talking to someone on the phone, but I had no idea who or what the hell I talked to them about.

Jesus. *What the hell happened last night?*

I could hear Avery's voice from across the hall, the girls running back and forth between the apartments, but I hadn't seen or heard Liv yet. If I felt this bad, I couldn't even imagine how horrible she must've been feeling.

My head lolled to the side, and I surveyed the room, realizing it was basically a mirrored version of Avery's. The living room was small and shaped like a square, with the couch against one wall, the TV, and two bookshelves lined up on the opposite side. The carpet was the same beige color as Avery's, the walls the same stark white paint that hers used to be before she begged me to paint them.

The bookshelves I vaguely remember helping her decorate last night held framed pictures of Liv and her husband with tiny Kennedy and colorful books that looked a lot like the romance section at the Target in Wilmington.

If my stomach wasn't so close to losing its contents all over Olivia's living room, I would have taken the chance to savor the sweet scent of vanilla and brown sugar that lingered in the air.

Before I could stand and take a good look around, movement in the hallway leading to the kitchen caught my eye. Kennedy poked her head around the corner, then looked behind her before tiptoeing over to where I lay completely still on the couch.

I knew I was probably overstaying my welcome, but the way the room seemed to spin if I moved my head too quickly had me plastered in place.

Kennedy stopped in front of the couch, crouching down so she was at eye level with me. "I'm not supposed to bother you."

I couldn't stop the smile from pulling at the corner of my mouth. Kennedy was so unintentionally funny that I found myself smiling more and more whenever she was around. Whether she knew it or not, Liv was doing an amazing job at preserving Kennedy's innocence. She acted just like every other child should at this age: shamelessly goofy with no care in the world.

"So what are you doing measuring my nose hair?"

Just like her mother, her face flushed a light shade of pink. But that was the only thing that clued me into the fact that she was embarrassed she'd been caught. Kennedy shrugged, like examining the nose hair of someone sleeping on your couch was the only obvious option to pass the time. "It's long."

I huffed out a laugh, running my fingers through my hair. "I'll make sure to pluck it for you." I was almost certain all of my nose hairs were a reasonable length, but I couldn't even remember the last time I really cared about my appearance, so it's entirely possible she and Nellie were correct.

She grinned, seemingly satisfied with the conclusion of that argument. Her voice lowered to a whisper. "Mom's gonna wake you up with breakfast. That's what she said to Avery. But—" she turned, looking down the hallway to make sure it was clear, "She already burned the toast and the eggs were too runny. You should tell her no."

How in the hell was Liv not kneeling over a toilet right now? I knew we went drink for drink, so there was no way she wasn't just as hungover as I was.

"And I think the milk is bad, too. So you should just say no," she added.

"Should I?" I asked, stifling a grin. I loved that Kennedy had no shame in critiquing Liv's cooking.

Kennedy nodded, her little green eyes wide. "You should."

Despite the churning in my stomach and pounding behind my eyes, I pushed myself up so I was sitting, swallowing the urge to vomit. "How about this?" I took a deep breath, letting the room right itself before continuing. "I'll run down to the diner, grab some breakfast from Barb, and be back here before she burns the next piece of toast?"

Her eyes lit up. "Sounds good to me! Can you ask her if she has French toast? I haven't had that since my daddy had his accident and I miss it."

I pushed myself off of the couch, ruffling her blonde hair. "You got it, kiddo." French toast wasn't on the menu; their food catered more to drunk people and semi-truck drivers passing through late at night or early in the morning. But if Barb couldn't figure it out, I'd go back into the kitchen and make some French toast myself.

Liv walked into the room, skidding to a stop when she saw me standing in the middle of her living room. Her blonde hair was tied up into a loose bun, one that started to slide down the right side of her head.

She wore a simple pair of black leggings that used to cling to her legs, accentuating the toned muscles of her thighs and calves. But even after just a couple of weeks here, they were loose. So much so that whenever she wore them to work this week, she was pulling at the waist constantly to keep them up.

My eyes moved slowly up her body, her baggy crop top stopping just before the waistband of her leggings, exposing a thin sliver of pale skin. I met her gaze, fighting a smile when that light shade of pink started at the base of her neck and slowly crawled its way up to her cheeks.

I hadn't meant to be so blatant about my slow perusal of her body, I blamed the hangover for that one, but I'd be lying if I said I didn't love seeing her squirm under my stare.

I might've felt a little more confident in my actions if it didn't feel like someone was trying to dig their way out of my brain with a pickaxe and my mouth didn't taste like something had died inside of it.

"You're awake." I felt a tiny twinge of pride swell in my chest at the breathless nature of her voice.

"I am." I cleared my throat, itching to run across the hall to Avery's so I could brush my teeth. I was almost certain she kept an extra toothbrush in the medicine cabinet above her sink. "What the he— *heck* happened—"

"Oh," she cut me off, her eyes dropping to her daughter. "Honey, why don't you run over to Avery's and get your bag from last night?"

Kennedy nodded, curious eyes shifting between her mother and me. "Okay." The two of us stood in silence, avoiding each other's eyes. I waited until the front door shut to meet her gaze again. "I don't have a clear memory of last night."

Liv nodded, rolling her lips together. "There was a lot of karaoke."

My hand scrubbed down my face. "Oh, god."

"We called Gia— Actually, I think technically, *you* called Gia. On my phone."

I lowered my voice. "Who the hell is Gia? How the hell did we get that drunk? How the hell do you not feel as bad as I do?"

I also had a history of running my mouth when under the influence of whiskey. I hoped that whatever I shared with the two of them wasn't that bad.

"Gia is my best friend from back home. I don't drink a lot, but I don't usually get hungover. I don't know, I think it's my special talent." She shrugged, her eyes flickering with amusement. "You, on the other hand…"

Her face twisted up, and if my brain hadn't felt like it was being gutted by a tiny little construction crew, I would've rolled my eyes. "Don't be a smart ass."

Liv snorted. "Avery said she has some stuff for you in her apartment if you wanna get cleaned up."

Thank god for my sister.

Kennedy came running through the door, Nellie and Avery following closely behind. Her expression fell when she saw that I hadn't left yet, meaning there wasn't French toast waiting for her.

"I'm going right now," I promised, looking up at my sister. "You still have that extra toothbrush?"

She nodded, pushing the girls out of the small hallway and into the living room. "Knock yourself out. Holler when you're done, I'll walk to the diner with you."

"Diner?" Liv's brows pushed together as she looked from Avery to me. Kennedy's eyes widened.

"I'm gonna run and get some breakfast for everyone. Ken requested French toast."

"Seriously, Kennedy?" Olivia turned to look at her daughter, but the scowl on her face softened when she noticed the death glare Kennedy was sending my way. She bit back a smile, shaking her head. "Let me get my card."

I shook my head. "It's fine. I got it."

"No, it's fine. Just give me—" I reached out to grab her wrist as she turned toward the kitchen where her purse sat on the table.

"Liv, she won't make us pay. You and I both know that. If she does, I got it."

"Okay," she breathed, her eyes jumping down to where my hand was wrapped around her. She swallowed, and the rise and fall of her chest picked up just enough for me to notice. "Thank you."

I wanted to explore the reaction that she had to me. I wanted to keep my hand wrapped around the smooth skin of her wrist and feel the way her pulse kicked up under my thumb. But Avery cleared her throat and pulled her lips between her teeth as she fought a grin.

So instead, I nodded, pushing past her and the girls and ignoring the smirk on Avery's face.

***

"So..." Avery drawled, nudging her elbow into my side.

I let out a deep sigh, swatting at the arm that still poked at my ribs. We hadn't even made it half a block before the meddling started. I at least thought we'd make it to the diner before she attempted to pry at my personal life. Or lack thereof.

A small part of me thought this could be about something else, but that hope was short-lived when the next thing to come out of her mouth was, "Olivia."

I kept my eyes focused on the sidewalk ahead, pulling the ball cap I'd stolen from Avery's bathroom down to cover my eyes. I'd given it to Nellie last year so the fit was a little off, but without sunglasses, it would have to do for now. I needed something to shield my eyes from the sun.

Ideally, I'd pick the blackout curtains in my room. But I promised French toast. And French toast I was going to deliver.

At least until I could figure out a way to teach Olivia how to make it herself.

"Hello?" Avery shoved my arm to get my attention. Clearly, I wasn't getting out of this conversation.

"I thought we talked about you meddling."

She scoffed, "I thought we came to an understanding."

"Which would be?"

"You tell me to butt out, and I start bothering you about it more," she teased, pulling a small smile from my lips.

I shook my head as we approached the diner, pulling the door open and letting her step through in front of me. "We're remembering this conversation very differently."

Avery laughed. "Sounds about right."

The pounding behind my eyes intensified the second we walked through the front door, the scraping of knives and forks against plates and the laughter and chatter amongst patrons sounded like it was playing through a pair of headphones duct taped to my ears. A wave of nausea rolled through my stomach, and I took a deep breath, closing my eyes for a second.

Avery came to stop beside me.

"You told me you'd be okay." She lowered her voice, taking a step toward me. "And I am."

Despite my eyes being closed, I could feel the eye roll she gave me. "You're practically green, Noah, and you reek of booze."

"I'm fine, Ave." I guess Liv didn't tell her I spent the night singing Taylor Swift karaoke and organizing her smut collection. "It was a good kind of drunk. We— We had fun."

I peeled my eyes open and avoided meeting the shocked look on her face as I walked up to the counter, Barb emerged from the kitchen with a neon pink smile spread across her lips. It faltered just a tad when she did a once-over of my face.

Barb had known my family for a long time; she was practically my grandma's best friend. She, like most of the other people in this diner, knew that yesterday was Adeline's birthday. But I wasn't about to go around and tell everyone that I spent my night shitfaced on Liv's couch.

However, she'd probably make her own assumptions since I was showing up, the night after dinner with Liv, hungover and ordering her breakfast.

"Noah Kent, you look like shit." She balanced a pen behind her ear and rested her elbows against the counter. "The usual?"

I nodded, gesturing to Avery. "Nellie and Ave's usual, too. Could you guys make French toast? Kennedy asked for some. I can make it if you don't." It would only take a few minutes to whip up, but I wasn't confident in my ability to fight back the nausea right now.

Barb exchanged a glance with my sister, one that told me they'd been gossiping about me and the receptionist that I couldn't seem to get out of my mind. But unlike Avery, she was gracious enough to keep her thoughts to herself. "I can do that. Give me ten."

Just as I did every time I entered the diner, I avoided looking toward the dining room and turned, leaning back on my elbows. "You know, she thought you were my wife."

Avery's mouth dropped open, and I almost wished I had thought to pull my phone out and start recording before I told her. She turned to face me, her copper ponytail slapping against my arm in the process.

"Shut the fuck up. Are you serious?!"

I grinned, unable to hold back my laugh. "Yup. She thought we were married."

"This whole time?"

"This whole time," I confirmed, nodding my head. Avery stood in awe, undoubtedly doing the same thing I did after finding out Liv thought we were married, which was picking through every interaction we've had in front of her and trying to figure out where the hell she would've gotten that from.

She shook her head, her face twisting up in disgust. "Gross."

"My thoughts exactly," I laughed.

Thankfully, our order was up quickly. We said our goodbyes and I grabbed a fortune cookie for Liv, earning a curious look from my sister as we headed out the front door.

I was expecting Avery to question me about Liv some more, but she stayed quiet as we made our way back toward the apartment complex. I shut down after Addie died. Avery was used to hearing just about every thought that crossed my mind, and I knew the lack of answers to her many questions was probably driving her insane, but there wasn't anything to tell. Not really, at least.

I cleared my throat, looking at Avery. "We had dinner together last night. I went into her apartment for a couple of drinks and passed out on the couch. That's all."

She rolled her eyes, her lips curling into a smile. "I didn't say anything."

"Yeah, but you're thinking it." I removed the ball cap, running my fingers through my hair before pulling it back on and using the bill to shield my eyes.

"Was not," Avery responded, shoving her elbow into my stomach.

I groaned and pinched my eyes shut while another wave of nausea churned in my stomach. "Low blow, Avery," I gritted out through clenched teeth.

She laughed and continued walking toward the apartment. "Stop being a baby," she threw out over her shoulder.

Chapter 14

Olivia

Honestly, I had to give it to him. Noah could fake his way through a hangover like no one I'd met before. Through all the giggling and screaming from the dining room table, he only looked like he was on the verge of throwing up once or twice.

I kind of felt bad for him. Maybe I should've warned him about the no-hangover thing before I poured his fourth glass of whiskey.

After he and Avery got back from the diner, he'd asked for a painkiller, downed it with a glass of water, got everyone's food set out around my table, and tossed me my fortune cookie.

Plant seeds of kindness, and watch a garden of warmth bloom around you.

Something about this breakfast had the sweetest feeling of contentment sweeping through my chest. It was like nestling into the warm feeling of a heated blanket after a cold day. Every time Kennedy and Nellie would giggle to themselves or Noah would nudge my foot under the table when picking on Avery, the hole in my chest stitched itself together bit by bit.

I never wanted this breakfast to end.

But soon, bellies were full, and the girls were running around the apartment, fueled by the pint of syrup they'd both consumed with their food. I definitely was not looking forward to the sugar crash that would inevitably follow in a couple hours, but it was worth it to laugh and feel whole for the first time in so long.

I dried my hands after putting the last of the utensils in the drying rack, overhearing Noah mention something to Avery about needing to go back to the shop. I felt my heart sink a little, hating that this morning was coming to an end so soon.

I missed Sunday brunch at my parents' house. I missed the smell of Dad's homemade biscuits baking in the oven and the sizzle of the bacon on the stove. I missed my brother, Jackson, and how he and Kennedy would always end up in trouble for almost breaking something of my mother's. I missed the chaos. I missed my family.

It was so hard to ignore the way my chest ached at the reminder of my family and everyone I ripped Kennedy away from when I moved across the country. Every reminder of how much I missed them was a harsh reminder of how much they hated me and how many texts and calls went unanswered.

But I didn't want the conflicting feelings building inside me to taint the peaceful morning I'd just shared with three people who had done nothing but make us feel welcome and at home. So I shook it off, making a mental note to call home tomorrow afternoon and pray that someone would finally answer. Instead of dreading the end of this brunch, I willed myself to be thankful it happened.

Even if it was partially due to Noah waking up hungover on my couch and my daughter's spectacular ability to get her way whenever she bats her eyes at anyone in the room.

Swiping Noah's keys from the counter, I stepped into the dining room and held my hand out.

"Thanks," he said quietly, stuffing them into his pocket.

"Thanks for brunch. Barb is really going to regret making that French toast. She's going to order it every time we go."

Noah chuckled, his eyes flickering over to where Kennedy and Nellie sat in the living room. "I'm sure she won't mind."

"Well, thank you again."

He smiled gently. "Sure."

He had this incredible ability to make the world around us disappear whenever his eyes locked onto mine. The maternal instincts inside me wouldn't let me lose track of Kennedy's voice and where it carried throughout the apartment or the shop, but if it weren't for Avery clearing her throat beside us, I would've forgotten she was there.

There was so much to decipher in Noah's eyes, so much to get lost in. I could see the sadness that he carried with him, I could see the guilt. I didn't know the details behind Adeline's death, but I did know that he didn't intend to forgive himself for whatever happened, even if the circumstances were out of his control.

Avery cleared her throat again, a smug grin plastered on her face as her eyes bounced back and forth between me and Noah.

I took a step back, cursing the blood that rushed to my cheeks. "I'll see you Monday."

"Monday," he responded, dipping his chin once, then rolling his eyes when Avery snickered from beside him. "Alright." He shoved her shoulder gently and yelled his goodbyes to the girls before heading toward the front door, my eyes shamelessly falling to his ass as he walked through my kitchen.

Avery waited until the front door shut to turn toward me, her hands immediately finding her hips. "So," she started, tilting her head slightly to the left, "Will you get coffee in the morning with me now that you know you're checking out my brother and not my husband?"

I groaned, slapping my hand against my forehead. Apparently, my poker face needed some work. "Oh my god. I would love to, but the fact that I'll never be able to look you in the eyes again would make that really hard."

She threw her head back and laughed, and I mentally berated myself for not noticing the subtle similarities between the two of them. Besides the noticeable difference in their hair color, which I'd found out today came from their mother's side of the family, they had the same slender nose and angular jaw. Their eyes were the same shade of golden brown and various hues of green. Now that I knew they were siblings, I almost couldn't believe I ever thought differently.

"I know we can be an intimidating crew. But we're not so bad when you get to know us. I'm serious about my offer for breakfast, though. Whenever you're ready. I don't brag often, but I am a little more fun to hang out with than that brood."

I smiled and looked over at Avery. "He's not so bad."

I half expected her to tease me for my answer, but her expression softened instead. "No, he's not."

"Actually." I turned toward the door, sliding my feet into my tennis shoes. "I actually had something to ask him about Monday. Can you watch Ken for a second?"

She waved me off and walked toward the living room. "Take your time."

Noah

"Noah!"

I whipped around entirely too fast for someone as hungover as I was, my stomach churning as Liv jogged down the short sidewalk toward me.

"I had something to ask you," she said nervously.

Her hands wrung together, her gaze shifting to the concrete beneath our feet. I lifted my index finger to tap the bottom of her chin, her eyes slowly traveling up to meet mine. "What's wrong?"

"No," she answered quickly. "Nothing's wrong. I just— You know, this um— I heard that—" She paused, taking a deep breath and squaring her shoulders. "The grief counselor at the hospital after Liam died told me that it was helpful to talk to people. People that might be going through the same thing as you."

I knew that. The grief counselor who was already waiting for me when the hospital doors slid open told me the exact same thing about four hours after I started zoning out while staring at the blank, white wall across from me.

He warned me about the stages of grief. Survivor's guilt. Depression. PTSD. There was a pamphlet for each one shoved in my hand while I sat on that tiny waiting room chair. Pamphlets that were promptly tossed right into the trash can as I left without my wife.

"I don't have anyone here." She paused to clear her throat, scratching at her cheek nervously, "And maybe you don't want to talk about it. I would understand if you didn't. But I'm always here if you do want to. I just think it would be…

I think it could help us both. Who doesn't love bonding over shared trauma?" Her question ended with a nervous laugh, her arms wrapping around her torso like she was trying to make herself smaller.

I bit back the first response that bubbled up my throat. On instinct, harsh words intertwined with a bitterness that Olivia didn't deserve begged to spill from my tongue. I knew she was only trying to help, but that isn't what stopped me from saying something I couldn't take back.

It was her eyes. They bore into mine, wide and full of nerves; an endless blue ocean of desperation, silently pleading with me. She needed someone. While a part of me was screaming from a small corner in my brain that she needed someone like Avery, not someone who drank themselves into oblivion after every painful memory, I couldn't do it.

I couldn't let Avery have her thoughts and feelings. There weren't many secrets Liv had shared with me, but suddenly I couldn't stand the thought of not knowing. I felt oddly possessive of her concerns, her nightmares, her bad days along with all of the good ones weaved in between.

From my standpoint, there wasn't much I could do. I hadn't figured out how to pick up the broken pieces of myself; there was absolutely no way I could assume the responsibility of doing that for her.

But the longer we stood, her eyes getting more and more desperate by the second, I knew she'd worn me down without even trying.

Liv was kind. If I told her no, she would leave it at that. There wouldn't be any pressure. She wouldn't keep pushing me to open up. She would flash a smile, probably throw in a shrug, and nothing would change. No awkward tension, no hurt.

Even knowing that, I couldn't bring myself to say no. Because *she* needed someone. And all of a sudden, I was dead set on being whatever she needed me to be.

I cleared my throat. "Maybe we could go to the diner for lunch or something and talk." Her lips parted in surprise. It was hard to miss the breath of relief that was released from her lungs.

"Yeah, that would be— we should. That would be amazing."

"Maybe less whiskey next time."

Liv let out a laugh and took a step toward the apartment. "Sounds like a plan."

Chapter 15

Olivia

My head jerked toward the direction of the front door as I rinsed off my toothbrush. My brows pulled together as I tried to figure out who would be knocking on our door before noon.

"Who's that?" Kennedy asked, the foam from her toothpaste spilling out of her mouth and splattering onto the counter.

"Jesus, Ken. Keep your mouth closed!" I laughed, wiping it away with a tissue. "I don't know, maybe Nellie left something last night. I'll be right back."

I headed toward the front door, checking my phone to see if Avery had texted me about coming over. I frowned when I found the screen blank. It wasn't super early. Thanks to Kennedy's impromptu sugar-crash-nap yesterday, we were both up until around one in the morning and had gotten a little bit of a late start. But I still had no clue who would be knocking on my door at ten.

I rolled my eyes when I leaned forward to glance through the peephole, remembering too late that we didn't have one.

"Liv?"

My brows furrowed. A nervous, yet excited feeling fluttered in my stomach as I reached for the doorknob and pulled the old wooden door open. Noah stood on the other side, looking a hell of a lot better than he did yesterday after waking up on my couch.

His dark brown hair was still damp from a shower and brushed out of his face, curling a little at the nape of his neck. I swallowed, trying to control the flush that burned through my body. He was wearing one of my favorite outfits. A simple black t-shirt that always looked a size too small and a pair of dark wash jeans that wrapped around his thighs and hugged his skin.

The black snake tattoo swirled and stretched across the exposed skin on his right arm, only bringing more attention to the corded muscles they were drawn on.

"Hey," I breathed, slowly bringing my gaze back up to meet his.

He smiled softly and my grip tightened on the doorknob as my stomach twisted with nerves. I honestly couldn't tell whether I loved or hated that being around Noah made me feel like a teenager again.

These butterflies had only ever been owned by Liam. For the first time since being in this town and working for Noah, the guilt in my chest had lessened to something of a dull ache and was almost completely overtaken by the excitement I felt knowing the smile on his face was meant for me.

"Hey." Noah shifted a little, bringing my attention to the bags in his hands. Several bags from the grocery store.

"What's up?" I asked, tilting my head and trying to take inventory of his bags.

He lifted them higher like I wouldn't have been able to notice them until now. "I brought groceries."

"I see that," I laughed. "Why?"

Noah nodded in the direction of my kitchen with raised eyebrows. "I'm going to cook for you," he stated, like this was a totally normal thing for him to be doing.

I stood in the doorway, frozen by the overwhelming amount of emotions rushing through me, trying to settle on just one but I couldn't.

A beautiful swarm of butterflies battled with a nervous mass of bees inside my stomach. Part of me wanted to swoon over this man who was standing in front of me while another part of me was terrified that he was capable of eliciting these feelings.

I was excited. I was scared. My heart was racing, and the grip I had on the metal doorknob was slipping as my palms started to sweat.

Noah shifted the groceries over to his left hand, reaching up and crooking his index finger under my chin, lifting my gaze to his. "I'm *just* cooking you breakfast."

"That's the— Yeah, I know."

He smiled sweetly, and I swear to God, my knees buckled in response. "You're panicking. It's just breakfast. Unless this is weird. I can turn around and go home. Up to you."

It's just breakfast. It definitely wasn't weird.

I wanted to scream at the way my body dared to deflate the *smallest* amount, disappointed that he insisted it meant nothing more. Pinching my lips together, I stepped to the side and gestured for him to come in, his hand dropping from my face.

He said absolutely nothing as he passed by. I closed my eyes and took a couple of deep breaths before pushing the door shut and joining him in the kitchen.

For the first few minutes, we worked in silence, unloading the groceries from the plastic bags and setting everything on the counter. Eggs, a loaf of Brioche bread, lots of cinnamon, milk, sugar, and butter. The bags were endless.

Kennedy joined us after a few minutes, dragging her feet in her slippers and her bed head sticking out in every direction. "Noah?"

He looked over his shoulder with a small smile. "Hey, kiddo."

"What are you doing?"

My eyes bounced between my daughter and Noah. He said it was *just* breakfast, but his being here still just didn't make sense to me.

"Showing your mom how to make French toast."

Kennedy's face lit up, her eyes widening. "Really?"

"Really?" I asked at the same time, my face probably resembled Ken's. However the excitement was definitely replaced with confusion. I should've figured out on my own what all the ingredients were for, but having him in my kitchen in the first place was too much of a distraction.

The small smile on his lips stretched into a grin. "Really. She'll be a pro in twenty minutes."

"Okay, don't give me *that* much credit. I burn eggs on a regular basis."

Noah winked and a breath caught in my throat. Thankfully, he turned back to the groceries on the counter before he could spot the blush forming on my skin or the way I struggled to regain my composure. I had no idea how to control these reactions to him.

"Can I watch TV?"

"Yeah. Yes. Go ahead. I'll let you know when it's ready, okay?" I cleared my throat and turned my attention back to the large man in my tiny kitchen.

"Do you have a shallow dish? Something we can dip the bread in?" He spared a glance over his shoulder as he waited for my reply.

"Yeah," I breathed, lifting my hand to point at the cabinet to his left. "Second shelf."

I shamelessly watched the ripple of his muscles as he reached up and pulled out the dish he was searching for, scolding myself in the process. He was here to teach me how to cook, and I was more interested in watching the way the veins in his forearm moved while he shuffled the never-ending groceries around my small counter to make room for whatever mixture he was getting ready to prepare.

It was hard to pay attention to what he was doing and easy to get lost in how effortlessly he started putting things together. Noah was a natural in the kitchen.

I wanted to tell him that, but something stopped me. I couldn't quite put my finger on what compelled me to withhold the compliment, but it felt an awful lot like the nerves that often accompanied insecurity.

My entire dating and relationship experience came from one man. I didn't know how to have a conversation with someone I found attractive. It was like all these years I had blinders on, only allowing myself to see Liam. Now, the blinders were off, and this man was standing in my kitchen, cooking breakfast for me and my daughter, and I had no idea how to approach him.

Almost all the conversations that I'd had with Noah consisted of cars, his sister, death, and grief. I wasn't sure I knew how to fall into a casual conversation with him.

Thankfully, we both seemed almost content with the thick blanket of silence that fell over us, and he was none the wiser of my inner turmoil. Noah worked on breakfast while I stood off to the side, tracking his every move and keeping an ear out for Kennedy.

He paused after lifting the half-gallon of milk, then turned to face me. "I'm not being a good teacher."

I smiled and lifted my shoulder in a shrug. "I was happy to just stand around and let you do all the work. We might actually have a properly cooked meal for once."

Noah huffed out a laugh, set the milk on the counter, and reached out, wrapping a hand around my wrist. He tugged me gently to the counter, stepping back to give me room. I tried *desperately* to pay attention to the words coming out of his mouth and not the way we both seemed to notice just how close we were standing.

He cleared his throat, and I curled my fingers into a fist to keep my hands from trembling as his breath ghosted over the skin at the nape of my neck. "Just uh— Pour about a half-cup of milk into the eggs and then we'll add the cinnamon."

"How does one eyeball a half-cup of something?" I asked, turning to look at him.

Noah's lips twisted to the side as he considered my question. "Well... Picture the size of a tennis ball. That's about a half-cup."

I must've looked at him like he was speaking Latin.

"Just—" he paused, gesturing to the milk. "Come on. A tennis ball. Pour."

"I have measuring cups, you caveman."

"I don't think cavemen had tennis balls," he argued with a smirk.

Pinching my lips together to suppress my smile, I turned back to the task at hand and poured milk into the eggs. I lifted the jug after a second and peered up at Noah, who tilted his head from left to right in a *so-so* gesture and then motioned for me to pour a little more.

I rolled my eyes and shook my head, lifting the jug to pour a splash more.

"That's good," he instructed quietly, taking the small jug of milk from my hand. Noah grabbed a spice jar of cinnamon and held it out to me. "Just add some into the mixture, and then we can whisk it."

I nodded, opened the jar, and turned it over, expecting it to sprinkle out. I gasped when it spilled from the mouth of the jar, quickly jerking it back upright and sending a cloud of cinnamon into the air.

My hand slapped over my mouth. Noah's face and shirt were dusted with a light layer of cinnamon. "Fuck, I'm sorry! I thought it would *sprinkle* out! I didn't know it was just one big hole!"

"*Some*, Liv." He laughed again, brushing the spice from his cheeks and chest. "Not the whole jar."

I rolled my eyes again, trying to play off the embarrassment, but I could already feel the burn in my cheeks. I shot him a playful glare over my shoulder. "This is why they invented measuring cups." My mental load seemed to lessen as we fell into a comfortable conversation. I wasn't worried about what to say next or if I was saying the wrong thing.

We'd eased into a comfortable back and forth, and it just felt so... natural.

He waved a hand at me and then twisted the cap back onto the spice jar. "Measure everything with your heart. The food is only good if the chef makes it with a little love." He smiled softly. "That's what my mom always says."

"Well, your mother can probably manage to scramble an egg without burning it. I'm almost convinced that I'd burn water if given the chance."

For the second time this morning, Noah's grin was aimed at me and my heart stuttered in response. I was so sure my reaction was plastered on my face, but he didn't seem to notice the way my composure was hanging on by a thread. His low chuckle vibrated through my chest, filling the hollowness with warmth. Something I'd been missing. Something that reminded me I was human and *alive.*

"Give me a week and you'll make the best boiled water anyone's ever seen. I'm talking front-cover-of-a-magazine amazing."

I nudged him gently with my elbow, laughing softly. Another deep chuckle filled the room, and it was almost as if I gravitated toward the sound. I closed my eyes, both surprised and terrified at the way my ears honed into his breathing.

Whether I wanted it to happen or not, little pieces of Noah were being seared into my brain. Similar to the way pieces of Liam had reserved a permanent spot in my mind when we started spending time together all those years ago.

It had been years, but I still remembered the butterflies and the nerves that would take over whenever he glanced in my direction or whenever he would stop at my locker after school.

I hadn't ever planned on these feelings making a reappearance. Being married for so long to someone like Liam didn't necessarily take the butterflies away, but the reason behind them certainly shifted.

The honeymoon phase eventually wore off, and the relationship wasn't new, but life with him was still so exciting and special. I'd still get those sweet, gentle butterflies after a good morning text or a post-it note with a sweet message. I felt them on our date nights or whenever I watched him with Kennedy.

With Noah, every anxious butterfly and twist of my stomach when he was around clued me into the start of a budding *crush*, all while carrying the weight of losing my husband.

But knowing that Noah had a similar past to mine eased a little bit of the nerves. I hoped that maybe if these feelings were reciprocated, they were just as new and confusing to him as they were to me.

I wasn't necessarily sure if Noah found me funny, but he'd laughed *at* me enough that I'd spill a hundred little jars of cinnamon if it meant he did it more often.

I waited for the guilt to kick in. I waited for the almost painful twinge of guilt that would dig into my sternum at the revelation that I was chasing the sound of Noah's laughter, or admitting to myself that I might be feeling *something* toward him. But it didn't come.

Not as he walked me through the steps of making the perfect piece of French toast. Not when his fingers brushed against my arm every so often, leaving behind the subtlest trail of goosebumps in his wake.

Not when he stepped aside and left me to finish up the cooking while he took the same plates I'd shared with Liam at our home in Wyoming and set the table so he could eat with me and my daughter.

It never came.

As much as I didn't want to admit it to myself, I kind of hoped it never would.

* * *

Kennedy wiped the maple syrup slowly sliding down her chin with the back of her hand, then leaned back against her seat, patting her belly. Her hair was a mess, and syrup was smeared across basically the entire surface area of her face.

I loved that little human with my whole heart, but man, kids were gross.

She grinned, her eyes blinking slowly from the food coma that started to kick in. "That was *good.*" Her green eyes found mine, and before she even had the chance to ask it, I knew what question was coming out of her mouth next. "Can Noah cook us breakfast every morning?"

Noah laughed, wiping his face with a napkin like a civilized human. "I think Barb would miss me if I stopped hanging out with her *every* morning." His tentative gaze slid to mine, an eyebrow arched *just* enough for me to read the unspoken question.

I didn't know how to decipher that. How I knew exactly what he was trying to ask me with just one look. Was I okay with that? Would it be weird for Noah to come over every weekend?

He'd reassured me this was *just* breakfast and there was no reason to make breakfast mean anything more than a meal shared between two friends. *And Kennedy.* Because that's what we were.

Friends.

Noah was teaching me how to not burn something as simple as eggs, and while I still hadn't quite figured out what he was getting out of a friendship with me, I'd happily throw every spice from my pantry at him until he figured it out.

I dipped my chin in silent approval and scolded myself for the way my stomach fluttered when he shot a wink in my direction. But I latched onto that feeling like it was a lifeline. It was foreign and weird but exciting at the same time. One wink and a promise of tasty, perfectly cooked breakfast every weekend and I was giving myself permission to feel things that I'd only felt towards Liam since I was a teenager.

"How about on Saturday mornings? We can make a little extra so you can warm it up on Sunday?" he offered up.

Kennedy's whole face lit up, her eyes wide as she sat up straight. "You mean it?" Her gaze bounced back and forth between me and Noah. "Really?"

I smiled softly. "Really."

And just like that, my Saturday mornings belonged to the broody mechanic who laughed at my daughter's scatterbrained thoughts with me and cooked some of the best French toast I'd ever shoveled into my mouth.

Chapter 16

Noah

I'd been made.

I knew I didn't have long before Nellie wandered outside and saw my truck in the driveway. Honestly, I was surprised she wasn't running out the front door the second my tires started to crunch against the loose gravel. But knowing my mom, Nell was probably elbow-deep in a mixing bowl of mashed potatoes or setting the table.

Dinner was *supposed* to start ten minutes ago.

Yet there I was, sitting in my truck and staring at my childhood home. I'd been avoiding it as much as possible for the past four years, declining invites from my parents to come over and share dinner or help Dad out in the garage. It was too hard.

Much like Avery, my mother's concern was displayed in every single one of her features, and my father's version of tough love was telling me I was wasting my life away and to get my shit together.

He might've been right, but I still didn't want to hear about it every time I walked through the door.

It was almost like everyone had their own timeline for how long I should be able to grieve and with every passing year, the pity in their eyes shifted meaning. At first, it was, "Oh, this poor man. I can't imagine what he's going through." Now, it was, "It's been four years, why hasn't he moved on yet?"

Grief affected no two people the same, and it was easy to pass judgment when you weren't harboring the guilt behind the death you were grieving.

So, I avoided their house to avoid the tears in Mom's eyes as she carefully watched and dissected my every move and the harsh words Dad would mumble as if the level of his voice softened the blow at all.

It'd been a week since Addie's birthday.

I might still shoulder the blame for my wife's death, but I could at least bury it deep inside of me for a few hours every week and try to enjoy dinner with my family.

If Liv can push through it and still be the amazing mother that she is to Kennedy, I could do this, too.

"Uncle Noah!" Nellie's smile was always contagious. Wide, toothy, and unscathed by the heavy gray cloud that seemed to follow me around. Addie loved her so much. On the days when everything was becoming a little too grim, Nell was always there with her weirdly personal questions and infectious laugh like a little lighthouse in a dark, stormy sea.

I pulled my keys from the ignition and pushed the door open. My feet landed on the ground about three seconds before Nellie was launching herself into my arms.

Nellie smelled like dirt, grass, and everything I used to enjoy as a kid. My parents used to have to drag Avery and me inside by our ears for dinner every night. This land was heaven for a kid.

We used to spend most of our time down by the creek, listening to the shallow water tumble over the mossy rocks. We would catch frogs and lightning bugs along the bank, and come home with muddy hands, and skin covered with mosquito bites.

I was happy that my parents still lived on this land all these years later and that Nellie got to grow up doing all the same things her mom and I used to do as kids.

I wrapped my arms around Nellie and held her tight.

"Hey, Peanut." I shifted her so she was resting on my hip and began walking toward the front door. I tickled her bare feet. "You should always wear shoes out here, Nell."

She scoffed. "My feet are invisible!"

"*Invincible*," I corrected with a smile.

"That's what I said!" She rolled her eyes and shook her head at me, making me laugh.

"You know, you're almost gettin' too big to be carried like this."

I swear her voice raised at least an octave. "You told me you were going to carry me like this forever!" she shrieked. "I knew your muscles were shrinking!"

"Hey!" I playfully pinched her side before digging my fingers into her ribs. "My muscles are just fine, thank you."

Nellie's laugh pierced through the open air around us and I couldn't help but grin. She flexed her bicep, placing a wet kiss on her arm. "I'm stronger than you!"

"Oh, yeah? Prove it. Let's arm wrestle." I walked up the old wooden stairs, setting her down on the front porch and gesturing to the small table and chairs sitting off to the side.

The old screen door creaked open and my mom leaned against the door frame, a dish towel draped over her shoulder. She smiled at me and the wrinkles around her eyes deepened. Her copper hair was slowly giving way to old age, a light gray taking over her roots almost completely.

Just like Nellie was a replica of Avery, Avery was a replica of our mom. They had the same smile and the same dimple on their right cheek. The same freaking mannerisms. And they were both *horrible* at minding their own business when it came to me and my personal life.

She opened her arms for a hug and I walked over, resting my chin on the top of her head as she squeezed me tight.

"Hey, Ma." She smelled like her signature lavender perfume and something warm and sweet, like– I pulled back, keeping my hands on her shoulders. "Did you make banana bread?"

Her smile widened. "I did. Whipped up a couple of loaves this morning once I heard you were coming for dinner. Thought maybe you could take some to that new girl you got working at the shop, too." She stepped back and avoided my eyes.

Mine narrowed on Avery suspiciously. She sat at the dining room table with her fingers steepled under her chin, a not-so-innocent smile pulling at her lips.

I hadn't mentioned anything about Liv to either of my parents, so that meant either Avery or Nellie spilled the news. It wasn't that I was keeping it from my mom, but I hadn't mentioned it for good reason.

Okay, maybe I *was* keeping it from her.

Avery was undoubtedly at fault for that little shimmer of hope in her eyes.

"I'm sure Olivia would appreciate that." I kept any semblance of emotion out of my voice just to be safe and dropped a kiss on the top of my mom's head before turning back to Nellie and flexing my bicep. "Arm wrestle?"

My mother stepped out of my grasp, swatting at me with the towel that was draped over her shoulder. "No, we're all waiting on you. Arm wrestle with your five-year-old niece *after* dinner."

Nellie groaned and made her way to the door, narrowly avoiding a towel smack of her own as she jumped out of the way, and giggled all the way to the dining room table.

Dad wandered into the room at some point, or maybe he'd been there the whole time and subconsciously, I'd chosen to ignore the judgment wafting from his presence. His hands rested on his hips as he regarded me over his bifocals. "Well lookie there. I *do* have a son."

"Otto," my mom warned in a low tone.

Avery's eyes flickered between us.

I met the sarcasm in his voice with a sharp tongue. "Startin' early tonight, huh?" Comments like that were another reason I stayed away.

What was the point in coming all this way if I was just going to be reminded of how little I visited the entire time I was here?

I wasn't sure where it all went wrong with us. Our relationship had never been this strained. Part of it was more than likely due to the things I didn't see when I isolated myself in that cabin. He was here, picking up the pieces while I was hiding and doing everything I could to numb the pain. Mom was a wreck, and Avery was, too.

And I was just gone.

Maybe he was waiting for a thank you. Maybe he was waiting for an apology.

Maybe some part of him knew what happened that night and he blamed me, too.

Given neither of us was prone to talking about our feelings, I wasn't sure if we'd ever get to the bottom of his hatred for me. But at this point, it was only hurting Mom.

"Well, considering you're now–" He lifted his hand, checking the time on his watch. "Eleven minutes late, I think I started right on time."

"I was busy," I snapped, clenching my hands into fists. All I wanted was a good night with my family. Why was he bound and determined to drive me away like this?

My mother stepped between us, fixing my dad with a stern glare. "He might be late, but he's here now. So both of you sit, and we're going to enjoy a nice family dinner for the first time in *months.*" Her voice cracked on the last word, and my entire body flooded with shame and guilt. "I miss my family and I'll be damned if your sour attitudes ruin this for me. So sit down, shut up, and find something nice to say to each other before the night is over."

The hard exterior molded over my father's aging face melted at the disappointment that dripped from her voice. He swallowed, his Adam's apple bobbing as his gaze fixed on me once again. "I like your beard. You heard the woman, let's eat." He cleared his throat and Avery snorted, draping a cloth napkin in her lap.

Nellie sat next to my sister, frozen and confused.

I wanted to laugh at the ridiculous compliment, but I rolled my lips together to hide my smile and sat across from Avery. We both spared a glance at the empty seat to my right, my eyes quickly cutting to the white lace tablecloth while hers lingered on where Addie used to sit.

She used to love sitting next to my mom. They'd be so lost in their own world that their food would get cold before they'd taken three bites of it. Avery and I used to have to threaten to separate them so they'd finally eat.

A small smile tugged at the corners of my lips as I pictured her sitting there, her laugh ringing through the small farmhouse while my mom told exaggerated stories from my childhood. I was surprised by the tendrils of warmth and happiness that blossomed within me, weaving themselves around my heart like a warm hug.

That memory... That flashback... It didn't hurt to relive.

Instead, it caressed the wall I'd built around my heart like a gentle reminder that something alive and worthy of happiness still existed behind the concrete barricade I was so adamant to leave up.

I swallowed against the emotion knotting in my throat, looking up at Avery. Her eyes shimmered in the low light, and the vulnerability I felt was bittersweet. It was like the whirlwind of emotions and memories that swept through me was all playing out on my face, and she was watching it like her favorite movie.

I liked Avery seeing that I wasn't just some rigid asshole and that the goofy brother I was before all of this still lived and breathed inside of me.

Some of the tension straining the muscles in my shoulders melted away, and I looked over to my dad and mumbled, "The lawn looks good."

* * *

There was no way to beat around the bush… Dinner was off to a rocky start.

But the first weird-ass question that Nellie asked seemed to melt away any residual tension. We made it through the whole dinner without a side comment from Dad, and Mom had that sappy, nostalgic look on her face for the rest of the night.

Everyone was happy.

Especially when Ma put her signature meatloaf on the table. It'd been so long since I enjoyed some of her cooking. Granted, she taught me everything I knew, so whatever I cooked was an extension of what she brought to the table. But there was just something about kicking your feet back and enjoying a home-cooked meal made by mom.

As he always did, Dad questioned me about the shop and how everything was running. It wasn't easy for him to step back and pass it over to me, but he just couldn't keep up like he used to and I needed the distraction at the time. Of course, his asking about the shop shifted into a conversation about Liv and Kennedy. I tried to change the subject once every few minutes, but Nellie could talk about her new friend for hours.

Every time Liv was brought into the conversation, I could feel Avery's eyes burning a hole into my forehead. I couldn't decide which was more incriminating... Making eye contact or staring at my plate until the subject changed.

"Noah... You're awfully quiet over there," Avery teased, kicking her foot gently against my shin.

I shoved another piece of meatloaf into my mouth and took my sweet time chewing it up.

The room fell quiet.

Avery smirked, my mom's eyes flitted between us, and Nellie was in a world of her own at this point, building a mashed potato moat around her peas.

Mom smiled softly. "Is there something going on between you and that Olivia girl?"

"No," I answered almost too quickly, my mouth still full of food. I glared at Avery, delivering the same soft kick to her shin under the table as a warning.

She rolled her eyes and stuffed a piece of meatloaf into her mouth. It was like I was sixteen again, arguing and kicking Avery's legs to keep her from blabbing about plans I probably shouldn't have had because she was vindictive and I ate the last dinner roll.

I finished chewing and wiped my mouth with a napkin, silently praying for one random-ass question from Nellie to shift the mood.

Sparing a glance at my mom, my chest tightened at the softened look on her face. "It's okay, Noah. If there is or if you want there to be, *it's okay.*"

Fuck.

Normally, I would be offended by the gentle tone she used. I didn't need soft words and small, reassuring smiles to placate me like a toddler being told no. But something in her eyes and the way she emphasized "it's okay" ripped through my chest like a rusty knife. I concealed the sudden wave of emotion with a cough, taking a sip of water and hoping the fake choking would cover the sheen of tears that clouded my vision.

Regardless of how many times someone told me it was okay to look at another woman or feel *something* for someone who wasn't my wife, I could never justify it in my mind.

It didn't seem fair.

I never fell out of love with Addie. She was ripped out of my life without a warning and I just couldn't wrap my head around how there could be room in my heart for something new when I was still so wrapped up in the past. Because if she was alive, we'd still be happily married. We'd probably have a kid. Imagining *that* future without her hurt enough. It felt like an insult to open up the possibility of having that future with someone else.

Tonight, the look in Mom's eyes pierced through that wall of uncertainty that barricaded my heart from ever being broken again.

It was almost as if I could feel this wall collapsing, and out of the rubble, bruised and broken, hope made a rare appearance.

I would always love Adeline. *Always.*

But that didn't mean I couldn't be happy without her. She would be so disappointed if she saw me today. Sulking, drinking, throwing myself into work. This wasn't the life she would want for me. She'd want the goofy guy who made her laugh until her sides cramped and spent Sundays at his childhood home, helping his parents around the house, and eating too much food. Not the one who locked himself away in a dirty garage and drank until he was numb.

Convincing myself that I *deserved* to be happy would be another problem to tackle. Right now, the warmth of her memory and the reassurance from my mom that it was okay to live life without her felt like a good place to start.

I coughed again, *really* trying to sell the fake choking and Nellie looked up at me. "Do you need the high-nick manure?"

Avery snorted. *"Heimlich maneuver,"* she corrected, shaking her head.

"That's what I said!" Nellie insisted, throwing her hands up in defeat.

I covered my mouth with my hand, holding back a laugh. But when I looked over at Avery and saw her face turning bright red, I lost it.

I threw my head back and roared out a laugh, clutching my chest to feel the vibrations against my palm. It'd been so long since the last time I'd laughed so freely.

Avery joined in next, and soon after, so did Dad. I think Mom would've too, but the tears in her eyes told me she was busy soaking up this conversation for an entirely different reason.

This was how it always should be.

I wondered how many weekends my mom spent on the porch, waiting for the sound of my tires to crunch against the gravel, or how many times my dad had to console her when I didn't show up. Looking at it from that perspective, I understood the hostility and constant bickering when I was around. He may not be a man of many words, but my dad loved my mom *fiercely*. My actions and my poor coping skills had inadvertently torn her down. She watched her child wither away for four years while refusing help from anyone, and my father had to watch the love of his life endure that loss every weekend. Every weekend for four years, my absence from this table crumbled the hope she'd built up over the course of the week. And while my mother was falling apart, my father became the brick and mortar keeping her together. All because I let my guilt fester and poison every good thing I had left.

The guilt and the overwhelming sense of responsibility for Adeline's death still lingered like a looming darkness haunting the halls of my mind. Their bloodlust and thirst for self-destruction was a heavy weight to bear on my own, but somewhere in the simplicity of this night, I'd found *something* to satiate their appetite. Or maybe something that was just enough of a distraction to lift the fog they'd left behind for the time being.

Maybe I couldn't hold them off permanently. But I could fight them for now. If only to hear my family laugh like that again, or see tears of *joy* in my mother's eyes instead of sadness.

That was another thing about grief's convoluted narrative. Every memory, every flashback, every fleeting moment when I forgot for just seconds that she was gone wove a deeper, darker path for me to follow. And I did so. Blindly.

So blind to the fact that not only was my family grieving the loss of my wife, but they were also grieving the loss of *me*. Or at least the me that I was before my carelessness ripped away the best thing that had ever happened to me.

Maybe the key to forgiving myself and moving forward with my life was shoving all the grief and anger so far into the back of my mind that eventually, it wouldn't be a temporary solution. At some point, the bitterness would have to fade and I'd be left with a dull reminder that all of these negative thoughts and feelings still resided somewhere within me, but everything good that I had left had the potential to overpower the obstructive nature of grief.

Or maybe all of this was a bullshit revelation and this was just the reality of healing that I was too stubborn to see before.

I'd never know.

But as I looked around at my family, I realized it didn't matter. It didn't matter how I came to this revelation or how I went about healing from this loss while still harboring so much guilt. It only mattered that I was going to try.

It only mattered that I was present.

For my family's sake, and maybe a little for my own, I needed to start focusing on right now.

Chapter 17

Noah

"Promise you won't be a stranger?" Her tone was light, but I could hear the plea buried beneath her smile.

I leaned down to kiss my mom's cheek, holding two loaves of banana bread tightly in my arms. "Promise." And I meant it.

It wasn't like all the other times I would wander out here for a quick, silent dinner, and leave with an empty promise of coming back soon floating in the air behind me. I wanted to come back. I needed to.

This time, she believed me. She reached up to pat my cheek with her hand. "Drive safe. Make sure Olivia gets that banana bread. Don't you dare keep it for yourself!"

Not that I would admit it to her, but I had actually considered keeping it for myself... At first, I had myself convinced that Liv would never know. She wasn't at dinner. She didn't know about my mom's tradition of sending us home with banana bread every weekend. But Avery did. And since Nellie fell asleep on the couch and my sister ultimately decided to just stay the night, the task of delivering the banana bread was transferred to me. So, I couldn't keep it to myself because Avery would *definitely* ask Liv what she thought of the bread, and then I'd be scolded for hoarding two loaves.

And probably chased out of town by Kennedy once she found out I withheld something that would cater to her sweet tooth.

"I can see you thinking about it, Noah Kent. Don't you dare!" My mother's voice was stern, her hands finding her hips as she narrowed her eyes.

I laughed, lurching out of the way when she reached over to swat my arm. "I won't, I won't! I promise."

"Alright, good. Now, go on. Get home safe."

I nodded, lifting my hand to wave to my dad before heading down the old wooden stairs on the front porch. The gravel crunched under my boots as I walked down the driveway, feeling a lot lighter than I did during those ten long minutes in my truck before I finally gathered the courage to go inside.

On nights like this one, I would normally leave my parents and stop by the only twenty-four-hour gas station about ten miles out of my way. I'd get a six-pack of beer and head home to drink away the image of Addie's empty seat and the pity in Mom's eyes.

But tonight was a good night. I had no desire to drink myself numb with a nineties sitcom playing in the background. And it felt good. It felt so much better to be weighed down by no less than five pounds of meatloaf and the exhaustion of a good night as opposed to suffocating under the weight of my grief.

My fingers drummed against the steering wheel as I made my way down the driveway toward the main road, my mom growing smaller in the rearview mirror as she leaned against the doorway. When I got to the end of the driveway, I sat with my foot on the brake and my fingers just barely touching the turn signal.

If I turned right, the road would lead me home. I could give Liv her banana bread tomorrow.

But... On the off chance that it somehow developed a thick layer of mold overnight just sitting on my counter... I should probably take it to her right now.

My eyes cut to the clock on my dash.

It was only ten... Was that too late? Too... Suggestive? It was *just* banana bread after all. Would she freak out and think it meant something else? Did I *want* it to mean something?

"Jesus Christ," I scrubbed a hand over my face, groaning at myself. How the fuck could I possibly be overthinking *banana bread* to this extent?

I stared into the darkness of the tree line across the street, my car idling while my brain ran a mile a minute.

"It's just banana bread," I spoke into the void, nodding my head with a false sense of confidence. I was taking it to her now because I didn't want it to go stale overnight. Mom's banana bread was top-tier. It would be a shame if Liv missed out. The urge to drive toward town had nothing to do with the faint, curious pull that I felt toward her or the voice in the back of my mind that kind of hoped she would invite me in to share it with her. *Nope.* Not at all. "Just some bread."

With that, I pushed down on my turn signal and slowly eased onto the main road.

* * *

This was stupid.

This was a *terrible* idea.

I stood in front of Liv's apartment door, my palms sweaty as I contemplated over and over whether or not to knock. I wanted to. But I also wanted to tuck my tail between my legs and run for the hills.

I looked down at the banana bread tightly cocooned in plastic wrap in my arms. This was *weird*.

Who the hell shows up on someone's doorstep to drop off *banana bread* at ten-thirty? A creep. That's who.

I could've given it to her at work. During the day. Like a normal person.

But before I could turn to leave, the handle twisted and the door pulled open. Liv jumped, dropping the garbage bag in her hand and cursing loudly. She looked up at me with panicked eyes before blowing out a slow breath and relaxing marginally. "Noah," she breathed. "Is everything okay?"

Over the course of her time working at the shop, I'd seen Liv in so many different styles of clothing. Business clothes. Old, bleach-stained leggings and paint-splattered t-shirts. Jeans. But I think this was my favorite.

She had a large, oversized t-shirt draped over her small frame with a tiny pair of sleep shorts. Her hair was pulled into that bun that was sliding down the side of her head, a few tendrils of light blonde hair falling out of the elastic and framing her face.

Unsuspecting. Relaxed. At home.

That was my favorite version of Liv. It felt like the real her. Not the version of her that pretended everything was always okay as soon as she crossed the threshold.

"Noah?"

I blinked, tearing my eyes away from the small hole in her t-shirt that exposed just a sliver of smooth skin on her collarbone.

I *loved* watching Liv squirm under my gaze and the light shade of pink that would coast across her cheeks. Right now, I could confidently say that I *hated* being on the other side of it.

She looked up at me expectantly, eyebrows raised in confusion with an underlying layer of concern, like maybe I'd gone off the deep end and was here in hopes she'd toss me a lifeline. Thankfully, the somewhat overgrown beard on my face covered most of the color that now painted my cheeks. "Hi."

"Hi?" Her brows furrowed as she did a quick sweep of the hallway. "What are you doing?"

My stomach was tossing and turning like I was on a roller coaster and anticipating the drop, my palms still sweaty as I thrust the wrapped loaf of bread toward her. "Bread. I– I brought you– *My mom* wanted me to bring you this bread– banana bread." *God.* I sounded like an idiot!

Liv's eyes widened as her teeth sank into her bottom lip. "Banana bread?!" she squealed, licking her lips as she eyed the loaf in my hands. She glanced down at the garbage bag on the floor.

"Here. Trade me. I'll take it out to the dumpster on my way out." I pushed the bread toward her again.

"Oh, you don't have to do that! It's fine."

I waved her off, holding the bread a little higher. "It's fine, I got it."

She reached out, wrapping her hands around the loaf, a tiny squeal escaping from her lips. "Banana bread is my *favorite!* My mom used to make it all the time. I swear, I've tried to recreate it *so* many times, but we all know how baking goes for me. It's burnt or never the same."

I chuckled, smiling at her excitement as she clutched it to her chest. "My mom tries to make it weekly. I can never get the 'secret ingredient' right. She *insists* that it's love. But it's gotta be something else."

Liv grinned, blue eyes twinkling in the fluorescent lights. It was the kind of grin that I dreamed of being able to pull from her, but I'd settle for coming in second to the banana bread if it meant lighting her face up like this. "It's drugs. There's no other explanation. I would literally eat ten loaves in a night if given the chance. I am very excited to find myself a banana bread dealer here."

I snorted, leaning down to grab the trash bag while making a mental note to have Mom make an extra loaf for Liv every weekend. "I know what you mean. It took a lot of convincing and the promise of a slap on the wrist to deliver this. I was planning on keeping it for myself."

She gasped, tightening her grip around the bread. "Noah! You wouldn't have gotten away with it. Avery would've told me!"

I rolled my eyes. "I know, that's why I brought it. Avery doesn't know when to keep her mouth shut."

Liv laughed, shaking her head. "What did you think of this batch?" she asked.

"I haven't tried it yet. I was saving it for when I got home."

"Oh," she said quietly. I watched the delicate muscles in her throat work as she swallowed. "Would you want to come inside? We could– We could share?"

I wanted to revel in the fact that I'd successfully made it back to the side of our dynamic that had *Liv* nervous and blushing as she looked everywhere but my eyes, but I wasn't given the chance. Because as exciting as that was, she'd asked me exactly what I'd hoped she'd ask me and I had no goddamn clue what to do next.

Did I want to go inside? Absolutely.

There was a side of her that was still a mystery to me. I knew the basics about her and her daughter, and I knew the reason she moved to Rose Hill, but I wanted to dive deeper. I wanted to know the most basic things about her, but also the most embarrassing song that she loves unironically. A secret hidden talent. Her go-to song to sing in the shower.

This time, there would be significantly less whiskey involved, so I had a better chance of remembering these small things in the morning.

"Sorry, I know it's late, I just–"

I cleared my throat and nodded. "I'd like that. If it's okay with you."

She pinched her lips together to smother a smile before saying, "Wouldn't have offered if it wasn't."

I shook my head before letting out a laugh. Clearly, she'd been hanging onto that one for a while. "Alright, alright. Let me take this out, and I'll be back."

"Okay," she said quietly, reaching back to open the door. "Do you like yours warmed up with some butter?"

One simple, seemingly innocent question tugged at my heart. Every second I spent with Liv was shifting this invisible string that pulled me to her into something almost tangible. Every little thing we had in common solidified this connection, and I wasn't sure how much longer I was going to be able to ignore it.

All because of some fucking banana bread. "I do."

"I'll leave the door unlocked, just come on in. Thank you for taking that, by the way. I hate going back there at night." She shivered like she was picturing what lurked in the dark alley behind the building.

In a town this small, it was more than likely a barn cat that'd wandered too far or a raccoon looking for its next meal, but I almost hated the idea of her going out there as much as she did.

"I can start taking it when I leave on Saturday," I offered. It would only take me a few minutes and honestly, my whole Saturday belonged to her and Kennedy, so it wasn't like it was a huge inconvenience.

"Oh, you don't–"

I shrugged, cutting her off. "I'll do it, it's fine. You shouldn't be going out there this late anyway. It'll give me a little peace of mind if I just take care of it Saturday."

"Peace of mind?" she questioned, the small influx of her voice made it sound like she was surprised I could be concerned about her well-being.

"Yeah. If I take the trash out, we don't run the risk of you trying to befriend that fat raccoon again and getting rabies. Could you imagine how berserk Sheila would go if you took time off to recover from rabies and someone quit answering the phones every day? Who would she talk to if you weren't there?"

Liv laughed, shoving my shoulder. "I never should've told you about that. He was *cute!* And hungry. I could see it in his eyes."

To her credit, technically *she* didn't tell me anything. Kennedy let it slip that Liv tried to feed a raccoon she saw hiding in the bushes behind the apartment complex and it charged at her.

"Uh-huh," I deadpanned, memorizing the playful shimmer in her eyes. "You're lucky he didn't eat one of your fingers."

"They don't eat meat," she argued, crossing her arms over her chest, the loaf of banana bread still clutched tightly in her fingers. "Like, only veggies and stuff like that."

"Liv," I laughed, shaking my head. "That is *so* wrong."

Her eyes rounded as she looked up at me. "No, it's not! They eat *garbage*. Like potato skins and banana peels!"

"And... snakes. And fish... And frogs."

She shook her head. "No. That's– They're too cute to eat shit like that."

"Well, you look it up while I run outside. Hopefully, that raccoon doesn't try to eat me. Because they *definitely* eat meat."

I knew I was right. You don't grow up right next to a creek without seeing a few raccoons fishing or snatching frogs out of the water. I had no clue where Liv got this idea from, but this was the kind of stuff I craved to know about her. All her quirks and terrible ideas. Like attempting to feed a fat raccoon that resided near a dumpster or thinking, for some reason, they only ate veggies and fruits.

I spared a glance over my shoulder as I made my way down the hallway, laughing when I saw Liv furiously typing something into her phone before disappearing into her apartment.

* * *

I thought the walk to the dumpster would have given me a chance to calm my nerves, but I was still wiping my sweaty palms against my jeans after several deep breaths. I half expected the door handle to slip from my grasp when I turned the knob.

I was so nervous that my stomach felt like it was twisting around my intestines. I knew I was overthinking the entire situation. But I also wondered if she was nervous, too.

Did she feel the same pull to me that I felt to her? Did the thought of spending time with me outside of work fill her with the same kind of nervous excitement as it did me?

I could've spent hours out there staring at the old wooden door that led to her apartment while mulling over the endless possibilities about what was happening in her head when it came to me. Or I could just go inside, talk to her, and figure it out for myself.

One of those options was significantly less terrifying than the other.

Even with the thought of enduring awkward small talk in the front of my brain, I couldn't ignore the fact that *something* told me to come here.

Whether it was an irrational fear of moldy banana bread on my counter or the want to see her for some reason that I couldn't quite put my finger on, I'd never know. But I was here. I'd chosen to turn left and take the road back into town, knowing exactly where it would lead it and who it would lead me to.

Nerves aside, I *wanted* to be here.

So, I twisted the handle and pushed through the door. The subtle, warm scent of Liv's vanilla perfume filled my nostrils, along with the sweet smell of the warmed-up banana bread, and my chest tightened. My ribs squeezed around my lungs and stole my breath as they cinched tighter.

It reminded me of home.

Or at least the home that I had before Addie died.

The warmth and the smell of something that wasn't so sterile and empty. From the candle flickering on the kitchen counter to the almost imperceptible underlying smell of cleaning products, it was familiar, yet completely different at the same time.

I'd been in Liv's apartment a few times at this point and never felt this kind of grief. If that was even what it was called. The familiarity of Liv's perfume mingling with the smell of banana bread had a different sense of home than Addie's perfume and the home we shared together. But it was homey in every sense of the word.

Liv poked her head around the corner that led to the living room. "You okay?"

"Yeah," I spoke on a short exhale like my lungs were trying to hold in as much of this cathartic experience as my brain was.

The concern in her eyes shifted as her features softened, a small, knowing smile replaced the furrowed brows and slight downturn of her lips. "What was it?"

"What?"

She swallowed, stepping around the corner and leaning her hip against the wall. "What made you think of her?" Liv asked quietly.

I took a deep breath through my nose, letting it out slowly as I tried to figure out exactly what it was about being here that made me think of Addie. "I'm not sure. I think– Just–" I had such a hard time articulating my thoughts when it came to my late wife. I had the right words at the tip of my tongue, but no matter what I said, it always came out twisted and incoherent as I stumbled over my words. There were so many thoughts and emotions that surfaced whenever she was brought into the conversation, and I'd spent so many years weighing them down and praying they would disappear that I struggled now that I was getting to the point of being okay with talking about her.

It was like losing muscle memory and then expecting yourself to just fall back into it.

I had to get used to including her again.

I had to familiarize myself with the weight of her name on my tongue again.

"It's the smell," I said weakly. "Your perfume, the banana bread. It's different than the home we had together, but it's still... *Something*. Everything I use now is scentless and perfume-less. Sterile. The candle, your perfume, the bread. It's homey. It reminded me of her."

Liv smiled softly then twisted her lips to the side. "You know the day when Deb called me, and I was crying at the desk, and you hugged me?"

I met her gaze and nodded.

"I asked for another minute because..." She swallowed, her cheeks turning a light shade of pink. "I thought maybe you used the same body wash that Liam used to and– and I just couldn't let you go." She laughed, shaking her head a little. "I realized later after spending some more time with you that you do not in fact use the same body wash or cologne, whatever it is. But I think that just smelling something even marginally close to the way he used to, in a vulnerable moment like that, made me cling to the idea that he was there. It's stupid, I know that. He's– Liam's dead. But I get it. Sometimes the memories, good or bad, just hit at the weirdest times and there's nothing you can do but ride it out."

There it was again.

That pull.

That invisible string that seemed to tug me right to her was wrapped around my heart, inching me closer and closer. Our struggles, while unique in their own ways, were tied together in the middle, and every conversation we had shortened the tether that connected us.

At first, I was reluctant to "join forces" and sip tea while crying over the people we lost, but if we learned to lean on each other, maybe we could both make it out a little better off than we were before.

"It gets exhausting," I muttered. "I feel like I've done nothing but ride it out for the past four years, and I'm just now able to see the light at the end of the tunnel. I'm trying not to focus on the fact that it still feels miles away."

She lifted her shoulder in a shrug, the corner of her mouth still tipped up in that knowing smile. "Don't. Because it's there."

I sighed, my shoulders falling with regret. This was all still so fresh for Liv. "I'm sorry. I didn't–"

"It's okay. Don't sell yourself short just because my loss is more recent. They both still hurt in their own ways. And if you can see it, there's hope for me then. Sometimes I think I see it. But then I get swept away by some painful reminder he's not here, and the progress is just gone. Just gotta keep riding it out, I guess."

I huffed out a laugh, scrubbing a hand down my beard. "Worst roller coaster *ever*."

Liv snorted, turning to head toward the living room. "Zero out of ten, do not recommend."

Chapter 18

Olivia

Noah sat on the couch across from me and most of the nerves that fluttered around in my stomach when he first magically appeared at my front door had dissipated. It was getting easier and easier to talk to him. For the most part, I found that absolutely terrifying. But it was nice to talk to someone who got it.

Someone who didn't have this bullshit expectation of me to be happy and cheery twenty-four-seven. He got the ups and downs of grief, the confusion, and the guilt. Noah understood me on a level that a lot of other people couldn't even fathom dropping to. Not quite rock bottom, but hovering just above the jagged, sharp reality of it being an arm's length away.

While he was taking the trash out to the dumpster, I checked on Kennedy to make sure she was still asleep, then sliced the banana bread up and microwaved it for just a few seconds before slathering some butter on it. My mouth was watering before the microwave even beeped to let me know it was ready.

I held the plate up to him, letting him steal a slice before setting it back down on the coffee table. "Is this our first official meeting of the Dead Spouse Club?"

Noah laughed, taking a bite of the bread and groaning, his eyes fluttering shut. "I forgot how good this shit was," he said through a mouthful of food.

I wasn't lying earlier when I said banana bread was my favorite.

It was basically the only thing I wanted when I was pregnant with Ken and then after I gave birth, the craving just never left. My mom mastered the recipe during my pregnancy if only to avoid a hormone breakdown, and I couldn't get enough. She made it for us almost every week back home.

If this didn't live up to the hype, I'd have to figure out some way to get her to talk to me and send a loaf or two in the mail. Shit, I'd pay fifty dollars for overnight shipping if I needed to.

"You're getting my hopes up, Noah. If this isn't as good as you're making it out to be, I'm gonna be *so* disappointed. I need you to understand the severity of this situation."

He grinned before shoving the rest of his slice into his mouth. "I'm not over-exaggerating."

I swatted at his arm. "You're worse than Kennedy! Keep your mouth closed until you've finished chewing, you barbarian."

Noah's grin grew but he stayed quiet as he chewed, using his fingers to lift the slice of bread in my hand closer to my mouth. He dipped his chin in encouragement, eyebrows raised to damn near his hairline with anticipation, and I took a bite.

As I chewed, I understood his reaction.

Holy shit.

It was dense, moist, and the perfect amount of sweet without being over the top, and quite possibly the best piece of banana bread I'd ever tasted.

Noah's arms shot up in triumph. "I told you!"

I threw my head back and laughed, forgetting for a moment that Kennedy was asleep just a few rooms over. The pride on Noah's face warmed my heart, but the thought of my daughter asleep in her room sobered me up quickly. I slapped my hand over my mouth and leaned forward to peek around the corner, both of us holding our breath to listen for any indication that she was up.

My shoulders sank with relief after a few moments of silence. *Thank god.*

She'd been fighting bedtime *so* hard this weekend.

I looked back up at Noah, feeling the intensity of his gaze on my cheek, and remembered I was leaning forward. Truthfully, I hadn't moved that much and we'd definitely been closer before, but his eyes dropped to my lips and I forgot how to breathe.

My brain was trying to process the closeness of his body to mine and the way he was looking at me with an expression I couldn't decipher. I could feel the blood rushing to my cheeks, my stomach fluttering for the second time tonight.

Would he try to kiss me?

Why else would he be looking at my lips?

Liam was the last person I'd shared something so intimate with. Was I ready to let go of that part of my life?

I swallowed as Noah reached up, swiping his thumb against the corner of my mouth and taking a crumb with it.

Oh my god.

My spine straightened and I sat back against the arm of the couch. The mortification and relief that swept through my body was fucking confusing, and mixing terribly with the banana bread that lodged itself somewhere between my esophagus and my stomach.

My mouth was dry, my face was undeniably bright red.

I actually thought he was going to *kiss me!*

Oh my god. For some reason, through all the confusion and panic, I'd also located the goddamn audacity to be *disappointed* that whatever just passed between us ended with a crumb being brushed off of my mouth and not with the knowledge of how his lips would feel on mine.

My stomach dropped at the realization that having that knowledge was something I actually wanted. My brain was telling me it was wrong, but at the same time, it didn't *feel* wrong. Or maybe it did?

There were a million different thoughts ping-ponging through my brain and I couldn't get them to slow down enough to form something coherent. "I'm gonna get some water. Want some?"

"Sure," he answered quickly, leaning back against the couch. He pulled his phone out and pretended to be preoccupied with it while I stood and rushed into the kitchen. I was so desperate to get away for just a second, I couldn't even find it in me to either laugh or be offended by the fact that his phone was upside down as he typed.

What was happening to me?

It was too soon to be excited by the prospect of his lips on mine and the way his scruff would scratch against my chin. It was too soon.

Right?

I reached into the cabinet and pulled down a couple glasses, using the rush of water from the faucet to cover up a couple of shaky breaths. Despite the fire burning in my cheeks, I resisted the urge to stick my face under the running water in an attempt to cool down.

Facing Noah after *whatever the fuck just happened* or get waterboarded? At this point, I was going with the latter.

I turned the faucet off and took a deep breath before grabbing the water and walking back into the living room.

Noah continued to type on his phone, though at some point while I was in the kitchen, he'd discovered it was upside down.

I took a large gulp of water, hating the fact that I didn't think to put music or some late-night TV show on in the background before he came in, because the only thing we had to listen to right now was the sound of this water making its way down my throat. Maybe if he listened closely, he could also hear the sound of me slowly dying inside.

Why did I think he was going to kiss me?

I wracked my brain for a million different things I could bring up to break the tension, but instead of a solution, all I could hear was the theme song to that kids' show with the blue Australian dog, and that certainly wasn't helping.

Though maybe I could've used some sage advice from the parents. They always seemed to have their shit together and what I was going through felt like the complete opposite of that.

Truthfully, the only thing that was keeping me from melting into the floor and becoming one with the earth underneath this building was the fact that Noah seemed to be just as flustered by whatever moment we had. I mean, the man blushed. That was *my* deal. Not his. He was always confident in whatever he did. Grumpy and annoyed also? Absolutely. But grumpy and annoyed *with confidence*.

To see him unsettled and struggling to compose himself seemed to level the playing field just a little bit.

At least instead of being alone in this confusion, he was right there with me.

I set my water down on the coffee table, fidgeting with a loose string on my t-shirt as Noah pocketed his phone.

The nerves that'd been calmed by small talk and easy laughter were back. Only this time, the sting of angry hornets buzzed around my stomach, replacing the once soft fluttering of gentle butterflies.

His gaze slid over to mine, slow and tentative. We stared at each other for no more than five seconds before a tiny little snort escaped from me. Noah's lips twitched with a smile, and soon, we were both doubled over in laughter.

I tried to get myself to stop. Kennedy was sleeping, and I truly didn't want to wake her, but I think at this point, it was inevitable. Honestly, I wasn't even sure what the hell was so funny because just moments ago, I was mortified, but I think that made it even funnier.

Noah laughed with me, his hand pressed against his mouth in an attempt to muffle the sound.

The sound of Kennedy's door creaking open had both of us sitting up straight. The muscles in Noah's jaw feathered as he fought to hold in another laugh.

I wiped a few tears from my eyes and rolled my lips to repress my smile as Kennedy's almost silent steps made their way to the living room. She stood in the threshold of the room, a hand covering her eyes to shield them from the lamp in the corner.

"Noah?" she croaked, dropping her hand and squinting.

"Hey, kiddo." Noah's voice was strained, his chest heaving as he held back laughter.

"Why are you here?" She walked over to me, climbing on my lap and snuggling into my arms.

He took a deep breath, smiling sweetly as he watched her get comfortable in my lap. "I was just dropping something off to your mom. I'm sorry we woke you."

She sniffed, her breathing getting deeper as her eyes fluttered shut. "S'okay," she mumbled as she fought sleep.

"Let's go get you in bed, Ken." I smoothed my hand over her bedhead and kissed the top of her head. "Why don't you go climb under the covers and I'll come to tuck you in in just a second."

It took her a second to stand up, but her eyes remained closed. She used to sleepwalk all the time as a toddler. It used to scare the shit out of me. But sometimes, like in this moment, it came in handy. I could tell she wasn't fully awake, which meant she wouldn't be up for hours tonight, and I'd be able to toss and turn about my *moment* with Noah without Kennedy's foot kicking me in the face.

"Okay," she whispered, smacking her lips a couple of times before stumbling a couple of steps and successfully trudging back to her room.

Noah wiped his hands on his jeans, smiling softly. "I think that's my cue."

I pushed off the couch, disappointment and relief clashing inside of me. The two very conflicting emotions swirled through my chest, unwilling to coexist, while I battled the mental repercussions of their fight to overpower the other.

I fumbled with what to say, part of me wanting to reassure him it would only take a second to get her back to sleep. The other part of me was relieved that Kennedy had ultimately decided how tonight would end.

I sighed softly, rocking back on my heels. "I think you might be right."

Noah stood, and I could see the conflict in his eyes, one similar to mine.

I missed having friends. I missed having *someone* to decompress with and laugh with at the end of the day. The look on his face told me that he did, too. I could fully recognize and accept the fact that I isolated myself by moving across the country. But just because I was alone in a new, unfamiliar city didn't mean I had to be lonely.

The goal when I moved was to regain my footing and heal. Maybe one day we'd make our way back to Wyoming. Maybe we wouldn't. But I was here now.

I wanted to *do* things and *feel* things.

Granted, all of this doing and feeling would have to wait until at least the morning because I had a four-year-old who needed to be tucked in and a loaf of banana bread to finish off before the clock struck midnight.

"Thanks for letting me crash your night. Sorry I dropped by so late." Noah palmed the back of his neck, a small, sheepish smile spreading across his lips.

"Ah, well. I think the only thing you crashed was a trip to the hospital. I was *definitely* going to feed that raccoon," I admitted with a grin.

I couldn't even lie about it. The thing was fucking cute.

"Lock up after me?"

One question and I found myself a victim to the same heart-skipping, mind-sobering rush of nostalgia that stopped Noah in his tracks earlier. He must've recognized the look on my face and seen the way my smile dropped. His brows pulled together, his expression melting into that same soft look he gave me outside the apartment complex the night of Adeline's birthday.

"I'm sorry." His voice was tender and barely registered in my ears.

It wasn't his fault. He had no way of knowing that was the last thing Liam said to me before he was killed. It was like his hug at the shop all over again. Just similar enough to strike a chord but lacking something so intrinsically Liam that the moment of remembering him was gone before I could savor it.

I honestly hadn't given much thought to the phrase over the past year, but somewhere in the rich timbre of his voice, I could hear my last moments with Liam.

I mustered up the best smile that I could at the moment, trying my best to stop my memories of Liam from bleeding into these moments I shared with Noah.

"He said that a lot?"

"Every night when he left for work." I cleared my throat, meeting his gaze. I always expected to see pity, but his eyes held nothing but understanding. Maybe a hint of sadness, but I doubt that had much to do with me. "It took me by surprise. That's all."

The corner of his mouth lifted into a knowing and somewhat melancholy smile. "I know the feeling."

I hated the reason we had so much in common. But I was thankful we seemed to settle into the silver lining of having each other.

The moment shifted away from the past and dragged me painfully back to the present, where I suddenly remembered that less than five minutes ago, I was staring at this man's mouth and hoping it would magically land on mine.

"I'll walk you out," I offered, then paused. "Well, I'll walk you to the door."

He chuckled and nodded, and the second he gave me his back, I stifled a groan and rubbed my hands over my face. I couldn't stand the nervous tension that was emanating from me. Honestly, I wasn't even emanating it anymore. It *was* me. The nerves sealed over me like a second skin, seeping into my bloodstream and embedding itself into the marrow in my bones.

My legs felt like poorly set gelatin, somewhere between somewhat solid and just plain liquid as I walked behind him to my front door. The hinges creaked as he pulled it open.

He hesitated in the doorway, and I held my breath, torn between asking him to stay and making sure he left. Noah turned, hazel eyes meeting mine. "I'm sorry for stopping by so late. And I'm sorry for–" He paused, his throat bobbing as he swallowed. "I'm sorry for touching you."

Oh, please for the love of god, someone sedate me. There was nothing I needed more than a nice coma right about now.

My cheeks flamed almost immediately, and the corner of Noah's mouth twitched, but he held back his smile, rolling his lips to keep them pressed firmly together. Happy to see that this was funny to someone!

I threw my head back and let out a fake sob before palming my forehead. "I'm sorry for freaking out."

Noah gave up on trying to hold back his smile, and the grin that spread across his lips was almost like a shock to my system. My heart squeezed, and the air rushed out of my lungs as he shrugged. "We can blame it on the banana bread."

I snorted, nodding in agreement. "It was definitely the banana bread."

"Next time I'll bring something less suggestive."

I hummed, resisting the urge to laugh. "Like fruitcake."

"Or cornbread."

My teeth bit into my bottom lip as I held back another laugh, shaking my head softly. "Thank you for coming over."

He waved a dismissive hand in my direction, backing into the hallway. "Don't mention it."

Something squeezed at my chest again, but this time, panic danced along the edges of my nerves instead of excitement. "Text me when you get home, please. I just– I won't be able to sleep until I know you're home safe." *And alive.*

I said that part in my head, but he knew the meaning behind my request.

Noah took a step forward and leaned down, his lips brushing against my cheek. I sucked in a small breath, holding it in my lungs. "Promise."

Before I could even process what happened and before he could see the shiver that rolled down my spine, he disappeared down the hall and toward the front of the building.

My fingers rested gently on top of where his lips met my skin, and I wanted to scold myself for playing into every rom-com love story cliche, but my cheek tingled as his kiss lingered on my skin and I let myself feel it.

I ignored the niggling sense of guilt that rapped its knuckles against the steel door I'd locked it behind, giving myself until the morning to remain guilt-free. Then, I'd release the hangry beast and let it ravage my false sense of confidence and control until there was nothing left but insecurity and chaos.

But tonight, I wanted to crawl into bed and replay the moment his lips touched my skin until my nerves finally settled and I could picture his perfect, lopsided grin without risking cardiac arrest.

I closed my front door and secured the deadbolt, smiling into my hands before walking over to Kennedy's room. Honestly, I was expecting her to be fast asleep and sprawled across her little bed in a way that could only be comfortable to someone with rubber bones. But her sleepy eyes remained open, blinking slower and slower each time.

Kneeling beside her bed, I brushed a few unruly locks of hair from her forehead. "Night, sweetie. I love you so much," I whispered, pressing my lips against her cheek.

Kennedy rolled onto her side, gripping my cheeks with her hands. "I love *you* so much." She ended her sentence with a yawn exactly two inches away from my face, but my heart still melted.

Her tiny hands dropped from my face, and I pulled the blanket up until it covered her shoulders.

"Mommy?"

My fingers traced the delicate curve of her chubby cheek before brushing over her hair. "Yes?"

"I like it when Noah comes over."

It was hard to ignore the way the butterflies in my stomach fluttered their wings at Kennedy's approval. Maybe it was silly to seek approval from a four-year-old, but she would always come first in my life, and if for some reason she didn't like having Noah around, he just wouldn't be around. It was as simple as that.

"Do you?" I asked gently, smiling down at my daughter.

She nodded with her eyes closed before a sleepy smile tugged at her lips. "He makes really good food. And you aren't so sad when he's here."

I cleared my throat, trying to summon up a response, but my words got stuck behind the emotion clogging my throat. I had tried so hard to shield Kennedy from my grief, and it pained me that I hadn't done as good of a job as I had thought.

She was only four. She shouldn't have to worry about whether or not her mom was crying again or if I'd smiled today. But I also didn't want her to think she had to hide her emotions or that grieving was something to be ashamed of.

These were the moments I truly hated about being a single parent. I didn't have anyone around to validate my thoughts or offer up another solution when I was doubting myself.

Thankfully, Kennedy was asleep before I had to figure out what exactly I was supposed to say back to that. I sighed, dropping another kiss on her forehead. I didn't want her to have to worry about me. I wanted her to be four. I wanted her to have good memories of her childhood that didn't seem weighed down by the loss of her father.

I wasn't even sure if that was possible, but I was going to try.

I closed her bedroom door gently before heading back into the living room.

When I was taking the trash out, I had every intention of coming back into the apartment and crawling into bed. But that loaf of banana bread was whispering my name, and I had several moments with Noah to overanalyze from now until he let me know he was home.

I knew I wouldn't be able to sleep until that text came through, so I grabbed another piece of bread and settled onto the couch. I was only a few minutes into my shitty reality TV show when my phone buzzed on my lap.

Noah: Home. Sorry again for stopping by so late and waking Ken.

Me: Don't worry about it. She's already asleep again! Thank you for letting me know :)

Me: Also.. While I have you... How should we go about tomorrow?

Noah: ?

Noah: What do you mean?

Me: Well, we obviously have to be super weird with each other now. So who initiates? Do you avoid eye contact first or do I?

Noah: …

Noah: Goodnight, Liv.

Me: Night :)

I laughed at the way our personalities seemed to shine through our texts. I was a firm believer in utilizing the exclamation point and basically every single expressive emoji. Noah's texts were to the point and ended with a period, lacking any emotion.

Even still, I could picture the small smile on his lips as he read my last text and the deep chuckle that would rumble through his chest. I clutched my phone in my hand, watching the texts from Noah dim before disappearing altogether.

Whether it was too soon or not, I was starting to think I was past the point of being able to stop it. The nerves, the disappointment when he *didn't* kiss me, the comfort that I felt when he was around… It all pointed to one thing. One thing that I was absolutely terrified of.

One thing that I desperately wanted to be reciprocated while simultaneously hoping it wasn't so I no longer had to battle a constant conflict of emotions.

The heart that once belonged to Liam was shattered when he died. And now Noah was here, unknowingly picking up each jagged piece and holding them together until the glue stuck.

I wasn't sure what was more terrifying.

Letting myself succumb to these feelings or placing my broken pieces into the hands of a man who was just as broken as me.

Chapter 19

Olivia

"I thought you were just taking care of him because he was drunk! I didn't know you *liked* him. Tell me more about this hot mechanic!"

"Georgia!" I scolded, my gaze jumping from the desk to the front door. Noah would be in at any minute, and I knew I had no business talking on the phone with her while I was in the same building as him. But after a few days of secret, playful stares, I texted my best friend for her advice. I should've known that not even half a second after saying hello she would skip the pleasantries and jump right into my text about Noah.

Did she have a filter? No. But she would always be the person to give advice based on my best interests and *not* her opinion on the situation or my life before Rose Hill.

"Oh-liv-e-uh." She sounded out my name with a sarcastic bite, probably annoyed that I called her by her full name. No one called her Georgia. Except for her mother. "Be serious right now. You text me to tell me you *might* have a crush on some grumpy mechanic and think I don't deserve more details? I need them all! Have you kissed? On a scale of one to Henry Cavill, what does he rate? This is for science, babe. Trust me! I can't make an educated decision on what I think you should do if I don't have evidence."

She took a breath and kept going before I could respond.

"I'm literally an author. I *live* for this shit. So tell me, where are we in the plot? First act? Have we gotten to the smutty part yet–"

"G! Slow down." I laughed, resting my forehead on my palm. "There is no novel. No first act–" I lowered my voice to a whisper. "*Definitely* not smutty parts."

"Boo," she huffed, probably with an eye roll. If I trusted her enough to have her on speaker, I'd opt for FaceTime. I missed seeing her every day, but she and her loud mouth were just going to have to stay put for now. "I'm sorry, babe. I just– I want you to be happy."

I sighed, massaging my temple with my free hand. "I know. I– I know that. I just don't know what to do. Or how to feel. He's grieving just the same as me, and I can't fully convince myself that it's a good idea to–"

The bell chimed over the front door, and Noah slipped in, bags of takeout and coffee cups balanced in his arms. I coughed, then cleared my throat, trying to clue Gia in on the fact that he was now in the room.

"To what?"

Noah walked over to the desk, plopping down the white plastic bags as I obnoxiously cleared my throat again.

My best friend cackled on the other end. "Did he just walk in?"

"Uh-huh. Yup. I hear ya," I responded with a nervous laugh, holding up a finger to my boss who started unpacking our breakfast and eyeing me with a curious expression.

Gia laughed again. "Oh god, this is the best morning ever!"

"I'm glad you think so," I clipped through clenched teeth, keeping this fake-ass smile plastered onto my face. Noah's stare grew increasingly curious, and I prayed to whatever higher power there was that he couldn't hear Gia on the other end.

"Look, babe. I'm just gonna say my piece, and then I'll leave you alone. Stop thinking about whether or not it's too early or you're too broken. If he makes you happy and you feel… some sort of way about him, whatever those feelings may be… Just let it happen. You've had the weight of the world on your shoulders for the past year, and from what you've told me, this man wants to help ease some of that burden. *Let him.* You don't have to be on your own to figure shit out again. You just need to be happy and content. And if he brings that to the table for you, so fucking be it."

I swallowed, blinking back tears. I could never have these conversations without the freaking waterworks. My throat felt like it was closing in as I swallowed back my emotions.

Noah's gaze shifted, his shoulders tightening as his brows pulled inward. I gave him a gentle shake of my head and waved him off for the time being, trying to reassure him it wasn't another call with Deb.

"I know this is hard to hear, but Liam was one of my best friends for *years*. He would want you to be happy. He would want to know that you and Kennedy are taken care of and doing more than just going through the motions. Let him make you happy. Let him cook for Ken because god knows that child will be living off of burnt crust and overly seasoned food for the rest of her life if it was up to you."

I laughed, shaking my head. "I love you, G."

"I love you, too." She lowered her voice and softened her tone as if her words weren't enough to drive her point home and bring me to tears. "Stop thinking about all the things that could go wrong and just lose yourself in the possibilities of everything that could go right. Stop planning. Just be. You've earned that right."

I cleared my throat, purposefully ignoring the intensity of Noah's stare as he burned a hole into the side of my face. "Ken."

Gia was silent for a moment, and I wished again that I could see her face so I could read between the lines. "Yes, there's Ken. But it's so important for her to see you grieving the man that you lost because no one will ever be able to replace her dad. You know that. She knows that. But it's also important for her to have a happy mom. It's important to show her that it's okay to lean on other people to get you through hard times. *I* understand why you couldn't do it here, but it sounds like you have this tiny community in Rose Hill, so lean on it. Let her see the good parts of grief, too."

I made a small, whimpering noise in the back of my throat as I held back the emotion trying to claw its way free. "Has anyone ever told you that you're really good with words? You should try writing a book."

"Okay. Clearly, honesty hour has reached its limit with you, so I'll let you go," she laughed.

I hummed in response and attempted to wave Noah off again. "You know me so well."

"That I do, best friend. I love you, Livie."

Smiling softly, I took a deep, cleansing breath. Or at least as cleansing as a breath full of gasoline fumes and motor oil could be. "I love you, too. Talk to you soon."

I ended the call and dropped my cell onto the counter, burying my face into my hands and scrubbing them over my cheeks.

"Are you okay? Who– What just happened?"

"I'm fine," I laughed. "Just an overdue phone call with a nosy best friend from home."

"Ah." Noah slid my breakfast across the counter until it was sitting in front of me and then passed over a fork and my coffee. "Hopefully it was a good conversation?"

I was afraid that if I let my gaze linger on him for too long, he'd be able to piece together that we were talking about him.

I always loved hearing from Gia, and we didn't talk nearly as much as we used to. But talking with her had done nothing to calm the nerves inside me. My heart rate still kicked up, and my palms still sweated when I thought about leaning into whatever invisible string was pulling Noah and me together. Indecision still clouded my thoughts, and even with Gia telling me that it was okay, I still needed *something* to tell me it really was.

So, the call was good in the sense that I got to catch up with my best friend and I heard all the things that I needed to hear. But I still didn't know if Noah felt this inexplicable hold he had on me or if the feeling was reciprocated.

I swallowed, dropping my gaze to the coffee cup in front of me and toying with the lid. "I think so."

My cheeks flushed, and I tried to use my hair as a shield, blocking him from seeing the nervousness so easily spelled out on my face, but then he took me by surprise and lifted his hand, tucking the strands that framed my cheeks behind my ear.

"Good." The corner of his mouth tilted into a small grin. "I was worried it was Debra. You were one tear away from me stealing your phone and blocking her number."

A laugh bubbled its way up my throat. "I don't think I'd put a ton of effort into stopping you, to be completely honest."

It'd been a while since I talked to Deb without Kennedy there as a buffer. If she called, Kennedy answered. If she texted, they went unread. I had enough to deal with on my own, and I was done letting her plant seeds of doubt in my mind. I had to protect my peace, and since my move, she'd done nothing but harm it.

I popped open the lid on my takeout container and grinned, then looked up at Noah. "You're fucking all of this up."

He choked on a sip of coffee, wiping the droplets from his chin. "Excuse me?"

"We're supposed to be weird toward each other now, and instead, you have Barb cookin' up strawberry crepes?"

I'd told Noah sometime last week crepes were something I'd always wanted to learn how to make. He told me that he'd add it to the list of recipes to show me, but I had no idea he'd somehow convinced Barb to offer them at the diner.

Noah laughed, leaning his hip against the counter and crossing his arms. "It's no biggie. She– Uh– She already knew how to do it. Just like pancakes, right? And the banana bread... We're past it already, right?" I drank him in and the way his eyes seemed to light up as his grin spread, his shoulders relaxed and shaking slightly as he chuckled. The grumpy and broody mechanic who said five words to me the first day we met was laughing at my jokes and bringing me breakfast every morning. He was attractive before, but there was something so goddamn enticing about the carefree, lopsided grin on his lips.

"Even if we weren't past it, technically, I am being weird," he insisted, quirking a brow as I cut into the soft pancake.

"How so?" I challenged.

He huffed out a laugh and uncrossed his arms, fingering the hem of his shirt before he began to unpack his breakfast.

Was he... *Nervous?*

"I'm being nice to you. That's pretty... Unusual for me, I guess."

My heart sank for the misunderstood man in front of me. I knew all too well what it was like to be drowning in grief. It was suffocating and unrelenting. He shut everyone out while he was being pulled under and healed like a broken bone that was cast without being reset. Beneath the surface, everything was still *Noah*. But he hadn't carefully put the pieces of his own broken heart back together the way he seemed to be doing with mine. After four years, everyone around him might've healed from the loss or even considered him to have been healed, but underneath a seemingly perfect (albeit grumpy) exterior, everything was jagged and slightly out of place.

I dropped my fork and reached over, placing my hand over his. "There is not a single part of me that believes you being kind is anything unusual, Noah Kent."

I think he was surprised by the conviction behind my words, his throat bobbing as he swallowed. He shifted on his feet, but I held his stare. I needed him to believe this. I needed him to know.

"Got it?" I asked, smiling up at him.

He dipped his chin in acknowledgment. "Got it."

We shared a few moments of comfortable silence before I slapped my thighs with my palms and exhaled loudly. "Okay, well. My job is done. I'll be putting in my two weeks no–"

Noah's laugh was loud and booming, addicting and warm. It cut my sentence off, filling the quiet of the lobby. This moment that we shared was something I wanted to latch onto and keep close to my heart.

"Not a chance. I'm spoiled now," he said with a laugh, grabbing his fork and cutting off a small piece of scrambled egg. "There's a fortune cookie, too."

"Oh!" I smiled and dug through the bag. The hopeless romantic in me loved that he remembered such a small detail about me.

He quirked a brow. "What's this one say?"

I cracked it open and slid the tiny slip of paper out. "Soon you'll discover that going with the flow leads to the most beautiful destinations."

Noah hummed, plopping another piece of food into his mouth. "Beautiful destinations? In Delaware? Unlikely."

I rolled my eyes. "Maybe you don't know because you don't go with the flow."

"Eat your freakin' pancakes."

We ate in silence, taking turns stealing glances at each other and laughing. As I popped the last bit of my crepe into my mouth, I found myself not wanting this morning to end. I wasn't ready for Noah to retreat into the garage and I certainly wasn't ready for Sheila's daily phone call that would come through in a couple hours.

The subject changed daily, but it seldom had anything to do with her car.

After a year of going through the motions and putting everything before myself, I wanted to sit down and soak up all things Noah. I wanted to bathe in the warmth of his laugh and memorize the way his eyes lit up at something I said.

My heart thrummed a nervous rhythm in my chest. Gia was right. I was tired of planning and overanalyzing. I was ready to just *be* and let everything else fall into place.

* * *

Sweat dripped down my temple as I fanned myself with an intake form. The temperature in the shop had been consistently rising for the past two hours, and Noah couldn't figure out what was going on.

I had worn a pair of leggings and an oversized t-shirt today in preparation for cleaning, but the second the air conditioner went out, I lost the motivation. Just sitting at the desk had me dripping in sweat. There was absolutely no way I was going to get any cleaning done without passing out due to heat stroke.

I swiveled in my chair as the heavy footfalls of Noah's boots made their way up the hallway from the garage. He was dripping in sweat, long fingers spearing through dark brown hair. His shoulders were tense, his jaw set in frustration.

"Nothing?" I asked, trying to keep the disappointment from seeping into my voice. It was fucking hot.

I hadn't expected late September to have so many days of ruthless summer heat. But there we were, more than halfway through the month and still getting highs close to ninety.

He shook his head with a sigh, resting his hands on his hips. "No, I'm sorry." His face twisted up as he took me in. All five-foot-five inches of me were covered in a sheen of sweat that had my t-shirt clinging to my body. Thankfully, I'd remembered to bring a hair tie with me this morning, so at least the birds' nest was under control.

Slightly.

I blew a puff of air out of the side of my mouth to move a strand of hair from my cheek, but it stuck to the sweat and stayed in place.

"It's okay," I promised.

He looked to the ground, shaking his head in frustration. "Let me give someone a call and see if it's even in the realm of possibility to get it fixed today."

I busied myself with menial tasks and things that didn't require a ton of movement while he was on the phone, praying that it could get handled quickly. I had no idea how I was going to last all day in that heat.

Several minutes and several quiet curses later, Noah was back in the lobby, wiping sweat from his forehead. He let out a deep sigh and rested his hands on his hips. I could see the frustration settling over him. He couldn't figure out what was going on and whoever he was calling to fix it clearly couldn't make it today.

Unfortunately, my knowledge of A/C units began and ended with knowing that A/C stood for air conditioning... So I brought absolutely nothing to the table.

I could, however, go to the diner, get us some water, and possibly swing by the convenience store for a couple of fans. "Let me run down the street to get us some water and I'll stop by Colt's place before I come back to see if he's got a desktop fan or a tower fan lying around somewhere. I'm sure he does."

"You're on a first-name basis with Colt already? That man hates most people that come into his store."

He wasn't wrong. The first dozen times I'd wandered into the convenience store, I was greeted with a blank stare and an almost imperceptible nod. He wasn't like most people in this town who went out of their way to be as welcoming and accommodating as possible. Though, I didn't fault him for it. I'd seen my fair share of haunted, but something was lurking in his eyes that didn't necessarily scare me, but told me he'd seen enough in his life to make him question every person that walked through the door. He kept to himself, and much like Noah, offered one-word answers and a series of caveman noises.

Before I bribed him for his friendship, the most I'd gotten from him was the day I started at Kent Automotive. He questioned me about the cleaning supplies, which I found completely understandable considering I felt like every third-grade math problem that everyone thought was too ridiculous to be true.

Olivia went into the convenience store to buy fourteen sponges, five bottles of bleach, three scrub brushes, and a face mask. How many total items did she buy at the store?

I scoffed at Noah, grabbing my purse and resting the strap on my shoulder. "Colt loves me. Between you feeding me on the weekends and me keeping this place clean, we're practically keeping him in business."

It felt like my lucky day with all the smiles I was coaxing out of Noah, though this one seemed a little tighter than the others. "Still. I grew up in this town. We were practically inseparable in high school. I haven't had more than a two-sentence conversation with the man in years. You've been here since what, July? And you're already on a first-name basis?"

Did I detect a hint of *jealousy* in his tone? My stomach fluttered, blood rushing to my cheeks at the thought.

There was a certain thrill that traveled through me at the thought of Noah being jealous that I was getting to know another man in town.

"Why do you say that like it surprises you? Until a month ago, I wasn't even sure you knew the English language. Both of you grunt like cavemen and brood in dark corners of the semi-dingy shops that you own. What about that screams 'great conversationalist'?"

Noah pinched his lips together and raked his tongue over his teeth.

"Still," he chuckled, rolling his eyes at my dig.

"What can I say? I'm just a very likable person." I shimmied my shoulders a little bit and Noah laughed. "Also, I may or may not have bribed him with a piece of pie from the diner."

Noah snapped and pointed his index finger at me. "There it is."

I feigned offense, slapping my hand against my chest with an over-dramatic gasp. "I would've eventually gotten him on my good side without food, thank you very much. I just... Sped up the process."

He shook his head, walking over and resting his hip against the front desk. "So you–" He paused to clear his throat and a tinge of red colored the tips of his ears. "You're interested in getting to know him?"

I matched his stance and leaned against the desk, my eyebrow arched in a silent question. Noah Kent was *jealous*. "What's it to you?" I narrowed my eyes in a challenge, waiting for him to admit it.

I crossed my arms and a muscle in Noah's jaw feathered. His lips parted marginally before snapping shut again.

I heard Gia in my head telling me to lose myself in the possibilities. To let myself *feel*. Noah's jealousy and his refusal to answer my question or admit what he was feeling were the last little confidence boost I needed.

Just be. Just feel.

"Are you... jealous, Noah?" I leaned forward *just* a tad, crowding his space a little more. My tone was light, but the tension in the room was anything but. I could feel the fear and nerves weaving their way up my spine as he remained silent in front of me, stoic and seemingly unaffected by what little space remained between us.

The flame of confidence that was just burning so brightly began to dim, embarrassment slowly creeping up to take its place.

I was definitely a little rusty. My most recent romantic interactions were with a man whom I met in *high school* and a raunchy novel where everything was described as heated and throbbing.

I began to pull away, my whole body splotchy and red, burning from the mortification that I had tried to be bold and it had gone so poorly.

Gia was getting a piece of my mind after this, for sure.

I let my gaze drift to the floor, and Noah's hand reached out, crooking his index finger under my chin to tilt my head back. I met his eyes again, my mouth dry as his nostrils flared.

"What if I am, Liv?" he rasped, his gaze dropping to my mouth for *just* a second. The moment was fleeting, gone before I could even be sure that it happened.

My lips parted with a small exhale, and his thumb rested just below my bottom lip, his calloused skin creating an addicting contrast between the softness of mine.

"Hmm?" he urged, gaining the courage to let his thumb slide a little closer to the curve of my lip. "What if I am, Liv? What if I *am* jealous?"

A small shiver traveled down my spine, and I swallowed, trying to use the two brain cells I had left to focus on coming up with a semi-coherent response. "Well," I started, my eyes flitting back and forth between his. "I would tell you that there's only room for one brooding asshole in my life and fortunately for you, the spot is yours." My voice was breathy and low, barely registering over a whisper.

Noah's lips twitched as he fought a smile, his fingers brushing along my jawline. I shivered again as his hand slid around to cup the back of my neck, kneading softly. "Good," he whispered, his gaze dropping to my lips again. This time there was no mistaking it.

My tongue darted out to swipe against my bottom lip, and he tracked the movement carefully. It was almost as if neither of us knew where to go from here or what we were ready for beyond this point. Truthfully, I was content as we were. Somewhere during our little standoff, we'd inched closer together, our chests kissing with each heaving breath. The temperature of the room was long forgotten, as was the desire to run.

Noah's chin dipped, his breath fanning across my nose. "Liv," he said quietly, his eyebrows pulling together as he studied my face.

The phone on the counter rang and we jumped apart, my heart racing for a completely different reason now. My hand slammed to my chest as I took a deep breath and Noah scrubbed a hand down his face before reaching behind him to grab the phone.

He kept his eyes on me the whole time.

"Kent Automotive," he ground out, his shoulders dropping with a sigh half a second later. "Hey, Sheila."

A laugh bubbled up my throat, and my hand came up to clamp over my mouth in an attempt to muffle the noise. Noah grinned when it failed, a deep chuckle rumbling through his chest. He pulled the phone from his ear and let his laugh loose, my chest tightening as I reveled in the sound.

Through broken words and loud laughter, he told Sheila the shop was closed and that we'd call her back tomorrow. Once the phone was placed back onto the receiver, he huffed out a laugh and shook his head, reaching up to tuck that stubborn piece of hair that stuck to my cheek behind my ear. The corner of his mouth lifted into a small smile, and I wanted a picture of this moment.

I wanted to remember the way he looked at me and the way he made me feel. I wanted to soak in the adoration pouring from his stare and the way he trusted me enough to relax and joke around. I wanted this moment to be tangible, something I could clutch in my hands and hold close to my heart.

A small, seemingly inconsequential moment to anyone on the outside looking in. But for me, for Noah, it was the first step toward becoming *more* than our losses.

He smiled at me for a beat longer before his eyes lit up. "How would you feel about pulling Kennedy out of school?"

Chapter 20

Olivia

"Lake day?" Kennedy asked, her tiny little eyebrow quirked as she adjusted the straps of her book bag. "What's a lake day?"

I should've known better than to mention anything before we made it out the door first. *Technically,* Nellie and Kennedy just so happened to have doctor appointments at the same time… On the same day… At a doctor in Wilmington.

Judging by the small smile on the receptionist, Rhea's, face as we signed them out, she knew it was a lie.

Avery met us at the door with Nellie, her index finger pressed to her closed lips.

Ken's eyes went wide as she pinched her fingers together at the corner of her mouth and twisted, sealing the lock and then tossing the key over her shoulder.

Rhea winked from behind the desk and waved to the girls as we pushed against the heavy metal doors to leave their school. "Do you guys do this often?" I questioned as Nellie and Kennedy giggled together like they'd gotten away with stealing a cookie out of the cookie jar.

Nell skipped forward, urging Kennedy to join her while Avery stayed back with me. "Only every summer. It used to be something our parents did with us. There's this tiny lake about thirty or so minutes outside of town, and we would go every summer from the time we were in daycare until we graduated from high school."

She paused and I could almost feel the nostalgia emanating from her, a distant look in her eyes as we trailed behind the girls. "Naturally, I kept the tradition going. This is the first year Noah's gone since Addie passed." She nudged my shoulder with hers. "Thanks for that."

"Oh." I could feel my cheeks heat. I looked down at the sidewalk and counted the cracks as we walked, unsure of what to say back. Avery laughed as I fidgeted with the hem of my shirt. "Well, I didn't break the A/C."

She scoffed, nudging my shoulder again. "We both know it has nothing to do with the broken A/C."

I could feel the color in my cheeks deepening. It felt unfair of me to claim the recent changes in Noah as something that I'd done or inspired. But at the same time, when I first moved into our apartment here, I couldn't remember the last time I'd genuinely laughed or shed tears that reflected something happy inside of me instead of something unbearably dark. So, maybe it was okay to claim a little bit of responsibility for the growing number of small smiles and breathtaking laughs.

"I haven't seen him like this in–" Avery paused, blowing out a slow breath and puffing her cheeks out. "I mean, it's been years, Olivia. You can say that it's not you, but the fact of the matter is, that man has laughed and smiled more in the past few months than he has since Adeline died and it's hard for me to ignore that."

"I don't need a thank you for being a decent human to someone." I wasn't sure what else to say. I hadn't done anything extraordinary or over the top to pull Noah out of his shell. Just existing in the same space as him and sharing the same struggle gave us something to bond over. Maybe that was what he needed all along. Someone who could validate his grief and guilt, someone to tell him that he wasn't crazy for *still* feeling the way that he did.

I wasn't sure at what point it shifted from sharing a similar bond to thumbs on lips and heated stares, but I couldn't find it within myself to feel guilty or ashamed about it.

We turned toward the pathway that led up to our building, the girls screaming and running toward Noah who waited for us at the door. He grinned, lowering himself to their level, and snatched them both up as they giggled and kicked their legs.

Avery gently pulled me to a stop. "It's more than that. Maybe you can't or don't see that. But I do. *We* do."

Avery slung an arm around my shoulder and sighed. "I hate the circumstances that got you here. And if I could make it so that you two didn't have to go through that, I would. But at the same time, I am also really glad that this was the town you stumbled across."

"Me, too."

I turned to look back over at Noah and the girls, Kennedy tossed over his shoulders while Nellie clung to his leg. He looked up, and the wide, crooked grin plastered on his face forced all the air from my lungs in one single breath.

I'd always thought that Noah was attractive. From the second I laid eyes on him in the shop, I was terrified of how drawn I was to him.

He reminded me of something like a stained glass window. Hundreds of shattered pieces soldered together to form something extraordinary. A beautiful piece of art, sturdy and breathtaking formed by the jagged edges of heartbreak and loss.

At this moment, I could see a glimpse of what Avery was talking about. Because Noah wasn't just surface-level happy. I could *feel* it. I could feel the warmth wrapping around me as his laugh carried through the breeze, I could hear it in the way he joked with the girls and in the way he talked.

This little town had already given me back so much of what I was desperately craving when Evergreen was sucking the life out of me. It felt good to know that maybe I'd done a little to pay that back.

"Are you guys done being all sappy yet or should we give you another minute?" Noah winked at me, and I was blushing for an entirely different reason now.

Avery rolled her eyes at her brother and urged me forward. "You're insufferable. Some of us *like* expressing emotions."

He twisted his face up as if there was nothing in this world he found more repulsive. "I can't imagine why."

"Sometimes you just need a good cry, Uncle Noah! Isn't that right, mom?" Nellie stared up at her mother with a grin, her arms and legs still wrapped around Noah's leg like a koala.

"That's right, baby."

He chuckled, lifting Kennedy off of his shoulder and setting her down. "Clearly, I'm outnumbered here. Come on, ladies. We're losing daylight."

* * *

Noah pulled off the main road and onto some kind of overgrown path that was *just* wide enough for his truck to ride along while avoiding any paint scratches from stray branches. I watched the road, amazed at how Noah even knew where to turn. The whole thing just looked like grass with a few patches of what looked like gravel here and there. There were no signs or reflectors to tell him which way to go, but he followed the winding road with ease, a lazy smile on his lips the entire drive.

He sat back in his seat, his right arm resting on the center console while his left arm was draped over the steering wheel as he drove. Avery, Nellie, and Kennedy were all in the backseat carrying on with their own conversation, laughing and singing along to the radio.

I closed my eyes and tilted my head back, soaking up the moment. Kennedy's laugh pierced through the air, and I smiled at the sound.

I no longer felt that pang of jealousy in my chest when she laughed so carelessly. She was only four. She deserved every ounce of that carefree feeling. I was beginning to see that despite noticing the cracks in my composure on a bad day, I wasn't stealing anything from her. I wasn't proving myself incapable of being a good mother just because I had bad days.

I still felt the ache of Liam's loss, and I don't think it would ever completely go away. But every day, the people in this truck gave me a reason to push through the pain.

When I felt a shift in the ground underneath us, I opened my eyes again. The trees began to clear, overhanging branches growing shorter and shorter while the distance between the trees grew wider.

Noah followed the path forward, driving toward the break in the trees. Sunlight broke through the canopy above and danced along the path in front of us. My jaw dropped a little when we finally made it through. "No beautiful destinations in Delaware my ass."

Noah put his truck in park and cut the ignition just shy of the shoreline, letting out a laugh. "Okay, maybe I forgot about this one."

My eyes swept over the lake, calm waves lapping at the shore gently. The water shimmered under the harsh sun as it moved with the breeze, ripples breaking across the surface in mesmerizing patterns. Large trees surrounded the entire body of water like a shield from the outside world. No wonder they came back to this place every year.

Avery worked on getting the girls out of their car seats as I pushed open my door and slid out of the truck.

Noah walked around to the bed of his truck and snagged the cooler with the sandwiches he'd made while waiting for all of us to get ready. "Liv, can you grab the towels?"

The girls piled out as I rounded his truck, snagging the beach bag with towels, sunscreen, and five different flavors of potato chips that Noah *insisted* we needed.

We had our own little picnic packed and ready to go. I wasn't exactly sure how long we were planning on staying, but given the girls' excitement and the amount of supplies we packed, we weren't leaving any time soon.

"Mom! Hurry! I wanna get in!" Kennedy and Nellie had Avery by the hands, dragging her toward the shoreline.

I laughed and followed closely behind, quickly laying a towel down as Kennedy practically buzzed with excitement next to me.

After a few minutes of sunscreen application and making sure Ken's arm floaties were secure, Avery was waist-deep in the water with the girls, and the once-placid waters came to life as they splashed and played.

"Come on, Olivia!" Avery's hands were cupped around her mouth as she yelled from the water.

"Yeah! Come on, *Olivia!*" Kennedy giggled as I scowled playfully in her direction.

I toyed with the hem of my crochet cover-up. It had been a long time since this yellow two-piece had made an appearance and an even longer amount of time since I was this nervous to wear it in front of a man. Liam had seen my body in every stage of life. From elementary school to the awkward stages of middle school and high school. He saw me pregnant with Kennedy when I was nothing more than a swollen body lined with stretch marks.

Liam was there when I brought Kennedy into this world and witnessed every weirdly amazing thing that happened to my body in the months and years after.

The thought that Noah could potentially no longer find me attractive after seeing me in this swimsuit had my stomach churning in a way that it hadn't in *years*. I didn't think he was the kind of man to get scared away by stretch marks and a mom pooch, but the worry still lurked somewhere in the back of my mind as Kennedy grinned up at me from the water.

I took a deep breath and reminded myself that this day wasn't about what Noah thought about me or any lingering insecurities. Today was about keeping that wide, toothy grin on my daughter's face and making the most of one last hot day before fall swept over this small town.

Before I could convince myself not to, I whipped my cover-up over my head, tossed it to the side, and then took off toward the water.

Chapter 21

Noah

I watched as Liv ran toward the water, her smile bright and wild around the edges. Her hair moved like golden silk in the wind, catching the sun in all the right places. She looked happy.

She caught up with Kennedy, scooping her into her arms momentarily before tossing her into the water again.

I rolled out one of the towels that Liv had carried over and peeled my shirt off, tossing it through an open window in my truck. I took my time getting settled and dug through the cooler until I found a beer. This wasn't exactly how I pictured my day going, but as I lowered myself onto the towel and took that first sip of cold beer, the stress and weight of my to-do list at the shop melted away in the sweltering heat.

If this had happened before Liv was working at the shop with me, I would've forced myself to keep working. I would've put in a call to see if James could stop by whenever he had time and suffered through the heat until the air conditioning was working again. But I heard the disappointment in her voice when I came up empty-handed and knew that I couldn't keep her there.

Especially when I was skating on such thin ice. The distance from the desk to the garage wasn't enough anymore. I could feel her presence in every room. Smell her sweet, vanilla perfume lingering in the air.

My mind flashed back to the heated moment we shared, the dangerous feeling of her lip against my thumb. My grip tightened on the beer bottle in my hand as if that would somehow help me regain the feeling of control that was slowly slipping away.

Fuck, I had almost kissed her. I *wanted* to kiss her.

I was so goddamn tired of being at war with myself. Two more unin-terrupted seconds and my self-restraint would've snapped. There was just something about Liv that was making it impossible to keep my distance. I wish I could read her mind and know every thought that accompanied her nervous stares and flustered reactions when I got too close.

Nellie squealed from the water, pulling my attention back to the lake. I took another sip of my beer and pulled my ball cap down to cover my eyes, kicking myself for forgetting my sunglasses. The little glances I stole while Liv ran through the shallow water and splashed around weren't enough.

I'd spent most of the drive over here straining to keep my eyes on the road. Every time she crossed or uncrossed her legs, my eyes tracked the movement, trailing the length of her exposed thighs. I could hear the leather of the steering wheel creaking under my grip as I fought the urge to reach over and settle my hand on her soft skin. The smooth skin of her thigh and the rough calluses on my hands would create the sweetest, most addicting juxtaposition that my fingers ached to discover.

There were about a million different swimsuits I had pictured under that tiny crochet cover-up, and of the many different images my overactive imagination drummed up, nothing compared to the real thing.

The Olivia that I met outside of her apartment door in July was not the same person splashing around in the water today. Emotionally or physically. Weeks of eating (mostly) balanced meals had filled out the curves that her clothes were once slipping off of. Her cheeks were round and full of life when she smiled.

As hard as I'd been trying to fight it, I caved and let my eyes drift over to where she stood in the water. I traced the softness of her curves, dragging my gaze down her body and lingering on the swell of her hips. The stretch marks peeking out from under that yellow two-piece were like a siren song to my hands.

Adeline and I fell in love hard and fast, and I never had this issue of being so captivated by someone that I shouldn't want. When I ventured past the grief and guilt, there wasn't anything inherently wrong with the way I felt about Liv. But there was also a lot that we didn't know about each other.

So I could sit there going back and forth with myself about how much I shouldn't want her, but when it came down to it, it had nothing to do with my lack of willpower. It had everything to do with the fact that once she knew the details of Adeline's death... She wouldn't want me.

The flustered feeling she got around me, the flush in her cheeks that I wanted to claim as mine... All of it would be gone.

Because no one wants a man responsible for the death of his wife.

* * *

"Alright." Liv walked over and rolled out a towel, plopping down on the ground next to me. She wiped the sand off of her feet and pulled her knees to her chest, resting her cheek on her knee as she turned to look at me. "What's wrong with you?"

I snorted out a laugh, setting my beer down in the sand. "Why would there be something wrong with me?" There was a multitude of reasons I'd been trying to keep my distance since we got to the lake a few hours ago, but the realization that eventually, I would have to tell Liv about how Addie died was what soured my mood completely. I couldn't fathom the thought of her looking at me differently.

She smiled softly, squinting her eyes against the blazing sun. I pulled the ball cap from my head and plopped it on hers, shielding her from the bright light.

She adjusted the bill of the hat with a grin. "Don't distract me with kind gestures." Liv reached over, snagging my beer from the sand and putting the bottle to her lips. She tipped her head back and took a long pull, draining the last of it.

I huffed out a laugh as she dropped the empty bottle onto her towel and wiped her mouth with the back of her hand. My heart thrummed a wild beat in my chest as she grinned over at me.

I twisted toward the cooler and lifted the lid, snagging two beers. "I'm not distracting you."

She reached over and grabbed a beer, twisting the top off and taking a small sip. Liv hummed a noise of disagreement in the back of her throat. "Fine. Keep your secrets, Noah Kent."

I knew that her words weren't meant to deliver such a harsh blow to my chest, but it stung all the same. She had no clue about the secrets I was keeping or the pain that I had caused.

I shifted, my shoulders sinking under the weight of the hypocrisy that settled over me. I carried this overwhelming need to delve into her past, yearning to uncover every intricate detail of her life, all while evading her inquiries of mine.

The unfairness of it all was not lost on me. That imbalance of expectations. I'd been trying to open up and offer more of myself, but the fear of falling short and exposing her to the truth of my past held me back.

We were in this vicious cycle of taking one step forward and three steps back. Just hours ago, I was inches away from finally closing the distance I had repeatedly put between us. And now, I was slowly inching myself away once again.

I'd spent a long time not caring what others thought of me, and yet, with Liv, I longed for her acceptance. I wanted to live up to every expectation that she held of me. I wanted to prove myself worthy of not only her trust but also her daughter's, and the second she learned that it was my carelessness that sent us flying off the road that night… The connection we had would shatter like delicate glass, irreparably fracturing our bond and leaving behind shards of broken trust.

Liv's gaze shifted to me once more, her eyes searching for an answer I wasn't willing to give. "Just tell me you're okay?"

Another twinge of hurt and guilt seared through my chest. She knew I was avoiding her questions, and part of me was terrified that holding back the answers she was seeking would sever the connection we'd established. But a larger part of me knew that if she got the answers she wanted, the connection would be severed regardless.

Liv sucked in a deep breath and blew it out slowly, lifting the beer to her lips. She accepted my silence, and I knew I should've been relieved, but the invisible claws of guilt tore at my chest, and I was desperate to make her understand, consequences be damned.

Clearing my throat, I took a swig of beer and let the crisp, citrus flavor dance along my tongue for a moment before swallowing. "I worry that if I tell you, you'll think less of me. I care about you, Liv, and the thought of losing this friendship..." Shaking my head, I turned my gaze to the water to avoid meeting her eyes. "I don't wanna lose your trust," I admitted, an unfamiliar grit gripping my voice.

She was silent for a moment, and I let curiosity pull my attention toward her once again.

"I don't talk about Addie. I don't talk about that night. But I can't..." I stopped, unsure of what I was trying to say or how much of myself I wanted to expose right now. "I just need *you* to know."

Her eyes softened, reflecting a shimmer of surprise as she recognized the vulnerability I was preparing to share. "Noah, listen to me," she said, her voice laced with sincerity. With a subtle shift in her posture, she closed the physical distance between us, her hand finding mine in the warm sand.

"You're a good man. And I hate that you either can't see that or just outright refuse to believe it. But you are. I don't scare easily. I trust you. If you wanna talk about it, I'm here to listen. But you are so much more than your loss. You're stronger than you give yourself credit for." Her assurance washed over me and soothed the doubts that had plagued my thoughts. The conviction in her voice ignited a tiny spark of hope within me that maybe, just maybe, she would be able to see past my mistakes and still choose to see me as this honorable man. Someone worthy of her time and trust.

I wondered if she held herself to the same standard that she preached to me. Did she realize that she too was so much more than her loss? Did she see the strength that she carried?

She was so happy to instill these feelings into everyone else. I needed to know she believed these things about herself, too.

The corner of her lip tugged into a soft, endearing smile. "Plus, if we get it all out in the open now, we can stop having these sad-ass talks and maybe talk about the weather for once. I never thought I'd be craving small talk. But I guess having death in common will do that to your conversations."

I chuckled, shaking my head while lowering my gaze to where our hands met in the sand. We shared a moment of silence before I flipped my hand, lacing our fingers together.

I heard Liv take a shaky breath, her voice soft, barely breaking over the sound of the water and the girls' laughter carrying through the still air. "I'm not perfect. I've never claimed to be. I know that I haven't handled Liam's death with grace. I know I've made mistakes." She looked up at me, her brows pulling together. "So I'm pretty sure I have no clue what I'm talking about. But you can tell me." She paused, shaking her head gently with a small smile. "Caring for someone doesn't mean you tuck tail and run when the going gets tough. You care for the ugly bits, too."

Keeping my hand wrapped around hers, I sat up straight and swallowed past the lump in my throat, summoning the last of my courage to push the words past my lips. "That night—" I rasped. "The night that Addie... Died. It was my fault."

My throat constricted, hindering my ability to speak. Olivia's body stiffened, but I kept my eyes trained on the sand by our fingers. I cleared my throat again, snagging my beer and taking another long pull in hopes of clearing the emotion clogging my throat. "I killed my wife."

Chapter 22

Noah

Four Years Ago

"Ad," I yawned, scrubbing a hand down my face. The shrill sound of Addie's phone jarred me awake. "Honey. Phone," I rasped.

She hummed in her sleep, rolling toward her nightstand. I kept my eyes closed, smiling softly to myself as her hand slapped against the wood in an attempt to find her phone. I turned my head, peeling one eye open as she swiped against the screen and lowered the device to her ear.

Her voice was thick with sleep when she answered. "Yeah?"

I glanced at the clock on her nightstand and rolled my eyes, knowing it was probably Winnie. We'd told her not to go out, but she was eighteen and hellbent on enjoying her last spring break as a high school senior despite the snowstorm blowing in.

Winnie was riding this streak of independence like her life depended on it, and normally, I wouldn't care. Everyone had a bit of rebellious spirit within them, especially at her age and in a town as small as Rose Hill. But it was always Adeline who got the call for help in the middle of the night, and my guess was that she was drunk and stranded at another house party.

Adeline sat up, her once sleepy eyes wide and attentive. "Win, slow down. What happened?"

Before she could even finish her sentence, I was throwing the covers back and moving to our walk-in closet to get dressed. I could hear Winnie's panicked and slurred speech over the phone and something uneasy settled in my gut. I yanked some jeans on and threw a hoodie over my head before walking back into our room and peering out of the window.

"Shit," I cursed softly, walking over to Addie's dresser to grab a pair of leggings and something warm. There was already at least six inches of snow on the ground. Hopefully, wherever Winnie was, she had heat. Because it was going to take us a while to get there.

Addie threw me an appreciative smile, tucking her phone between her shoulder and her ear as she pushed off the bed and grabbed the leggings I had already laid out. "How long ago did they leave you?"

There was an edge to her voice that made me want to cower. There were a lot of things I admired about my wife, but her protectiveness over her family was something high on that list. If someone in this town abandoned her little sister in the snow, they would have to answer to her tomorrow.

"Christ, Winnie. It's like twenty degrees outside!" Addie put the phone on speaker and dropped it onto the bed, pulling the crew neck over her head.

Her sister's slurred voice poured through the speakers. "I know, Addie! I'm sorry. Jas said she was going to give me a ride, but she darted when Amber's parents came home."

"Can you go inside?" I asked, clearly hearing her teeth chattering in between sentences.

"Her parents said no."

I sighed, shaking my head. Her parents might be angry at Amber for having a party, but they couldn't leave her outside to freeze.

Addie scoffed, grabbing her phone from the bed and walking to the dresser to grab a pair of socks. "Go knock on the damn door. Tell Krissy that Noah and I are on the way, and if she doesn't let you in the house, I'm gonna tell Mom to fry her hair next time she goes to the salon."

Living in a small town had its perks. For instance, knowing exactly who Amber's parents were and being able to make oddly specific threats if they piss you off because you unwillingly know too much about their personal life.

"Addie, I don't want to! She's already so mad," Winnie whined.

"Gwenyth. Go up to her door and tell her that I'm on the way. If you don't, I'm going up to her door when I get there and shoving my foot up her ass for kicking you out in the first place."

I laughed, quickly concealing it with a cough when Addie's glare shifted from her phone and landed on me. "I'm gonna warm up the truck."

I retreated through our house, down the long hallway that separated our bedroom from the rest of the home, and aimed for the front door. Moonlight poured in through the living room windows and reflected off the dark wood floors, lighting my way through an otherwise dark house.

I sighed, realizing my truck was still propped up on the lifts in the garage, neglected amidst the chaos that winter brought to our shop. The promise to install the snow chains on Addie's old truck had also slipped through the cracks; another task left unfinished. The winter months were without a doubt the busiest months at the shop, demanding my attention and pulling me away from personal responsibilities. The irony of it all struck me - here I was, working tirelessly to ensure the safety of everyone else in this small town while our own vehicles remained untouched and unprepared for the harsh conditions outside.

I should've listened to Addie last week when she told me it was too early to take the chains off in the first place.

A pang of remorse tugged at my conscience. Working at the front desk of Kent Automotive, Addie understood the demands of the season and never complained or voiced her frustrations. But it didn't alleviate the guilt. I would never forgive myself if something happened to her because I'd been so concerned about everyone else's cars that I failed to make sure my own wife was driving safely through such harsh weather.

After toeing on my boots and shrugging on a jacket, I snagged the keys for Addie's truck. If Amber's mom, Krissy, was really hellbent on not letting Winnie inside, there wasn't time to get my truck down. Not to mention, I hadn't addressed the power steering issue yet, so I'd much rather take my chances on a lack of snow tires over the power steering going out while driving down an icy road.

I could hear the almost silent footfalls of Addie's socked feet as she made her way through the house. "We'll be there in twenty. Go up to the house, ask Kris if you can hang out. She's not gonna leave you in the cold, hon."

She smiled up at me as she walked through the living room, her blue eyes tired yet worried. They would stay that way until Winnie was in the backseat. I held up her coat and waited for her to push her arms through the sleeves before turning her around and zipping it up.

"Yeah, I'll see you soon. Okay. Love you, too." She hung up, sliding her phone into her pocket. "I need to have a talk with her. I just wanna go one weekend without getting woken up at three in the morning to fetch her drunk ass from some random farmhouse because her shitty-ass friends left her behind again."

I tucked the keys into my pocket and raised my hands to cradle her face. She leaned into my touch, smiling softly. "You, Adeline Kent, are the most selfless human being I've ever met." I slid my hand around to cup the back of her neck, tangling my fingers in her hair.

"I kind of am, aren't I?"

"And ever so humble."

She laughed, curling her fingers into my jacket and pulling me closer. "I love you. Thanks for waking up with me every weekend to rescue her from random ditches throughout town."

Leaning down, I pressed my lips to the tip of her nose. "I'll follow you to every random ditch in the country if you keep looking at me like that." I would forever chase that look of adoration in her eyes, whether it be through grand gestures that would steal her breath or small acts of kindness that softened her gaze and made her heart skip a beat.

That little twinkle in her eye belonged to me and me only.

"Alright. Come on, Casanova. My sister's gonna get frostbite. And I'm gonna kick Krissy's ass."

A few minutes later, Adeline sat in the driver's seat, the heat blasting while I cleaned the snow from the windshield. Not that it was doing much. I looked up, massive snowflakes tumbling down from an inky black sky almost faster than I could clear them. I used the brush to swipe at the last dusting of snow before tossing it into the bed and pulling the driver's side door open.

"You want me to drive?"

She looked up at me with gratitude, all the nervous tension bleeding from her shoulders as she relaxed. "Please. I'm sorry, babe. I wasn't gonna ask... But..." Her voice trailed off as she unbuckled her seat belt to move over.

"You hate driving in the snow, I know. Scooch." I climbed into the truck, yanking the hat off my head and blowing hot air onto my cold fingers. "You picked a horrible place to settle down for someone who hates snow," I teased.

"Well," Addie sat back against the old leather and crossed her legs. "There was this guy. He asked me to prom ages ago and you know, I thought he was kind of dorky—" She squealed as I pinched her side.

"Buckle up," I ordered with a laugh, throwing the truck in reverse and slowly backing out of the driveway.

"Anyway," she continued, though we both knew how this story played out. "I kind of had plans to leave, went to college and everything. Then, he asked me to marry him, and I just knew that I wasn't going anywhere. Little did he know, he was going to spend the rest of his life driving me around in the snow and picking up my drunk teenage sister from house parties."

I spun the steering wheel in my hand and put the car in drive, the air inside the cab shifting, and the road in front of us was almost imperceptible under the blanket of snow. "Ah, fuck." I flicked the wipers on and eased onto the gas, praying that the tires were able to get enough traction without chains.

Addie wrung her hands together as she leaned forward, narrowing her eyes at the falling snow. "I can't believe Krissy wouldn't let her stay, that fucking bitch."

I let out a low chuckle at her insult, but it was strained. That same unease from earlier was churning in my stomach once again. I normally wouldn't so much as take the trash out in weather like this, let alone drive in it. But I couldn't let Winnie stand in the cold, and I wouldn't let Addie drive in this alone.

"Just... Go slow, babe." I could hear the tightness in her voice, equally as concerned about the lack of visibility as I was.

Thankfully, this wasn't the first time I'd ventured over to Krissy's in the past month or so, and I was familiar with the route. But it wasn't the familiarity that was digging at me.

I straightened my back, leaning into the steering wheel as we eased down the winding road, my knuckles blanching as my grip tightened. I was only going around ten miles an hour, but even that made me nervous.

Addie's phone rang, spearing through the silence of the car and I jolted. That tiny surge of adrenaline sent my heart into a gallop as I blew out a controlled breath.

"Win?" Her spine straightened almost immediately, and the on-edge feeling that I'd been battling with since I woke up buzzed around my gut like a swarm of angry hornets.

There was too much going on in front of me to worry about the conversation she was having with her sister. I just hoped that Krissy let her come inside. At this rate, we wouldn't make it for another thirty minutes.

I tuned them out as I continued down the windy road, the windshield wipers swiping aggressively across the glass as the snow continued to race from the sky. The tires struggled for traction as I turned, slipping and sliding as I eased us around the curve. The wind howled, and I found myself oddly thankful for the noise.

I felt the thunk of Addie's phone against the leather seat and spared a glance in her direction. "She okay?"

"Krissy's a raging bitch, but she let her inside. Told her she couldn't stay so someone had to come get her. Apparently, Amber's getting the ass-chewing of a lifetime." She mumbled something about that being nothing compared to the way she was going to rip into Krissy, and I let out a small laugh, relaxing marginally.

I eased onto the gas, telling myself it was okay since the road would be empty this time of night.

"My guess is thirty or so minutes."

Addie flopped back into her seat and crossed her legs once again. "Gives me time to go over the shit I'm gonna yell at both Krissy and Win."

I huffed out a laugh, trying to force myself to relax. Winnie was fine. We were fine. I just needed to relax, and we'd be back home and warm soon.

"Careful, there's a—"

"Hill. Yes, I know, Ad."

Even without seeing it, I could feel her eyes roll in my soul.

"Sorry, I'm just nervous. I don't know how you can even see the road."

The leather of the steering wheel creaked under my grasp. No way in hell was I telling her that I actually couldn't see shit in front of or around me. I acknowledged her with some kind of grunt in the back of my throat and kept my focus on the flurry of snow falling around us.

Carefully, I put a little more weight on the pedal, gritting my teeth as the tires spun, losing their grip on the road as I tried to get us over the hill.

Leather groaned as Addie shifted, her fingers curling around the seat. My body tensed, both of us feeling the shift in the ground as it happened. "Noah," she warned, her voice nervous and frantic around the edges.

"I know," I ground out. The bed of the truck began sliding left, the cab of the truck sliding right. Addie gripped the seat harder, and I sucked in a breath through my teeth. "We just have to get over the hill."

It wasn't a big hill. Not even big enough to make your stomach drop if you drove over it too fast, but in this weather, one wrong move and we would go flying off the road and into the embankment. The second we cleared the top, I eased onto the brakes, the tires fighting for purchase, the whole truck shifting and skidding across the snowy ground.

I adjusted the steering wheel, trying to correct the tires and slow us down, but as we coasted down the hill, we only gained speed. My heart pounded against my ribs, my pulse roaring through my ears as I tried to regain control.

Adrenaline surged through my veins as time seemed to slow, Addie's panicked, shallow breaths were the only thing I could focus on.

I cursed, trying again to correct our course, but it was no use. I was blinded by the falling snow, with no idea which direction we were facing or where we were headed. I was at the mercy of this old truck, and the only thing we could do was hold on as we careened through the wintery chaos.

"Noah!" Addie's shriek pierced through the howling wind, but it was too late.

My throat tightened at the panic in her voice, at the complete lack of control I had. I couldn't do anything.

I watched helplessly as bright headlights illuminated the cab, and the last thing I saw was the panic on my wife's face as the sickening crunch of metal cut off her scream. The impact of the other car reverberated through the cabin, sending a tremor of pure horror through my body.

The world spun as the truck circled faster and faster.

Another loud crunch of metal pierced my ears, and for a moment, the car felt weightless. I saw flashes of black hair in my peripheral before we crashed back down to the snowy ground, glass shattering and metal groaning as we rolled. My head smacked against the unforgiving surface of the driver's side window, pain exploding through my skull for a split second before the world around me went black.

Chapter 23

Olivia

My grip tightened on Noah's hand, fingernails biting into his skin, but I don't think he noticed. Completely oblivious to the world around him, I listened in horror as he recounted that terrible night with Adeline.

Slowly, and with each gruesome detail, the color had drained from his face. His lips quivered as he took a steadying breath, and I, too, was blind to everything that existed outside of this cocoon we'd created. There was no beach, there was no Avery, or sandcastles being built on the shoreline. There was only Noah and this guilt that was eating him alive.

He blamed himself.

He *genuinely* thought that he was to blame for the death of his wife.

There was so much about Noah that seemed to make a little more sense now and my heart ached as the pieces fell into place. The way he tortured himself and withheld pictures of their time together simply because he thought he didn't deserve it.

It'd been four years since Adeline's accident. And he'd spent every single second thinking he was at fault. I couldn't fathom the weight of this emotional toll that he'd been enduring, this deep-seated anguish that had been tearing at his soul and poisoning his heart for the past *four years*.

I knew that Noah didn't need or want my tears, but they flooded my eyes anyway.

He cleared his throat and I blinked back the moisture building on my waterline. "I woke up sometime later to Adeline screaming." His voice cracked and I wanted to tell him to stop. I wanted to beg him to understand that nothing about this was his fault, that accidents like that just happen.

But something told me that this was the first time he was allowing himself to process this moment and I couldn't be the one to take that away from him.

"I wasn't sure how long I'd been out, but she was screaming for me and I— I couldn't do a single thing to help her. We were upside down after rolling down the embankment and the only thing I could see was the blood dripping—" He paused, swallowing hard and training his gaze on the water that lapped against the sand. "There was already so much and it was coming out so fast, but I just... I just sat there. I couldn't move. My legs were trapped, the seat belt was stuck and the only thing I did was hold her hand while she..." Noah's voice trailed off, and I choked back a sob that was clawing its way up my throat.

"By the time the paramedics got there..." he sniffed, a muscle in his jaw feathering as his molars ground together. "It was too late. All because I didn't make time, Liv. If I would've just spent twenty extra minutes in the garage, I just— I know she would still be here."

I shook my head, swiping at a tear before he could see it. "No, Noah. You don't know that. There's no way for you to know that."

His hand relaxed around mine, but I refused to let go. Not now. "The tires— They wouldn't have spun out like that if they just had chains. I had the fucking chains. *I had them.* But I was so busy... I let my wife's life slip through the cracks."

I released his hand from my grip and turned, pushing myself up onto my knees, and making sure we were eye-to-eye. My chest cracked at the agonized look on his face. "Noah. Listen to me." I lowered myself a little as he tried to look away, locking our eyes once again as my hands took on a mind of their own, gently bracketing his face. "It's not your fault."

I could read the resistance in his expression, his face twisting up as his eyes filled with tears. "It is. I had—"

"It is not," I reiterated, my tone resolute and offering no room for argument. "I know how absolutely unbearable it is to live in this world without the one person who understood you the best. I know you're angry and think that torturing yourself with this guilt is the only way because you harbor the blame, but *it's not your fault*. You could've fixed your truck and taken it, and it still could've happened. You could've put the chains on her tires before you left and your tires *still* would've spun out."

Noah allowed one tear to slip free and I wiped it away with my thumb. "Do you blame her sister?"

"No, absolutely not," he answered quickly.

"If you don't blame her, you can't blame yourself, Noah."

"It's not the same."

I sat back on my heels, dropping my hands to my thighs, but Noah's eyes stayed locked on mine. "It's not. But it's still not your fault. What happened to Adeline— to both of you— was tragic. But Noah, you have to understand that there is nothing you could've done. You can't continue to let this guilt eat you alive."

I paused, my eyes dancing back and forth between his. "Life is a cruel son of a bitch doling out tragedy after tragedy, all of them riddled with uncertainties. It is *not* fair for you to hold yourself responsible for her death."

His gaze softened, his breathing evening out as he took in my words. I could see the conflict playing out in his mind, an unfair battle between self-blame and the desire to let go of this soul-crushing feeling.

I brushed his hair out of his face. My nose burned, tears pricking at the corners of my eyes. "You deserve peace, Noah."

A strangled sound ripped through his throat, his eyes welling with tears again.

I wasn't sure how long we sat there, my knees pressed against the outside of his thigh and my hand softly brushing against his cheek. But I broke the silence with the four words he was struggling to believe. "It's not your fault."

I swiped my thumb against his cheek, wiping away another stray tear, but when he looked up at me I could almost feel a shift. This invisible string pulling us together just knotted itself around my heart, and I had no clue how to unravel it.

He took a deep breath, shutting his eyes for a moment and leaning into my touch. And this time, when those hazel eyes locked on mine, they held a glimmer of acceptance. Noah nodded once, a silent acknowledgment to the truth in my words and maybe he didn't completely believe them, but I knew this was a step in the right direction. A step closer to the closure that he needed.

"Thank you," he mumbled.

I smiled gently and opened my mouth to respond, but Noah surprised me by winding his hands around my waist and pulling me into his chest. I hesitated for a moment, a wave of conflicting feelings crashing against my ribs. But I shoved them aside, my arms wrapping around him as I melted into his embrace.

He buried his face into the crook of my neck, and my fingers weaved through his hair like we'd done this a hundred times before and I didn't let myself overthink it.

We sat there on this small beach in Delaware, holding each other tightly as the weight of the world seemed to melt from his shoulders. He held me closer, and I fought the shiver that raced down my spine as the warmth from his hands seeped into my exposed skin.

It became abundantly clear that this connection between us went far beyond the mere friendship we shared. I wasn't sure how to define it in that moment, and there were a million other things to consider, but there was something deeper, something undeniable and profound that tethered us together.

He loosened his hold, his hands lingering on my waist as I pulled back. "Thank you, Liv."

With a gentle smile, I met his gaze. "I'm always here to listen. Okay?"

Noah nodded with a smile and took a deep, cleansing breath as I eased back onto my towel and extended my legs out in front of me.

"So," he said quietly, looking over at me with one eye squinted shut as he faced the sun. "What time next week?"

"Huh?" I met his gaze, furrowing my brows in confusion.

"Well, this was our second official meeting for the Dead Spouse Club. Might as well get it penciled in now. They seem to be happening whether we want them to or not."

I laughed and nudged him with my shoulder. "Pick the time and date, and I'm there."

* * *

Noah threw a little sand onto the bonfire, snuffing out the last of the glowing embers. I knew it was time to go. Honestly, the girls were up way past their bedtimes, I had consumed three too many beers, and Avery looked dead on her feet. But I didn't *want* to go.

It was like this whole day existed in some kind of rose-tinted bubble, and I wasn't ready for it to burst. I wasn't ready to go back to our apartment.

The conversation I had with Noah weighed on the day for all of ten minutes before we were ushered into the lake by two demanding little girls, and it was like I could see the strain in Noah's muscles dissipate with each step he took toward the water.

And when he turned to look over his shoulder at me, the grin on his lips had my head swimming almost as much as the beer racing through my veins did right now. Too distracted by the carefree joy in his eyes, I had failed to notice his playful intentions until it was too late. Until he was moving toward me, closing the distance that separated us in a few easy steps. With one swift motion, he hauled me over his shoulders, large hands splayed across the backs of my thighs.

My whole body flushed under his touch, fire licking at my veins as I tried to control my breathing. Noah tossed me into the water like I weighed nothing, and the coldness failed to register against my burning skin.

I could still feel the warmth of his touch like a brand on my skin as we made our way to the truck hours later.

Noah loaded Nellie into the car, fastening the buckles of her car seat straps as her head lolled to the side, exhaustion fluttering her eyelids. "Uncle Noah," she whispered, her yawn stretching his name out.

He pulled the straps tight, brushing a piece of tangled hair out of her face. "What's up?"

"This was the perfect day."

Kennedy lifted her head from Avery's shoulder. "The bestest."

My throat tightened, tears welling in my eyes as I clutched the damp towels draped over my arms closer to my chest. I didn't miss the way Noah's gaze locked on mine as he responded, "It was, wasn't it?"

I blinked quickly, severing the moment that we were sharing. I hated shying away from the intensity, but it was far too meaningful for the amount of alcohol fogging my brain.

"Don't you think, mommy?" Kennedy asked sleepily, fixing her tired eyes on where I stood just a few feet away. She looked absolutely adorable drowning in Noah's sweatshirt.

I swallowed the knot forming in my throat, not wanting her to misinterpret the emotion that swept over my features. "The bestest," I whispered, my voice catching. I could feel Noah's eyes lingering on me as I stepped closer to my daughter, stretching my hands toward her. She smiled, ignoring the towels on my arm as she reached out and settled into my grasp. "It was the best, sweet girl."

Avery climbed into the back seat, squeezing between the girls. "They're both gonna be *knocked* by the time we get home."

I smiled and lifted Ken into her car seat, Avery swatting at my hands as I tried to buckle her in.

"Go throw the towels into the back, I've got her."

I nodded, sweeping my fingers over Kennedy's cheek before backing away and shutting the door.

Noah was raising the tailgate as I circled around his truck, the towels landing inside the bed with a wet thunk as I tossed them over the side. As I turned back toward Noah, the warmth of the beer mixed with the cold breeze sent a shiver down my spine.

Noah's figure stood tall and strong against the backdrop of the trees, the moonlight casting a soft glow on his features. He was so effortlessly captivating, a steady anchor in the chaos of my thoughts. But it wasn't just his physical presence that held me; it was the genuine care he showed for his family, the tenderness in his eyes when he looked at his sister and his niece, and the way he had welcomed me and Kennedy into their lives.

It was more than just attraction or infatuation. My heart craved this sense of normalcy that he brought into my life after over a year of grappling for solid ground. Little by little, we had unknowingly formed this connection, and I wasn't sure what that meant. For me or for him. For Kennedy. But admitting that to myself was scary, and my mind struggled to sort through the feelings, leaving me slightly unsteady on my feet. Or maybe it was the beer.

Noah tilted his head to the side, a soft smile tugging at his lips. "You okay?"

I couldn't tell if it was the alcohol that I could still taste on my tongue or if I was just so damn tired of being miserable. But I wanted to tell him every thought that raced through my mind, to pour my heart out and let him know in a blubbering rant of twisted words and confusing confessions that I wasn't exactly sure what I was feeling, but that I was feeling *something*.

But the words tangled in my throat, choked back by the fear of being vulnerable.

I still had no idea how to navigate this life that I'd been forced into, and even though he'd been so honest with me tonight, the liquid courage wasn't enough to push me over that edge. There was too much I felt like I needed to figure out on my own.

I could hear Gia telling me that I didn't *need* to figure it out on my own, but in my short time here, I'd already leaned on Noah for so much. Sorting through whatever was happening with my mind and heart should weigh on me and me only.

"Yeah, I'm fine," I replied, my voice slightly wobbly. "Just a little tipsy, that's all."

He stepped closer, his fingers lifting to brush against my jawline. "You sure?"

I nodded.

"Do you need help getting into the truck?" The corner of his mouth lifted into a playful smile, and I rolled my eyes, smacking his shoulder.

"No, smart ass. I'll be fine."

His eyes dropped to my lips for just a moment, tracing the curve of my smile, and my stomach came to life in a delicate dance of butterflies. It wasn't the same heated look we'd shared earlier. This one was lingering and soft like he had no intention of forgetting the small details in my smile, and that only made me grin wider.

"Alright," he responded, jerking his head toward the front of his truck. "Let's get you guys home."

***

The drive *away* from the lake carried a different sort of uncertainty than the drive *to* the lake did. These butterflies inside of me that were once painted in various shades of gray and weighed down by hopeless thoughts, turned bright and vibrant, fluttering around weightless in their confidence that something had changed between me and Noah.

Or maybe I was drunk off of four beers and finally letting myself relax for the first time in over a year.

I wasn't sure.

But regardless, the glances we stole and the secret smiles we shared didn't go unnoticed by the other.

A quiet smile tugged at my lips, dappled streaks of soft moonlight lining our path as we eased through the thick trees and toward the main road. I could feel Noah's gaze flicker over to me and linger for just a few short seconds before he was focusing on the road again.

With everyone in the back seat slowly giving in to sleep, Avery included, I gave in to the persistent curiosity poking around in my brain.

My head rolled against the headrest, and I took a second to watch him, my eyes tracing the long tail of the tattooed snake on his arm until it disappeared under the sleeve of his t-shirt. There were a few smaller tattoos sprinkled throughout the entire piece, all of them shades of black and gray. I'd never really taken time to study them, but from here, I could see the flowers, greenery, and Roman numerals clear as day.

The one that always caught my attention was the snake.

It was beautifully detailed with deep black scales highlighted in white ink that seemed to glow in the moonlight. The tattoo roped around his forearm and ended at his wrist, the snake's head shaded with varying hues of gray and black. I wondered if it meant something to him.

Noah's head turned slightly, catching my eyes before I had a chance to turn away. He smiled softly, flexing his hand on the wheel before looking back at the road. "Do you have any?"

I shook my head. "No. I've always been too scared. I don't think I have a very high pain tolerance."

"Eh, they aren't too bad. After a minute, you kind of get used to the pain."

I snorted. "Believe it or not, that does not make it sound enticing. At all. Actually, I think I want one even *less* than I did before."

Noah laughed, easing onto the brakes and signaling his turn as we got closer to the main road. "I got my first one at eighteen and swore I'd never get another. It hurt so bad. Here I am, sixteen years later with a sleeve."

I let my eyes drag over the snake one more time. "Do they mean anything?"

He tilted his head from side to side in a *so-so* motion as he turned. "Some of them do. Some of them are just fillers to connect the piece together."

"What about this guy?" My finger traced a few inches of the black ink. The touch was so innocent, so gentle. But I shivered as my fingertip smoothed over his skin.

He cleared his throat, flexing the fingers of his right hand a couple of times before explaining with a hushed tone. "After the accident, I needed... Hope. I needed something to look forward to. The snake is a symbol of healing and rebirth because of its ability to shed its own skin." He paused, fidgeting slightly in his seat.

"When I saw it on the artist's sketchpad, it felt like a sign. I'd been given a second chance at life. Do I feel like I deserve it? No. But it was a reminder of what I'd been through and what I'd lost. It was a reminder to make the most of the second chance that I was given. After everything—" He paused to clear his throat, fingers flexing around the steering wheel again. His voice lowered. "It should've been me. But it wasn't. So I have to make that mean something."

"Noah," I whispered his name, something hot burning its way through my chest. The thought of him believing it should've been him instead was one that I could relate to, but hearing him voice that about himself broke my heart.

I took a shaky breath, once again finding myself unsure of how to be on the opposite end of the conversation. My head was swimming with things to say, but they all felt wrong. They all sounded like things that would end up pissing me off instead of settling the grief that ran rampant within me.

I knew exactly what he was feeling, but I couldn't articulate a worthy response. My chest ached, the heel of my hand rubbing against my sternum as if to alleviate the discomfort, but it remained, bubbling hot and uncomfortable like heartburn.

I swallowed, shifting my gaze back to him. "You know, I thought after experiencing death firsthand, I'd get better at these conversations and offering advice, but I never know what to say," I admitted honestly.

The corner of his mouth tipped up. "To be fair, I don't think anybody really knows how to respond, which is probably why most people end up talking out of their ass."

I hummed my agreement. "I have the profound ability to do that in any conversation. Especially when beer is involved."

Noah chuckled softly, shifting in his seat again before sparing a glance in my direction. "Did you have a good time today?"

My sleepy eyes found his, a slow grin spreading across my lips. "The bestest."

Chapter 24

Olivia

Gentle fingers stroked along my jawline and then my forehead, brushing damp, tangled hair out of my face. My neck ached, and my left leg was asleep from the weird way it was folded underneath me.

Slowly, I peeled my eyes open, straightening all of my folded-up limbs with a yawn, unsure of when exactly I'd fallen asleep on the drive home. Noah smiled down at me, backlit by the one streetlight in the parking lot and I wanted to roll my eyes at the fact that he looked so good in such terrible lighting. Figured. He was all hard lines and breathtaking features and I had mascara smudges around my eyes.

I rubbed my eyes and sat up, turning to find the backseat empty.

"Kennedy is already settled at Avery's. Figured you might want the morning off. Avery said she'd stop by before school to grab some clothes. I changed the shop's voicemail from my phone to let everyone know we'd be closed tomorrow, too. No sense in going in until the A/C is up and running again. A hangover in eighty-degree weather is a special type of torture."

I blinked. Once. Then twice. My chest tightened, throat clogged with emotions I didn't quite know how to explain. "I don't get hungover."

He shrugged. "Maybe. But ya know, just in case it does happen… Everything's handled."

Noah's brows pulled together just enough to clue me into his confusion before tears flooded my eyes and he became a watery blur.

"Shit, I'm sorry. I overstepped, didn't I? Shit. We can go get her right now–"

I reached out, grabbing his forearm with more force than I intended to, my fingernails biting into his skin. His eyes were wide with panic, one foot already moving toward the apartment building. My mouth opened, but the words were caught in my throat, so I settled for shaking my head.

I knew that the alcohol had a lot to do with the emotions currently winding around my rib cage with a suffocating grip, but there was just *so much* relief and so much gratitude because *he* made that call for me.

I'd grown up in a small town just like this one. I'd gone to school with every single person who stood off to the side and watched me drown in my own grief as I fought to keep my head above water. They knew all of my secrets, just as I had known theirs.

But none of their kind, placating words ever meant anything. None of their flowers, none of their casserole meals. I was lost in a sea of self-serving people who only helped when it fed into their own selfish narratives.

And here I was, in this small town in Delaware, surrounded by a town of people who didn't know a single thing about me, feeling stronger and more capable than I ever did in Evergreen.

Noah was the last thing I expected when I moved across the country, yet somehow became everything that I needed.

It all felt so silly that this small, seemingly unimportant thing could reduce me to tears, but for the first time in a long time, I felt *seen*. Not just as a grieving widow or a single mother but as Olivia. As *Liv*. The woman that existed behind all the roles and responsibilities and grief.

It was a stunning realization to finally see that what I predicted was right this whole time. That what I needed to heal this hole in my chest didn't exist within the city limits of Evergreen, Wyoming. I needed something new. Something that saw all the ugly, shattered pieces inside of me and just *knew* they could be crafted into something beautiful. There were parts of me that had changed. There were parts of me that would be forever tainted by a loss so life-altering, but Noah saw all of it, every tattered, broken part, and refused to let it define me as a whole. He was helping me understand that healing wasn't about erasing the pain and proving to everyone that you could do it alone. It was about learning to live with it and leaning on people that gave you the strength to recognize your own resilience.

I wanted to say all of this to him. I wanted to make him understand everything that I was feeling. I wanted to thank him.

But I blame the beer and the fact that I was still a little groggy from falling asleep for the words that actually managed to make it out. "I'm just really looking forward to talking about the weather," I choked out.

His brows furrowed, and then his face softened with understanding. And maybe I couldn't articulate everything that I was feeling right then, but Noah put it together all the same.

We both just wanted to be happy.

Noah's knuckles brushed against my cheek, catching a tear as it trickled down. "Me, too."

I took a deep, shaky breath and let it out slowly. "I think I need to go to bed."

His shoulders shook as he laughed, his hand reaching around to unbuckle my seat belt. "I think so, too." He offered his hand and I took it, sliding out of his truck. Such a simple gesture, but my stomach fluttered anyway. Thankfully, my brain was too fuzzy to be embarrassed about the ungraceful way my top half seemed to be moving faster than the bottom as I stumbled off of the seat and gripped his forearm for balance, the other hand still securely wrapped in his.

I didn't miss his chuckle or the way my heart floundered about in my chest as a result of that tiny laugh, because I'd spend the rest of my days making a fool out of myself if that was my reward.

He snagged my beach bag from the floor of his truck and turned, hazel eyes jumping to where our hands joined. I thought for a second that he would pull away. But instead, with one little shift in movement, our fingers laced together.

I could feel my heart punching against my ribs, so sure that in the silence of this parking lot, he could hear each nervous beat and see my skin vibrate with the harsh rhythm of my pulse. If he did, he didn't let it show.

Noah started guiding us toward the door, and my chest wound tight as it braced for the disappointment that would wrack through my body when he pulled away. I held my breath and walked through the door with him, my chest squeezing tighter like it was trying to hold onto this moment in any way that it could.

But the moment didn't end.

His hand stayed wrapped around mine, thumb stroking incoherent patterns against my skin. Each step that we took toward my apartment put me further at ease. I stole *several* glances as we neared the door and fought a smile at the way his lips tipped up when he caught me staring.

"Subtlety eludes you, Olivia Brooks."

I tried to find it within myself to be embarrassed. I waited for that fateful blush to creep up my neck and take possession of my cheeks, but it never came. Just like the guilt, I pushed that feeling of embarrassment into the far corners of my mind, refusing to let it claim even a square inch of space.

I did, however, scrunch my nose up at him. *Olivia.*

He huffed out a laugh, snagging my keys to unlock the door. "What's that look for?"

"You called me Olivia."

His head tilted in confusion as he pushed my door open, gesturing for me to walk inside. "That's your name."

"Yeah, but–" I walked into my apartment, tripping over the transition strip in the doorway and catching myself on the wall, earning an exasperated sigh from Noah. "Everyone calls me Olivia. Or Livie."

I turned around as my front door shut, Noah hanging the beach bag on one of the poorly hung hooks by the front door. His brows pinched together as he fidgeted with the hook, clearly disapproving of the shoddy job I'd done hanging them up.

He turned to face me, apparently deciding they were a problem for a different day. His hands landed on his hips. "You lost me."

I wracked my brain for an explanation that I couldn't seem to find. My brain was fuzzy, and I had no eloquent way of expressing the jumbled mess that was my thoughts. "You know, Olivia belongs to everyone else… Liv—" I paused, swallowing thickly. "Liv belongs to just you."

My chest and cheeks warmed, something I wasn't really able to conceal with a swimsuit and my hair tied up on the top of my head, and that realization only made me blush harder.

His lips curled into a smile, his eyes softening as I started to open my mouth. I had no clue what was going to come out, but then his fingers reached up to brush a piece of hair behind my ear. A shiver tingled its way down my spine, my shoulders visibly shuddering as I let out a shaky breath.

Noah's voice was low and warm, tinged with a hint of amusement. "Just mine, huh?"

I looked down at my feet, my heart fluttering. "Sorry, that was– That was weird."

"No," he responded immediately, his thumb tracing a feather-light path along my cheekbone. "Not at all."

Twisting my lips, I chewed on the inside of my cheek for a moment before meeting his gaze again. "It feels...." *Weird. Stupid. Pitiful. Embarrassing.* My voice trailed off, unable to settle on a word.

His hand dropped back down to his side, and I had to physically stop myself from chasing the warmth of his touch with my face. Pathetic? Absolutely.

"Liv." The weight of my name on his tongue made my heart race with something I hadn't felt in so long. Something that burned through my body and swirled low in my belly. "I like having a little piece of you that's just mine." His voice was low and husky, carrying a possessiveness that had the temperature of my blood skyrocketing.

"You do?" I rasped, my chest heaving with each shaky breath.

He stepped *just* a little bit closer, and I could feel the warmth of his breath coasting across my cheek. "I do," he whispered, his mouth twitching into a smirk.

I nodded weakly, my head buzzing with a sensation that felt an awful lot like how TV static looked. It was almost too much. "Okay," I whispered.

We stood in the tiny little entryway to my apartment, breaths mingling in the limited space between us. I wanted to close the distance. I wanted to press my body against his and tangle my fingers in his hair as I tasted him on my tongue. I wanted to feel the warmth of his hands on my skin and surrender myself to every little part of him that called out to me.

As much as I didn't want to sever this tension between us, I knew it was coming sooner rather than later. Noah was sober. I wasn't. I licked my lips in anticipation of a kiss that I knew would not come.

Just as I predicted, he took a step back, clearing his throat and dragging a hand over his face. He looked at me with a tortured mix of desire and restraint and despite the pang of disappointment in my chest, I understood. I was thankful he carried the restraint that I didn't seem to possess.

He took a deep breath. "Let's get you to bed."

I could feel the exhaustion sweep over me as the tension between us ebbed, my limbs almost as heavy as my eyelids. "Sleep sounds amazing."

He jerked his chin and placed his hand on the small of my back, guiding me through my small apartment.

"My room is a mess," I blurted out.

Noah's deep chuckle vibrated through my chest. "I don't care."

"I'm not a slob."

"I know." There was a lightness to his voice that told me if I spun around, he'd be grinning ear to ear.

"I'm serious!"

He chuckled again as I reached for my bedroom door, twisting the handle and pushing the door open. I swallowed nervously as I took in the room before me.

It was so fucking sad. So small and bland. I hated the yellow walls. I hated the fact that I still had so many boxes to unpack. I worked so hard to make this place feel like home for Kennedy, but I wasn't sure how to do the same for me.

There were clothes strewn about and shoes that had obviously been kicked off at the door and forgotten about.

I waited for Noah to say something, but his hand just pressed against the small of my back, urging me into the room. "Go get changed. I'll wait for you out here."

"You don't have to wait for me."

"I'll leave the second you're in bed." His grin melted into a soft smile. "You tripped like three times in between my truck and this room. I won't be able to sleep without confirming that you made it to bed first before I go."

I laughed and rolled my eyes, attempting to take a step back and tripping over a pair of shoes.

Noah's brows shot up as if to say *See?*

"I'll be back," I grumbled, turning and disappearing into the en suite while he laughed to himself.

I took a second to change, throwing my swimsuit and cover-up into the bathtub and snagging my pajamas from last night from the floor.

Okay. Maybe I was a little bit of a slob.

A few minutes later, I flipped off the bathroom light and walked back into my bedroom. Noah, who was perched on the edge of my mattress, quickly stood and rubbed his hands against his thighs.

Before I could tell myself not to, I walked over and wrapped my arms around his neck, pulling him into a hug. He smelled like the outdoors, like the trees and the earth, and something spicy that belonged to only him.

His hands slid around my waist, and I tried not to overthink the way he sank into my touch.

"Thank you," I murmured, my lips dangerously close to his throat.

I felt him chuckle and held my breath as his lips brushed against my temple. "I think I'm the one who should be thanking you." I shrugged, pulling back just enough to meet his gaze. All the amusement seemed to melt from his eyes, replaced by something more intense. "I think–" He paused to clear his throat, his voice surprisingly thick with emotion. "I needed to hear most, if not all, of the things that you said to me today. I didn't realize just how... Paralyzing it's been. And I– I might still struggle to accept them, but I needed to hear them."

I moved my hand to his cheek, fingertips brushing against the skin just above his beard. "Well, a wise old grump once told me that the only way to get over it is to get through it and you, my friend, would not give yourself enough grace to get through it. You kept yourself trapped in this horrible, guilt-ridden purgatory, torturing yourself for something that wasn't your fault. I meant what I said, Noah. You deserve peace."

He swallowed, a slew of emotions playing out over his features. Conflict, guilt, acceptance. I knew that he felt undeserving of this kind of truth, but I hoped that somehow he could find it within himself to let go of the blame he shouldered.

"You know," he started, a new flare of amusement surging through his eyes. "You're saying a lot of very coherent things for someone with half-closed eyelids."

I laughed, smacking his chest lightly. "Alright, alright. I can take a hint. Enough sappy shit for one day."

He grinned that perfect, crooked smile that never failed to steal the breath in my lungs.

"Goodnight, Noah." I stretched onto the balls of my feet and pressed my lips to his cheek, his beard scraping against my skin as I pulled away.

"Night," he responded gently, the floorboards creaking as he turned to leave.

I climbed into bed as he opened my bedroom door, one more loose-lipped question blurting out before I could stop it. "Noah?"

He stopped, turning to look at me as he gripped the door handle. "Yeah?"

"Earlier at the shop... Did you– Do you think you might've kissed me? If the phone didn't ring?"

My questions hung in the air between us, my room silent aside from the sharp intake of breath that Noah drew in through his lips.

He licked his lips as he processed my question, probably trying to figure out if I would even remember this conversation in the morning. "Yeah," he answered, his voice breathy and wavering a little around the edges. "I think I might've."

I took a shuddering breath as the corner of his lip pulled up into a small, curious smile like he was imagining our moment at the shop with a completely different ending.

When the question burst into my mind, I knew I wanted an answer to it. But the confirmation of my suspicions had stolen any semblance of a response from my mouth. My heart rate kicked up, a mess of the most beautiful nerves tingling in my stomach.

"Okay," I whispered, my cheeks flushing.

OKAY? This gorgeous, tattooed man just admitted that he wanted to kiss me and I said okay?!

Hazel eyes jumped up from the floor to meet mine. "Night, Liv."

I swallowed, my mouth dry. "Goodnight."

The latch clicked, Noah's footsteps disappeared down the hall, and I flopped back onto my pillow with a wide grin stretched across my lips.

Because he wanted to kiss me. And dammit, I wanted to kiss him, too.

Chapter 25

Olivia

If it weren't for the whole dead husband thing, I might've considered calling myself lucky. For the first time in what felt like a long time, I woke up with the same goofy grin stretched across my lips that I fell asleep with.

I hadn't gotten around to hanging curtains in my room, so I was up at dawn, and the same hiccuped heartbeat that lulled me to sleep was back to gently coax me awake. There was a small bit of embarrassment slithering around the edges of my happiness, poking and prodding, searching for a weak spot. But I wouldn't let myself focus on that. I wouldn't let it in.

I refused to let myself be embarrassed about asking Noah if he would've kissed me. I had lived in this perpetual state of confusion and guilt, curious about the attraction that pulled me to him while telling myself it shouldn't be happening in the first place. Seeing him just as affected as I was told me I wasn't alone in these feelings.

Noah wanted to kiss me.

And that little tidbit of information had me traipsing around my apartment all morning with a grin on my lips. My cheeks were actually starting to get sore. But I did nothing to wipe it away.

I felt light and happy. The pessimist inside of me was bracing for the other shoe to drop, and maybe it would be soon, but until it did, I was going to enjoy whatever was happening now.

I was going to just *be*.

And because every good morning is incomplete without Taylor Swift blaring in the background, I pressed play on my phone and wet my toothbrush, dancing to myself while I brushed my teeth. As much as I loved having a second alone, I did find myself wishing Kennedy was here to get ready with me this morning.

She deserved to see me like this.

Almost right on cue, three light taps knocked against the front door, and I danced my way across the apartment, damp hair from my shower flopping around. I flung the door open and kneeled down to hug my daughter, almost choking on the toothpaste foam in my mouth when I came face to face with a crotch.

Not just any crotch.

My wide eyes trailed upward, taking in the black t-shirt hugging his narrow waist and stretching across his broad chest. I fought the urge to swallow, my toothbrush still hanging out of the corner of my mouth as my eyes slowly met his.

Noah's mouth was cocked into a smirk; his head tilted to the side as he looked down at me. "Whatcha doing?"

"Fuckin' peephole," I mumbled, a tiny glob of toothpaste foam spilling from my mouth and plopping onto the floor in front of his black boots.

I shot up, combing my fingers through my hair and wiping the minty spit from my chin. "I thought you were Kennedy," was what I wanted to say. But it came out sounding more like "I foff ooh er Kenny."

His smirk spread, as did the blush that started on my chest. I could feel the blood rushing to my cheeks and to the tips of my ears.

"You seem to be feeling fine."

I started to talk but quickly closed my mouth around my toothbrush and offered a simple nod instead.

The muscles in Noah's neck strained as he fought off a laugh, scrubbing a hand down his face. "Why don't you go take care of that."

I nodded several more times and held up my index finger before darting out of the entryway and down the hall to my room. I threw open the door to the bathroom and whimpered when I saw myself in the mirror.

Toothpaste foam leaked out of my mouth and onto my chin, and remnants of mascara bled from my eyelashes.

I looked like a mess. Less than twenty-four hours ago, this man was ready to kiss me, and I greeted him at my door this morning with spearmint drool and clown makeup. I might've missed the eye makeup when I showered, but at least my hair was clean.

Quickly, I pulled myself together as best I could, trying to focus on literally anything other than the man waiting for me in the kitchen. Or the living room?

Shit. I didn't even invite him inside.

I groaned, slapping my hand against my forehead before diving into the closet and pulling on a pair of denim shorts and one of Liam's old t-shirts. I tucked it into the front so it looked less like a dress and wiped my under eyes with a washcloth.

Put together. *Kind of.*

My whole body felt… Twitchy. I felt alive with some kind of anxious energy, one that had weaved its way around my spine and attached itself to each and every nerve ending with tiny little alligator clamps.

I thought after last night, I'd be nervous about seeing him, but instead all I could think about was going back out there, burying my nose into his shirt, and sucking in a breath full of his cologne.

Not that I was planning on doing that… But in theory… It sounded like a great way to start my morning.

Snagging my phone off the counter, I paused the music and *calmly* made my way back to the front door where Noah was currently waiting. I was right.

I hadn't *technically* invited him in… So there he was, arms crossed across his chest, shoulder leaning against the door frame. That crooked smile was back the second I rounded the corner, and it turned my insides to something that resembled the soft, gooey butter cake my mom used to make growing up.

"Taylor Swift, huh?"

I leveled him with a look, eyebrows just about touching my hairline. "Don't you *dare* say a word against our lord and savior."

He snorted out a laugh, the white plastic bag around his wrist dropping into the crook of his elbow as he raised his hands. "You won't hear that from me. I love Taylor Swift."

I stared at him through narrowed eyes. "Favorite song?"

Noah took a sharp breath, his eyes widening. "Just one?"

I decided to humor him. "Okay, top three."

He tilted his head back and stared at the ceiling for a second while he contemplated his answers. "Enchanted. Cardigan. Evermore." Noah paused, tilting his head back and forth like he was trying to shake another song loose in his brain. "Honorable mention to Tim McGraw."

I didn't even try to hide my surprise. My mouth dropped open, and his lips slid into that perfect, easy grin. "I'm actually impressed."

"I'm a total Swiftie," he said with a scoff and then tilted his head to the side. "And what I mean by that is Nellie is a total Swiftie, and I got pulled into the movement." Noah shrugged. "Can't say that I mind. She's a lyrical genius."

Fucking *swoon*.

"Wow. If it didn't sound like such a threat coming from me, I'd offer to make you breakfast this morning. But… The best I can do is offer to pay and then have Barb shove my card back into my face."

He grinned. "That is an offer I can get on board with."

***

An hour later, the kids were dropped off at school, and I was searching deep for that same antsy energy that was humming just beneath my skin earlier, but it was gone.

Every step we took toward the diner had my stomach rolling over and my hands slick with sweat. At first, I thought it was the hangover catching up to me. But after several narrow-eyed glances and one seemingly knowing smirk from Avery, I knew it wasn't the alcohol.

We'd all had breakfast together before, but something about this morning felt so different. Like Noah and I had this secret that Avery was intent on figuring out. Maybe he had said something to her before he came over. Or maybe after he made sure I was in bed? I knew he stayed the night at her place, but the way her eyes kept swinging back and forth between us told me she was either making wild assumptions or knew something that I didn't.

Maybe she could see the way his eyes would linger on mine for just a fraction too long. Or the way I took a shaky breath when his hand brushed against the small of my back, gently guiding me out of the way so he was between me and the road.

She cast another look my way, her eyes bouncing between me and Noah a few times before focusing on the path ahead once again. I could feel my cheeks warming, the rhythmic tapping of Avery's heels on the pavement matching up to the rapid beat of my heart.

I fought back the urge to laugh.

I felt like a teenager on my way to being scolded by my prom date's mother.

Well, maybe not scolded. But definitely interrogated with questions that would raise my blood pressure to a dangerous level when I didn't know how to answer them.

If Avery started questioning the nature of our relationship, I wasn't quite sure what kind of answer I would give.

Or what answer Noah would give.

The urge to laugh was back, bubbling up from the pit of my stomach. It took an insane amount of effort to swallow it down. Because what in the *hell* was going on with my life?

Here I was, a twenty-eight-year-old widow raising a four-year-old daughter almost two thousand miles away from a family that hated me. Our apartment wasn't the worst place we could've ended up, but it certainly wasn't the two-story house I'd left behind in Wyoming. In the midst of all those changes, I found myself pondering the intricacies of my "relationship" with a man who just so happened to be my boss. Honestly, I probably didn't even have the right to be questioning anything. Because the most we'd done so far was share a few lingering glances and admit that *maybe* we'd like to kiss each other.

A mess.

I could practically hear Gia in my head telling me not to overthink it, but I wasn't just some single woman moving on from a harsh breakup. I was married a little over a year ago, and my life was on a completely different path. Every fiber of my being was itching to overthink *everything*.

Noah's elbow nudged into my arm. "You alright over there?"

I nodded and smiled, pressing my lips together to keep myself from saying what was actually racing through my mind, like how I was scared of Avery and the embarrassing fact that I had *noticeable* pit stains on this shirt when it was only seventy degrees outside.

Logically, I knew that I had no reason to actually fear Avery. We knew each other well enough. Our kids got along just fine. We were already friends, and she was easy to talk to. It certainly helped that the two of us had *several* things in common, including a brief fixation on learning how to crochet before ultimately giving up after the first failed stitch. I was almost a hundred percent sure we both still had the supplies shoved into a closet corner, but neither of us would admit it.

Avery helped me feel less lonely. Especially as a single parent. Our circumstances were different, but the struggles were still similar.

But none of that mattered if I was totally misinterpreting these little glances and in reality, she didn't approve of whatever was happening between Noah and me.

Avery was the first one to walk in, her hand lingering on the door to keep it open for Noah before she walked over to greet Barb at the counter.

Noah sidestepped to let me go in front of him, but when I tried to walk around, his finger slipped through a belt loop on my shorts, pulling me to a stop. I watched as the door slowly eased shut before he stepped in front of me, his large frame blocking my view of the diner.

Everyone inside could see us.

I knew that.

He knew that.

But there was no hesitation when his hand lifted, index finger hooking under my chin as he tilted my head back. I met his gaze, hazel eyes catching in the sunlight, strands of green weaving through swirling hues of golden brown.

The corner of his mouth lifted, his hand dropping back down to his side. "You're freaking out."

It wasn't a question.

I blew out a breath, cheeks puffing on the exhale as my hands found my hips. "Freaking out seems a bit intense. Just... Mild overthinking."

His expression softened, eyes flitting across my face. "About?"

"I think just a little bit of everything."

Noah shrugged, eyes dancing with amusement. "So nothing crazy."

"Exactly," I said, unable to stop the smile from forming on my lips. "Do you think Avery knows that..." My voice trailed off, mouth closing and opening twice before Noah finished the sentence for me.

"That I *might've* kissed you?"

I swallowed, my eyes dropping to his lips as I nodded. "Yes, that."

He chuckled softly, the sound sending a warm shiver down my spine. "If she does, she hasn't said anything to me. I think she has her suspicions."

My gaze snapped back to his, a little surprised by the nonchalance in his tone. "She has suspicions that you might wanna kiss me?"

"Yeah, Liv," he said with a grin. "Honestly, I think everyone in this nosy-ass town does."

"What?" I asked breathlessly, resisting the urge to let my eyes wander to the diner windows. I didn't need to look; I could feel the stares of everyone inside. "Why? How?"

Noah's grin melted into something softer, something that felt vulnerable and honest. He raised his hand, fingers swiping absently against my cheek before sweeping a strand of hair behind my ear. "Because I haven't looked twice at anyone in this town for almost five years and for some reason, I can't seem to stop looking at *you*."

My heart skipped a beat, and the breath I attempted to take lodged itself in my throat as I struggled to come up with the words. It was one thing to make assumptions or to hear soft words meant to placate drunk thoughts, but hearing it out loud— this thing that I'd been hoping for had materialized into spoken truth— I had no clue what to do with it.

I was so confident last night, so sure I wanted to kiss him. Even this morning I was so sure I was ready. But the confidence I'd been feeling was clashing with the confusion and the fear of so much being unknown, and every answer I thought I had was just... Gone.

I felt like a fish out of water as I struggled to find what I wanted to say. Because I wanted to say something. *Anything.* But every word that bloomed at the tip of my tongue wilted and withered away just as quickly as it came to me.

Noah's gaze held mine, and I could slowly see the realization wash over his features. His disappointment masked as understanding.

God, I wanted to tell him how much that meant to me. I wanted to tell him that his vulnerability wasn't in vain and that there were so many confusing feelings all meshed together in my chest and I couldn't pinpoint which one I wanted to hash out first. But the more desperate I became, the more twisted my words seemed to get.

He cleared his throat as the diner doors pushed open, offering a small, polite smile to someone I didn't recognize. And with that, my time had run out.

Noah held the door open, gently pressing his free hand to the small of my back. "Come on. Let's get you something to eat."

My shoulders fell. "Noah."

He gave me the same polite smile he'd offered to the lady rushing past us just a second ago and fuck if my heart didn't ache at the sight. Because I didn't want his polite smiles and friendly gestures. I wanted the smiles that stretched his lips wide and the laughs that pulled at something in my chest.

"Noah–"

His hand pressed against my back again, urging me forward. "It's alright," he reassured me, his voice gentle. "Come on. I'm sure if you asked Barb, she could get you some more of those crepes."

The iron fist around my lungs tightened its grip at his patience and understanding, even if I could see right through it.

With a reluctant nod, I let him guide me into the diner, ignoring the curious stares of half the town. I looked at Avery first, who had that same knowing look on her face now that she did on the way here. That is…. Until her eyes shifted to Noah. The second they landed on him, she twirled around, resting her forearms against the aluminum counter.

He cleared his throat again, the warmth of his hand disappearing from my back and like some kind of love-sick puppy, I wanted to nuzzle into his side until I was rewarded with his touch once again. But instead, he pulled his phone out of his pocket and pressed it to his ear. "Why don't you guys go sit? I'll be right there."

Before Avery or I could protest, he made his way back outside.

Avery turned slowly, her hazel eyes wide. "Everything okay?"

I blinked a few times, shaking my head in an effort to clear the haze that Noah always seemed to leave behind. I smiled, but I think even Barb could see through it. "Yeah."

"Crepes?" Barb offered with a neon pink smile.

Avery scoffed. "Crepes? Seriously? I've known this lady for almost thirty years, and she hasn't offered to make me crepes *one time!*"

Barb rolled her eyes, shooing us away with a wave of her hand. "I didn't even know how to make 'em 'til Noah came in to teach me. That boy was here before I was, waitin' outside of the door with a bag of ingredients before the sun was even in the sky." She paused, giving Avery a pointed look. "I'm only offering because I have leftover batter."

I made a small whimpering noise in the back of my throat because it was almost too much. The image of Noah showing up in front of the diner just like he did at my apartment, arms full of ingredients, to teach Barb how to make something just for me. I pressed the heel of my palm against my sternum, unable to bear the way this seemed to crack my chest open, exposing everything soft and vulnerable inside of me.

He told me she already knew how to make them, leaving out this crucial piece of information that would've left him feeling just as exposed as I did.

I wished I could be the same person that Noah put to bed the night before. I was nervous, yes, but I was confident in the way I felt and so sure I was ready for whatever he could give me.

"You sure you're okay?" Avery asked, interrupting my thoughts.

I forced myself to swallow past the knot forming in my throat, offering a few tight nods. "I just really like crepes."

Barb and Avery exchanged a look, and I knew it was innocent enough, but I shied away from the small smirks tugging at their lips.

Avery hooked her arm around mine. "Come on. Let's go sit. He'll be back," she reassured me, casting a glance at the diner doors before dragging me to a booth toward the back.

Once we settled in, Avery was doing everything she could to keep herself busy. She fiddled with a napkin and stacked a few packets of jelly, her lips rolling together as if to stop her from asking every question that popped into her mind.

As she attempted to distract herself with the straw wrapper, I found my thoughts drifting back to the look on Noah's face and the feeling that speared through my chest when the words got lost on my tongue. I knew that he didn't expect anything from me, but he had hoped. Hoped that we were on the same page and hoped that I would be ready to take this next step with him.

The truth was, I wanted to be. I thought I was, given the way my smile stayed plastered on my face at the thought of kissing him. I wanted to unravel all the tangled thoughts and emotions that wove us together, to lay them all out and smooth my hands over the wrinkles until they all made sense. I wanted to bask in the warmth of this fire he lit in the most hollow parts of me and keep it kindled, letting it fill every little corner of me that was once cold and hopeless.

But there was this fear of letting go and once again placing my heart into the hands of someone who had the power to completely destroy it. I wouldn't be able to survive another heartbreak. I'd been so sure about letting myself enjoy the possibility of Noah, but when I was faced with the reality, I saw just how terrifying it really was. *Would we be able to pull through if it blew up in our faces?*

Avery ripped through another napkin. "Olivia," she said softly, dropping the remnants of her latest paper slaughter onto the table. "I know I'm no Gia." She paused and chuckled nervously, her hands wringing together. "But you can talk to me. You know that?"

I smiled softly, reaching across the table to still her nervous hands. "Yes, I do. I'm sorry– God, I'm honestly the world's worst company today."

Her lips rolled together. "Is it– Did something happen with Noah?"

My hesitation was enough of an answer.

Avery leaned across the table, lowering her voice. "We can talk about it. If you want." She gave me an amused smile. "I know my brother's an idiot. I'll never take his side."

I huffed out a laugh, a fleeting smile tugging at the corner of my lips. "I appreciate that. It's– It's nothing like that. I just–" Blowing out a breath, I leaned back against the red vinyl seat. "It's like everything has changed and I don't even know where to start with figuring it out. I have this puzzle in front of me, and it seems so simple, but I can't figure out how the pieces fit together."

A slow blush crawled its way up my throat and splayed across my cheeks. I might not have said it outright, but it felt an awful lot like I'd laid all my cards on the table.

Avery shrugged, crossing her arms over her chest as she leaned back against the seat. "Even the easiest puzzles take time. There's no need to solve it all in one go. You lay it all out on the table, and you take it piece by piece. Could take a few hours, could take a few days, or weeks. But regardless, it's not something you figure out without a little time and patience."

"Yeah," I said quietly. "I guess you're right."

"I'm always right," she said with a laugh. "Plus, a lot of things *have* changed. For both of you. And puzzles are supposed to be *fun*. Challenging? Yes. *But fun.*"

I smiled, the tightness in my chest loosening just a notch.

Avery took a sip of her water, swishing it around in her mouth for a second before swallowing. "Can I just say one more thing?"

I snagged my water from the table and took a slow sip to buy myself a few seconds before responding. "Is it gonna make me cry?"

"How the hell am I supposed to know that?"

"Oh, come on! If someone said it to you, would you cry?"

Avery shrugged. "Maybe?"

"Maybe?" I deadpanned.

She sighed dramatically and took another large sip of water, staring me down while she swallowed.

My leg bounced under the table as my curiosity bloomed because *of course*, I wanted to know what she had to say!

Avery's eyes narrowed, and my resolve cracked. "Fine! What? Just say it!" I chucked a wadded-up piece of shredded napkin at her. "You peer pressure-er."

She grinned in response, and while I knew she was happy, there was something deeper in her eyes. Something that shimmered with gratitude. "I meant what I said to you yesterday. Before the lake. This change that we see in him... It's you, Olivia."

My ribs cinched around my lungs at the look on her face. I was searching for the lie. Some kind of tell that would reveal she was lying or maybe over-exaggerating, but I saw nothing but honesty.

"He smiles. He laughs. He *talks*. And I'm not saying you have to fall in love with the guy, but there is clearly something he sees in you that has helped him more over the past couple of months than anyone has been able to in *years*. Just– I really think what he needs most is a friend. And I think he has that in you."

I let out a shaky breath, my hand running along my breastbone again like I was trying to soothe the ache made by her words. Despite the conflict and hesitation that lingered beneath, it was the best kind of ache.

I blinked furiously, a poor attempt at holding onto my tears. But one by one, they fell.

"Whatever you're doing is clearly working because my brother knows how to smile again and your daughter is thriving."

I couldn't talk. I was scared to breathe. Like one little shift in movement would have me falling apart.

Avery's eyes softened as she reached across the table, placing her hand over mine. "Also, in case no one has told you recently, you're doing a good job."

A small whimper escaped from my lips, and I cleared my throat. She smiled as I blew out a controlled breath and wiped the fallen tears from my cheeks. "That was more than one thing."

She shrugged and slid her hand away from mine, steepling her fingers under her chin. "Okay, enough with the sappy." She leaned to the left, craning her neck to look outside. "Noah's still on the phone. Tell me more about Gia."

I laughed, wiping my cheeks one last time. "Oh my god, you're gonna love her."

Chapter 26

Noah

I was a coward.

I knew it.

Once Avery and Liv found out I wasn't coming back, they'd know it.

Based on the look she gave me when I all but ran from the diner, Barb knew it, too.

I had become a master of evasion, dodging my problems time and again. This was no exception.

I sat at the shop, stewing in sweat and my own shitty mood for half an hour, unable to convince myself to go back to the diner. It was all a bit ridiculous, I knew that. I pushed too far, too fast and Liv just wasn't ready. I didn't fault her for that. I couldn't.

So I ran. Even if she was ready for… whatever we seemed to be edging towards, Liv needed someone that I knew I couldn't be. So did Avery for that matter. They needed someone who could stick around and handle all the messy shit. I should be happy that they found it in each other.

But instead of being relieved at the thought, I was constantly checking my phone wondering if Liv would ask where I was or if I was planning on coming back.

It wasn't easy to lay myself on the line like that and I knew that this was newer for her than it was for me, and I had every intention of giving her the space she needed. But it was difficult to keep my own insecurities at bay.

She insisted that Addie's death wasn't my fault... But what if she didn't mean it? What if, every time she looked at me, all she could see was the blood on my hands? That would certainly explain part of her hesitancy outside the diner.

I let out a frustrated sigh, spearing my fingers through my hair as a few tools clanked around in the back of the shop. I spun slowly in the chair as James's heavy footfalls sounded against the concrete floors behind me.

His toolbox landed on the floor with a loud thunk. "That thing is fifteen years old."

I stared at him with a bored expression, lifting my brows in a silent question as he removed his blue ball cap and wiped at the sweat beading along his receding hairline.

I hated having him in my shop.

James's old work shirt hung loosely over his thin frame. A couple of missing buttons exposed dirty, pale skin underneath. His pants had seen better days, the hems ragged and uneven lengths. He wore boots caked with god knows what, the laces loose and dragging behind him with each step.

If there was someone else in this town who knew their way around an HVAC, I'd call them in a heartbeat. But for years, I'd been stuck with the same grease-stained man.

He grumbled something under his breath, wiping a greasy hand across his chest. While he wasn't someone in this town I knew well, he was the only person in a twenty-mile radius who could work on the HVAC within a forty-eight-hour time frame. Mostly, he kept to himself, only showing his face when he was called upon, and even then, he wasn't someone people liked to spend a lot of time with.

Maybe it was the comb-over. Maybe it was the way he only left three inches of space between him and whoever he struck up a conversation with.

Regardless, the sooner he figured out what was wrong, the sooner he could leave. "Ya need a new one. It crapped out."

"Shit," I mumbled, scratching my beard. "How much?"

He shrugged. "Probably lookin' at eight to ten."

It wasn't so much about having the money for it. Between Addie's life insurance and the fact that Kent Auto was the only mechanic shop in town, I got by just fine. Ten grand would still put a dent in the business account.

I would force myself to work here without A/C, but I wouldn't do that to Liv.

"Alright just do what you have to do." I sighed again. "The sooner the better."

James leaned over to pick up his toolbox, wheezing out a breath as he stood. "I'll do what I can. Probably lookin' at a week turnaround."

"Fine."

My stomach grumbled and I cursed myself for turning around and walking to the shop instead of getting myself something to eat. I checked my phone again, getting ready to type out a text to Avery when the door was pulled open.

My head jerked up, and the bad mood that had been festering all morning eased when Liv walked through the door with a white plastic take-out container in her hands, two cups of coffee and a fortune cookie balanced right on top.

Everything in my head screamed at me to pretend it meant nothing, to make sure she didn't think I was coming on too strong, but then her cheeks were painted that dusty rose as a sheepish grin spread across her lips. Every ounce of my attention was held by her.

Liv made her way over to the desk, tendrils of blonde hair escaping the hold of her clip and framing the delicate features of her face. My gaze lingered, trailing the length of her legs, mapping out every inch of satiny skin. Her eyes flickered over to James before carefully setting the takeout container down on the counter and sliding over a cup of coffee. "Figured you might be hungry since you didn't go inside," she whispered, giving no indication aside from the flush in her cheeks that she'd caught my slow assessment.

My stomach grumbled on cue and I looked up at Liv with a smile. "You figured right. Thank you."

A subtle shrug accompanied the faint deepening of pink in her cheeks. Fuck, I wanted to dip a paintbrush in that color and blend it into the sky. It was slowly becoming my favorite color. "It was nothing," she dismissed. Curious eyes shifted over to James again, a momentary crack in her polite facade set off a niggling feeling in the back of my mind, one that spiked my blood with adrenaline. I looked over my shoulder to find his gaze lingering on Liv for a beat too long, his lips unfurling into an appreciative smile.

I turned, positioning myself to block her from his view. "You're parked out back, yeah?" My tone carried an unexpectedly protective edge, one that felt foreign to my own ears.

James's eyes narrowed before his smile shifted into a smirk. "I'll let you know when it's here and we'll settle up then."

"Great," I clipped, jerking my chin toward the hallway he'd just ventured from. "You know the way out." I waited until his back was turned to flip back around. "I'm gonna lock up after him."

Liv nodded once, twisting her lips to chew on the inside of her cheek. Lifting my hand, I nudged her chin with my knuckle. "Be right back."

The strain in my shoulders alleviated at the smile that graced her mouth. My eyes lingered on her lips. Soft. Tempting. A delicate canvas of rosy pink that my thumb begged to drag across. "Okay." I swallowed, turning away from her before I did something stupid, like pull her mouth to mine and find out if that pink on her lips tasted as good as it looked.

I followed the pungent trail left behind, resisting the urge to plug my nose at the heady mixture of sweat and body odor permeating through the shop. I pushed past the swinging doors that led to the garage and waited until the heavy steel door sealed shut behind him before flipping the lock.

I forced myself to take a moment to catch my breath in preparation for Liv. To give myself the reminder that this morning was already too much and I needed to keep my distance. The rhythmic thud of my boots against the concrete seemed to echo in beat with my racing heart.

With each step, I mentally rehearsed what I would say to her. How I would keep it light and casual, trying not to disclose just how much her being here affected me.

But I rounded the corner, and those practiced words seemed to evaporate from my mind.

Liv leaned against the counter, twirling a piece of hair between two fingers as she read her fortune cookie, and my hand flexed at my side, desperate to pull that clip from her hair and watch it fall down her back. I wanted to trace the curve of her jawline and thread my fingers through beautiful waves of golden silk. The soft glow of the overhead lights played on her features, casting a warm halo around her. I took a fortifying breath as she looked up, soft lips curling into a delicate smile.

Everything about her pulled me in. And that was precisely the reason I chose to sweat in this stuffy-ass garage over breakfast in an air-conditioned diner with her and my sister. I needed the space. I hated thinking that I made her uncomfortable.

Liv lifted the lid of the takeout container and snagged a piece of bacon, ripping off a chunk with her teeth. "I don't like him," she mumbled as she chewed, pointing her bacon toward the back.

I huffed out a laugh, stealing a piece of bacon for myself. "Me neither."

She took another bite, and my eyes moved to her mouth on their own accord. Her tongue swept across her bottom lip. Such a simple gesture in theory, but you wouldn't know that by the way my pulse picked up at the sight.

Every time I thought I had a grip on my emotions, she managed to unravel me again, leaving me stumbling over my thoughts.

I cleared my throat and rolled my shoulders, forcing my eyes back to hers. "What's it say?" I gestured to the folded fortune on the counter.

She hummed, wiping her hands on her shorts before picking it up. "Plant the seeds of kindness, and in the garden of reciprocity, unexpected blooms of favors shall grace your path."

"Do these ever make sense for you?"

Liv shrugged. "Sometimes. But sometimes I think it's less about them making sense at the moment and maybe just something you should keep in mind for the future."

"Interesting."

She grinned. "Liam used to say fortunes were the universe's advice column. I still think he's full of shit, but sometimes I think he was onto something."

I smiled and rested on my elbows. "Thanks for this." I flicked my hand out, gesturing to the food on the counter.

Liv shrugged again, then rested her chin on her palm, her eyes gleaming with amusement. "It wasn't purely selfless." Her nose scrunched in the most adorable way.

I raised an eyebrow, intrigued by her words. "Do tell."

Her mouth twisted from side to side before snatching the bacon from my grip and taking a bite. "I have a little favor to ask."

"Alright," I responded with a smile. "I'm all ears."

"Well," she started, standing and resting her hands on the edge of the counter. "I was talking to Avery, and she mentioned that *maybe* you had painted a room or two for her in the apartment and convinced me that *maybe* it would be fun to tackle an apartment project today since we weren't working."

"Oh, did she?" I knew that Avery was meddling, and for the first time in my life, I didn't care. I was grateful for the extra push.

Her hands slapped down onto the old laminate countertop before wrapping around mine. *"Please?* Pretty please? I've seen Ave's apartment, and you did a great job."

Her cheeks flamed, and she rolled her eyes as a grin slowly spread across my lips. "I know that yellow is supposed to be a happy color but honestly, it's depressing as fuck. It reminds me of cheese. I need it gone. *Please.*"

I let out a laugh as she lifted her hands and clasped them beneath her chin. "Pretty please?" Liv whispered, her brows lifting as her teeth sank into her bottom lip.

My fingers twitched with a burning desire to reach up and pull it free.

I was going to help her. The second she said she had a favor to ask, whatever plans I could've had for the day were rendered moot. I'd paint this whole fucking town for her if she asked.

But I'd be lying if I said I wasn't enjoying this.

She blew a puff of air out of the side of her mouth, a tuft of hair swinging out of her eyes before falling right back down.

I reached up, tucking that stubborn piece of hair behind her ear. "Sure, sweetheart."

Liv beamed. Her blue eyes shimmered with excitement and I realized I'd do just about anything to coax a smile like that out of her again. "Really?"

"Really."

She let out a little squeal and shimmied her shoulders. "Oh my god, you're amazing! Okay, finish that–" Liv aimed her finger in the direction of my food while backing away toward the door. "I'm gonna run back to the diner before we go to the store. I have to pick something up. 'Kay?"

I smiled, peeling the fork out of its plastic wrapping. "Okay."

***

"How often do you take him pie?" I asked, looking down at the small container Liv held in her hands.

She shrugged. "I don't know. I don't keep track. Maybe every other time I go to the store?"

I made a noise in the back of my throat, unaware if my curiosity was born of jealousy or a genuine interest in understanding the motive behind her trying to befriend Colt.

Years ago, he was someone I would've considered family. We were inseparable in high school, doing all the stupid shit that we could get away with in a town this small. Colt was the brother I never had.

I knew he hadn't had an easy life. His mother died when he was young, and in a shocking series of events that rattled everyone in Rose Hill, Colt's older sister Cora was one of three teenage girls who went missing while we were in high school. To this day, no one knows what happened. It shocked the whole county. Shit like that just didn't happen in towns this small. But first, it was Jennie Seager, then Summer Higel. At that point, a strict curfew had been put into place, no one under the age of eighteen was allowed after dusk without an escort.

Everything was fine for a few months.

Until Cora snuck out to go see her boyfriend. Colt was the one who found her bedroom empty. Her boyfriend said she never made it.

After that, Colt went silent. The happy, goofy, boy I'd grown up with was gone. Local authorities said they did their best, but none of the girls were ever found. Eventually, they were all three declared dead, and the case went cold.

Neither he nor his father were ever the same. The second we turned eighteen, he disappeared. His Dad told me he took off to some city near Yellowstone and did a lot of volunteer work for the local fire department and Search and Rescue team. I tried to reach out. I called and texted him once or twice a month until his number no longer went through.

But then my whole life was flipped upside down.

I think he would've stayed away for the rest of his life. Until fate took another deadly turn. News of his father's passing brought Colt back home, like a ghost from the past. I remember seeing him for the first time in many years, standing on the porch of his father's old house, a shadow of the boy I used to run around with. An unruly beard, and unkempt hair– he was almost unrecognizable.

He sold his childhood home, used the money to settle into a small cabin in the woods, and took over the general store. I knew what it was like to find peace in solitude, but that didn't mean it was healthy. I saw that now. Thankfully, I had people to pull me out of the darkness. Colt was content to become one with the shadows, making no attempt to reconnect with the people he'd left behind.

Maybe the jealousy I felt wasn't so much about Liv and Colt getting to know each other. There was a time when we shared everything, but lost years and tragic circumstances had forced us into these different versions of ourselves and I lost a friend. A brother. So maybe this curiosity was a strange blend of longing for the past and jealousy that Liv was somehow finding a way into a part of his world that was lost to me.

Liv nudged me with her elbow, a playful gesture that pulled me back to the present. "Jealous?" Her tone held a touch of amusement, a small smirk tugging at her lips.

I let out a soft laugh, glancing down at her as we neared the general store. "Maybe at first," I confessed. "But he deserves to have someone in his corner."

Her question was gentle, laced with empathy. "Did something happen?"

"Yeah," I confirmed quietly. "A lot."

Her brows pulled together, eyes softening with genuine compassion. A silent understanding of the burden he was carrying. "You said you used to be friends?" she inquired softly.

"Like brothers."

"What happened?"

I exhaled slowly, shoving my hands into my pockets. "He lost a lot. First his mom. Then his sister. He disappeared for... A long time." My eyes flickered to the glass door of the general store before finding Liv again. "Then his dad."

"Oh," she breathed, swallowing thickly. "That is... Horrible." Her hand lifted to her chest as she massaged her sternum like it physically hurt her to think about everything Colt had endured. I knew I needed to keep my distance, but fuck, that little movement made me want to pull her into my chest.

"So," I cleared my throat, rocking back on my heels. "Maybe I was a little jealous at first. But he could probably use some pie."

Liv pulled her shoulders back, took a deep breath, and slapped on a grin, one that radiated joy and warmth. I followed closely behind as she headed toward the store, struggling to make sense of this feeling blossoming in my chest. Liv's heart was a ray of sunshine, bright and balmy to my dark and bitter cold. Every little selfless thing she did melted a little bit of the ice inside of me.

I held the door open for Liv. The jingle of the rusted bell overhead was dull, but it did the job just fine; Colt's head snapped up from the book he was reading. His gaze settled on Liv for a moment before shifting over to me, his eyes narrowing marginally, brows pulling together. He was curious.

I didn't blame him.

Liv bounced over to the counter with a smile and I redirected my attention, eyes sweeping over the rows of shelves neatly lined with an assortment of goods. Over the years, it'd adapted to being the only store within a twenty-five-mile radius, Colt keeping it stocked with a wide variety of things to save people unnecessary trips to Wilmington.

Canned goods, fresh produce that he collected from a farmer's market a few towns over every weekend. There were power tools lining the back, cleaning supplies, and toiletries. He did a good job making sure he had what everyone needed.

There was even one of those tiny libraries out front where someone could take a book or leave one behind.

Most recently, a professional-grade paint mixing machine was installed in the back corner, a rainbow of swatches displayed next to it.

I wandered toward the back, Liv and Colt's hushed conversation fading to the background as I flipped through a few sampler cards. Ever since Liv rolled into town, I'd spent several mornings and evenings here, grabbing what I could for breakfast with Liv and Kennedy, and the most conversation I'd gotten out of him was a monotone "good morning".

But when I glanced over, his mouth was hooked up into the smallest of smiles. It wasn't fake or used to placate Liv as she talked with him. It was real.

Olivia Brooks had Colt Everest smiling in public for the first time in probably years.

Her whole life had been turned upside down a little over a year ago and even still, she couldn't dim the light and the warmth that was thawing even the most guarded hearts. She had this uncanny ability to break down walls, to find the humanity in people, and draw it out.

Colt leaned against the counter to look at something on Liv's phone, his normally stiff posture more relaxed than I'd seen it since high school. The shroud of tension that always seemed to hang around him had melted away, if only for a moment. And in its place was a glimpse of the person he used to be, the friend I lost all those years ago.

There was this small, irrational part of me rearing its ugly head, planting seeds of insecurity in the back of my mind. I was finally seeing the light at the end of this dark, long tunnel, and I wanted to keep it. I wanted to keep her smile and her laugh. I wanted to keep the breathless fumbling of words and that dusty pink flush that grew up her neck like a vine every time I looked at her too long.

It was foolish. Selfish. Sure, this morning she was a little overwhelmed, but her friendship with Colt had nothing to do with my own fears. She'd told me that once before. However, emotions rarely bowed to logic, and the small voice in my head persisted, whispering doubts and insecurities.

Metal scraped against the linoleum floor, and I spared a glance as Colt stood and rounded the counter. He made his way over with Liv, and that small voice of insecurity hung around until I met her eyes. She smiled, something soft and reassuring. Something that reached inside of me and untangled every thread of doubt that lingered in my mind.

As they approached, her fingers brushed mine, a soft touch that sent a shock of warmth up my arm.

Colt cleared his throat, arms crossing over his chest. "I hear you're painting." His eyes flickered over to me for a moment before returning to the sample cards.

"So I'm told," I responded, smirking down at Liv.

She rolled her eyes and reached forward, swiping a light gray swatch from the array of colors. "So you were asked. *Very* politely, might I add?"

I hummed my response, grabbing a few paintbrushes, a roller, a paint tray, and a drop cloth.

Colt's lips twitched as he moved around us, reaching for a can of paint and primer. "Find a color?"

Liv sighed, her head tilting to the side as she considered her options. "Something neutral, I think." Her slim fingers picked through a few different colors before snagging a light blue. She ran her thumb across the smooth card, then put it back, skimming a few more shades of blue before snagging another, this one closer to navy.

Colt got work on my right, using a paint can opener to pry the lid open, setting it in the machine before tapping a few buttons on the screen. He cleared his throat and looked over at me. "H-How've you been?"

I almost didn't think he was talking to me. Fixing the look of shock on my face, I looked over at my childhood best friend. "Good," I responded, rolling my shoulders to loosen the tension. "You?"

He palmed the back of his neck, his hand resting just beneath the blonde bun tied at the nape. "Fine."

I nodded, raking my tongue over my teeth before responding. "Good. That's good."

Liv slowly pulled another swatch from the wall, her eyes shining with amusement as they bounced back and forth between the two of us. She shook her head and mumbled. "Cavemen" under her breath.

I stifled a laugh, shoving my finger into her side as she squirmed away, her lips spread into a wide smile.

Liv stared at this color card and something calm settled over her features. I watched every little muscle tick in her face as she took it in. Her brows pulled together marginally, her mouth tilted into an introspective smile. I had no clue what she was thinking, but I knew this was the color she wanted. She flicked her finger against the card and held it up. "What do you think?"

It was a nice slate color, on the lighter side of blue but more like the sky after a rainy day instead of on a sunny one. I couldn't put my finger on it, but there was something about it that was just so intrinsically Liv. It just made sense. After a look like that on her face, even if the color was neon green, I would've told her I liked it. I smiled and nodded, taking the color from her pinched fingers and handing it to Colt. "It's great."

Her lips twisted to the side as she watched Colt press a few buttons, the machine whirring to life. "I think so, too."

Colt turned, his eyes dropping to the small amount of space between me and Liv. "It'll just be a few minutes. I'll ring y'all up while you wait."

Liv worried her bottom lip for a second before holding up a finger. "Just a sec, I wanna grab some stuff."

Colt raised his brow at me as she darted off, moving through the small store quickly. I shrugged and she dropped a tomato onto the ground, disappearing behind a shelf. She shot back up, her cheeks painted pink. "I'll pay for that still."

I chuckled, moving to the counter and dropping the paint supplies on top.

"Don't you dare use your card Noah Kent!" she hollered, snagging a can of something and struggling to balance it on top of her armful of grocery items.

Colt smirked as he walked around to his place behind the counter, typing a bunch of numbers onto a register that had to be from the late nineties. The same register his dad used when it was his store.

I looked down at the book he'd been reading when we walked in. *When The Lights Go Out* by Gia Taft. "Any good?"

He bagged a few things, eyes shifting down to the hardcover book. "If you like thrillers. Someone put it in the library out front. Thought I'd give it a try." His voice was gruff, deeper than I remembered now that he'd said more than four words to me.

Liv made her way over, dropping several items onto the counter. "It's pretty good if I do say so myself." Her voice was light, teasing, earning an eye roll from Colt.

"I'd say you're a bit biased."

She grinned, lowering the last of her produce. "Maybe."

I looked at her, my brows pinching together. "Biased?"

"That's Gia's book!" she said excitedly, "You know? Nosy best friend who asks too many questions."

"Ah," I said, nodding slowly. "When you said she was an author, I pictured something more..."

"Pink and frilly with a naked man on the cover?" She quirked a brow in my direction.

"Something like that." I looked down at the black cover again, white words sticking out against the dark background, fake blood spattered across the glossy material.

"Gia has been dark and twisted since we were kids. *Really* into true crime growing up. She just released this last year. Hit the number one spot on the bestseller list in two months." She paused, jabbing a finger into my ribs. "And there's nothing wrong with pink and frilly. Or reading books with naked men."

I swatted her hand away as she moved to poke me again. "I didn't say there was!" I insisted, lifting my hands up in surrender. "Bestseller, though?" My brows shot up. "That's impressive."

Somehow, she smiled wider. "She's a genius."

"She's alright," Colt grumbled, tucking Liv's items into a bag before I had the chance to inspect them.

Liv scoffed. "She's more than alright, you grump."

"Yeah, yeah," he mumbled beneath his breath, a small smile tugging at his lips. "Eighty-four even."

Before I could take my wallet out, Liv had cash in hand, quickly sliding it over to Colt with a satisfied grin. "I'm gonna pay for my own paint, Noah."

"*Fine*, Liv," I taunted, easing the bags off of the counter.

Colt plopped back down onto his stool as he counted her change before handing it back.

"Thanks, Colt! Enjoy the pie, I'll come by next week with another book."

I turned to face him, lifting my brow. His face grew red as he looked down and mumbled his thanks.

Following behind Liv, I looked over my shoulder at Colt. "Take care."

He nodded once, quickly averting his gaze. I barely heard him respond with, "You, too" as I walked out of the door.

Chapter 27

Olivia

We hadn't even started yet and I was over it.

Not a single swipe of paint had made it onto the wall and the towel was wadded up in my hand, ready to be thrown. Figuratively. Because in reality, that was the towel I was using to wipe the sweat from my forehead, seriously kicking myself for leaving so many packed boxes in my room.

I shoved the last box into the bathroom and pulled the door closed, wiping the back of my hand across my forehead and facing Noah. I was wearing the same t-shirt and shorts I'd thrown on earlier and already sweating my ass off, while Noah wore a pair of thick, dark jeans and a black t-shirt with ease. He moved a majority of the boxes and hadn't even broken a sweat.

He pulled the drop cloth out of its plastic packaging to shake it out. "Need a break already?" Noah teased with a grin.

I shot him a playful glare and met him in the middle, taking the other half of the drop cloth and laying it down over the carpet in my room.

Honestly, I was a little surprised he was even helping me in the first place. I still felt guilty about our interaction– or lack thereof– outside of the diner and could tell he was keeping his distance. The closest we'd gotten was at the store when my fingers gently brushed against his, and I thought that maybe it would show him that the awkwardness from earlier was only a result of me being locked inside of my own head, too busy catastrophizing to enjoy the moment.

But no matter where we were in this tiny two bedroom apartment, he made sure to stay out of my way. And I hated it. Because just hours ago, I'd woken up so relieved and practically humming with anticipation. The moment Noah called my anticipation into question, I'd frozen. Instead of melting into the way that he reassured me and telling him that I felt it, too, I'd planted this tiny seed of doubt into his mind.

Given the way he was interacting with me as we maneuvered past each other through the apartment, that tiny little seed had sprouted roots and borne down.

I wasn't sure where we went from here. Do I back off and give him space to lick his wounds and repair his ego? Was I even correct in assuming his pride had taken a hit? Regardless, he didn't strike me as the kind of man who would wallow in self-pity, but I was too nervous to push my luck.

Noah lifted the can of paint from the doorway and set it down by the paint tray, using his keys to pry it open. I smiled at the beautiful shade of slate blue that clung to the lid as he peeled it away.

"It's a nice color," he said quietly, tilting the paint can into the tray and pouring it out.

It *was* a nice color.

When we'd stepped into the store earlier, I had no idea where I wanted this project to go, only that I wanted the yellow gone.

This blue... I wasn't exactly sure how to describe what it made me feel in comparison to the yellow, but it was calm. Subtle. It was the color of the solitude that I found in this small town; it was the dark, cloudy sky settling after a cleansing storm.

Gia would call it depressing. The color of sadness and grief.

And maybe it was to some people, but to me, it meant so much more.

"It's the perfect color for me," I finally said, my words carrying a weight of sincerity.

I glanced over at Noah as he pushed the roller through the paint, his movements steady and methodical. I *definitely* wasn't watching the way the corded muscles in his arm flexed as he lifted it from the glossy paint. He stood, holding the foam roller in my direction. "Would you like to do the honors?"

I took in the smell of fresh paint, my fingers brushing against the warmth of his yet again as I grabbed it. I shivered at the contact, my hand lingering in mid-air, waiting for the connection to sever. And *god*, I didn't want it to.

My stomach came to life with a flurry of butterflies, and it felt so silly but at the same time, I couldn't get myself to pull away.

Noah swallowed, his eyes locked onto where our fingers overlapped. "I thought you could roll and I'd cut the edges." He spoke quietly, like if he talked too loud, it would spook the tendons in our hands.

"That works."

He smiled, soft and warm, and I found myself a little frustrated that the feeling in my chest was something fleeting. I wanted something tangible. I wanted the feeling that the warmth of his smile pulled from the depths of my wounded soul woven into a soft blanket. One that I could drape around my shoulders and sink into whenever the weather got cold or my thoughts got too cloudy.

My mouth dried as I considered the possibility that what I was searching for was him. His touch, his comfort, his warmth. I had something tangible right in front of me, painting my bedroom on his day off simply because I'd asked.

I blinked when he cleared his throat; lips tilted into a smirk that told me we'd been standing here in the middle of my room with my hand lingering on his for a moment too long. Curious but confident eyes traveled across every inch of my face, and my heart was a kick-drum in my chest, each pounding beat rattling through my bones.

With shaky hands, I eased the roller out of his grip, swallowing past the dryness in my throat. "There's a– Uh– There's a step stool in the hall closet if you need one." I tucked my chin to my chest and shied away, trying to hide the furious blush crawling up my neck, but I knew he saw it.

Every time that rush of pink filled my cheeks, there was a flare in his eyes that told me he enjoyed every second of it.

Pressing the roller against the wall, I busied myself with the task at hand, a welcome reprieve from his steady gaze. It was like my body was fine-tuned to every little movement or sound he made. The breath that he released from the center of the room might as well have coasted over my skin with the goosebumps left in its wake.

We were a ticking time bomb and even as nervous as it made me, I found myself anxiously awaiting the countdown to reach zero.

His socked feet carried him to the hallway closet where he pulled the step stool out after a brief battle with haphazardly hung winter coats, and then he was back in my tiny little room, drawing my attention with every shift in movement.

Noah dipped his brush into the paint tray, and I used his moment of distraction to let my eyes wander back over to him. And *Jesus*, who could blame me?

His black t-shirt stretched across the broad line of his shoulders, sleeves hugging the curve of his biceps as he lifted his arm and moved to make his first paint stroke. I traced the length of the snake that curled around his arm, all the way to where it bared its fangs on his wrist.

He really was way too attractive for his own good.

Noah angled his body to face the corner of the room, his arm raised to paint a line where the ceiling met the wall and I struggled to breathe as his shirt lifted, revealing a sliver of taut, tanned muscle underneath.

My grip on the paint roller trembled, fingers aching to trace over his skin – and *oh my god* what was happening to my brain?

I sucked in a deep breath, my head swimming. I couldn't tell if it was the paint fumes or Noah's cologne *or* the heady mixture of both in this small, poorly ventilated-room. But regardless, I was standing on wobbly legs.

I rolled my shoulders and steeled my spine, attempting to regain some semblance of composure. He was *just* Noah. But as I glanced back at him, there was something about the ease of his smile that made my stomach flutter, and my heart started racing again. I pressed my eyes shut and shook my head, pushing aside the distracting thoughts so I could focus on finishing what we started.

* * *

For the last two hours, we'd worked mostly in a comfortable silence.

Music flowed from the speakers of Noah's phone, filling the lull whenever it appeared, and in some ways, I felt as if the gaps in our conversations told me more about him than the actual talking did.

There were songs by Taylor Swift, Michael Jackson, Elton John, and Fleetwood Mac, some of which were clear reminders of Adeline based on the distant look he got in his eyes.

It was an afternoon of stolen glances and lighthearted conversation, shy smiles, and cheeks painted pink. It carried none of the nervous, frantic energy that I was expecting and instead, offered a peaceful segue into this new chapter I was opening myself up to.

It was comfortable and mildly terrifying but in all the best ways.

I'd been trying to work up the nerve to ask Noah if he'd be interested in staying for dinner tonight, but every time I looked over at him, the words dried up on my tongue. I wasn't a hundred percent certain that my cooking skills had improved enough to compete with whatever he would make at home or grab from the diner. Just this morning, I'd opted to buy us something instead of cooking whatever I had in the fridge, but after today, I wanted to try.

After my fourth or fifth glance in his direction, he was prepared, his eyes already waiting to lock with mine. My cheeks flamed, and I bit back a grin, once again losing the nerve to ask.

I turned my attention back to the roller in my hand, sliding it against the wall slowly. But the room was almost done and soon, I'd lose the distraction. Noah took a few steps toward me and leaned down, dipping his brush into the paint. My heart rate kicked up as two more of his large steps easily closed the gap between us, his breath tickling against the hairs at the nape of my neck.

"Liv?" he asked, his voice a low, gravelly rumble against my skin. I could feel the heat from his body radiating against my back, a shiver twisting down my spine.

I made a noise in the back of my throat, something high-pitched and quite frankly, embarrassing. That still didn't stop me from wanting to melt into his touch, sink into his chest, and breathe in the almost intoxicating blend of his cologne and laundry detergent.

"Is there something you wanna ask me?"

Letting out a shaky breath, I shook my head gently before clearing my throat. "Nope."

"*Liiiiiiv...*" He dragged out my name, his tone light and teasing. "You're lying to me." His voice dropped and my body shuddered. "Wanna know how I know?"

I dipped my chin once, my lungs barely expanding as I sucked in short, shallow breaths.

Noah's finger brushed against the apple of my cheek until he curled a strand of hair behind my ear. "This pretty pink color tells me you're nervous about something."

Every single one of the bones inside of my body melted into a puddle at my feet. "I don't know what you're talking about."

He clicked his tongue and took a step closer, warm breath coasting across the back of my neck. "Liar," Noah whispered, and I gasped, the cold tip of his paintbrush swiping against my cheek.

I spun around and Noah backed away with a shit-eating grin, blue stained paintbrush dangling from his fingers. Reaching up, I swiped my fingers against the wet spot on my cheek, my lips splitting into a surprised grin at the paint now smeared onto my hand. "Noah Kent!"

His smile only widened. "Olivia Brooks," he mocked, wielding his brush like a sword. "Tell me the truth."

I lifted the roller in a challenge. "I am."

I wasn't. But he didn't *really* know that.

My heart fluttered at the boyish look on his face, his eyes sparkling with mirth.

Noah used my distraction against me, lunging forward to swipe the paint across my nose. I jolted back with a laugh.

"Noah!"

He let out a loud, boisterous laugh. One that moved through the air like a tendril of warmth and coiled around me like one of his hugs. It was lovely. It was secure and addicting. A high I never wanted to stop chasing.

"Tell me the truth or I'll do it again."

"Don't you dare." I tried to sound at least a little menacing, but the laugh in my voice made it impossible.

Noah tilted his head, the playful glint in his eyes shifting to something mischievous. "Or what?"

"I will turn you into a walking canvas," I threatened with a grin.

He chuckled. "I'd love to see you try, Brooks."

Before he could finish his sentence, I rushed forward, swiping the roller from his stomach up to his neck, staining his black t-shirt and most of the exposed skin under his chin. I pulled away, my mouth wide as I laughed.

Noah stared down at the paint, and I used the momentary diversion to drop the roller into the paint tray and sink my hands into the thick, cold liquid, coating my fingers in that pretty blue color that now covered my walls.

I wiggled my fingers at him as his hand slapped against his chest. "This was my favorite shirt."

"I'm pretty sure you order those in bulk from Walmart. Cry me a river, Kent." I lunged for him again, fingers outstretched. He tried to evade me, but I managed to smear a streak of blue across his cheek. His laughter filled the room, rich and vibrant.

"Oh, you're in for it now," he declared, lowering himself so he could dip his hands into the leftover paint. I shrieked and turned to run, but long, strong arms wrapped around my torso and pulled me to his chest, blue handprints making their mark on my shirt.

His fingers jabbed into my sides as I let out some of the most horrific sounds, laughing and yelping as I twisted in his grip.

Chest to chest now, I reached up, gently slapping both of my hands against his cheeks. He groaned as the paint dripped down his face and onto his neck, another loud laugh bursting through my lips.

And because I wasn't quite ready to let him go, I slid my hands along the strong cut of his cheekbones and quickly inched my way back, threading my paint-covered fingers through his dark hair.

Noah's hands sat heavily on my waist, and only then did I realize just how close we were. The pleased smirk on my lips slowly faded as I swallowed, my eyes flitting back and forth between his.

Our chests kissed with each breath and his fingers curled into my shirt, the *want* in his eyes and on his face almost as prevalent as the restraint.

Noah lowered his forehead to mine, our breath mingling in the space between us. My heart thudded against my ribs. There was a question in his eyes. One that I assumed would have such an easy, obvious answer, but his hesitation told me otherwise. The self-doubt that I planted earlier had shot into the forefront of his mind and he was frozen. He was stuck in this place of questioning my every move, replaying every touch in his mind to see if he was misreading this situation.

He wasn't.

My tongue darted out, swiping against my bottom lip. This time, I craved the kiss that the alcohol had deprived me of the night before. I needed it. Like lungs needed oxygen. Like plants needed sunlight. It was a desperation that I'd never felt before.

The room around us seemed to blur as time slowed, Noah's fingers tightening their hold on my waist, pulling me even closer.

The tip of my nose brushed against his as I tilted my head back, my eyes fluttering shut. I felt Noah take a shaky breath, and I leaned into the moment, paint-covered fingers holding his hair firmly in my grasp.

One final tug on his hair snapped his resolve and sent it crumbling to the ground. Noah's lips met mine in a gentle, tentative kiss, one that was guarded and riddled with vulnerability. I sighed against his mouth and melded to his chest as one of his hands slid up my back and sifted into my hair.

This kiss felt so much like him. Soft, yet firm. Intense and profound, but in the most subtle manner. His lips moved against mine in a way that was all-consuming. Every nerve in my body tingled with awareness, goosebumps skittering across my skin. I grappled for control as my mind spun, my thoughts a twisted, excited mess of short-circuiting wires.

As many times as I imagined this happening, nothing that I dreamt up compared to the real thing. To the feeling of his fingers tangling in the hair at the base of my neck and the heat of his hand on my back. And I wanted it to be slow, I wanted to take my time. I knew we had so much to figure out, but Noah kissed me with such fervent purpose, he kissed me like he never wanted to stop and *fuck* I was right there with him.

His tongue swept out against the seam of my mouth, and I slowly parted my lips, meeting him with a gentle, curious swipe of my tongue. All the blood in my veins rose to the surface of my skin, hot, molten lava taking its place. What started slow and gentle, quickly morphed into a collision of emotion and desire. Our lips moved hungrily together, seeking, tasting, drawing out contented sighs and gasping breaths.

I lost track of time, lost myself in this new sensation of him. My hands slid from his hair, skimming the rough texture of his scruff, then down the hard plane of his chest. The softness of his lips and the way his tongue curled against mine was a beautiful contradiction I couldn't get enough of.

Noah pulled away, keeping his forehead pressed against mine and I cursed my lungs for the air they needed to breathe because I never wanted this moment to end. The silence in my apartment was only disturbed by our panting breaths as my eyes slowly peeled open and lifted to his.

The corner of his mouth twitched before he dipped down and brought his lips to mine in one more lingering kiss.

I stared up at him, memorizing the deep flecks of green buried within the golden amber, a slow grin stretching across my face.

He lifted a brow at my amusement. "What?"

I let out a chuckle, pressing my forehead to his chest for only a moment before I remembered the wet paint I'd smeared on his shirt just a few moments ago. Lifting my head, I groaned as my skin briefly stuck to his shirt, the blue paint transferring onto me.

Noah grabbed my wrist when I went to wipe it away, reminding me that my hand was still covered in drying, sticky paint.

"Thanks," I laughed, wiping my hands on my already-stained shorts. "I was just thinking that I should lie to you more often."

Noah's laugh echoed through the empty room as he threw his head back, my stomach flipping at the sound. He met my eyes again, his paint-stained thumb brushing against the curve of my bottom lip as my grin widened. "Liv," he said with a sigh, the amusement in his expression melting to something so tender my heart squeezed in response. "I think I've wanted to do that for a lot longer than I realized."

I rolled my lips together, trying to stifle the enjoyment I felt hearing those words, but the rush of warmth to my cheeks gave me away regardless.

The adrenaline of the moment started to seep away, exposing the weight of what just happened and what it meant for both of us. I searched his eyes for any trace of regret, but I saw none. I thought the realization that my last kiss no longer belonged to Liam would weigh a little more heavily on my chest than it did, but I felt nothing but peace.

I swallowed and drew in a steadying breath through my nose. "Me, too."

Slowly, we peeled our sticky hands from each other's clothing, both his t-shirt and mine ruined by blue handprints and streaks of paint. I laughed as my eyes drifted to his cheeks, and then to his hair, which now stuck up in several different directions. Every other strand was coated in blue and in the process of drying.

"We should probably get cleaned up," I said with a laugh, the dry paint on my cheeks cracking as I grinned. "I have some of Liam's old clothes if you wanna shower?"

"You sure?"

I nodded, letting my eyes wander around the newly painted room. I soaked up the slate blue color that covered the walls, a sense of pride blooming in my chest. It looked good! The room felt bigger and less depressing. Maybe it was the new color, or maybe it was the kiss we just shared, but the overwhelming urge to unpack my life and finally settle into the apartment washed over me, and my fingers itched to get started. "They're in a box in the closet. Let's–" I held up a hand and gestured vaguely to the mess we'd made over the past couple of hours. "Get all this paint stuff sorted before we do any more damage, and then we'll clean ourselves up."

He laughed, his hands landing on his hips as he surveyed the room. "Sounds like a deal."

Chapter 28

Noah

An hour later, my mind was still reeling from our kiss. I replayed the way she melted into my arms and the way her eyelids fluttered closed as she tilted her head back in anticipation, waiting for my mouth to press against hers.

I could still taste her on my tongue and feel her hair twisted in my fingers. And her lips... *Fuck.* Her lips. So soft, and utterly intoxicating, pink and swollen from our kiss. And that one kiss, as perfect as it was... It wasn't enough. I wanted them all.

I stood in her bathroom, wringing the water from my hair as she moved things around in her room, carefully avoiding the newly painted walls. I kept waiting for the guilt to creep in. For my brain to ruin this moment of bliss by reminding me of the broken human I'd been just a few months ago, but thankfully, it never came.

I wasn't foolish enough to think that one heart-to-heart with Liv magically welded all of the broken pieces inside of me together. There were still plenty of things I needed to work on on my own, but there was this... calmness that settled within me. It stilled the racing thoughts of 'what if' and allowed me to focus on what was happening right here, right now.

I was okay with being okay. I could let go of this guilt and hold onto everything good and I was determined to hold onto it for however long it was mine.

I hung the towel over the shower curtain rod and turned to leave, steam billowing out of the bathroom as I pulled the door open.

Liv tossed a pillow onto her bed and smiled up at me, making a sweeping gesture across the room. "I told you I'm not a slob."

There was a small stack of broken down cardboard boxes in the hallway outside of her bedroom, the top of her dresser decorated with a few picture frames and a small porcelain structure that looked like the branch of a tree, a couple bracelets, and a necklace hanging from the ends. There was a lamp on her bedside table now, a few throw pillows on top of a neatly made bed.

The new color on the wall suited the dark wood on her furniture better than the dingy yellow. It suited *her* better.

"You got a lot done in ten minutes."

After getting all the paint supplies gathered and tucked away in her hall closet, I helped her pull the bed frame and mattress back into the room, as well as move the boxes from the bathroom back into her bedroom. She took a shower while I'd busied myself with the hooks in her entryway, making sure they were tightened to the wall instead of dangling loosely.

Honestly, while I showered, I'd expected her to just rearrange the boxes. Maybe move them out of the way. I hadn't expected her to unpack anything, let alone transform her room.

Her chest rose and fell with a deep sigh as she surveyed the room. "It was about time for this place to feel like home. Living out of boxes was getting old."

My lips tilted up into a small smile. "Well... Welcome home, Liv."

She bent a little at the waist in a bow as she chuckled. "Thank you, Noah."

"So." I walked over to sit on the edge of her bed as she dug into another box. "You never did tell me what you were lying to me about."

I watched with satisfaction as her cheeks flamed pink.

"It's stupid," she murmured, pulling out a stack of folded sweaters. "It's just– I mean, it's nothing." Liv gave me her back as she leaned down and pulled the bottom drawer of her dresser open, stuffing the sweaters inside.

"I promise it's not." I hadn't the slightest idea what she was so scared to ask me, but I knew without a doubt that if she was this worried about something, it wasn't stupid. It wasn't nothing.

She stood with another sigh and turned to face me, the words flying out of her mouth almost too quickly for me to understand. "I bought some stuff at the store to make spaghetti for dinner, and I was wondering if you'd let me cook for you tonight. For dinner. Tonight. It's nothing special. Just an easy recipe. Did you know they put recipes right on the side of the box? It seems pretty simple. So... If you– I mean, only if you want–"

"Liv," I cut her rambling off as I stood, though part of me kind of wished that I wouldn't have. There were a lot of things that I found adorable about her. The rambling was one of my favorites.

I stood in front of her and lifted my hands to her face, my thumbs swiping against her cheekbones as nervous blue eyes stared up at me.

I knew that one kiss, no matter how captivating, didn't give me the right to hold her like this. But now that I had knowledge of the way she felt in my arms, the way she leaned into my touch, so soft and pliable... I couldn't resist the urge to hold her now.

"I would love to stay for dinner." The tension melted off of her shoulders, her head falling to the side as she leaned into my palm.

"Yeah?"

"Yeah."

"You're not scared of my cooking?"

I snorted. "Absolutely terrified. But all good things in life are a little scary, right?"

She scoffed, her fingers curling into my shirt. "I can't promise that it'll be any good."

My shoulder lifted in a shrug. "I'm willing to take that risk."

We hadn't talked about the kiss yet or what it meant for us. We hadn't talked about what we felt or where we would go from here. But I'd eat raw pasta if she put it on my plate, if it meant spending a few more hours with her.

My arms dropped and her eyes flickered to my mouth, her fingers tightening around the fabric of my shirt. Liv's tongue darted out to wet her lips, her breath shaky. "We kissed," she stated simply.

"We did."

She drew in a deep, fortifying breath. "I think I wanna do it again."

A surge of anticipation rushed through me at her words, and I couldn't help but smile. She took a step forward, and my fingers ached with want. Want to trace her skin, weave through her hair, and pull her lips to mine.

I'd spent so much time concerned about the pace we were going and whether or not we were ready for something that felt so... inevitable. But it was like the dam had been opened. The blockage, the wall I'd so carefully erected around my heart was gone. The reluctance to find something beautiful in the shitty hand I'd been dealt had dissolved, and almost everything inside of me was dying to go full steam ahead.

There was still something scratching at the back of my mind, reminding me of the hesitation written all over her face this morning, but it wasn't enough. It wasn't enough to stop me from taking what I wanted.

My hands slid into her damp hair as I slanted my mouth over hers, swallowing her gasp of surprise. Her lips were so soft, melding perfectly against mine. And just like the first one, I never wanted to let her go.

Heat blazed down my spine as her hands splayed across my ribs, her head tipping back, lips parting with a whimper. My hand slid down to the small of her back, pulling her closer. I could feel the frantic beat of her heart against my chest.

All of the questions and hesitations buried themselves in the back of my mind, and I savored the taste of her lips, my fingers trailing up the curve of her spine. I wanted to spend the rest of the day with my mouth on hers, my hands exploring every soft curve of her body.

But her apartment door swung open, the doorknob bouncing off the drywall as Kennedy and Nellie's laughter filtered through the apartment. Liv's cheeks flushed, her fingers pressing against her mouth.

She gently eased me away, her brows pulling together as a panicked look formed in her eyes. "We shouldn't– I don't wanna confuse her. We can't–"

I took another step away, creating a little more distance. Shaking my head, I gave her a reassuring smile. "It's okay. I understand," I whispered, lifting the step ladder from where it leaned against the door and carrying it out into the hallway right as the two girls rounded the corner.

Nellie beamed up at me, tossing her book bag to the floor. "Uncle Noah!"

I opened the hall closet and shoved the ladder inside before turning to my niece and scooping her up into my arms. "Hey, Peanut!" Her small arms wrapped around my neck as Kennedy hugged my legs.

"Hi, Noah!"

I looked down at Liv's little girl, her wide smile warming my heart. Squatting down the best that I could with Nellie hanging off of me, I playfully pinched Ken's cheek between my fingers. "Hey, kiddo."

Avery rounded the corner; one copper brow arched high. "You're still here."

Not a question. But I wasn't going to be the one to confirm her suspicions.

I stood and set Nellie down, and she and Kennedy took off to the living room. "Yup."

My sister crossed her arms and leaned her hip against the wall. "You have wet hair."

"There is not a single thing that gets past you, huh?"

"Don't be obtuse," she scolded with an eye roll.

Liv emerged from her room, her neck and cheeks flushed my favorite shade of pink. She swallowed, her eyes flickering back and forth between me and Avery.

Avery's eyes narrowed on Liv. "You have wet hair."

I took a lot of pride in my capability to leave Liv flustered with her cheeks flaming, but nothing that I have ever said or done had left her looking like *that*. Her face was well past pink, quickly shifting to bright red as she grappled for something to say.

I cleared my throat and glared at my sister, hoping the sharp edge to my tone was enough to get her to back off. "I stupidly set the paint can on the step ladder and elbowed it off. It got a little messy. We had to get the paint off."

She nodded slowly, her eyes still narrowed in suspicion, but to her credit, she backed off.

Liv muttered something about going to see Kennedy before she hurried down the hall and out of sight.

"Seriously?" I hissed, reaching over and lightly shoving Avery's shoulder. "I mean, what the hell was that?" I loved my sister, but I swear, sometimes we still bickered like we were teenagers.

She grinned, flicking her hair off of her shoulders. "*That* is what I like to call… Meddling. You're welcome."

***

Another loud bang sounded from the kitchen, Kennedy's eyes shifting over to me. I dragged my hand over my mouth as Liv cursed under her breath, trying my best to conceal my grin.

"Do you think she needs help?" Kennedy whispered. The pink crayon in her hand hovered over the coloring sheet on the coffee table.

I shrugged, trading my blue crayon for a green one. My crossed legs were shoved in the space under the coffee table, Kennedy sitting across from me as we colored some beach scene from a princess movie. Avery and Nellie headed out to my parents' house about an hour ago, and Liv got started on dinner, insisting she didn't want any help... So I set up camp in the living room with Ken, and we'd been listening to Liv curse and bang around in the kitchen ever since.

"Do you think I should help?"

It was Kennedy's turn to shrug. She looked toward the kitchen and lowered her voice. "I like your cooking better. But don't tell her that."

I zipped my lips and pretended to throw the key over my shoulder. "Your secret's safe with me."

"She's getting better. Daddy used to cook at home. Before his accident. He had a cutter thing that made the french toast and pancakes look like a heart." She paused for a moment before letting out a little sigh. "I miss Daddy." Her green eyes flickered up to me. "Did you know him?"

My heart squeezed, and I offered her a sad smile. "No, I didn't. But he sounds like a good dad."

She grinned. "The bestest."

The silence as we colored was filled with noises of Liv moving around the kitchen and the soft scrape of our crayons against the paper. After a minute or so, Kennedy's small voice broke the quiet. "Noah?"

"What's up?"

"You make my mommy smile more, you know."

I paused, surprised by her statement. "I do?" I asked, my voice barely more than a whisper.

She nodded, her blonde hair bouncing slightly with the motion. "Yup. Whenever you come over, she's always smiling after you leave. She thinks I can't hear, but she says nice things about you when she talks to Aunt Gia on the phone."

I couldn't help but smile at her words, a warm, fuzzy feeling spreading through my chest. "Well, Ken, your mom makes me happy, too."

Her smile mirrored mine as she picked up a purple crayon and started coloring again.

"So it's okay that I come over sometimes?"

"Yeah," she answered after a moment. "I think so."

I smiled to myself, feeling a sense of achievement wash over me. While it was one incredibly amazing accomplishment to believe that Liv and I were making good progress, it was reassuring to hear that both Liv and Kennedy felt even a modicum of the same relief and happiness that I felt whenever they were around.

Liv's head poked around the corner, something sweet and gentle flickering through her eyes as she watched me color with Ken. Her mouth pulled into a smile, red sauce smeared across her cheek. "Dinner's ready."

* * *

"It's nothing special really. Like I said, the recipe is on the box, and the sauce was easy. Just some seasoning and I made sure to–"

"Liv–" I hated cutting her off, but I hated hearing her talk down about herself even more. "It's good. *Honestly*. You did a good job. Thank you for cooking."

Liv took a breath, her fork toying with the last few noodles on her plate as her cheeks flushed. "You're sure?"

I offered her a wide, sincere smile as Kennedy slurped up her last noodle. "I promise."

"It's really good, Mommy!" she reassured, leaning back in her chair and patting her stomach.

"Thank you, honey. Thank you, Noah." The pink in her cheeks deepened, and she looked down at her hands, a shy but contented smile playing at her lips.

Kennedy yawned, and I knew my time here was coming to an end. I didn't want to leave. Liv and I... We dove head first into uncharted territory today, and there was nothing else I'd rather do than spend all night exploring what that meant for us, but it was late. Ken had school in the morning, and Liv needed to get her ready for bed.

The look on her face told me she was coming to the same realization as I was.

I used a napkin to wipe my face and looked at Liv. "Go get her ready for bed, I'll clean up."

"Oh, you don't have to do that."

"You cooked. I'll clean. Besides–" I reached over, swiping Kennedy's napkin over her sauce-stained mouth. "*Someone* could use a bath."

She giggled and swatted my hand away. "*You* need a bath!"

Liv grinned and pushed her chair away from the table, standing to her feet.

"He's right, kiddo. You have pasta in your hair. Go get a towel. I'll meet you in the bathroom."

Kennedy took off without another word, and Liv looked over at me. "You don't have to clean up."

I shrugged. "I'm going to."

Before she could argue anymore, I stood and began gathering our plates and silverware. "Go," I jerked my head toward the hallway. "I'll take care of everything here. You get her ready for bed."

It'd been a little over a year since Liam died. A little over a year ago, she was used to having a support system, used to having someone to take care of her, and now, I was beginning to think she was getting used to the idea of needing to do everything on her own.

We hadn't talked much about what her life in Wyoming was like, but based on the conversations I'd witnessed with Debra, there was probably a small part of Liv that felt like she had something to prove. But I wanted her to know that if she ever felt like her load was too heavy to carry, I was here to bear some of that weight.

Hanging around to wash up after she cooked me dinner felt like the bare minimum.

She looked down the hall to make sure Kennedy was out of sight and stretched up on tiptoes, swiping a kiss against the corner of my mouth. "Thank you."

I smiled as I watched her disappear around the corner and got to work in the kitchen.

* * *

"She's out," Liv announced gently as she leaned against the wall, her arms crossed over her chest.

I dried my hands on the towel hanging from the cabinet under the sink and turned to face her. She'd replaced the claw clip in her hair with an elastic and piled it all on the top of her head, a few runaway strands framing her face. They accentuated the sharp cut of her cheekbones in the low light, like golden arrows directing my gaze straight to her full, rosy lips.

I leaned my hip against the counter with a smile. "That was quick."

Liv let out a small, melancholy chuckle. "She's a big girl now. She doesn't want me to stay with her until she falls asleep anymore." She sighed, but her smile remained.

"She wants a bath, a chapter of *Charlotte's Web*, and then to put herself to bed."

"I'm sure that's very bittersweet."

"Incredibly."

Dinner was over, and the dishes were done. Her room was painted, and the hooks by her door were now secure. My purpose here in her apartment was fulfilled. The day had drifted into night, and we both knew it was time for me to leave, but neither of us seemed to have any desire to speak that truth out loud.

We stood in the soft light of her kitchen for another quiet moment, soaking up the peaceful atmosphere. There was nothing but the faint hum of her refrigerator and the distant hoot of an owl until I finally spoke up. "I should probably head out."

The disappointment in her eyes mirrored mine. "Probably," she said with a sigh.

I pushed away from the counter and wiped my hands against my jeans. "Walk me out?"

Liv smiled and nodded, angling her body so I could pass through. I pulled the front door open and stepped out into the hallway, turning around to face her. Leaning against the door frame, I reached up to brush the hair out of her face.

She cocked her head to the side. "What's your favorite vegetable?"

I snorted out a laugh. "Favorite vegetable?" Of all the things I expected her to say, that wasn't even in the top ten.

Liv nodded, lifting her brows expectantly.

Dragging a hand over my mouth, I contemplated my answer. "Weirdly enough, probably Brussels sprouts."

Her face twisted with disgust. "*Brussels sprouts?!* Who the hell *enjoys* Brussels sprouts?"

I laughed. "You have to eat the ones my mom makes up. Crispy, seasoned to perfection, sprinkled with Parmesan. They're the best."

"I'll take your word for it." She let out another laugh, her eyes shimmering with amusement. "What's your middle name?"

"Anderson."

"Anderson?" she questioned.

I nodded. "Family name."

She let out a sound of surprise. "I like it. It's... Fitting."

"What about you?"

"Claire." She took a step closer, her arms folded over her chest and brushed against my stomach, her chin tilting up to meet my eyes.

"Olivia Claire," I said softly, "I like it."

"Thank you," She murmured, her cheeks warming as she averted her gaze.

"Any more questions?" I teased.

She tapped her finger to her pursed lips. "Favorite color?"

I blew out a breath. "Do adults have a favorite color?"

Liv gasped, slapping a hand against her chest. "*Obviously!* Who doesn't have a favorite color?" she scoffed. "Brussels sprouts? No favorite color? Who are you?"

I rolled my eyes with a laugh. "I guess I've just never given it much thought." Except I had. But how the hell do I tell her that my favorite color is the soft, almost peachy pink that paints her skin when she's embarrassed? Her smile was stretched wide, and my hand moved of its own volition, my thumb ghosting over the plump curve of her bottom lip. Slowly, my gaze roved over her features, so effortlessly beautiful and captivating.

There was something so enticing about the way her eyes sparkled with humor and how her lips held the memory of a laugh so carefree and happy.

Her breath hitched as my thumb reached the corner of her mouth, and my eyes slowly traveled back to hers. I wanted to lose myself in the beauty of her gaze. She stared back at me, bright cerulean eyes pulling me in.

Her eyes were a vast sea of adoration and hope, and all I wanted was to succumb to their depths. Maybe I had more than one favorite color.

"Blue," I finally answered, my voice soft. "I think my favorite color is blue."

The corner of her mouth twitched under my thumb. "A sensible choice."

"Very sensible indeed."

She sighed, something light but wistful as she leaned into my touch. "Let me know when you get home?"

I splayed my hand across the side of her throat, my thumb moving to stroke her jawline. "Of course. Leave your bedroom window open for tonight, 'kay?"

"Ooh, are you gonna sneak in and ask me to the prom?" she teased.

I rolled my eyes and leaned in, dropping a kiss on her cheek. "No, smart ass. If you breathe in nothing but paint fumes all night, I might lose out on all your witty remarks. So do me a favor, and preserve your brain cells by leaving the window open tonight. *Please.*"

Liv grinned. "Fine, but only because you asked so nicely."

"Goodnight, Liv."

"I won't be able to sleep until you tell me you made it home. So... tell me goodnight then." Her eyes moved to my lips, then flickered back up to meet mine. "Do I get a goodnight kiss?"

"Do you want one?" I asked, my voice low and filled with a longing I didn't even try to conceal.

"Yes," she whispered, unraveling her crossed arms and curling her fingers into my shirt.

Her pulse quickened beneath my palm as she pressed against me and I was thankful she felt the same surge of nerves and anticipation that I did. Her eyes fluttered closed as our faces drew closer and closer, the air between us crackling with an electric charge.

Finally, our lips met in a slow, burning kiss, our bodies inching closer. I felt the gentle rise and fall of her chest, the subtle quiver in her breath, and the tightening grip of her fingers on my shirt. The taste of her lips was a sweet revelation, like the first sip of a fine wine. One that only got better and more addicting every time it passed my lips.

At one point in time, my hands had begged me to keep her at a distance. And now, they only pleaded to pull her closer. They longed for the comfort of her skin and the familiar warmth that she offered, and who was I to deny them of such delicacy?

I surrendered to the hunger that grew between us, one hand cradling the nape of her neck, tilting her head back as my tongue gently parted her lips. I slid my other hand along the graceful curve of her waist, daring to slip beneath the hem of her shirt where my fingers met soft, smooth skin.

She shivered under my touch, swiping her tongue out to meet mine. I could stand here all night, learning what each and every small sigh and whimper meant. I wanted to watch her skin flush in an obvious statement of the desire we shared. I wanted to say fuck it and forget about the logical side of my brain that was screaming at me to take things slow, to resist the urge to push her back into her apartment and press her against the wall.

Somehow, I managed to latch onto that logical part of me. I summoned a willpower I didn't even know existed within me to pull away from her. Warmth flared in my chest at the small noise of disappointment that left her lips.

We stood at the threshold of her apartment, foreheads pressed together as we fought to catch our breath. I memorized the warmth of her skin and gave myself a few more seconds to hold her close before I moved away completely, knowing that if I didn't do it now, it'd be all too easy to let myself fall back into her embrace.

She swallowed and let out a shaky breath before lifting her eyes to meet mine Those perfect, kiss-swollen lips tilted into a shy smile, heat blossoming across her cheeks. "Thank you... For the paint and– and for the kissing. Today was a good day."

I grinned as the flush in her cheeks deepened, then backed away and shot her a wink. "The bestest."

Chapter 29

Olivia

It was time to bite the bullet and just *do it*.

It didn't matter that I was terrified of her reaction. It didn't matter that whatever scream was going to tear through her vocal cords would inevitably burst my eardrums.

I had to do it.

I had to call Gia. I had to tell her that I kissed the hot mechanic.

I'd been putting it off for days, letting myself bask in the secret moments and stolen kisses. Not that we'd spent a ton of time together this week. The shop was still technically out of commission until Monday, so most of our encounters had been brief and furtive.

I'd only run into Noah at the diner when I met Avery for breakfast in the morning. After that, since Kennedy was in school for most of the day, I spent my afternoons unpacking and re-organizing. I had officially moved into my apartment here in Rose Hill. Friday had come around quickly and I had no doubt the weekend would fly by as well. And by Monday, everything would be back to normal.

Normal, plus the added bonus of being in the same building with Noah... alone... from nine in the morning until I picked the girls up from school after two.

I had no idea how I was going to keep my hands to myself.

But that was the least of my worries. At this moment, I had to worry about calling my best friend and admitting that this crush had *clearly* evolved into something more. Even if neither party knew exactly what that meant. I didn't know why I was so nervous about calling her. Maybe it was because she would be the first person I was really admitting this to out loud aside from the person I was kissing.

Realistically, I knew Gia would be happy for me. Happy was probably even an understatement. But it was still scary.

I plopped down onto the couch and pulled a throw pillow onto my lap, letting out a deep sigh before unlocking my phone. My thumb hovered over Gia's contact for a moment, my stomach churning with nerves.

Finally, I pressed down on her name and raised the phone to my ear.

She answered after a few rings, and the first thing out of her mouth was a sigh of relief. "Thank fucking god. I miss you so much. I can never decide if I call you too much or too little. I've been thinking about calling you all morning."

I chuckled and leaned against the cold leather of my couch. "I miss you, too, G. And you can never call me too much. It's not possible."

"Trust me. It's very possible." Gia sighed again. "How are you, my love?"

I bit my bottom lip, suppressing a grin and the urge to loudly and very excitedly tell her just how fine I really was. There was a rustle of blankets from her end and then a door opening and shutting with a creak.

"Hey," she said, her voice gentle. "It's okay if you're not okay. I know you've been having–"

"No, G." I interrupted, shaking my head with a smile that refused to be contained. "I– I'm *really* good. I'm happy."

There was nothing but stunned silence from her side of the phone.

Instead of waiting for her rapid-fire questions, I decided to just offer up the answers.

"I finally unpacked. Like... everything. Um... I painted my room. I cooked a pretty decent meal without anyone's help and–" I paused, closing my eyes for a second before the next sentence rushed out of me. "I might've kissed the hot mechanic. More than once. To be honest, I've kind of lost track of how many times at this point. And I kind of never wanna stop."

Gia's hand slapped against something hard and I was met with more stunned silence.

I heard a couple gasping breaths like she was opening her mouth to start a sentence and then cutting herself off.

"Gia?"

And then it happened. The shriek of excitement that I'd been anticipating. I pulled my phone away from my ear and waited for it to die down, stifling a laugh as a slew of *oh my gods* filtered through the speaker.

"Livie! *Oh my god, Olivia!* You *kissed* him?! Like actually kissed him? Tell me *everything. Everything!*" She squealed and I laughed. "How the fuck did you go from him cooking for you to *kissing*?" Another loud squeal. "Did you make the first move? Did he? Was there tongue? Spill it!" Gia's voice crackled with excitement.

I settled back into the couch, staring up at the ceiling as I began spilling every interesting detail.

We spent the next hour on the phone, Gia listening with rapt attention as I shared every detail of this newfound... *relationship*... that Noah and I had formed. I told her everything. From each awkwardly endearing moment to the stolen, passionate kisses when we found ourselves alone. She would occasionally interject with well-timed playful commentary, gasps, or giddy laughter.

It felt like we were in high school again and I was lying on my bed, my see-through landline cradled against my cheek as my legs kicked behind me. Part of me was waiting to hear Jackson on the other end, grabbing the phone from the kitchen wall to make kissy noises while I confessed my crushes to Gia.

But as my recount came to an end, there was no one but me and G. No more playful laughter or teasing remarks. Just a deep, quivering breath before she said, "Livie... I'm so happy for you."

The conviction in her voice rattled me. I was never one to take advantage of our friendship or forget just how lucky I was to have someone like Gia in my life, but this was one of those moments where it struck me just how fortunate I truly was. No one, not even my parents, talked to me with this kind of genuine love and happiness. No one from home checked on me as much as she did. No one in my life made me feel *normal* for the way that I was processing everything that had happened to me over the past year and a half. Everything that she said stuck with me. Even from thousands of miles away, she was there for me, day and night, without a single ounce of judgment.

Gia was the sister I never had. And I missed her. I couldn't even articulate the words to describe just how much.

"Thank you," I said quietly, my voice thick with emotion. "I love you, G."

"I love you right back. I'm so incredibly jealous of you. But I love you."

I huffed out a laugh. "Jealous? Why on earth are you jealous of me?"

She let out a wistful sigh and I could almost see the back of her hand resting against her forehead like something out of a rom-com. "You're living out my small-town romance dreams, babe. Passionate kissing with a broody, dark-haired, tattooed mechanic? He makes you and your daughter breakfast? He's broken, but has a soft spot for you and only you? Come on. That's enough to make anyone swoon."

"Okay," I replied sarcastically. "Let's not forget about the whole dead spouse thing and how everyone from my hometown, aside from you, seems to be holding a grudge against me."

"Right, well…" Her voice trailed off. "You're happy, Livie?"

There was no hesitation, no bent truths, or lies. "Yes," I answered confidently. "I am."

"Good," she replied, her voice watery. I knew this was all she wanted for me, even if it meant only seeing each other through a phone screen for now. I just wished everyone else could see it that way, too.

An alarm blared from Gia's side of the phone and she cursed. "I gotta go, babe. I've got a call with my agent in five."

I didn't miss the dejected tone or the sigh that followed. "Okay, well… We're gonna follow up on that later tonight. So be prepared to hear from me again." A lot of our conversations had been so centered around me and what was going on with my life that I hadn't bothered to ask how her book was coming along.

By the sound of it, not well.

"Yeah, yeah. I'm gonna get a verbal lashing from Anna. I don't need one from you, either."

I scoffed. "I would never!"

Gia sighed again. Clearly, things were not going well. "I know. I gotta let

Kevin out before she calls. Call me tonight?"

Fucking Kevin. Who in their right mind named their dog *Kevin?*

"I hate that name so much."

"I know." She laughed and I swear I could hear her grin through the phone.

"Love you, bye!"

"Love you, bye."

I ended the call and rested my phone on my chest, staring up at the ceiling with a stupid grin tugging at my lips. I always felt so much better after phone calls with Gia.

Thoughts of Noah danced through my mind and I felt my smile grow.

I saw him yesterday. Truthfully, I was expecting to see him this morning, but he'd sent me an early text to tell me that he was meeting James at the shop to install the new A/C, and he wouldn't be at the diner.

It was just after noon… I would have to get Kennedy and Nellie from school at two-thirty and everything that I needed to do around the apartment today was done almost an hour after I'd returned from breakfast with Avery.

Obviously, the clear choice here was meandering over to the shop to see what he was up to and praying that he was just as anxious to see me as I was him. Maybe I could convince him to take a break and grab lunch with me at the diner.

Rolling off of the couch with a new rush of anxious, excited energy, I slid my sandals on and snagged my keys from the counter.

* * *

I honestly don't think I'd ever moved so fast.

I made it to the shop in record time, excitement bubbling in my stomach as I pulled the door open. The familiar scent of motor oil and gasoline greeted me at the same time a wave of heat hit my face. *Jesus*, it was hot in there.

I walked up to the desk, the faint sound of clinking metal tools traveling to the front. A chill raced down my spine at the thought of being in the same building as James. I had no clue who he was or his history with this town, but there was one thing I knew for sure: no part of me wanted to be in the same building with him alone.

A light sheen of sweat formed on my hairline as I leaned against the desk, tapping my finger against the bell that sat on top. My lips curled into a small smile when I remembered the old bell that sat here just a few months ago, so rusted that it made absolutely no sound.

Truthfully, there was no need to replace it. Whenever I was here, I was up front. And it wasn't like many people *actually* came into the shop. If anyone needed work done, they called to make their appointment now that the phone was hooked up and working, and when it came time for those appointments, they would drive around to the alley and knock on the door back there to let Noah know they'd arrived.

The bell was pointless.

But I liked having it regardless.

The shuffling of boots against the concrete replaced the sound of metal clanking, and almost immediately, my stomach sank to my feet. Maybe it was weird that I knew exactly what Noah's steps sounded like, but I'd gotten used to the sound of them coming up behind me during the day, and I knew he didn't drag his feet. I also knew that his jeans didn't drag against the ground as he walked, and as James made his way to the front of the shop, the sound of his dirty, worn khakis trailing behind him only sent another wave of discomfort coursing through me.

I took a couple steps away from the desk as he slowly made his way down the hall, his face shifting from one of boredom to something that made my skin crawl. His gaze traveled slowly down my body and I hated the fact that I'd worn something even remotely revealing.

Something told me that even if I was wearing a thick wool sweater and baggy jeans instead of a t-shirt and a pair of cutoffs, he'd still be looking at me like this.

James's eyes lingered on my chest before slowly dropping down the length of my bare legs and my face twisted into a scowl. I hated that I didn't think to message Noah before I got here.

Clearly, he wasn't in the shop. And based on the reaction he had last time I ended up in this shop with James, he never would've let me be alone with him.

Slowly, his gaze moved back up to meet mine. A perverted smile curled at his lips.

"Is Noah here?" I bit out, taking another step toward the door.

James rubbed his chest with his hand, leaving behind a smear of something dark on his shirt. "Nope."

That was my cue to leave.

"Okay." I took another step back. "Have a good day."

"Now, hold on." His raspy voice grated against my skin and sent an unwelcome shiver up my spine. "He said he'd be right back. Maybe you should stick around for a few minutes. So you don't miss him, ya know?"

That was the last thing I wanted to do. I didn't know where Noah was heading or what he was doing, but I had no desire to hang around here for a second longer than I needed to. I would go sit in the diner by myself and wait for Kennedy to get out of school before I stayed in this building with him.

"Oh, no. That's alright. I should go." I offered a polite smile because as a woman, that was what I was trained to do. To hell with my discomfort as long as his ego wasn't wounded.

James began to round the desk, the hems of his dingy pants scraping against the floor and a surge of adrenaline rushed through me as I took another step back. I hated the blatant appreciation in his eyes as they wandered my body again. "Tell me a little about yourself, angel."

I reached into my pocket to grab my phone as he took another few steps in my direction. Maybe he wasn't actually trying to scare me, or maybe he wasn't as much of a threat as my intuition was telling me he was, but I didn't want to stick around to find out.

Just as I began swiping through my messages in search of Noah's contact information, the front door swung open, and relief crashed through me. I stumbled back as James's face fell with disappointment, Noah's large, firm hands gripping my biceps.

"What's going on?" Noah gritted out, his fingers tightening around my arms.

James ground his molars together, a look of pure disdain etched onto his face. "Just being friendly."

There was a pause. One that told me Noah didn't trust a thing that came out of James's mouth. "Liv?"

I cleared my throat and tried my best to respond in a calm manner, but my voice shook when I answered. "Everything's fine."

"See?"

Dark, beady eyes did another slow perusal of my body before he turned and Noah's anger turned feral. I couldn't see his face, but I could feel his body tense behind me, his voice low and dangerous. "James."

"Yeah?" he called out over his shoulder, only turning once he rounded the desk.

Despite the rage coursing through his veins, Noah gently moved me to the side, carefully angling his body so he was in front of me. "If I *ever* catch you looking at her like that again, I'll knock your fuckin' teeth out."

The old man's face twisted with anger and confusion. "What are you goin' on about?"

"Get out," Noah ground out through clenched teeth. "You're done."

James scoffed. "You ain't gonna find anyone else to fix this within a week."

"I'll manage. Get your shit and get out."

It was neither the time nor the place to have such a visceral reaction to his words, and honestly, I didn't even know this hardened, possessive side of Noah was something I'd be so fucking attracted to. The deep, rumbling timbre of his voice flitted across my skin and sent a spark of awareness down my spine. My body shuddered for a different reason this time.

James gritted his teeth but bit back his retort, his face turning a deep shade of red before he made his way to the back of the shop again.

The second the doors to the garage were swinging shut, Noah was moving out of the shop and taking me with him. His hands still held my arms in a tight grip.

Noah's normal stoic look of disinterest had shifted to an ice-cold rage, and my spine stiffened as his jaw ticked in irritation. "Don't move."

"Wait, Noah—" I wrapped my hand around his wrist and attempted to pull him to a stop as he yanked the front door open. His anger was palpable, surging across the surface of his skin like an electric current.

I disliked James just as much as the next person, but some unwanted attention from him wasn't worth Noah spending the day in the county jail, and judging by the look on his face, this conversation wasn't going to end well.

"It's fine," I insisted, giving his arm a gentle tug.

His expression softened. "It's not fine. Don't do that. I'm just going to make sure he gets his shit out of my shop. That's all. I'll be back in a second."

"Promise?"

Noah brushed his lips against my hair. "Promise."

I released him of my death grip, mumbling an apology at the indents my fingernails left behind before he disappeared into the shop again.

There was no way the shop could stay closed for another week while he found someone else. He was losing income by keeping it closed and now, he'd have to pay yet another person to come out and finish what James started.

I should've just avoided the shop. I should've called him instead of just stopping by.

Regret and unease gnawed a pit in my stomach as I peered through the glass, my eyes fixed on the swinging doors that led to the garage. A few minutes ticked by, each stretching out longer than the last and I resisted the urge to ignore his request to stay put.

And because the pessimist inside of me loved putting me through absolute *hell*, I also started picturing just about every horrible scenario that could be happening out of my sight.

I used to do this with Liam.

He would leave for work around eight with the promise to drive safely and send a text the second he walked through the doors. But he worked at a hospital. Sometimes he would be bombarded the second he pulled into the lot, and I would wait over an hour for a text. Then, and only then, was I able to relax.

Eventually, I'd gotten kind of used to the late texts and stopped letting myself get so worked up over the possibility of something happening to him on the way. We lived in a small town after all. The worst thing that happened to people in Evergreen was the occasional fox stealing from the chicken coop or a rabbit helping themselves to someone's garden.

People didn't drink and drive because almost everywhere that served or sold alcohol was within walking distance of most neighborhoods.

If someone drank too much, they walked. Or they hitched a ride with one of the two taxis in town.

I let myself stop worrying.

The night that Liam was run off the road, I'd tucked Kennedy into bed and asked her what she wanted her Daddy to cook for breakfast in the morning. I'd poured myself a glass of wine, unloaded the dishwasher, and settled onto our couch to watch some romantic comedy from the nineties.

I told myself not to worry when his text didn't come. That something more important came up and he wasn't dead in a ditch like my anxiety told me he was.

The knock on my door an hour later filled my stomach with lead, and I just *knew*.

So standing here now, it was almost impossible not to assume the worst. Because the one time I told myself it was ridiculous to worry, the universe laughed in my face and tore my life to shreds.

The second I put my hand on the door, ready to race inside, those swinging doors pushed open, and Noah was making his way back over to me.

My heart leaped in my chest, and I did a careful once-over, my shoulders sagging with relief when I determined he'd been untouched.

I could hear James's old truck turn over in the alleyway as Noah stepped out onto the sidewalk, the scowl on his face giving way to relief when his eyes moved up from the ground and landed on mine.

Strong, sturdy hands framed my face, his thumbs sweeping across my cheekbones. "Are you okay? What did he say to you? He didn't touch you, did he? I should've asked that before I let him go." His eyes flared.

"Fine," I breathed, now extremely aware of the fact that we were standing outside of the shop for everyone in this town to see. My hands circled his wrists. "Hey. No, he didn't— he didn't touch me. He was just..." I shivered, thinking once again about the way his eyes lingered on my chest. "Creepy."

A muscle in his jaw ticked. "I should've fired him that first day he looked at you funny."

"You shouldn't have fired him at all, Noah. I mean— What about the shop? I could've stayed away from him until he was done. You can't go another week without being open. What about the money?"

"I can and I will. I'll call around, see if I can get someone out sooner rather than later, but I don't give a shit about the money. I'll take the hit. He doesn't get to make you feel like that and keep his job. He's lucky that's the only repercussion."

"But—"

He cut me off. "No. *You* are non-negotiable."

I swallowed, trying to clear the knot of emotion tangling itself in my throat.

His mouth quirked. "I really wanna kiss that sweet look of surprise off of your face."

My heart tripped over itself. Everyone knew everyone in this town, and if they saw Noah kissing me, the word would spread through Rose Hill like wildfire during dry season. It would be fast and uncontrollable.

Granted, the way we were holding each other now wasn't exactly inconspicuous.

Despite the nerves, I managed a smile. "So do it," I challenged.

Both brows shot up in surprise, his eyes doing a quick scan of the street behind me. "You sure?"

"Yeah," I breathed, my eyes flickering down to his mouth right before it landed on mine.

I smiled against his lips, pushing away all of my concerns about the watchful eyes of this tight-knit town. I was so tired of letting the fear of judgment stop me from being happy. It almost killed me in Evergreen.

I wasn't giving anyone that power over me again.

Chapter 30

Noah

Two days.

The news of our kiss in front of the shop took two whole days to get to Avery. Honestly, I think that might've been the slowest news had ever traveled in this town.

But now my five-foot-two little sister was standing at my doorstep, the blood in her cheeks rivaling the color of her hair.

She reached out to slap my shoulder. "You kissed her!? You kissed her and I had to find out from *someone else?!*" Her voice was all high-pitched and squeaky, clearly pissed off, and a little hurt, despite how happy I knew she really was underneath it all. "I'm quite literally never going to live that one down, Noah! I found out from *Pamela*, who heard from Harvey, who heard from Barb. Mom and Dad know, too. I'm supposed to hear gossip about *other* people! I'm not supposed to hear gossip about my own brother *from* other people. I'm supposed to hear it from *you!*"

I yawned, scratching my bare chest with a mask of indifference.

At some point, I'd probably have to outgrow this urge to mess with my younger sister, but today wasn't that day.

"I don't kiss and tell, Ave."

With a roll of her eyes, she shoved her way into my house and aimed for the coffee pot on the counter.

"You kiss and tell *me*. I'm the exception to this rule. I have no social life. You have to tell me when interesting things happen. I'm like Tinkerbell." Avery poured herself a cup of coffee, snagging the creamer from the fridge. "I need drama like she needs applause. It's the air that I breathe." She sighed. "It's the only good thing about living in this town, honestly."

I lifted my coffee from the counter and took a sip. "I think you're taking this a little too seriously."

"You're not taking this seriously *enough*." She blew on her coffee and glared at me over the rim. "You kissed someone."

I sighed. "Yes, Avery. I did. And last I checked, my mouth and who it kisses is my own business."

Avery groaned but her features softened. "You kissed someone." She smiled and took a sip of coffee to distract from the tears misting over her eyes, then cleared her throat. "How are — I mean, shit. I don't know, Noah. All I've wanted is for you to be okay. Does this mean— Are you okay?"

Something in the sincerity of her voice drove away my desire to toy with her. I'd been a shit big brother since Adeline's death. In more ways than one, Avery acted as the more responsible sibling. She was the one with her head screwed on right. She didn't run when the going got tough; she picked herself up and got her life together.

Her concern hit me right in the gut.

A few weeks ago, I honestly don't think I would've been able to answer this question without lying. But today, when I thought back on all the secret kisses and shy smiles I'd coaxed out of Liv recently, telling my sister that I was finally okay was the complete and honest truth.

"Yeah, Ave. I'm okay. I'm better than okay."

Her shoulders seemed to relax marginally.

Who knew how many years I'd taken off of Avery's life by holing myself away and drinking myself into oblivion? I didn't know how to lean on people when I needed support. I only knew how to suffer in silence.

But Liv made me want to learn.

I couldn't preach to Liv that leaning on the people around her was okay if I hadn't been doing it myself.

Avery's lips rolled together a few times as she blinked furiously in an attempt to keep her tears at bay. "I'm just glad you have something good in your life again."

Turning to face my sister, I gently knocked my fist against her shoulder. "I had plenty of good in my life before Liv and Ken. I just think... I don't know. I was too stupid to see it. Too far gone."

Her mouth tugged into a small, knowing smile. "Well... I'm just glad you found your way back."

I smiled and took a sip of my drink, but the warmth that spread through me had nothing to do with the coffee.

Avery reached out and squeezed my arm. "You should bring her to Mom and Dad's tonight."

I gnawed on the inside of my cheek. "You don't think it's... too soon? You don't think she'll freak out?"

Avery shrugged. "It's apple picking day. Nellie's already out there. Obviously, she'd have to bring Ken. Market it as more of a friendly thing with her and Nell, just something to get them out of the house today." She paused, lifting her shoulder in another shrug. "If she thinks it's too soon and doesn't want to stay for dinner, they can leave after all the fun stuff."

She had a point.

The apple orchard toward the back of my parent's property had rows and rows of trees that were almost all ready to be picked. They did most of the picking on their own, but once or twice in the fall, we'd all go out there and spend hours picking every ripe apple from the trees.

Our "payment" was a lifetime supply of apple butter and apple pies every Sunday until they eventually ran out. It was something Avery and I had been doing since we were kids. Just like the lake day, Avery was adamant about continuing it with Nellie.

Avery slurped her coffee loudly, dragging me back to our conversation. "Just go ask her. Judging solely by the way she looks at you, she'll be just as excited to spend some more time with you as Kennedy will be to pick some apples."

"How does she look at me?" I hoped to god she couldn't see the eagerness that I felt stirring my gut play out across my face.

She rolled her eyes. "The same way you look at her."

I sighed. "Which is?"

"Like you both finally see the light at the end of a very dark tunnel."

Avery's observation hung in the air around us, and my chest tightened. Because that was exactly how I felt about Liv. She *was* the light at the end of the tunnel. The breath of fresh air. The break in the clouds after weeks and months of endless storms.

She was everything I needed and everything that I was terrified of.

As if sensing my thoughts, Avery softened her tone. "I know it's scary, but you both have been through so much. Try not to overthink it, okay?"

I offered her a smile and rubbed my hand over her hair. "No promises."

She shoved me away, leaning against the counter and doing a not-so-subtle sweep of my kitchen and living room. "I mean, Christ. Would it kill you to make a mess every once in a while? Someone could perform surgery on your countertops."

I followed her eye-line, knowing she was telling the truth.

Things around here certainly got a little less homey and a little more... sterile after Addie. In the days when I would find her in the simplest of things, I rid myself of every opportunity to be heartbroken. I got rid of her clothes, her perfumes, the air fresheners she'd dropped in every outlet around the house, and the one too many candles she bought every time we went to Target. I changed my laundry detergent, and even the hand soap in the bathrooms. I couldn't stand it.

Everything reminded me of her and every reminder of the life we used to live just sent me into a turmoil of broken emotions. Eventually... I just left. I bought a cabin out near Colt's place and tried to forget.

When I came back and found out it wasn't any easier three years later, I got rid of everything. Our bed, our sheets, and every piece of furniture that we collected during our time together, and replaced with something new.

My gaze trailed along the dark, wood floor that ran throughout the whole house until it landed on the living room. One sad beige couch sat in the middle of the room, aimed at the TV. There was a coffee table that I got from Pamela's thrift store about six months ago and a lamp next to the couch. Addie always hated using overhead lights. I guess it was just something that stuck.

Avery was right about the kitchen.

The stark white cabinetry and butcher block countertops lacked the warmth that they used to carry now that our stuff wasn't strewn all over them.

It was exactly how I wanted it.

Cold. Bare.

I sniffed and lifted my shoulder in a shrug. "It's minimal. Plus, I don't have a lot of stuff."

Avery hummed, drinking the last of her coffee while she took another judgmental look around my house. Her eyes flickered back over to me. "You're happy?"

My lips tilted into a grin. "Gettin' there."

She stared at me for a moment longer before nodding and placing her cup in the sink. "Good. See ya tonight. Thanks for the coffee." Avery strode by me and patted my shoulder, leaving almost as abruptly as she came.

* * *

An hour later, I was knocking on Liv's door. I thought about calling first... But if I had done that, I wouldn't have gotten the chance to witness that cute little look of surprise on her face when she opened the door and saw me standing there.

Her blue eyes were rounded with surprise as she gazed up at me, blonde hair twisted into her usual bun on the top of her head. Her usual oversized t-shirt was replaced with a thin, barely-there camisole and my mouth went dry as my gaze methodically traced every inch of her smooth, flawless skin. My eyes trailed the freckles on her shoulders and followed the slow blush moving up her neck until I met her eyes again. Fuck. Those tiny sleep shorts were going to be the death of me.

I watched the muscles in her throat work as she swallowed.

"Hey," I said quietly, flashing her a crooked smile.

"Hey," she breathed, a slow grin spreading across her lips.

I leaned casually against the door frame, crossing my arms over my chest. "You have any plans today?" I kept my voice down, hoping to steal a few more moments alone with Liv before Kennedy inevitably tackled me to the ground.

She let out a frustrated breath, rolling her eyes in irritation. "Screening calls from my mother-in-law, it seems."

"Do you plan on answering?" I asked.

Her mouth twisted from left to right as she contemplated her answer. "I don't know. I know that I need to let her talk to Kennedy or things will just get worse. But Ken's birthday is coming up in a couple months and she'll be wanting answers about that and I just— I don't have them. I don't know what we're going to do and I don't want her anger or resentment to influence my decision-making process. But I also know that my daughter needs her family."

I let out a deep sigh, trying to decide just how thin of a tightrope I was balancing on. Would I be overstepping if I spoke my truth?

She raised a brow at me.

"Permission to speak candidly?"

Liv scoffed with a smile. "At ease, soldier," she muttered sarcastically. "The floor is yours."

"I'm not gonna sit here and say that Kennedy doesn't need her family. The decisions you make will always be in her best interest. I know that. You know that. So maybe Kennedy needs her family, but what she really needs most is a happy mom. And if Debra steals even an ounce of the happiness you have reserved for your daughter, don't answer the phone."

I bit my tongue and waited with bated breath while Liv's eyes raked over my face.

She was silent for a beat longer before her lips curled into a thoughtful smile. "You know," she started, "you have this amazing ability to make every seemingly complicated decision in my life sound so simple."

I shrugged. "It's not that they're simple." Lifting my hand, I brushed my fingers against her cheekbone. She leaned into my touch. "You've spent a long time putting everyone's feelings ahead of your own. And I know that you'll always put Kennedy first, but sweetheart, you gotta *at least* start putting yourself second. You can't pour from an empty cup."

Liv's eyes held mine with a mixture of vulnerability and gratitude. "There you go again." Her voice was strained as she let out a watery laugh. "Making everything sound so simple."

My thumb traced a path along the freckles on her cheek. "That part *is* simple."

I glanced over her shoulder to make sure that Kennedy hadn't magically appeared, then leaned down, and brushed a kiss against her lips.

Her hand moved to the back of my neck and slid into my hair as she pulled my mouth back to hers. "Thank you," she mumbled against my lips.

Liv pressed her body against me, each soft, supple curve melting into the contours of mine. My hands slid down her waist and settled on her hips, fingers digging into the painfully thin fabric of her shorts. My thumbs grazed the small amount of skin left exposed on her side and I resisted the urge to let them feel *more*.

It was so easy to let the world around us fade to nothing, but the moment we started to drift a little too far, Kennedy was always just around the corner, ready to pull us back.

"Mommy!"

Liv pulled back quickly, pressing her fingertips to her lips as she bit back a smile. "Yeah?"

"Gigi is calling again. Can I answer it?"

She closed her eyes, her chest expanding as she drew in a long breath. "Sure!" she finally called out, slapping on a wide grin, one that dripped with annoyance and sarcasm.

Her hand lifted, and she massaged the bridge of her nose. "I'm sure you didn't come by to listen to me complain about my mother-in-law." Liv chuckled and dropped her hand back to her side. "What's up?"

"Well," I started, resuming my previous position against the door frame. "First things first, I'd listen to just about anything that came out of that pretty mouth, Liv."

I paused just long enough to enjoy the deepening shade of pink stretched across her cheeks and nose.

"But you're right, I did come to ask you something else. Would you and Ken be interested in picking some apples today? My parents have an orchard toward the back of their land. We go out once or twice in the fall to collect as many as we can and make a whole day out of it. Apple pie, apple butter, apples in the salad at dinner. Basically apple everything until you can't eat it anymore."

I flashed her a grin and tacked on the last bit of important information. "Avery—and my parents— were wondering if you two would like to come over for dinner tonight when the picking is done."

There was a brief flash of surprise and panic in her eyes. "Your parents?" She squeaked out.

"I promise, it's not as scary as it seems. Word travels… fast around this town, as I'm sure you can imagine. They'd like to meet the woman everyone can't stop talking about."

Liv scoffed. "You mean the woman you were caught kissing in the middle of town in broad daylight two days ago."

My smile grew. "There's that, too."

The hesitation was there, the nerves too. I half expected her to say no. Maybe more than half. Her lips twisted from left to right as she contemplated her answer.

"Listen," I said gently, lifting my hand to cup her chin. "There's no pressure. You guys can come out for the day, pick some apples, and leave before dinner. Or you can stay."

"Are you— Do you *want* us to stay for dinner?"

"Of course I do. Liv, I know that this is new and I know that neither of us is in the place to rush into anything and I'm not asking for that. But—" I paused, the words I wanted to say getting twisted on the tip of my tongue. My hand dropped from her face, and I scrubbed it over my beard.

I'd spent too many years keeping my emotions under lock and key, and now that I needed them, it was like the skills that I needed to properly express what I was feeling had atrophied from lack of use.

Somehow, I think she knew, and my heart clenched at the patience in her eyes.

Liv's gaze softened as she looked at me. "But what?" she asked, her voice quiet, almost vulnerable.

"But," I continued, clearing my throat. I could feel my cheeks warm as I sorted through the jumbled words in my head. "I want you to know that I care about you and Kennedy. And I'd like the chance to get to know you both better. If you're comfortable with it, I'd love for you to meet my parents. They're good people, and I think you'll like them. But most importantly, I just want to spend time with you. And I'll take that however I can get it."

Liv took a moment to consider, her eyes searching mine for sincerity. "What if they don't think I'm good enough for you? I mean, they're gonna ask questions— if they don't already know why I came to town and—" Her voice grew small. "What if they think I'm too... damaged? Or what if they don't think you should be with someone who has a kid?"

My brows pulled together as her teeth worried her bottom lip. "Do you actually believe those things?"

A deep sigh punched from her lungs, her shoulders falling with what looked like defeat, and I instantly understood that Debra was to blame for this. How many times had she made her feel like she wasn't capable of being an extraordinary human being despite the wounds inside of her? Or that no one would want her and Kennedy?

Anger simmered in my blood, my fingers flexing at my side. I took a long, fortifying breath. "Liv," I said earnestly, "Avery and I, we're like the definition of damaged. They're not going to judge you for your past or make you feel like you're anything less than the incredible woman and mother you are. You're strong, resilient, and loving, and those are the qualities that matter."

I bent a little at the waist, dropping to her eye-line. "And they don't have Debra in their ear like you do whispering a bunch of bullshit that couldn't be further from the truth."

Defeat settled a little deeper into her muscles. "Why do I let her do that?"

"Because you are every bit of good that she is not."

I stood, snagging her hand and tucking her into my chest. "There's no pressure. It's whatever you wanna do. Promise. Just apple picking? I'll bring you back before dusk. But if you guys do decide to stay for dinner, and my parents get to meet two incredible ladies I've come to care about, I have no doubt they'll be just as blown away as I am."

Her arms slid around my waist as she sighed into my t-shirt. "Thank you," She mumbled against my chest. Her chin lifted and landed on my sternum as she glanced up at me. "At what point do we stop doing this?"

"Doing what?"

"Bringing each other to the point of tears."

I chuckled and gently ran my hand up the arch of her spine. "Maybe when it starts snowing and the weather starts giving us something to talk about instead of our feelings."

Liv snorted. "I can't wait for that day."

Kennedy laughed at something from the living room, and Liv reluctantly stepped out of my arms at the reminder that her daughter was just a room away.

She pulled her bottom lip between her teeth. "You'll bring us back if I get too nervous?"

"In a heartbeat."

"Okay," she breathed, pulling her shoulders back and standing tall. "I just need twenty minutes, and then we'll meet you out front."

I couldn't stop the grin that stretched across my lips, matching the excitement that bloomed in my chest. "See you in twenty."

Chapter 31

Olivia

I was antsy.

It was the good kind of antsy. The kind that fluttered softly through my stomach and grazed across my skin in little sparks of electricity. Honestly, I had no clue if I would stick around long enough to meet Noah's parents. The thought was terrifying.

He turned off of the main road and the asphalt underneath us shifted to loose gravel as we crawled down a long driveway. I smoothed down the skirt of my sundress, drying my sweaty palms as Kennedy sang loudly to the song on the radio from the backseat.

I could feel his eyes on me. Every time my hands swept over my dress, or I shifted nervously in my seat, his gaze would linger. His hand flexed where it rested on the center console like he had to physically retrain himself from reaching over to settle my nerves.

He'd also reminded me several times on the thirty-or-so-minute drive that he would take me home the second I wanted to leave and that there was no pressure to meet anyone I didn't want to. I was still on the fence, but I dressed the part just to be safe.

I couldn't remember the last time I'd worn a dress. It wasn't anything special, but it made me feel… pretty. Feminine. It was a soft pink color made of a light, flowy cotton fabric that fell just below my knees. I paired it with a simple set of open-toed sandals that also hadn't seen the light of day since my move from

Wyoming.

It took me longer than my predicted twenty minutes to get myself and Kennedy ready, but Noah was patient. By the time I'd changed my outfit four times and applied some makeup to my normally bare face, almost forty minutes had gone by.

Given the way his eyes flared when I stepped outside, it was worth it.

I could tell he was struggling to keep his hands off of me and I kind of loved it.

We slowly edged over the hill, and his childhood home came into view. I smiled, leaning forward to soak it all up.

His parents' house was nestled among tall trees, surrounded by a well-kept garden. There were wildflowers planted all along the right side of the house, surrounded by a white picket fence but divided up the middle by a little dirt path.

The weathered, wooden exterior was a warm shade of honey and had vines of ivy crawling up the front and along the sides. There was a large, welcoming porch that wrapped toward the back of the house and ended with a little wooden swing that rocked in the breeze.

A dark red barn rested a little further back on the property, surrounded by a thick, wooden fence, and inside— I gasped, sitting forward a little as Noah drove toward the end of the gravel driveway. "Goats?! Your parents have goats?!"

He let out a soft chuckle, maneuvering his truck around a smaller, older truck and a car that I knew belonged to Avery before he stopped and parked behind a golf cart.

"*Goats?!*" Kennedy shrieked, and I flinched, covering my ears.

"You're gonna scare them away if you keep screaming like that," I teased.

Noah released my seat belt and then his. "I don't think she was any louder than you." He winked as he climbed out of his truck and I rolled my eyes with a grin.

I slid out and pulled Kennedy's door open, her little legs tapping with excitement as she waited for me to unfasten her from the car seat.

"Ready to pick some apples?"

She beamed up at me and squealed. "Yes!"

I laughed and set her down, Noah moving to my side.

"So this is where you grew up, huh?" I took another look around, scanning the trees and the fields that ran behind them. I could hear the chickens clucking and the faint, faint sound of babbling water in the distance.

Noah's family had their own little slice of paradise here in Delaware.

His eyes followed the same path as mine, a small smile tugging at his mouth like he was thinking the same thing.

"This is it."

"It's beautiful."

"It is."

Someone stirred in the house, a curtain falling back into place and catching my eye. My stomach churned nervously. I knew from a few brief conversations with Noah that he didn't come out here much. I hated thinking that I was keeping him from seeing his parents.

Clearing my throat, I nudged him with my elbow. "It's okay—" I paused, jerking my head toward the house. "If they wanna come out and see you. It's okay."

He smiled softly and once again, that urge to reach out was back, but with Kennedy right there, I knew we both needed to keep our distance. "It's not me they want to see, trust me."

My cheeks warmed. "Careful. It's starting to sound a lot like you oversold me."

He blew out a breath, gentle eyes mapping out every inch of my flushing face. "I've been very careful to respect your privacy when it comes to them," Noah said softly. "So any positive opinion they have formed about you is something they've heard from someone in town... Or Nellie. That girl talks about you and Kennedy nonstop." His index finger tapped against my chin. "Don't undersell yourself."

Kennedy tugged on Noah's jeans. "Can we go pick apples now?"

He rustled her hair. "We sure can, kiddo. Grab one of those buckets over there—" He pointed to a stack of wooden buckets sitting next to the golf cart. "We're gonna take the cart out to the orchard. Avery and Nell are waiting for us out there."

She grinned and skipped over, grabbing each of us a bucket and struggling under the weight as she moved them to the golf cart.

I stood back and watched as Noah followed behind Kennedy, chuckling as he took the buckets out of her hands.

"How many apples do you think you're gonna pick?" he asked, setting them down on the back of the golf cart and looping some kind of rope around them to keep them in place.

Kennedy tapped her finger against her chin as she thought carefully. "Probably a thousand."

"Whoa!" Noah laughed, extending his hand and helping Kennedy onto the golf cart. "That's a lot."

"I can do it," she stated confidently.

He tousled her hair again. "I know you can."

I smiled and gleaming hazel eyes met mine with a warm grin. "You comin'?"

"Absolutely," I replied, excitement for the day ahead bubbling inside me as I climbed onto the golf cart.

* * *

The ride back to the orchard was a lot shorter than I thought it would be. We followed a dirt path worn through the bright green grass, the seemingly permanent smile on my lips only growing when I imagined Avery and Noah coming down this same path as children, doing the exact same thing back then that we were planning on doing today.

My smile faltered a little when I pictured Noah bringing Adeline back here. They'd been together for just as long as Liam and I had, and a small part of me felt like an intruder. I could see her sitting in this exact spot next to him, her hair blowing in the wind as they drove out with his parents, prepared to spend the whole day together.

Would my being here infringe on the precious memories he had of her? I couldn't help but wonder if he ever looked at me and saw all the ways in which I couldn't quite measure up to the woman he'd loved for so long. The thought nagged at me like an itch I couldn't scratch.

But then I glanced at Kennedy, her eyes shining with excitement, and Noah's easy smile as he navigated the cart down the path. I listened to their conversation and their laughs, and I pushed those doubts aside. It was easy to let myself fall into a dark place riddled with self-doubt, but the truth was... I would never be Adeline. Whatever feelings Noah had for me might not ever compare to how he felt about his wife, and that was okay.

I wasn't here to replace her. Just like he wasn't here to replace Liam. All we could do was create our own place and find our own way.

Judging by the smile on his face, he wasn't interested in making these comparisons I was attempting to force onto myself.

Instead, I turned my focus onto the drive as the mid-morning sun filtered through tall trees. I tilted my head back, enjoying the breeze through my hair and the warmth of the sun on my face.

The golf cart slowly came to a stop after another minute or so, Nellie's laughter reaching our ears before we even saw her.

There were rows and rows of apple trees lined up before us, surrounded by a wooden fence. There was a small, worn sign that read "Kent Orchard" on the gate and another stack of wooden pails ready to be filled.

Nellie emerged from behind a particularly leafy apple tree, her face beaming with excitement as she waved enthusiastically.

"Hey!" Nellie called out, her voice carrying through the orchard. "Took you guys long enough!" She sprinted toward the fence, hopping up on the bottom rail. "Kennedy I found a worm in one of the apples! You gotta come look."

Noah and Kennedy exchanged grins, and she climbed over me, practically jumping off the cart, eager to join her friend. The two girls met in a whirlwind of giggles and excited chatter like they hadn't seen each other in weeks rather than just a day or two.

Avery ducked under a branch and stood, wiping sweat from her forehead. "Jesus, I thought we were gonna have to pick this whole orchard ourselves."

I looked around, taking it all in.

Noah's parents truly did have a ton of land. It sprawled for acres, each corner harboring something different. They really made the most of it.

He rolled his eyes at his sister and hopped off of the cart, walking around the back to grab the extra buckets we'd brought with us.

Nellie and Kennedy took off and disappeared through a row of trees. I stood quickly, trying to keep her in my line of sight.

Avery glanced over her shoulder with a roll of her eyes. "I got 'em. You guys catch up when you can! Hi, bye!" She took off in the direction the girls went, and after just a second, I couldn't see her anymore either.

"I don't know what I would do without your sister," I said with a laugh.

Noah lifted a pail in my direction. "You and me both."

I took in a deep breath of fresh air and grabbed my bucket.

"Ready?"

I grinned. "Let's go get some apples."

* * *

"I'm totally beating you," I teased, reaching up and snagging another firm apple from a tree branch.

Noah scoffed from a few trees over, a few thunks following the noise as he tossed more apples into his bucket. "In your dreams, Brooks. I've been doing this since I was in diapers. Plus," he paused, tossing in a few more apples. "You can't even reach past the first branch."

I laughed, proving him wrong by snagging a few apples from the branch just above the lowest one. "You know, this orchard I went to back home had a step stool you could carry around with you. You might wanna bring that up to management." I bent over and grabbed my bucket, dipping below a branch and stepping out into the row between trees.

I wasn't exactly sure how far we'd ventured from the front gate, but we would have to turn back soon to empty our buckets.

"I'll make sure to put that in the suggestion box," he teased, ducking underneath a branch and slowly stepping out from the cover of the leaves. Noah's bucket thudded against the ground, and he wiped his hands against his jeans. "Sounds like a liability to you, though. I don't think I've ever seen you walk a straight line without tripping over your own feet."

Grinning, I made a show of carefully placing one foot in front of the other, my arms extended out from my sides, as I made my way over to where he stood. "I'll have you know, I have mastered the art of graceful stumbling. It's a skill that takes years to perfect."

Noah chuckled, leaning over and snagging an apple from his bucket. He inspected it closely before shining it on his shirt and taking a bite. My eyes fell to his mouth, his tongue swiping out to catch a droplet of juice that lingered on his bottom lip.

How the hell did he make something like eating an apple look so fucking attractive? I watched as the muscles in his jaw feathered as he chewed, hazel eyes staying locked on mine. The green was more noticeable today than the warm whiskey color.

Maybe it was the grass and trees surrounding us sharing some of their pigment. Maybe it was the light happiness of being here at his family's orchard and doing something so familiar and close to his heart. Whatever it was, his eyes shone with an extra layer of vibrancy that warmed through me after each smile.

I did a quick scan of our surroundings to make sure the girls hadn't managed to sneak up on us, then took another step closer. "You know," I said softly, taking another step so I could feel the warmth of his body against mine. "We're alone."

Noah's eyes flickered to my lips, lingering for a moment before he lifted his gaze back to mine. "We are," he responded, lifting the apple-free hand to toy with a piece of hair that framed my face.

I had no idea how he did it, how he made me feel all of these beautiful and scary things. His fingers trailed the curve where my shoulder met my throat and I shuddered, feeling this budding warmth blossom on the skin just beneath his touch.

His finger wandered up the length of my neck, his eyes following with rapt attention and I knew he was watching the blood crawl up my skin and flood my cheeks.

Normally, I hated the attention it brought to me. Right now, I loved the way it kept his eyes on me.

His palm settled just below my jawline, and the way his lips quirked into a smile told me he could feel the frantic rhythm of my pulse.

Noah continued to hold my gaze as he raised the apple in his hand, letting it hover just above my lips. I could smell the sweet, crisp aroma, my mouth watering as I imagined the taste on my tongue.

His eyes flared when I licked my lips, and my heart stuttered in my chest, a rush of heated electricity surging through me. His voice, a deep, velvety murmur, caressed my skin like a gentle touch. "Want a bite?" he asked.

I offered a gentle nod, trying to wrap my head around how something so simple could feel so intimate and bold. His smirk only deepened as he brought the apple closer to my waiting lips, my breath catching in my throat as his thumb trailed along my jawline and rested on my chin. With a gentle tug, he parted my lips, the apple's smooth skin brushing against them.

My teeth sank into the fruit, and its sweet, slightly tart flavor exploded on my tongue. Noah's darkened eyes remained fixed on me as I chewed, lingering at the corner of my mouth where I felt a droplet of juice slowly trickling down my chin.

He waited and watched, his gaze flickering back up to mine after I swallowed.

"Don't get me wrong," I breathed, "I think it is very sweet of you to ask before you kiss me... But Noah, how long do we have to be doing this before you just take what you want?"

He moved so quickly that my mind didn't even register what was happening at first.

The discarded apple landed in the soil and grass by our feet with a thump. His hands squeezed at my sides, the fabric of my dress bunching in his fists as his mouth landed on mine.

I smiled against his lips, my hands sifting into his hair, want spreading through my body like molasses, sticky and sweet as it moved through my bloodstream.

I would never tire of this. The way his body felt against mine or the way his tongue would always sweep so gently against my mouth, seeking something that I was so willing to give.

His hand glided up my waist and then the arch of my spine. I was hot all over, and my pulse was fluttering. I was burning from his touch, his taste, and the groan building in his chest.

Noah eased me back into one of the trees, soft leaves tickling my arms as we disappeared through the low-hanging branches. The rough bark scratched against the skin left exposed by my dress, but I didn't care. I only wanted more.

We were a mess of tangled, searching limbs and gasping breaths, his fingers bruising against my hips as my nails scraped his scalp.

Eventually, we came up for air, but Noah dipped down, his mouth hot against my throat, choosing my skin over the air in his lungs. His teeth nipped at my collarbone and a moan slipped through my lips as heat pooled between my thighs.

"*Fuck*, Liv." His curse was muffled against my throat as he worked his way back up to my mouth. Noah's hands smoothed their way down my body, then slid down my thighs and lifted, pressing me against the tree.

All of the softest parts of me were melded to the hardest parts of him, his hips rocking into mine and I was dissolved into nothing but liquid heat. My mouth searched for Noah's, hot and hungry before he swallowed the whimper building in my throat.

I moaned when he pulled my bottom lip between his teeth and then soothed the bite with a swipe of his tongue, stealing my thoughts as he pressed into me.

His hands were rough on my hips, his mouth angling over mine. Noah was everywhere all at once, each touch setting off a chain reaction inside of me. It'd been a long time since I'd felt this desperate for someone, my mind spinning with each frantic and fevered touch.

I wanted to erase the space and fabric between us, to slide my hands against the taut muscles under his shirt. A needy fog blanketed my brain and I moved against him, chasing a friction that was just out of my grasp.

His mouth pulled away from mine and I whimpered at the loss, my eyes pressed shut, head thrown back against the tree.

In my haze, I felt his mouth against my ear, his mumbled words taking a second to register. "Avery's coming."

My head snapped up, my eyes peeled open, and I heard what he said, but all I could focus on was the warmth of his hands on my ass.

"I gotta set you down," he warned with a chuckle, and my ankles uncrossed as he lowered me back to the ground.

I frantically swiped at my dress, smoothing out the rumpled fabric, Noah's cheeks flushed a deep red.

He reached down to adjust himself and an almost hysterical giggle bubbled out of my mouth. My lips were swollen, and my hair was tangled and sprinkled with bark from the tree. My left shoe was gone?

We looked like a mess.

His hair was sticking out in ten different directions, disheveled and tangled from my fingers. I laughed again as he combed his hand through it in an attempt to get it under control.

He pinched my side with a grin. "Turn around so I can fix your hair."

I heard Avery call out Noah's name, thanking the gods above that she was still several rows away.

I turned, and Noah's fingers expertly untangled my hair, swiping any lingering tree bark away.

"Fuck, Liv. I'm sorry. Why didn't you say something?"

"What?" I asked, turning to look over my shoulder.

His index finger trailed down my back. "Your back's raw."

I chuckled softly, vaguely remembering the bite of the bark against my skin. "I was a little distracted."

He grinned against my shoulder before pressing a light kiss to the scratches on my back. The tenderness of his lips sent a shiver down my spine, and I couldn't help but lean into his touch.

Avery's voice grew closer, and I twisted in his arms. We exchanged a knowing look before Noah whispered, "We should probably get back before my parents send out a search party for us."

I nodded, reluctantly pulling away from his warm embrace, my body still thrumming with need. My legs felt shaky, and my brain was still a little foggy, but I couldn't stop the grin that spread across my lips.

Just a few months before, I was wishing away the days. I would wake up in the morning and find myself craving the fall of night and the comfort of my bed. Every day was too long.

The more time we spent together, though, the more and more I found myself cursing the sun when it slowly dipped into the horizon. I hated when our breakfasts came to an end or when he dropped us off at my door after work.

Every moment felt too short-lived. There wasn't enough time in the day to learn all the things about him that I wanted to.

Noah's hand was heavy on my back as he led me through the tree branches and out into the open, our secret moment no longer protected by the cover of the leaves.

I slid my sandal on and looked down at the now browning apple that we shared with a grin. "You wasted a perfectly good apple on that kiss... I hope it was worth it."

He grinned and pressed a kiss to my temple. "Always."

Chapter 32

Noah

The sun had disappeared into the horizon, the last bit of reds and oranges bleeding into a dark navy sky as we made our way back from the orchard. My dad swung by about twenty minutes ago to collect our harvest, Avery and Liv taking the girls back out to grab one last bucket before we called it a night.

I knew Liv was still on the fence about meeting my parents, so I figured one last chance to fill a bucket would keep them away long enough to help my dad load up the back of his truck.

Kennedy sat wedged between me and Liv in the front, and Avery and Nellie sat in the back chatting about the first thing they were going to make with their apples. I smiled to myself as we rounded the gravel pathway that led back to the house, this sense of normalcy settling into my chest. Everything felt... right.

My dad was still warming up to my presence around the house again, but I'd give him as much time as he needed. I understood now just how hard it was on him when I checked out. I hated knowing I hurt the people I loved while trying to process my grief. Based on the snide comments and the look of surprise on his face whenever I walked through the door, it was just going to take time to convince him I was around to stay.

I smiled as I glanced down at Liv and Kennedy, both of them engrossed in animated conversation. Liv's smile was warm and genuine, and it filled me with a sense of contentment.

The house slowly came into view; the once sun-lit path now illuminated by solar-powered path lights. The porch was bathed in the soft glow of the wall sconces, my mother's silhouette moving through the house while she prepared dinner.

I came to a stop by my truck, Avery grabbing the last batch of apples and balancing the bucket on her hip. "See you guys inside?" It was hard to miss the edge of excitement in her tone, but I didn't want Liv to feel any pressure to come inside if she didn't want to.

There was a pause, Liv worrying her bottom lip for a moment.

"Are we going inside, mommy?" She looked down at Kennedy's hopeful eyes, and I saw the second she caved.

She was still a little apprehensive, but with the prospect of apple pie hanging in the air, I also knew she wouldn't want to disappoint Ken by going home.

"Sure," Liv answered, her lips curling into the sweetest smile. "You guys go ahead, I'm gonna grab something out of Noah's truck."

Nellie squealed and grabbed Kennedy's hand, dragging her toward the house.

Avery turned to look over her shoulder; her brow lifted as her eyes shifted between Liv and me. "Behave, you two."

Avery's comment earned a light chuckle from the both of us, the flush in Liv's cheeks visible beneath the moonlight. "Always," I replied.

As the girls disappeared into the house, their laughter and excited chatter fading into the background, Liv and I were left standing by the truck in the quiet evening air. It was a moment of stillness, and I took the opportunity to close the gap between us, my hand finding hers.

Her hair shifted in the breeze, tiny goosebumps erupted across her skin as she shivered, and my mind flashed back to the moment we shared earlier, the way she shuddered beneath my touch. I could feel her nails gently scratching my scalp, the warmth of her body pressed against mine.

It was so easy to get pulled back into the moment, to let the warmth of her sweet, vanilla perfume wrap around me and pull me under. I wanted to lose myself in Liv and forget to come up for air.

"You better lose that look on your face," she smirked while running her nails up my arms, letting her own arms drape loosely over my shoulders. "We were told to behave."

I grinned, settling my hands low on her hips. I wanted to fill every second of alone time we had with my hands on her body and her lips against mine. I didn't want to behave.

I wanted to press her against my truck and feel her melt against me. I wanted to feel the way her pulse kicked up and hear her breath catch in her throat.

Liv brushed her lips against the corner of my mouth. "Come on, Casanova. I need to make a good first impression. Plus, I already have points docked for the scratches on my back." Her arms dropped to her sides, but my fingers remained curled around the fabric of her dress.

"My mother already loves you," I noted, remembering the way her eyes lit up every time Liv's name was spoken the last time I was here.

"Because I had a small part in extending your vocabulary from caveman grunts to full sentences," she teased.

"Alright." I jabbed my finger into her side, and she squealed, twisting to get out of the way. "That's enough out of you."

Liv laughed as I unlocked my truck and grabbed a worn crew neck sweatshirt with Kent Automotive printed across the chest. I shut the door and held it out to her. "To cover the scratches."

Her lips quirked into a smile. "I don't wanna look frumpy." Bunching up the sweatshirt, I took a step closer and pulled it over her head. "You could never." Liv rolled her eyes and wiggled her arms through the sleeves.

I couldn't help but smile as she settled into the sweatshirt, running her hands over the front to smooth it down. The word frumpy wasn't even in my vocabulary when it came to her.

I grabbed a handful of fabric and gave in to the surge of possessiveness that rushed through me, tugging her to my chest. I always told myself those sleep shorts were going to be my undoing. But seeing her in something of mine unraveled me in the best way.

My lips found hers in a soft, lingering kiss, and I nearly groaned at the way she softened against me. Liv sighed against my mouth, her fingers curling into my shirt as the night around us faded into nothing.

I no longer heard the crickets in the grass or the barn owl that screeched in the distance. All five of my senses were redirected from the world around us and honed into her.

The taste of her lips, the scent of her perfume, the warmth of her body pressed against mine, the gentle sound of her breath, and the way her fingers traced over my skin all combined to create an intoxicating symphony I never wanted to end.

Time seemed to stand still, as if the universe finally felt compelled to give us one little uninterrupted moment together. But reality eventually called us back, and with a reluctant sigh, we pulled away, our foreheads still touching as we caught our breath.

Liv whispered, "We should go inside." And I knew she was right, but I couldn't get myself to move, to surrender this moment with her.

"We should," I replied softly, my shoulders falling slightly as the screen door creaked open. So much for being uninterrupted.

I stepped away from Liv and peered over the bed of my truck, my mother waiting at the door with her arms crossed and an eyebrow arched to the heavens.

She rolled her eyes and shook her head in a playful manner, slinging that dish towel over her shoulder as she pushed away from the door frame and walked back inside.

"Ready?" I looked over at Liv with a smile.

"Ready."

She was nervous. Her hands shook, and the smile on her face faltered, but she took a deep, steadying breath and put one foot in front of the other. Knowing she didn't want to be affectionate in front of Kennedy quite yet, I reached over to squeeze her hand one time in silent reassurance, then trailed closely behind her as we made our way up to the house.

"Oh, before we go in." I cleared my throat and peered around her to make sure the coast was clear. "Ignore anything... Untoward that comes out of my father's mouth."

Liv twisted to look at me, her eyes widening with a flash of panic. "Does he already not like me?" she demanded in a hushed voice.

"What? That's not— No, that's not what I'm insinuating." I let out a humorless laugh. "It's me he doesn't like right now."

Her brows furrowed. "Did something happen?"

I sighed, running my fingers through my hair. "Nothing big. Just a lot of little things. After Addie died, I didn't know how to grieve. I only came around when I needed something, and it hurt my mom. I think he's just waiting for me to disappear again."

She offered a warm smile, reaching over to squeeze my hand. "I'm sorry. Grief is... Impossible. You did the best you could. He'll come around."

I wasn't sure about either of those things, but I kept that to myself.

Liv smiled sweetly, her fingers sweeping gently against my cheek. "We should go inside before we get in trouble."

I dipped my chin and gestured for her to lead the way, hoping my dad could keep this resentment he held toward me in check for just one night.

I pulled the old screen door open for Liv, the hinges creaking loudly. Everyone's heads turned as she stepped through the threshold, a ripple of silence running through the room.

My dad was off to the left in the living room, his feet reclined in his old La-Z-Boy with a ball game playing softly in the background. Avery sat at the dining room table, slowly peeling a freshly rinsed bowl of apples.

Liv slid off her sandals, her hands wringing together as she looked around. There was a softness in her eyes as she took it all in, a small smile tugging at her lips.

Mom poked her head over a tall bucket of apples on the counter, and I could tell she was trying to rein in her excitement. Her eyes lit up, her cheeks rounding as the smile she was trying desperately to conceal warmed her face. "You must be Olivia."

Liv nodded and lifted her hand in a small wave. "Hi, Mrs. Kent. It's so great to finally meet you!"

Just like I knew she would, my mother waved Liv off and made her way around the counter. "Please. Everyone around here calls me Jo. We're normally a huggin' kind of family if that's alright with you." She walked over to Liv with open arms, and after the slightest hesitation, Liv accepted her embrace.

I met my mom's watery eyes over Liv's shoulders and gave a small smile as my dad's recliner creaked, heavy footsteps making their way over to where we stood.

He stood next to my mother, nodding in my direction. "Son."

"Hey, Dad."

Liv took a step away and looked over to greet him. "Mr. Kent, hi! I'm Olivia. It's so nice to meet you."

She extended her hand in his direction. There was a pause.

Realistically, I knew this pause only existed for a brief moment of time. Half a second at most. But I held a breath in my lungs and the seconds seemed to stretch out for an eternity.

I could only hope that he wouldn't treat her with the same disregard that he felt toward me.

Then his hand wrapped around hers, and a warm smile that hadn't been aimed in my direction for *years* graced his lips. My shoulders relaxed, and I blew out a gentle sigh of relief.

"Olivia. Welcome to our home. And please, call me Otto."

Liv's gaze bounced back and forth between my parents. "Well... Jo, Otto, thank you so much for letting us be a part of this day." Her eyes flickered over to where Kennedy and Nellie stood by the sink rinsing apples. "Kennedy had a lot of fun, so I really appreciate it."

My mom tossed her hand towel over her shoulder. "You two are welcome anytime! Now," she paused and cast a glance around the room. "Do you want peeling duty or chopping duty?"

Liv looked over at me with a smile. "Whatever gets me put with you. I want all the embarrassing middle school stories." She winked and my mom let out a loud laugh, her hands resting over her heart.

She grabbed Liv by the hand and towed her to the kitchen. "Chopping duty it is!"

I watched as she leaned down a pressed a kiss to the top of Kennedy's head and then turned to my mom, accepting the apron in her outstretched hands. She looked ridiculous with my sweatshirt covering most of her dress and the "No Bitchin' in Grandma's Kitchen" apron, but I knew I wouldn't be able to poke fun at her even if I tried. There was nothing in my smile but adoration as I watched her fit so seamlessly into the family I'd been tiptoeing around for years.

My dad stepped up next to me, just an inch taller than my six-foot-three, and crossed his arms over his wide chest. I'd listened to everyone in this town tell me over and over again while I was growing up that I looked just like him and I never believed it until I hit my twenties.

Now, in my thirties, I saw it even more. I saw it in the harsh lines on my face and the few strands of gray hair sprinkled through the dark brown. I saw it in the way I stood and in the way I laughed.

I knew when he was trying to be intimidating, and I knew when he was trying to be approachable.

Right now, I didn't necessarily think he was trying to be either of those things. But he didn't walk away... So that told me he was trying *something*.

He gently cleared his throat. Loud enough for me to know that he wanted my attention but low enough that the other ears in the room didn't pick up on it. "So," he started softly.

Dad's eyes flickered over to mine and then back to Liv. "She's the one that brought you back, huh?"

My throat constricted, and I swallowed, trying to clear past the emotion weighing my words down. "I didn't ever really leave, Dad."

His chest expanded slowly, then fell with a deep sigh. "Maybe. But... Before—" He paused, a ghost of a smile tilting his lips up. "We couldn't get you to leave. Son, you've seen us maybe three times since Addie died." He nodded in Liv's direction. "She shows up in July, and you've been out three times just since then. That means something."

I let my gaze wander over to Liv again, letting the weight of his words sink in. They hung heavy in the air around us, and it was hard to deny the truth of it all. It was like I'd been living in a haze for years, comfortable in the misery, but then she came along and everything was clear again. The fog had been lifted, and this life that I'd been living of going through the motions just wasn't enough.

I thought that I was content. I thought that it was what I deserved, but now that she was here... I just wanted more.

I was tired of the disappointed sighs and the sad eyes.

Liv made it easier to breathe, easier to smile.

She made me want to live again.

Dad's eyes softened as he watched me. "Noah," he said gently, breaking the silence between us but keeping his voice low, "it's good to see you smiling again.

Your mom and I, we've missed that."

I nodded, the tightness in my chest slowly dissipating. "I've missed it too." It was a simple admission but one that had taken years to utter.

Dad clapped a hand on my shoulder, a rare display of affection. He cleared his throat again and tugged at the hem of his T-shirt. I knew this conversation probably wasn't an easy one for him to have and the nervous fidgeting made it very obvious. "It's never too late to come home. Just don't disappear again." His eyes moved back to the kitchen, warming when he finally settled on my mother. "I don't think she would survive it."

I knew he wasn't saying that lightly. It wasn't an insult or a jab in an attempt to make me feel guilty. It was the truth. But I knew I wasn't going anywhere any time soon.

Dad clapped me on the back once more. "Well, go on. I've got a game to watch. Join 'em in the kitchen. It looks like they could use some help with those apples. You guys did good this year."

I nodded, a sense of warmth and belonging filling me as I headed toward the kitchen. Liv glanced up, her eyes brightening as she saw me approach.

"Looks like you guys have been accepted into the Kent family fold," I teased as I joined them at the counter. Kennedy stood at the sink with Nellie, rinsing apples and then tossing them into a colander to dry.

Liv grinned, her hands still busy with the apple peeler. She tucked her chin into her chest as her cheeks filled with color. "Well, it's a great place to be."

I smiled and snagged an apron from a hook by the fridge, joining Liv and the rest of the family at the kitchen counter.

We worked together, peeling and chopping apples, swapping pointless stories, and sharing laughter. It was a simple night, but it held a profound significance.

As we prepared the apples for pies, I stole glances at Liv. She seemed at ease, chatting with my mother and sister as if she had always been a part of our lives. The sleeves of my sweatshirt rolled up and bunched around her elbows, her hair slowly falling out of the hair tie Avery had tossed her way. Her presence brought a warmth and lightness to the room that had been missing for far too long.

Kennedy, who had been somewhat reserved earlier, started to open up to Mom. They exchanged stories about school, the goats in the barn, and much to

Liv's dismay, her lack of cooking skills.

Liv fell into place here so easily.

In the midst of the apple peeling and pie-making, I found a moment alone with her by the sink. She was drying her hands on a towel, her hip leaning against the counter.

Her skin was flushed, but not with embarrassment or discomfort. She was beaming.

Nellie and Kennedy had retired to the playroom upstairs after the last batch of apples were dried, uninterested in helping any longer than they needed to. Avery was in the living room, and Mom and Dad had taken the golf cart to the barn to check on the animals before they turned in for the night.

I couldn't resist the temptation of even two seconds of her undivided attention. I reached out and gently touched her hand, the simple contact sending a rush of warmth through me. Liv turned to me, her eyes meeting mine.

"Thank you," I said softly, my voice filled with genuine gratitude.

Her smile was bright and wide as she replied, "For what?"

"For bringing me back here," I answered. "For helping me find my way home."

Liv's eyes sparkled with emotion. She took a second to scan the room, then leaned in to kiss me. It was sweet and tender, something that conveyed feelings that words alone couldn't capture.

She smiled up at me, and I couldn't help but feel like the luckiest man in the world. I'd done so many things wrong. So many bad decisions that were made out of anger at the world and the shitty hand I'd been dealt. And there I was, standing in the kitchen at my parent's house, looking at a beautiful woman who had shown me the beauty of life despite every imperfection.

I never felt deserving of a second chance. And then Liv waltzed into my life with Kennedy in tow, and suddenly, after years of struggling to care, I felt like I had *everything* to look forward to.

Chapter 33

Olivia

The night was slowly coming to an end. The sweet, spicy scent of apple pie wafted through the house, carried by the slight breeze from the open windows in the kitchen.

Kennedy was curled onto my lap, tired eyes slowly giving up on the fight to stay awake. Nellie had passed out on the recliner with Otto thirty minutes earlier, and Jo had declined every single one of my many offers to help clean up after dinner, so I sat at the dining room table with Noah and Avery while they battled it out in an intense game of Uno.

Noah's laughter disrupted the quiet house, and I looked over to see him grinning at Avery's triumphant Uno win, her arms thrown into the air as she cheered as quietly as she could.

His eyes flickered to mine, bright and full of amusement, a wide smile stretching across his lips. My heart stuttered in my chest, that dimple poking through the scruff on his cheek. He was becoming so much more than a crush; he was becoming a vital part of my life. An essential piece of my everyday routine.

Our night might've been coming to an end far sooner than I wanted, but I also knew this was just the beginning of something new and exciting.

***

Noah carried Kennedy out to his truck an hour later, and I lingered on the front porch, the screen door propped open against my foot.

Jo stacked four apple pies in my arms and promised to make a drive into town in the morning to drop off a fresh loaf of banana bread and some apple butter, and as much as I wanted to tell her it wasn't necessary, I couldn't force the words out. I would do ungodly things for a loaf of her banana bread and if she wanted to drive it into town… Who was I to stop her?

She did reassure me that she had pies to drop off to Barb at the diner, so that made me feel a little bit better.

I balanced everything in one arm as she extended her arms in my direction, accepting another loving, warm hug. She smelled like lavender and gardenias, like a garden in the spring, and it was such a comforting scent. There was a pang in my chest that made me miss home, and somehow, I think Jo knew. Her arms squeezed a little tighter and she held on until the door of Noah's truck gently clicked shut, and then her hands were on my shoulders.

There was a glossy sheen over her hazel eyes, a wobbly smile tugging at her lips. She squeezed my shoulders gently. "Thank you, Olivia," Jo whispered it so quietly that I almost didn't hear her. "Thank you."

Noah's footsteps crunched against the gravel as he made his way back up to the porch.

I knew that she was saying thank you for something so much deeper than just helping pick apples, but with Noah approaching quickly behind me, I couldn't tell her just how thankful I was in return. For this day, for her warmth and hospitality. For raising Avery and Noah to be such selfless human beings.

I didn't have a second to reassure her that there was nothing to thank me for and that eventually, he would've found his way back to them. He just needed a little push in the right direction.

So I just settled for a smile, one that I hoped portrayed all of the things I couldn't say at the moment. "Thank *you*, Jo." Noah's boots hit the stairs and I felt the heat of his chest against my back. "Kennedy had so much fun today, I can't thank you enough for letting us come out here."

Another smile warmed her face. "You two are welcome out here anytime. And you know, Nellie likes to come out here on the weekends, play in the creek, and whatnot. Normally she's too tired to make it back home. Maybe one of these weekends, Kennedy can join her. Give you a night to yourself."

"She would love that. I'll talk with Avery and we'll coordinate."

"You just let me know. Don't be strangers."

"We won't be, promise." A small part of me knew that her comment was directed at Noah, too.

He scooped the pies from my arms and leaned over, pressing a kiss to the top of his mother's head. "Bye, Ma."

She reached up to pat his cheek. "Drive safe. Watch for deer."

"We will," he promised, taking a step back, and then looking down at me. "Ready?"

I nodded, lifting my hand to wave at Otto as he crossed the dining room and headed toward the kitchen. He offered a small nod to Noah and leaned against the counter, waiting for Jo to shut the door.

"Thanks again, Jo."

She grinned and shot me a wink that reminded me so much of Avery. "Anytime."

Noah led me to his truck, his hand a persistent heat on the small of my back. He opened the door and helped me inside, setting the pies on my lap after I buckled. Kennedy was snoring softly in the backseat, a tiny pink blanket wrapped around her legs and tucked in at the sides.

I told myself that he already had that blanket for Nellie and that he didn't buy it just for my daughter because she got cold on a drive in his truck one time, but then I looked at the corner of the blanket that dangled by her feet.

There, in perfect, white calligraphy, "Princess Kennedy" was embroidered onto the blanket, a tiny little tiara hanging crookedly from the P. My chest squeezed, and the driver's side door opened, Noah meeting my watery gaze as he climbed in.

"You okay?" he asked gently, settling into the seat. He reached over, resting his hand against my thigh.

I tried not to be distracted by the way his thumb traced the skin just above my knee or the heat of his palm pressed against my skin. I tried to ignore the flutter in my stomach and the warmth that spread through me when his grip tightened.

He had this astonishing ability to overtake every square inch of my brain with his presence. I'd already given myself permission to stop overthinking and just let whatever happens, happen. But there was such a stark difference between the possibility of this progressing and the sudden realization that it already had.

"You got her a blanket?" I whispered.

It was dark, the only light in his truck coming from the soft glow of the moon overhead, but I still saw the way his ears tinged pink. He palmed the back of his neck and let out a nervous laugh. "She said she was cold last time we were in the truck... There's a uh— One of my mom's friends embroiders and I asked her to make it. It's nothing."

I laid my hand on top of his, swallowing the knot of emotion that was building in my throat. "It's not nothing, Noah. Please know that. Thank you."

His hand twisted, his fingers lacing with mine. "I know neither of us really know what pace we're supposed to be taking this, but Liv, I need you to know that I'm not going anywhere." Noah's eyes lingered on where our hands rested on my thigh like he was afraid of what he would see written across my face if he looked up. "I've spent too much time unhappy and unsure of what was next for me. But you two— You have changed *everything* for me. I can see clearly for the first time in a long time and whatever happens next, wherever this goes, I know that Kennedy comes first and I will never put you in a position to believe otherwise. I just know that I want to keep exploring this with you."

I met Noah's gaze, my heart swelling with a mixture of hope, fear, and this overwhelming sense of possibility.

"You don't think I have too much baggage?"

Noah let out a surprised laugh. "Are you seriously asking me that question?"

I rolled my eyes and leaned my head back against the headrest. "I'm serious! I mean... I have a kid. My parents won't talk to me. My mother-in-law hates me. I can't cook for shit and I'd eat my weight in banana bread if given the chance."

Noah turned his head, glancing back at Kennedy as she slept in the backseat. "I love your kid, Liv. She is amazing, kind, and funny. She is not baggage. I don't give a shit about the rest of it. It doesn't matter. And who *wouldn't* eat their weight in banana bread if given the chance?"

I let out a small laugh and the small amount of relief that I felt eased some of the tension in my chest. The roar in my ears slowly faded to nothing as his thumb gently swept over mine. I watched the gentle movement for a moment before meeting his eyes again.

"But you want that? You want us?" My voice trembled and if my hand wasn't held so firmly in his, I knew it would've been shaking, too.

"All of it," he assured me, lifting our hands to his mouth. His lips pressed softly against my skin and I choked on the emotion building in my throat.

"Okay," I whispered.

He used my hand to shield the smile that tugged at his lips. "Okay."

Chapter 34

Olivia

The drive home was short and quiet. Normally, I would've fallen asleep no less than ten minutes into the drive. But with Noah's hand still securely wrapped around mine, it was the only thing I could focus on. The heat of his palm against mine, the calluses on his skin, and the way his thumb traced the same invisible pattern over and over again until we pulled into the parking lot.

He reluctantly slid out of my grasp as he shifted gears and turned the engine off. "You want me to get Ken or the pies?"

"Pies," I answered, twisting to set them on the center console. I wanted every last moment I could get to hold her.

God, the thought of Kennedy getting any bigger physically hurt my chest. I wasn't ready for her to be too big to carry inside or too independent for my help. I remember so vividly wishing I would keep her tiny forever when she was an infant, and thinking back on that now, I couldn't even process just how quickly time had flown by.

Years always seemed to pass in the blink of an eye when watching the little person you created grow up.

I slid out of the passenger seat and shut the door behind me, quietly pulling her door open and releasing the clips of her car seat.

I settled her against my chest and she sighed in her sleep, somehow managing to lift her arms just enough to circle my neck. Kicking the door shut, I turned and followed Noah up the sidewalk and through the front door of the complex.

Our footsteps were soft against the carpeted hallway, and I couldn't help but steal glances at him as we walked, wondering if he felt the same stir of anticipation that I did.

Would he want to come in? I knew it was nearing eleven, and *I* might not be going to work in the morning, but I knew that Noah was planning on showing up bright and early so the new company he'd hired to take care of the HVAC was able to get an early start. So would that mean he'd want to head home?

I was back to feeling like we didn't have enough hours in the day.

We stood at my doorstep and he twisted the keys in the lock, gently pushing the door open. "Go get her settled, I'll put these away and wait in the kitchen."

He dropped a kiss to the top of my head and waited for me to walk past before following me inside.

I walked Kennedy to her room, strategically stepping over toys, blankets, and discarded clothes on the way to her bed. I made a mental note to get some chores done around the apartment in the morning instead of chasing Noah around town like a love-struck teenager.

She stayed fast asleep when I laid her down and slipped her shoes off, her little lips smacking together before she rolled onto her side and buried her face into her pillow. I smiled softly and pulled her princess blanket up to her shoulders, brushing a kiss to her temple. I pressed the play button on her sound machine, then switched on the nightlight by her door.

I stood in the hallway outside of her door; my palm pressed firmly against my chest as I counted every frantic beat of my heart.

I could feel it. This invisible string that tied us together. It looped around my heart in a tangled mess of knots and ties. It was laced with big emotions that I was terrified of feeling again but redolent of all things new and exciting.

Except right now, it didn't feel invisible. Right now, it was almost like I could see it stretching out in front of me, burning a path right from my chest to where Noah waited for me in the kitchen, tugging on the other end.

So I followed the pull, walking toward the kitchen and peeling Noah's sweatshirt off in the process. My heart rate kicked up as I turned the corner, Noah's large form easily overtaking the small kitchen. He was leaning against the counter, corded arms stretched behind him, and my eyes swept over his chest. The kitchen light was off, but there was a soft glow emanating from a lamp in the living room, and the shadows it cast played along the contours of his muscles, highlighting each ridge and curve. I followed the inky black snake that coiled around his arm until it disappeared under the sleeve of his black shirt and then slowly lifted my gaze to his.

There was a quiet confidence in his posture. His lips were curled into a playful smirk, his head cocked slightly to the side.

I took a shaky breath and tried to steady my racing heart. The air between us crackled, brewing like a dangerous storm. I was acutely aware of the chemistry that simmered in the space, drawing us closer together.

Noah's gaze never wavered, and it felt like he could see right through me—like he knew the effect he had on me. The temperature in the room became almost unbearable; my skin flushed pink. The small smirk on his lips deepened as his eyes trailed along my chest, following the path of warmth that climbed up my throat and fanned across my cheeks.

His weight shifted and a large hand extended in my direction. I took it without hesitation, squeaking out a laugh when he yanked me into his chest, taking his sweatshirt from my arm and tossing it onto the counter behind me.

His stance widened and I settled against him, thick thighs bracketing mine. I couldn't stop the sigh that fell from my lips when Noah reached up, pulling the elastic from my hair. He watched with a satisfied smirk as it toppled down my back. His fingers sifted through the hair at the nape of my neck, massaging against my scalp. My eyes fluttered shut as I leaned into his touch.

His other hand settled low on my back, pressing my body closer, and I shivered when the warmth of his breath coasted across the shell of my ear. "So beautiful," he murmured, his lips brushing against my skin.

My breathing turned ragged, my head spinning as he slowly dragged his lips against my jaw. The grip I had on his arms tightened, my fingernails biting into his skin.

His nose dragged against the side of mine until our lips lined up, and I drew in a long breath, holding it in my lungs.

Slowly, my hands raked up his chest, the steady rhythm of his heart thumping against my palm. For the life of me, I couldn't understand how he was so calm.

I was so sure he could hear the way my pulse thundered in the quiet of my kitchen.

The air in my lungs trembled out of me, adrenaline spiking in my blood as the hand in my hair shifted to tilt my head back.

I peeled my eyes open and found myself locked in his gaze, his eyes burning with the same unmistakable hunger that coursed through my veins.

"I'm having a hard time taking this slow with you. Everything in my head is screaming at me to hold back, and I just don't know if I can," he whispered, his eyes sweeping over my face. I knew he was searching for hesitation. He was waiting for me to back away from his hold and tell him that slow was what I needed, and maybe that was what should've happened, but it didn't. I knew he wouldn't find what he was looking for.

"Then don't."

I didn't want slow. I didn't want gentle hands to hold me like I was made of glass. I was tired of being fragile.

I wanted fire and heat, rough hands on soft skin. I wanted to feel the scrape of his teeth against my lips and fight to catch my breath as he stole it for himself.

I stretched onto my tiptoes, gently grazing my lips against his. "I want it, Noah. All of it."

His eyes flared, and then his mouth slanted over mine, giving me everything I wanted. His fingers slid from my hair and down the arch of my spine as his tongue slipped between my lips.

Noah's hands were rough and warm, fingertips digging into my hips as he walked us backward. He kept his mouth moving against mine, tasting vaguely like the mint he chewed on the way home and the finger of whiskey he'd sipped on after dinner. It was so unbelievably intoxicating, my body was buzzing as if the whiskey were flowing through my veins instead of this deep, insatiable need for him.

I hit the counter behind us, and for the second time today, his hands were sliding down over the curve of my hips and wrapping around the backs of my thighs. Noah set me down on the countertop, and my legs instinctively hooked around him, yanking him closer to my body.

We were a blur of fervent energy: hands hungry and searching, nothing but bruised lips and clashing tongues.

He nipped at my bottom lip and pulled me to the edge of the counter. A rush of heat surged through me and settled between my thighs as he rocked into me.

All of the air in my lungs rushed out with a breathy moan.

Noah pressed against me, sliding his hands under the hem of my already bunched-up dress.

His mouth dragged down my throat, fingers trailing dangerously close to my lace underwear, and the only coherent thought whirling around in my mind was *more*.

My nails scraped against his scalp, and he groaned against my skin, slowly working his way back up to my mouth.

The sound of Kennedy's door gently opening seemed to echo through the apartment, and my body went still, Noah's lips hovering above mine. We stayed frozen, her almost silent footsteps dragging against the carpet before I heard the light switch in the bathroom flick on. I held my breath, waiting until the bathroom door clicked shut to exhale, my forehead lowering to Noah's shoulder as he shook with silent laughter.

"Jesus Christ," I muttered against his shirt, shaking my head slightly as a smile tugged at my lips.

Noah snorted out a laugh, and I reached up, pressing my palm against his mouth, my index finger slamming against my lips, gesturing for him to stay quiet. His eyes shimmered with amusement, crinkling around the edges as he grinned behind my hand.

The toilet flushed. The sink ran. One door opened. Then another.

The latch clicked as she pulled her bedroom door shut and my rigid body went limp against Noah as we both fell into a fit of silent laughter.

I buried my face into his chest to muffle any noise, his lips pressing against my temple with a grin.

With a final, almost silent chuckle, Noah gently disentangled himself from me, his hand lingering on my cheek for a moment. "I should go," he whispered. I could see the disappointment in his eyes and hear the hesitation in his voice.

I didn't want him to go almost as much as he didn't want to leave. There was one flimsy foot of space between us, and it was like every single one of my nerve endings was reaching for him, pleading for him to stay.

It was desperation in the simplest meaning, an ache that settled deep in my bones, put there by the fiery look in his eyes and the gentle sweep of his hands over the curve of my hips.

There was a split second of silence, his words dangling in the air between us, but I refused to acknowledge them.

Slowly, my hand reached out and curled into the thin fabric of his t-shirt. I ignored the tremble in my fingers and the way my breath shook as I gently forced it out of my lungs. "Stay," I murmured the word so quietly I was almost certain he didn't hear me.

Noah's muscles tightened under my fingers as they grazed the skin near his hip.

My gaze stayed fixed on his chest, afraid of what I would find if I looked up. I wasn't known to be bold. I wasn't known to put myself out there, and yet, I found myself doing just that over and over again when it came to Noah.

A small part of me would be devastated if I looked up to see the hesitation he felt about leaving shift into something else completely. But a larger part of me wasn't scared of rejection when I knew it was coming from someone so kind and understanding. Someone who constantly put my needs before his own.

He cradled my jaw, thumb swiping along my bottom lip. "Are you sure?"

"Yes," I whispered, a little louder this time, finally summoning the courage to lift my eyes to meet his. "Stay."

"Okay." His voice was all gravel, any hint of hesitation gone as his eyes bounced back and forth between mine. His features were soft, something tender warming his eyes and it made my chest swirl with an assortment of emotions.

I took his hand in mine and tugged softly, guiding him through the darkened hallway until we reached the door to my room. There was a brief pause, one that couldn't have lasted longer than a second or two, but he noticed. Because *of course*, he did, and I felt the heat of Noah's body against my back as he stepped closer.

My head tilted to the side as he swept the hair from my shoulder, his lips pressing softly against my skin. "I can go home," he whispered.

A shiver curled its way down my spine as his breath washed over me. "I don't want you to go." My voice was barely audible.

"We don't have to rush anything, Liv. I promise."

I shook my head, twisting to look up at him. "This doesn't feel like rushing."

"What does it feel like?"

There were a lot of things that whirled around my brain, but none of them felt significant. Nothing felt sufficient. My hands slowly slid up his forearms, taking in every inch of corded muscle as I went. "It just feels... *right*."

Unfortunately, the word I settled on felt incredibly lackluster, but I couldn't put it into words. I couldn't describe the feeling that bloomed in my chest whenever he smiled at me or the way he seemed to lift the weight from my shoulders with something as simple as a kiss.

"Does it feel like we're rushing to you?" I asked, suddenly worried that I was pushing him to do something *he* wasn't ready for.

His thumb paused its delicate sweep, landing at the corner of my mouth. "No," he answered confidently.

"What does it feel like to you?"

"It feels like I'm exactly where I need to be." His grip moved to my waist, sliding down to settle on my hips. "So unless you want me to go, I'm here."

"I don't want you to go."

"Okay."

I wasn't sure which of us moved first, but his lips caught mine in a rough kiss, fingers tightened in a bruising grip at my hips. My hands found their way into his hair as he backed me into the door, and when his tongue swept across my bottom lip, I felt it all the way down to my toes as they curled against the carpet.

Noah grabbed at the fabric of my dress, slowly sliding it up my thighs with gentle, teasing movements. The higher his fingers went, the faster my breath pushed out of my mouth.

He pulled my hips flush with his, and want rippled through my body at the feeling of his erection pressed against me. There was a nervous flutter in my stomach, but with the nerves, there was also excitement—a rush that came with experiencing all of these things for the first time again.

I reached back and fumbled around for the doorknob as he traced a burning trail along my jawline with his lips. His tongue flicked out against my skin and every coherent thought scattered in my brain.

"Noah," I breathed, dragging his name out as his hands followed along the curves of my body. I gasped, my head lolling back against the door, his thumb brushing the underside of my breast.

I was burning, fire licking through my veins, and I should've been searching for the door handle, but every thought in my brain was fleeting, fizzling to nothing before I could force my limbs to act.

Somewhere between his tongue on my throat and his teasing hands on my skin, I managed to choke out the word "door."

He reached down, twisting the door handle and pushing it open. We stumbled into the dark room, a low chuckle vibrating against my skin as he kissed his way back up to my mouth.

Noah gently kicked the door closed, hands moving to my waist as he backed me further into the room. I hit the bed, and we came to a stop, our chests brushing with each ragged breath.

His eyes searched mine, moonlight filtering in through the window and casting a soft glow across his face. Gentle fingers traced a path up my arms, leaving a trail of goosebumps in their wake. A smile curled on his lips, mirroring the warmth in his eyes. "So beautiful."

Before I could return the sentiment, his fingers sifted into my hair and tipped my head back, angling his lips over mine.

My hands trembled as they wandered under the hem of his shirt and splayed across solid, warm muscle. He let out a harsh breath, shivering when my fingernails scraped against his skin. I used it as an opportunity to slide my tongue against his bottom lip, and his hands pulled out of my hair, fingertips trailing down my throat until they stopped at the straps of my dress.

My stomach fluttered, and he pulled away, his breath ragged.

One finger slipped under the strap on my shoulder.

Noah's gaze moved to mine, his eyes riddled with hesitation. "Are you sure?"

"Noah." I took a step closer, a rush of heat surging through me as our bodies stood flush against each other. "For over a year, everyone in my life has treated me like I'm on the verge of breaking. Like I am just some fragile piece of glass that they have to handle with care."

I swallowed, his eyes falling to my chest as I moved one of the straps off of my shoulder. "I want this. I want you. And as long as you want me, I'm sure."

Chapter 35

Olivia

Noah moved one strap off of my shoulder at a painstakingly slow rate. His fingertip trailed against my arm as my dress fell into a puddle of cotton at my feet.

A muscle in his jaw feathered as he swallowed.

"God, Liv," he murmured, the awe in his voice rendering me speechless.

Large, rough hands met the soft, bare skin at my waist in a gentle but possessive touch. I shivered under the heat of his darkened gaze, my breath hitching as his thumb followed the curve of my breast.

My brain was fuzzy. My hands shook. It had been far too long since his lips moved against me. There weren't a ton of coherent thoughts being formed in my brain but I was convinced that his mouth would do wondrous things to soothe the fire lapping at my skin.

I toyed with the hem of his T-shirt before gently easing it over his head, revealing the taut muscles and the intricate ink of his tattoos. I traced the designs that wrapped around his arm, the intimacy of the moment nearly overwhelming. His body was a canvas, a work of art, and *god* I was eager to explore every inch of it.

He pulled me into his body, winding his arms around my waist and holding me tight against him as his mouth crashed into mine. He stole my breath with a swipe of his tongue, a hand roving down my back, cupping my ass as he eased me onto the bed.

He settled on top of me, my legs parting to cradle his hips between my thighs, and a whimper built in my throat as the heat of his mouth traveled to my jaw. "*God*, Liv." Noah's deep voice smoothed over my skin like a gentle caress. "I can't—" His head gently shook back and forth. "I can't think straight around you. You steal every logical thought right from my head."

I let out a breathy laugh. "I know what you mean."

My hips moved of their own volition, rolling against him to chase the friction I craved. A breath hissed out of him as he moved lower, teeth scraping gently over my collarbone.

It was like my hand was wrapped around a live wire, every single nerve ending firing to life under his touch. Every brush of his lips, every gentle press of his body against mine sent jolts of electricity through my veins.

Noah rocked into me, a rough hand cupping my breast, thumb stroking over my nipple. His name rushed out of me with a moan. I arched against the bed, his lips hot and wet against my skin.

It was too much.

It wasn't enough.

He moved down my body, planting kisses against the stretch marks that lined my stomach before he was tugging at the waistband of my underwear. I lifted off of the bed and he eased the scrap of lace down my thighs.

I thought I heard them land softly somewhere across the room, but his hands were on the inside of my thighs and I couldn't concentrate on anything else but his warm breath against my skin.

Noah kneeled at the end of my bed, strong arms wrapping around my legs as he pulled me to the edge. Right as I peered down, his mouth lowered and I fell back against the bed as I gasped for air.

"*Oh, my god.*" The words fell from my mouth in slow motion, fingers digging into the comforter on my bed.

A sound of pure desperation clawed its way out of me, and my hands moved to his hair, fingers threading between the soft strands.

My body wound tight, his groan vibrating against me as his fingers dug into my thighs. I knew there would be bruises decorating my chest and legs tomorrow, but I couldn't find it in myself to care.

Holy shit.

It felt like I was underwater, my pulse drumming a wild beat in my ears and drowning out the breathy moans and frantic sounds pouring out of me. He took his time learning what each moan or sharp breath meant, taking me right to the edge before gently easing me back down with kisses and sweet nothings whispered along my inner thigh. It was the best kind of torture.

Noah let out a chuckle at my frustrated, deprived groans, finally relenting after a strangled plea fell from my lips. My spine bowed against the bed as I came apart, the grip on his hair tightening as waves of blinding pleasure rolled through me.

My vision darkened around the edges; my chest heaved as I fought to catch my breath.

The heat of his mouth pressed against the crease of my hip and then up to my stomach. My heart squeezed as he made sure he spent a few extra seconds peppering kisses against the stretch marks I knew stood out against the slight tan I'd developed over the summer.

He never ran out of ways to make me feel seen and wanted.

His mouth was on my breast, my throat, my jaw, and then I was tasting myself on his tongue.

I fumbled with the button on his jeans, but Noah stilled and then pulled away.

"I don't have a condom," he rasped.

The haze that clouded my brain was suddenly cleared, and my hands paused on the waistband of his boxers.

I swallowed, my tongue darting out to swipe against my lips. "I— Uh. I have an IUD. There hasn't been anyone since..." My voice trailed off, and I cleared my throat. "I'm clean. There's nothing to worry about in that... Arena."

The corner of his mouth twitched. "There hasn't been anyone else for me either. Are you sure?"

I nodded, dragging my fingers down his back. "I trust you."

He pushed himself up, rising to his feet at the foot of my bed. His hands moved with purpose, undoing the button of his jeans. In the dim light, I could see a hunger in his eyes that sent a flush to my cheeks as he gazed down at me. He pushed his jeans down his thighs and let them drop to the floor with a casual kick to the side.

Noah's lips were tilted into a smirk as he kneeled on the bed, his mouth grazing my nipple as he kissed his way back up to my lips. He paused when he reached my jaw, his breath coasting over the shell of my ear. "I love it when you blush for me, Liv. So fuckin' pretty."

His words unfurled something hot inside of me. It started low in my belly and bloomed into my chest, and I wanted to say something back to him. Anything, really. But his breath, hot and demanding, washed over me in ragged exhales, followed quickly by the heat of his mouth on my throat, and the words dissipated from my brain before they could even form into something logical.

My legs wrapped loosely around him, and when he angled his lips over mine, I melted under the softness of his touch. His weight shifted, and my hands moved back to his hair, teeth sinking into his bottom lip.

My breath stilled, Noah's shoulders tensing.

He pulled back, hazel eyes locking onto mine, a shiver twisting down my spine. He hovered *just* above my lips, *just* out of reach and when he slowly eased inside of me, I understood why.

He stole my breath with a sharp inhale, the deep greens in his eyes flickering as he watched me with rapt attention. His gaze swept over my face, tracing the furrow of my brow and the way my lips parted with a sigh. Noah's deep, throaty groan vibrated through my chest, and I clawed at his back as he gently rolled his hips into mine.

"Fuck, Noah," I breathed, arching into his body. My nipples brushed against the light dusting of dark hair on his chest, and I trembled as I waited for him to move. "More. *Please.*"

With another shift of his weight, Noah hooked his arm beneath my leg, my calf resting against his shoulder as he drew back. He yanked my hips closer, and my mind splintered into a million different pieces.

I think he whispered my name, or maybe he yelled it. I wasn't sure. My pulse was thundering in my ears, my heart clattering around in my chest. He lowered his mouth back to mine, my toes curling as I panted against his mouth.

God, I never wanted this to end. Noah's deep voice sent a jolt of electricity skittering across my skin as he brought my thoughts to life. "I'll never be able to get enough of you."

His kiss was hungry, tongue delving into my mouth and curling against mine. He still tasted a little like whiskey and mint, but mostly like me and that revelation had the coil inside of me winding a little tighter.

His forehead dropped to the crook of my neck, lips dragging against my collarbone. Noah mumbled a curse into my skin, and I arched off of the bed when his hand slid between us, stroking me with slow, torturous movements.

My brain was done, disconnected from my vocal cords, focused on nothing but the slow roll of heat that was consuming every inch of my nervous system.

"*Liv.*" My name was gritted out through clenched teeth, his tone carrying the inflection of a warning.

My nails scraped against his scalp, my lips moving against his as the pressure inside of me neared a breaking point. I knew he was close, too. I felt it in the slight shudder of his arms and the ripple of his muscles as he tried to hold back. "I'm with you," I said softly. We sat together at the precipice of coming undone, dangerously close to toppling over the edge. Then his mouth slanted over mine, and my eyes fluttered shut, his tongue following the same steady stroke of his fingers. He grunted against my lips, driving his hips into mine one last time, and together, we unraveled.

I shuddered through the waves of rolling pleasure, sinking my teeth in his shoulder to muffle the noises I couldn't hold back.

There were so many emotions flitting around in my chest as I fought to catch my breath, so many warm, soft, and beautiful things that I thought were long buried in the rubble of my past. His limbs stayed tangled with mine, lips dragging over my heated skin.

Noah lowered himself onto the bed beside me, his arm draping over my waist. I smiled at the ceiling, then rolled into his chest, coming face to face with the same cheesy grin on my lips, plastered onto his.

He traced the curve of my spine in soft, delicate touches that had me shivering in his arms.

I searched for something to say, something profound and meaningful to describe everything that was billowing in my chest, making me feel so full and content, but nothing substantial came to mind.

"You make me feel human again." His voice was all gravel and strained like he was struggling to find the right words. "Sometimes I think that my heart forgot how to beat until you came into my life."

My chest cracked open, exposing everything raw and real, and I shuddered out a breath as his lips slipped against mine.

It was way too soon for his words to bury so deep into my bones like they did and it was way too soon for the word 'love' to flutter at the edge of my consciousness. But when he said things like that to me, it was impossible to ignore the way they made me feel.

The way *he* made me feel.

He was the sun, bringing so much light and warmth to a life that I thought was doomed to darkness. I poured so much of myself into my daughter that I hadn't even realized I had nothing left to offer.

Until him.

There were pieces of who I used to be that still existed inside of me, but they existed in fragments. Noah was this constant presence, this gentle flow of sand that filled the empty space between the broken parts of my former self and made me feel whole again.

His arm tightened around my waist, pulling me into his chest and I melted into his warmth. I slowly pulled my gaze up to his. "I hate what happened to the people we loved..." My voice trailed off, and his eyes softened with a heartbroken understanding. "And I hate how badly it tore us both up. But I feel so lucky that it brought me to you."

Noah's smile was watery, his lips gentle as they pressed against my mouth. "Me, too."

I nestled a little closer, and he caged me in. Of all the endings this day could've had, this was the one I least expected. But as we lay here, the steady rhythm of Noah's heartbeat beneath my cheek, I knew that it was the ending we both needed.

Chapter 36

Olivia

I groaned, the shrill sound of my alarm jolting me awake. It was so goddamn early; the sun hadn't even crested the horizon yet. But somewhere between the shower we'd taken on wobbly legs and our heads finally hitting my pillows, we'd determined it was better for Noah to sneak out before Kennedy woke up for the day.

I didn't particularly like keeping this secret from her, but I also wasn't sure how to explain it. So for now, Noah sneaking out was the best option I had.

Reaching over to silence my phone, I straightened my legs and yawned, letting out a gasp when Noah pulled my naked body against his.

Warm lips moved against my shoulder, a large hand splaying across my stomach. I wanted to spend the whole day tangled in my sheets, feeling him pressed against me as my name spilled from his mouth. But all too soon, he was pulling away, leaving my back exposed to cold air and my body desperate for his touch.

I pulled the comforter up over my bare chest, snuggling into the leftover warmth from Noah's body as he moved around the room, grabbing his discarded clothes from various spots on my floor. He shimmied into his jeans, his head cocked to the side as he looked over at me.

"Stop looking at me like that." His voice was gruff and thick with sleep but tinged with amusement.

"Like what?" I asked innocently, batting my eyelashes.

His tongue raked over his teeth as he shook his head. "Like you're thinking of ten different ways to get me back in your bed."

I smiled. "Only five, actually. I can be very persuasive."

Noah chuckled, pulling his shirt over his head. He wandered back over to the side of my bed. "I wholeheartedly believe that."

He leaned down, and I rushed to pull the blanket up over my mouth, shaking my head furiously.

His brows dipped in confusion. "What?"

"Morning breath," I mumbled from underneath the thick fabric.

Noah rolled his eyes but moved to kiss my forehead instead. "I'll be back in a few hours. I'm gonna shower, *brush my teeth*, and I'll come back with breakfast."

I scrunched my nose, though he could only see the upper portion of my face. "I promised Avery I'd meet her at the diner after drop off." I desperately wanted to spend more time with him, but Avery and I were becoming quite close, and I wouldn't be able to handle the guilt if I skipped out on our plans while sneaking around with her brother.

"I'll come get you for lunch, then." His lips brushed against my temple before he stood, and I made a mental note to grab him a toothbrush at the store so he had one here. "Come lock up after me." He snagged my robe from the back of the bedroom door and held it out.

I threw back the covers and eased out of bed, Noah's eyes fixed on the ceiling.

"You can look at me," I teased.

"No, Liv. I *really* can't. If I look at you, I won't be able to stop myself from getting back into bed and we both know that can't happen." His eyes pressed shut as I took a step closer. I let out a laugh and twirled around, sliding my arms into the awaiting robe.

He cursed under his breath and disappeared into the hallway while I secured the tie around my waist.

When I joined him at the door, his eyes fell to my chest, a low groan building in his throat. His eyes pinched shut, and he sucked in a deep breath. I couldn't help but laugh, though his restraint was commendable.

Noah knew that I wasn't going to kiss him, so his fingers brushed against the edge of my jaw in a feather-light touch. "I'll text you when I get home."

My heart squeezed, his promise placating the panic that lingered at the edge of my thoughts every time he walked out of my apartment. "Thank you."

He winked, and I watched until he disappeared down the hall, then slipped back into my apartment and pushed the door shut behind me.

I brushed my fingers over my mouth, a wide smile blooming across my lips. Noah made me feel alive in a way I hadn't felt since I was a teenager, all those years ago when everything was new and exciting. His touch, his smile, the way he constantly invaded my thoughts.

I had long forgotten the rush that came with all of these developing feelings and the fascination of discovering someone new, someone who had the power to turn my world upside down.

Silently, I made my way to Kennedy's room and carefully pushed her door open. I poked my head through to make sure she was still fast asleep and then wandered down the hall to my room.

I knew it would take Noah about twenty minutes or so to get home, so I walked into the bathroom to wash my face, unable to wipe the grin from my lips.

I rested my hands on the edge of the bathroom counter, staring at my now clean face, a faint glow from my night with Noah still painted across my cheeks.

My chin tucked into my chest as I laughed, and then my eyes caught on the rings still sitting on my finger. Before, they had felt like a part of me. Like they were welded to my skin, a permanent piece of my marriage I never wanted to part with.

I stared at them now, and they felt different. They weren't just symbols of love; they were reminders of loss and heartache. They were reminders of how I almost drowned in the depths of my grief. A part of me hated that something once so sentimental could weigh on my chest so heavily now.

The longer I stared, the heavier they felt, and my throat tightened with the grief that never seemed to completely fade. I missed Liam every day, even as I moved forward with my life and explored my feelings for Noah.

My fingers trembled as I carefully slid the rings off, one by one, the cool metal leaving an imprint on my skin from years of wear. Tears welled up in my eyes as I held them in the palm of my hand, glistening in the soft bathroom light.

With a deep breath, I closed my fingers around the rings and walked to my bedroom. I pulled the top drawer of my dresser out and dug around for a second, locating the ring box Liam held out to me at eighteen.

The velvet was worn and patchy, one of the hinges in the back barely hanging on. I smiled through the tears as I gently lifted the lid and placed two of the three rings inside. The one he gave to me when he got down on one knee and asked me for a forever that would end all too soon, and the one he gave me on the day of our wedding. I kept the third one closed in my fist as I lowered the lid and placed it back into the drawer.

The third ring, the one that Liam had given me the day I brought Kennedy into the world, slid onto the ring finger of my right hand. Its presence there felt different from the other two, a symbol of the beautiful life we had created together, despite the heartache that had followed.

I pushed the drawer shut and traced the indent left on my finger with my thumb, unsure of how I felt about the vacant space. There was a pang of guilt and sadness in my chest, a realization that my chapter in life that revolved around Liam was done.

My hands pressed against my sternum as I took a shuddering breath, trying to remind myself that I wasn't erasing the memories of Liam. I was just making room for more.

I walked back into my room and plopped into bed, texting the only other person who would be awake at this hour.

Me: You up?

Gia: Obviously

I knew she would be. Wyoming was two hours behind Delaware, and five in the morning for me meant three in the morning for her and I knew my best friend well. Gia hadn't even attempted to go to bed yet. She was probably slouched over her laptop, dark brown hair piled into a crazy bun on the top of her head while she downed some kind of caffeinated beverage.

Her sleep schedule sucked most of the time, but with the deadline of her book looming over her shoulders, it was even worse now.

A few seconds later, my phone was buzzing in my hand, Gia's beautiful smile filling my screen.

I swiped to answer her FaceTime and rolled onto my stomach.

"My sweet, angel baby. How are you?" She rested her chin on the heel of her palm, her glasses resting on the bridge of her nose. She was lit up by the soft light emanating from her laptop screen.

I snorted out a laugh. "I don't— I don't think I know how to answer that. I mean, I do. But... There are a lot of conflicting things."

Gia's desk chair creaked as she leaned forward. "What's wrong?"

I sighed, chewing on the inside of my cheek as I tried to make sense of everything. "I don't think... I mean— Nothing is *wrong*. I—I took my rings off just now."

"*Oh?*" Her raspy voice held a mixture of shock and concern.

"Yeah," I responded quietly.

Gia was silent for a moment and I watched her face shift through several different expressions. "Because of Mr. Sexy Mechanic?"

An unexpected laugh bubbled its way up my throat and burst through my lips. "He might have something to do with it." Might was a weak word.

"This is—" She paused and blew out a deep sigh. "Wow, babe. This is *big*."

Gia knew a few details here and there about what had been going on with Noah and me, but the time difference and the fact that she was on a deadline for her next book left us with little time to catch up. There were a lot of things that I'd been feeling but hadn't had the chance to fully share with her.

Her mouth popped open, her eyes widening comically. "You totally boned him."

"Boned? Come on. We're pushing thirty."

Her hand slapped over her mouth and I was beginning to think her jaw might've locked in place. "*Holy shit*. You totally had sex with him!"

She squealed, her feet rapidly tapping against the hardwood floor. "*Oh my god*, so this *is* big! I mean, monumental. Wait—" Her excited smile faded into something serious. "*Is it big?*"

"Georgia!" I laughed at her innuendo, dropping my face onto the bed.

"Come on, you can't blame a girl for asking."

I looked back up at my best friend, her smile so wide, her eyes kissed at the corners. Gia propped her phone up on her desk and leaned back into her chair.

"How are you feeling? *What* are you feeling?"

I sighed. "Is 'everything' an appropriate answer?"

"Yeah, babe. It is."

"I don't know how to explain it, but I haven't felt alive in a long time. It's like a second chance at happiness just fell into my lap, and it scares the shit out of me because it means letting go of a huge chunk of my past."

Her voice on the other end was soft and understanding. "Honey, you deserve this. You and that little girl have been through so much, and from what you have told me, so has he. You're not *letting go* of anything. Liam will always be a huge part of your life. That is something that will never change. But it's okay to chase after something new and exciting. It's okay to want something that makes your heart race."

Tears welled up in my eyes as her words sank in. "I know, but it's just… It's complicated. Kennedy wouldn't exist without Liam. How do I just move on? Ya know? I never stopped loving him."

"Nobody's saying you have to forget Liam or what you had with him. That love will always be a part of you and if you choose to remarry at some point, the love you share with that person will be just as real as what you had with him. It sounds fuckin' harsh, but life goes on, and you have the right to find happiness again, even if it's different and scary. Liam would want that for you."

I nodded and her eyes misted over. A few tears trailed down my cheeks, and I swiped them away. "I know you're right."

"I'm almost never wrong."

I responded with a laugh, wiping away another tear. "Unfortunately for me, that has often proven to be the truth."

Gia had a knack for providing clarity and comfort in moments during some of the most confusing and painful moments of my life.

"Thank you."

She grinned. "What are best friends for, if not answering middle-of-the-night calls about boys?" Her chair creaked again as she tucked a leg underneath her. "You sure you're gonna be okay, champ?"

"Yeah," I answered with another laugh.

"Good, because the lack of details I have received is *astonishing*. I'm gonna need you to spill!"

"God, I miss you." I sighed, not intentionally avoiding the topic of my newfound sex life, but she didn't press.

Her grin melted into something softer. "I miss you guys, too."

"You know, Kennedy asked the other day when you were going to be moving here. I asked her why you would do that, and she said 'Because it's Aunt Gia, Mom. You guys do everything together.'"

She threw her head back and let out a fake sob. "Fuck, I love that kid. You can't tell me this shit."

I rested my chin on my palm. "I know, I'm sorry. She just misses you."

There was a twinge of guilt that twisted through my chest at the way her face fell. Here she was feeling guilty for the distance that *I* had created.

"I'm gonna come visit soon, I promise. It's just— I mean, between the book and my mother hounding me to 'get a real job', I feel like I haven't had a second to breathe."

"I know, G. It's not your fault, you know that. I'm the one who packed up and moved across the country anyway."

"This is true." Her mouth curled into a small smile. "Anywho. Doesn't that hunky boss of yours give you any PTO? You could always come home." The inflection in her tone made it sound more like a question.

Gia's brows pulled together apologetically when I winced.

"It's— It's not that I don't want to. I miss Evergreen. I miss… *Almost* everyone there. But I just— I feel like I'm in such a good place right now and—"

"Your family," she surmised with a sigh.

"Right," I said quietly. "I just feel like we're finally *happy* and I know the second I go back, everyone will do everything in their power to take it away. I need to make sure I'm able to stand my ground when the time comes. And I'm just not ready to have to fight for it yet. I just want to enjoy it for a little."

She was quiet for a second, brown eyes softening as her smile grew. "You really like him, huh?"

That nervous flutter was back, sweeping through my stomach and turning my cheeks pink. "I do."

The sigh that fell from my best friend's lips was one of happiness. Contentment. "As much as it pains me to say this… If staying away is what keeps that grin plastered to your face… I kind of hope I don't see you for a long time."

Chapter 37

Olivia

"Where's your bookbag?" Right as the question left my mouth, the front door swung open. I swear to god, the hand holding up that gaudy, pink, and purple bookbag glowed and the angels started to sing.

"Got it!"

I sighed, my shoulders deflating with relief. Thank fuck for Avery Kent. Kennedy must've left it at their place after dinner last night. If my hands weren't preoccupied, I probably would've trapped her tiny little freckled face between them and plopped a kiss right on her nose.

I was standing in the hallway that leads to my front door in a bra and jeans with my t-shirt dangling over my arm while I pulled Ken's hair up into a bun. Given my current state and the fact that the school was a five-minute walk and the first bell rang in three, hunting down her bookbag would have sent me into a spiral that I did not have time to succumb to.

Avery walked over, swatting my hand away and taking the hair tie from my wrist. "Go get dressed."

"God, I could kiss you," I threw out over my shoulder, running back to my room to quickly roll on some deodorant (Noah could thank his sister for that later) and run my brush through my hair before yanking it into a haphazard bun that would probably have to be rearranged at least ten times throughout the day.

I threw on my t-shirt and took an extra second I didn't have to swipe some mascara onto my eyelashes.

"We gotta go!"

I rolled my eyes and laughed, giving myself a quick once-over in the bathroom mirror before pulling on my white sneakers and meeting everyone in the hallway. "Avery Kent. Did you just use your mom voice on me?"

"I did!" She ushered the girls out the door, shooting a wink over her shoulder as she lowered her voice. "People that sleep through alarms after a *boy* sleeps over get the mom voice, Olivia."

I swiped my keys and jacket from the hooks by the door and resisted the urge to roll my eyes at her again. "One time. I'm late *one time*," I muttered under my breath, locking the door behind me as Avery and the girls hustled down the hall.

Kennedy's laughter filled the hallway, Nellie following closely behind as Avery chased after them. I couldn't help but grin.

We were definitely going to be late. And I didn't care.

* * *

"Alright, girls. Here we go." I ushered Kennedy and Nellie toward the door of the school, tugging my jacket closer to my body. September and October came and went in such a rush, and I could barely wrap my head around the fact that we were nearing Thanksgiving.

We were just past that weird point in the fall where sweaters were encouraged in the morning and by mid-afternoon, you were shredding layers one after the other to keep up with the rising temperatures. The way the cold air nipped at my cheeks told me it was only a matter of time before the coldest temperature of the day became the warmest. Not that I really minded.

I watched as a few parents and their children bustled around me, the kids all wrapped up in sweaters and jackets they would discard almost immediately once they started moving around. It was nice to see we weren't the only ones running late this morning.

Up until today, I thought I was starting to get the hang of mornings. Scratch that. I got the hang of them. I made school mornings my bitch. I was doing just fine! But this new routine that I'd fallen into with Noah and Avery was making me *too* comfortable.

I was sleeping better, laughing more, and much to Noah's credit, my cooking had improved a ton. Also to Noah's credit, my clothes started to fit the way that they used to. Gone were the days of yanking my pants up constantly.

I would almost argue they were borderline snug. Something I thought I would be insecure about, but it became a happy and welcome reminder that I was alive and doing well.

However, Avery did politely let me know that my punishment for sleeping in was dragging the girls to school while she ran ahead and sat at the diner without us to enjoy a cup of coffee alone.

Life was back to being hectic. I thought I would hate it, but in reality, it was comforting. I didn't feel like the new kid anymore. Rose Hill had welcomed us with open arms, and it was evident in the friendly faces and warm greetings. We were... Comfortable. We had a routine, and Kennedy had friends. *I* had friends, and I had Noah, too.

Noah certainly wasn't helping with the need to oversleep.

We were still being careful around Kennedy, but in order to do that, we were spending a lot of late nights together... And early mornings.

It was a delicate dance. Kennedy's sleep schedule was wildly unpredictable most days, and I never really knew when she was going to be up at five for the day or fighting tooth and nail to stay in bed and skip school. So far, Noah had managed to do a good job at sneaking out before dawn. But I hated the fact that he was getting up so early after staying up so late.

I knew we couldn't keep this up forever. Kennedy was sharp. She paid attention to every little detail and sooner or later, one of us would slip up. I didn't even know how to go about explaining a relationship to a soon-to-be five-year-old. But I was going to have to figure it out soon.

In the meantime, we just had to be cautious.

I struggled to admit that a part of me was nervous to tell Kennedy because of Deb. Despite her making me out to be this monster, I still wanted her to have a relationship with Kennedy. And because I was adamant about maintaining that relationship, they talked frequently.

I had a lot of faith in Kennedy, but keeping secrets wasn't her strong suit.

Just the thought of asking her to keep something from Deb in the first place left a sour taste in my mouth. But the more time I spent with Noah, the more evident it became that she would have to know soon.

I pulled on the bright yellow doors to the Pre-K side of the building, guiding the two of them through the entrance by the handles of their book bags. Kennedy was moving so slowly this morning, her feet dragging against the tiled floor while Nellie skipped to the desk.

I pressed my hand to Ken's forehead just to be sure she hadn't spiked a fever overnight.

We shuffled up to the front desk behind Nellie and the receptionist, Rhea, who I'd gotten to know more and more over the past few weeks, had her hands folded under her chin as she grinned down at the girls. Half of her long, black braids were pulled up into a bun, the other half draped over her shoulders. There was a dark purple blush swept over the apples of her cheeks, her deep brown skin glowing with a golden highlighter. Kennedy loved trying to predict her makeup for the day. She cycled through various shades of purples and some dark reds now that we were getting into the fall season, so every morning before we walked to school, Kennedy would predict red or purple lipstick. On days that we were on time, she would tell me after school whether she was right or wrong. Honestly, sometimes I think she gave me a hard time in the morning for the sole purpose of being able to talk to Rhea before school. She was so great with all the kids.

"Hi, Ms. Kennedy. Hi, Ms. Eleanor." Rhea scrunched her nose, and Ken dragged her feet to the counter. Nellie's face twisted up at the use of her full name.

"Hi, Ms. Rhea." Ken's voice was unusually soft, but Nellie made up for the lack of enthusiasm just fine.

"Hey, Ms. Rhea!"

Kennedy rested her head against my hip, and I looked down at her, dark circles under her eyes.

Kneeling down, I swiveled her so she was looking at me. "You feeling okay?"

Kennedy shrugged. "Just tired, Mama."

That set off another alarm in my head. She never called me Mama. Not anymore. I raised my hand to feel her forehead, but she still wasn't warm. "You sure?"

She nodded and yawned as if to emphasize her point. There was a tiny part of my brain that told me to just scoop her up and take her home for the day, sick or not.

Rhea leaned forward, resting her forearms on the desk. "Are we maybe a little hungry? I may or may not have saved some French toast sticks."

Kennedy perked up, turning to look at Rhea.

"Really?"

"Really."

I stood and scribbled my name onto the sign-in sheet, shooting Rhea a look of appreciation, hoping she wasn't saving those for herself. "She had some toast earlier, I promise. I tried to get her to eat something else, but she wouldn't."

Rhea waved a perfectly manicured hand at me. "I know how kids are. Avery texted me and asked me to save something for her. I don't think the kindergartners have eaten yet, so Nellie should be fine." She rolled her chair to the mini-fridge and bent over, snagging a paper plate. "I know Ken is never one to refuse French toast." She slid it into the microwave before turning back to us.

"Thank you, Ms. Rhea." I always made sure to call her Ms. Rhea around the kids.

"You are so very welcome, Mrs. Brooks."

"Olivia," I corrected, pointing my pen at her. "You make me feel old."

She snorted. "Fine, fine. Olivia. You're welcome, *Olivia*."

I beamed, helping Kennedy shrug off her bookbag. "Why don't you go put your stuff in your cubby and hang your coat while we wait for the French toast?"

She nodded and walked off, her shoulders slouched and her feet still dragging.

"Will you call me if she doesn't perk up? She seems off." I turned back to Rhea, who was writing Kennedy's name onto the late pass in perfect cursive.

"Of course. I'll write something on her pass, so her teacher knows to call me if she's falling asleep or something."

"You are an angel, thank you."

She smiled and slid the pass across the counter. "No problem."

Kennedy trudged back to us and peered over the counter right as the microwave beeped.

A few seconds later, she was sitting at a small table, dipping her French toast into a small puddle of maple syrup. I kneeled to her level. "I'm gonna go, okay? I gotta take Nellie to school."

She nodded and wiped the syrup from her mouth. "Okay." She stood, wrapping her arms around my neck.

I buried my face into her hair as I hugged her close to my chest. "Bye, baby. I love you."

"Love you the mostest," she offered with a weak smile. I pushed a few baby hairs out of her face.

Rhea spoke up. "I'll call you if she needs to go home. Promise."

"Thank you, I owe you one."

I stood and turned to Nellie. "Alright, kid. You ready?"

She nodded, waved goodbye to Rhea and then to Kennedy, and we were off.

Chapter 38

Olivia

"Opinion."

Before I could respond to Avery's statement that one hundred percent should've been a question, her phone screen was shoved into my face. Which didn't end well for either of us, considering I was approximately four inches away from my mouth with a spoonful of yogurt that I now wore on my cheek.

I glared at Avery, swiping at my face with a napkin before setting my spoon down into the bowl and stealing her phone from her grip.

"Meh." I shrugged, swiping through this stranger's assortment of pictures. "He's a farmer. And he's over six foot. But he's forty-seven miles away. Are you really considering going on a date with someone who's basically an hour away?" I eyed her over the top of her phone, raising my brows. "Forty. Seven. Miles. And it's not even toward the good stuff. Try Wilmington."

"Have you seen this town? We live in bum-fuck Delaware, Olivia. My options are Eddie, Harvey, or a farmer who lives forty-seven miles away. I think I'll take my chances on the farmer," she deadpanned, shaking her head while she snatched her phone back. "Guys in Wilmington are never any good."

I snickered, picking up a piece of bacon. "I could talk to Eddie for you. From the stories I've overheard, he's a *very* talented man."

I didn't think it was possible for someone to *actually* turn green, but whatever shade Avery's face just shifted to was damn near close. Her eyes flickered over to the elderly man sitting at the counter, dabbing his gray mustache with a napkin.

Her mouth dropped open in horror before she clapped her hand over it. "Olivia. Jail. You are– Oh my god. Gross."

I threw my head back and laughed, tears forming in my eyes as she continued to scold me, her voice muffled by her palm. Being scolded by Avery in her mom voice was slowly starting to become my favorite thing.

Selfishly because it meant that I was laughing again.

"I'm swiping right on the farmer."

"What farmer?" I jumped as Noah appeared out of thin air and snatched her phone from her hand. He jerked his head to the side, gesturing for me to move over.

"Would it kill you to say please?" I rolled my eyes and scooted to the left, scoffing as he swiped a piece of bacon from my plate and took a bite. "Manners, Noah Kent."

He ignored me, all of his focus going to the phone in his hand. His thumb swiped against the screen as he looked through the same pictures I'd just gone through. "No."

Avery snorted, reaching across the table to steal her phone back. "Big, burly man say no," she mocked, dropping her voice to sound like the caveman I often compared Noah to. "Newsflash, Noah. You can't control my dating life. Not anymore. Not since high school."

Noah chewed on *my* bacon for at least twenty seconds too long before stealing a swig of orange juice from *my* cup. "He farms celery." His arm draped around my shoulders, and a wet kiss landed on my temple.

"Hey, sweetheart," he murmured for my ears only. His breath coasted across my neck and sent a shiver down my spine.

Avery used her coffee to stifle a grin while my face burned a bright shade of pink. I don't think I would ever get used to this. These simple, nonchalant gestures grabbed the attention of the entire diner and had everyone in the room sharing secret smiles that were, unsurprisingly, not that secret.

I loved the normalcy of it all, but the casual way he would kiss me in front of a room of people never failed to kick my heart into overdrive. I wondered if he felt the same erratic nerves buzzing around in his stomach that I did.

"And?" I asked, reaching over and dragging my food in front of me. Would it stop him from stealing it? No. But it was worth a shot. "What's wrong with celery? Someone has to farm it."

Avery rolled her eyes like she already knew what he was going to say.

"Those who can't farm, farm celery," he said very matter-of-factly.

My eyes bounced back and forth between the siblings, trying to figure out what the fuck he was talking about. "Am I supposed to know what that means?"

"It's a quote from a TV show." Avery rolled her eyes again. "A fictional TV show, Noah. You don't even know anything about farming!"

"I know enough," he responded, not even trying to hide the defensive tone.

I loved watching the two of them interact. They reminded me so much of me and Jackson and the way we would bicker constantly about everything and nothing all at the same time. It was like a little piece of home here in Rose Hill.

"I'm not completely ruling him out *just* because he farms celery."

"You know that means he probably won't relocate because his farm is more than likely wherever he lives."

Avery paused like she hadn't considered that and chewed on the inside of her cheek. She sighed, slouching against the red vinyl seat. "I feel like every conversation we have leaves me in a horrible mood. Go to work. Let us finish breakfast in peace. You get her literally every other hour of the day."

I hid my grin behind my cup of orange juice, earning a glare from Avery.

"Hey." Noah reached over, grabbing a piece of sausage from Avery's plate like he wasn't waiting on a to-go order for himself. "You stole my breakfast buddy. Liv was mine first and now I eat breakfast alone. It's sad, really. So, sue me for wanting someone to talk to over breakfast."

Avery's hand swept over the table, gesturing to our food. "*This* isn't even *your* breakfast! You're just stealing our food while you wait for yours!" There was not a single ounce of remorse in her body for stealing me away from Noah. "Also, you guys eat lunch together every single day. And breakfast on the weekends. And don't think I don't know what goes on behind closed doors." Her eyebrows raised as she pointed a piece of sausage at us. "I think it's only fair that I get her for *one* meal."

"Oh my god, I'm like a child of divorce." I laughed, looking back and forth between Noah and Avery. "Please don't make me choose."

Noah rolled his eyes, scooting out of the seat when Barb called his name. "You know she'll choose me." He winked, then turned and made his way to the counter, and damn, I'd be lying if I said I wasn't tracking his every move.

Avery cleared her throat, crossing her arms over her chest with an eyebrow arched in my direction. "Could you be less obvious about checking my brother out when you're with me?"

"I don't physically think that is possible," I whispered, picking up my orange juice to take a sip. I thought maybe it would hide the way my skin flushed from being caught ogling Noah, but judging by the way Avery was laughing, it didn't.

Thankfully, my phone started to ring. I loved Avery, but discussing the intimate details of my life with her brother just seemed to cross a line.

Maybe she was right. The ogling would have to be kept to a minimum when she was around.

Rosy Cheeks Pre-K and Daycare flashed across my screen, and I groaned. A phone call right after school started could only mean one thing. Especially given my conversation with Rhea and the way Kennedy was acting.

"Hello?"

"Hey, Olivia." Rhea's voice dripped with sympathy.

"No, don't say it," I groaned.

"I'm so sorry, but I'm going to need you to come and pick up Kennedy. She started throwing up, and from the looks of it, I don't think it's coming to an end any time soon."

I held back another groan. I should've known this was coming. I was hoping that it wouldn't, but there was a newsletter sent out last week about a few kids in her class coming down with some kind of stomach flu, and I hoped and prayed that Kennedy wouldn't get it.

As much as I hated it, I couldn't help but be thankful it wasn't lice.

"Shit, okay. I'll be right there. Give me a few minutes."

"Okay, she'll be in the nurse's office waiting for you. Thanks, Olivia." Rhea hung up, and I let out a fake sob.

Noah stepped back over, his eyebrows pinched together. "Everything okay?"

"I have to go. Kennedy's puking. Are you gonna be okay without me there? I don't– Can I use a personal day or something? Do I have those? I don't actually know." I grabbed my purse and dropped a ten on the table, knowing it would be returned to me later. But that didn't stop me from trying.

"Just go, don't worry about it. I did run the shop by myself for the past four years." I think it was his attempt at teasing me, but the underlying tone of concern had the joke falling flat.

I shot him an appreciative glance, climbing out of the booth. "You're the best, thank you."

"The stomach flu?" Avery scrunched her face up, gathering her things.

"Yeah, I got a letter last week that a few kids caught it. But I was hoping we'd make it out unscathed. Apparently not. Hopefully, it's just a quick twenty-four-hour thing. Thanks for the company, don't swipe right on the farmer." I shifted my gaze to Noah. "Sorry, you're on your own for lunch."

I failed to mention that he would probably be on his own for the next few days. Because if there was one thing I'd learned since becoming a mother, it was that sickness does not stop with the child, and pretty soon, it would be me running a fever and dry heaving into the toilet after drinking a sip of water.

But we'd cross that bridge when we got to it.

Noah snagged his food from the counter. "I'm just gonna run to the shop for a minute. Call Jane and let her know I can't take her car in today. I'll meet you at your apartment? I can stop by the store and grab some..." His voice trailed off at the confusion on my face.

"What? No. You can't close the shop."

His mouth quirked. "I can and I will." He paused, shifting nervously on his feet. "If you want me to. Sorry, I don't want— I'm not trying to overstep."

My heart squeezed at the reminder that I didn't have to do this alone if I didn't want to, and I reached over, rising to my tiptoes to brush a kiss against his cheek. "I can't even tell you how much that means to me, but it's probably for the best if I tackle this alone for now. I don't want you to get sick."

He shook his head. "I don't care about that, Liv."

"I know, but it's okay. We'll be okay. Promise." My reassurances did nothing to smooth out the crease in his forehead.

Avery waved as I walked away, but Noah followed me out of the door, wrapping a hand around my wrist to pull me to a stop as I pushed out of the diner. "I'm serious, Liv. Call me the second you think you might need me. I don't care what time it is. I don't care about getting sick. I'll be there."

"I know you will." I smiled softly, lifting my hand to his cheek. "I'll call you, okay?"

"Okay." He bent to kiss my forehead. "Let me know when you get back to your apartment."

It only took me a few minutes to walk over to the school, and I found Kennedy right where they said she would be, sitting in the nurse's office, cradling a small puke bag to her chest. She had tears in her eyes; her face was flushed and splotchy. I hated it when she got sick, especially if there wasn't anything that I could do to help her.

"Hey, pumpkin. Not feeling too well?" Her little chin quivered as she shook her head, and my heart sank. "Come on, let's get you home."

I signed her out and made it approximately ten feet out of the door before she asked to be carried. I only made it about five more feet when she threw up all over my shoulder and down the front of my shirt.

This was going to *suck*.

* * *

I'd never been covered in that much puke. Not since Kennedy was an infant, at least. The acrid stench clung to my skin, and my fevered body ached. For the last twenty-four hours, it felt like I'd been glued to the bathroom floor. Whenever Kennedy wasn't puking, she was crying. Whenever she wasn't crying, she was sleeping, but those moments of rest were few and far between. I was drowning in exhaustion. And vomit.

I desperately wanted to prove that I could do this alone, that I was capable. But my stomach churned relentlessly, and I was ninety-nine percent sure I was running a fever.

The icing on the cake? Kennedy woke up about two minutes earlier and vomited down the front of my shirt. I was reaching a breaking point. Tears welled up in my eyes as Ken profusely apologized, her own tears streaking down her face, and now more than ever, I needed help.

I needed a shower, something to break my fever, and someone to tell me it was going to be okay.

My phone taunted me from across the bathroom. I knew it would only take one call or text to get Noah over here, but the guilt digging into my chest had me holding back.

In the past, whenever Kennedy got sick, I'd rely on my parents for help that Liam couldn't provide. My dad was retired and my mom worked flexible hours, so whenever I needed help, I would call them to lend a hand. I never felt guilty about asking them for help. But I felt guilty about asking Noah. I couldn't ask him to take that risk. I couldn't ask him to chance getting sick just because I couldn't handle being a single parent.

"Mommy, I don't feel good." Kennedy's voice was hoarse from crying, her face bright red and tear-stained.

My soiled shirt clung to my skin, the smell sending a wave of nausea through my stomach. But I stroked my hand over her hair, swallowing back the urge to throw up. "I know, baby. I'm sorry. Do you need to throw up again?"

She sniffled and wiped her nose with the back of her hand. "I think so."

I gently positioned her in front of the toilet, trying and failing to suppress my own roiling stomach.

Oh, god.

"Ken—" My hand clasped over my mouth. "I'll be right back."

After making sure she was in front of the toilet, I pushed off the floor and ran into my own bathroom, emptying the contents of my stomach.

Fuck the stomach flu.

The door flew open, and Kennedy stood in the doorway, tears flowing down her face. "Mommy—" Before she could finish whatever she was going to say, her eyes widened, and she threw up on the floor at my feet.

The first tear slid down my cheek. And then another. And soon, I couldn't see through the steady flow of tears flooding my eyes.

I was so unbelievably tired. My bones ached, and my stomach was churning in dangerous waves. All I wanted to do was take a shower and lie down. I wanted to be clean. I wanted Kennedy to be taken care of so I could take care of myself.

I wanted Noah. I wanted his hands on my face while he told me everything was going to be okay. I wanted to curl against him and let the heat that radiated from his body soothe the ache in my bones.

I wiped the tears from my cheeks and stepped over the vomit on my floor, then scooped a crying Kennedy into my arms and made my way to her bathroom.

Noah answered before the first ring had finished trilling. "Liv?"

I had no clue what came over me. But the deep, gruff sound of his voice fell over me like a thick blanket of comfort and security, and uncontrollable sobs wracked my body.

Kennedy was crying, I was crying. This was not what he signed up for, but I was on the verge of puking again, and I couldn't do this by myself. I just couldn't.

"Baby, what's wrong?" The softness of his voice sent another wave of emotion crashing through me.

My voice quivered as I confessed, "I think I need help." The sentence came out through a series of hiccups and sobs, each word heavy with the weight of vulnerability.

Beep. Beep. Beep.

My brows furrowed, and I pulled my phone away from my ear, staring at the home screen.

He hung up on me.

My lips quivered, and right as I was on the brink of losing it completely, three soft knocks sounded on the front door.

Kennedy was softly crying on my shoulder, her tiny arms wrapped around my neck and clinging tightly. I made my way over on shaky legs and flipped the deadbolt, easing the door open.

Noah stood in the hallway in front of me donning his signature uniform of a black t-shirt and dark wash jeans. His hair was all sorts of disheveled, sticking out in several different places. It hadn't even dawned on me to check the time.

"What—How did you get here so fast?"

"I've been sleeping on Avery's couch in case you needed me."

"You— You've been sleeping on your sister's couch? In case I needed you?"

I half expected him to be offended by the disbelief in my voice, but all he did was smile. Kennedy sniffled in my ear, and the soft look in Noah's eyes turned sympathetic.

"I didn't want to overstep." He reached out to brush his knuckles against my hot skin. "You said you wanted to do it alone and I will never make you feel like you aren't being heard. But I wanted to be close by... Just in case." I took a moment to study his face; the deep concern etched into his features, the warmth of his gaze soothing the panic in my chest.

The tears that welled in my eyes were no longer formed from a combination of exhaustion and despair. This time, the tears I shed were ones of relief.

He reached over and gently took Kennedy from my arms, paying no attention to the puke that had transferred from my shirt to hers, and tucked her against his chest. "Go take a second. I got her."

Chapter 39

Noah

Avery's couch was unbearably uncomfortable.

My back hurt, there was a kink in my neck that had been there all day, and if she weren't on the verge of kicking me out, I'd probably offer to buy her a new one.

It was driving me crazy to be away from Liv and Kennedy. I hated being kept at arm's length for the sake of not getting sick. The few texts I'd gotten from her were about Ken but she said nothing about how she was doing and it was killing me. I assumed by the suspicious lack of information that whatever Kennedy had was passed onto her and she didn't want to tell me she wasn't doing well.

Since she was clear about her want for me to keep my distance, I settled for the second-best option: staying on Avery's couch. I felt a lot better about being a few feet away if she needed me versus all the way across town.

I stood at the kitchen counter and poured myself a glass of water, yawning as Avery shuffled into the room. She only had one eye open, but I felt the weight of her glare regardless.

"Did I wake you?" I asked, taking a sip from my glass.

She sighed. "Thin walls. Nellie doesn't normally move around at night."

"Sorry," I grumbled.

Avery leaned her hip against the counter across from me. "You're stinking up my apartment with your broody man-ness."

I glanced up at her, blinking slowly. "I took a shower this morning. Yesterday morning. Recently."

She rolled her eyes. "Just go over there."

"She asked me not to."

"Since when do you actually listen to people?" She crossed her arms and quirked her brow. "You've been moping on my couch for like two days, and you're not helping anyone here."

"Sorry, what was that?"

"Har-har." She made her way over to where I stood and pulled her own glass down from the cabinet. "But seriously. Just go over there."

I sighed, running my fingers through my hair.

It didn't feel that simple. I wanted to, more than anything. But Liv had been adamant that I should stay away, so I had reluctantly obliged. It was hard to suppress the instinct to rush to her side, but I also didn't want to be overbearing. Things were still relatively new with us. I knew how I felt about her and had a pretty good idea that the feelings were mutual, but I was scared to overstep. She's had to deal with Debra breathing down her neck for the past year, the last thing she needed was someone else ignoring her wishes and making her feel inadequate.

But then my phone vibrated on the counter next to me, and I don't think I'd ever answered a call faster. Her gut-wrenching sob tore me in two. She was crying so hard that the words were barely audible, but the second she said she needed help, I was already on my way out the door.

I could see the exhaustion written all over her; her hair was sticking together at the ends where Kennedy's throw-up had dried it into one piece. Her bloodshot eyes filled with so much gratitude that I was kicking myself for not coming over sooner.

I knew how important it was for her to know she could do everything on her own, but this was killing me. Especially since I was just a few feet away the whole time. I wondered how many times she looked at her phone and fought the urge to call me.

I sat with Ken in the bathroom while Liv took a few minutes to change clothes and pull her hair up, and once she felt like she could stand for a few minutes without puking, she came to run Kennedy a bath while I cleaned.

It was thirty or so minutes later when I loaded the last bit of laundry into the washer, and Liv had successfully tucked Kennedy into bed with a puke bowl on the floor just in case.

Exhausted and worn down, Liv stood in the hallway outside Kennedy's room. Her eyes, heavy with fatigue, flickered with appreciation as she whispered, "Thank you."

Throwing her bed sheets and a few towels into the washer felt like the least I could do. I made my way over to where she stood, but she took a step back when I tried to pull her into my chest.

"I don't want you to get sick," she protested, her voice wavering around the edges.

I took a step closer. "Come here, Liv."

Her eyes filled with fresh tears as she stepped into my arms and I wasn't sure if it was exhaustion, frustration, or the fact that she didn't feel well, but I was going to do whatever I could to take it all off of her shoulders.

I pressed my lips to her forehead and rubbed slow circles on her back as she cried into my shirt. "What's wrong?"

She sniffled and rested her cheek against my chest. "I just—" Liv paused, shaking her head. "I hate not being able to do things on my own. I hate that I need you so much. I should be... I should be able to stand on my own."

I shook my head, slipping my finger under her chin and tilting her head back. "You don't give yourself nearly enough credit. You are doing an incredible job, and it kills me that you don't think so."

I pushed a loose strand of hair out of her face. "You can hate a lot of things. Being sick, Brussels sprouts, the color yellow." The corner of her mouth barely moved, but I took it as a win. "But please don't ever hate needing me. I'm not going anywhere. I promise."

She stepped back into my arms, and I continued to stroke her back. "It's okay to lean on others. You're still a fantastic mom, and Kennedy is lucky to have you. I'm here because I want to be, not because I think you can't handle it."

Her shoulders relaxed marginally as she sank into my chest. "Thank you. I wish I had something better to say, but I think the fever has fried my brain."

I snorted out a laugh and pulled away, keeping my hands on her shoulders.

"Thank you for the reminder. Tell me what you need."

Liv sighed, pinching the bridge of her nose with her thumb and forefinger. "I don't— I'm not even sure where to start. I'm so tired, but I need to shower, and the bathroom floor—"

"Is taken care of. Mopped and disinfected."

"I don't deserve you."

"At the risk of sounding cheesy, you deserve everything I have to offer and so much more."

She smiled softly, her eyes fluttering with exhaustion. "Would I be completely disgusting if I went to bed without showering? On a scale of one to ten, how likely are you to stop coming over after seeing me like this?"

"I think the fever really did fry your brain if you think this will send me running. I'm in it for the long haul, Brooks. Puke and all. Plus, Kennedy is good for my ego. She's the only one around here who laughs at all of my jokes."

Liv laughed, the blues in her eyes gaining back a little bit of their vibrant hue.

"Now... Go sleep. Shower when you wake up, and we'll handle the rest as it comes. 'Kay?"

"Come with me?"

I wanted to stay out here and clean Ken's bathroom for her. Maybe wait for the washer to finish up, but her eyes did that adorable little sleepy flutter, and I knew exactly where I needed to be.

* * *

"Mommy?"

A tiny little voice stirred me from my sleep, Liv's feverish body clinging to mine. I rolled at an awkward angle and looked up to see Kennedy standing in the doorway.

I slid out from underneath Liv, careful not to disturb her. It'd only been a few hours since we fell asleep, but she'd been up at least three times to puke so I wasn't surprised that she was out cold.

She needed the sleep.

Still dressed in my jeans and T-shirt from the day before, I tiptoed across the room. "You okay?"

Kennedy looked past me to her sleeping mother, her green eyes brimming with a touch of concern. She looked so much like her mother. I crouched down and held out my arms, and she immediately walked into the embrace.

"Is Mommy okay?" she asked in a hushed voice, her words barely more than a whisper.

"She's just sleeping," I reassured her, brushing a lock of hair from her forehead. "She needs to rest so she can feel better. And so do you. You feelin' okay?"

Kennedy shrugged, her wide eyes darting to the bathroom. "Maybe still a little pukey."

Her little hands clutched my T-shirt tightly. I patted her back gently. "Maybe a little pukey, huh?"

She sniffled but nodded. "I don't think I ever want to be sick again."

"I'll tell ya what, kiddo. I don't think I ever want you to be sick again either." I stood, lifting her into my arms and resting her on my hip.

After I gently eased the door to Liv's room shut, we made our way to the bathroom, where I sat on the floor and listened to her tell me about all of her favorite stuffed animals in between bouts of throwing up and crying. My heart tugged at the fatigued look on her face. I held her hair back, helped her wash her face, and rinse her mouth. Once she was clean and feeling a little better, we settled into the living room.

"Do you wanna watch a movie?"

Kennedy stifled a yawn behind her hand. "*Moana* always makes me feel better when I'm sick."

I wrapped her in a blanket and made sure the movie was playing before I stole some saltine crackers from Liv's pantry and convinced Ken to give them a try.

She climbed onto my lap and snuggled into my chest, her little hand resting over my heart and I was woefully unprepared for the rush of emotion that flooded my chest.

"Hey, Noah?"

I looked down at the little girl who had stolen a huge chunk of my heart and cleared my throat, attempting to clear away some of the emotion that pulled my vocal cords taut. "What's up?"

She took a deep, tired breath, her eyes fluttering closed and for a second, I thought she'd fallen asleep. But then she looked up at me, green eyes dancing in the low light from the TV and even without the words she uttered next, I knew that I would move Heaven and Earth to give her and her mother every ounce of happiness that they deserved in this life. "Thanks for taking care of me." She snugged a little closer. "I love you."

I took a staggering breath, the sting in my nose intensifying when her lips curved up into a smile. "I love you, too, kiddo." My voice was strained, rasping in my throat as I fought to hold myself together.

Kennedy's smile grew a little wider as her eyelids fluttered again. She snuggled closer, and after a few minutes, her breathing evened out, and I knew that she was fast asleep.

I gazed down at her, letting that mix of emotions swirl through me raw and unfiltered. Liv and I were navigating this path with care, step by step and day by day. But despite the odds, I knew what I was feeling. It was too soon, too fast, and yet, it was irrefutable. I knew without a shadow of a doubt that my heart beat solely for the two people in this apartment and that I was head over heels in love with Liv and her little girl.

Chapter 40

Olivia

Death.

This had to be what death felt like.

I didn't even have morning sickness this bad when I was pregnant with Kennedy. There was absolutely no way the universe wasn't punishing me now for every hangover I've avoided in my life.

That had to be what it was.

Because never in my life had I felt so absolutely worn down. I was mentally and physically *drained.*

At some point, while I was sleeping, Noah disappeared from my bed, and honestly, I couldn't even find it within myself to be upset.

There was puke in my hair, I hadn't showered in almost two days, and despite the fact that I was brushing my teeth *religiously,* a horrible taste lingered in my mouth from my time spent bending over the toilet.

Somewhere in the beautiful tales of parenthood, people seemed to leave out the fact that no matter how many precautions you take, their tiny little illnesses would still find a way into your home and absolutely wreck you in the process.

I managed to pull myself out of bed, one arm clutching my stomach, the other pushing aside tangled, unwashed hair from my face. The morning— or afternoon light streaming through the curtains was like an assault on my senses. I stumbled into the bathroom, clutching the counter for support, and peered at my reflection.

My stomach was calm at the moment, so I took a second to brush my teeth and untangle the elastic from my hair before wrapping it into another bun. I was a little surprised by the fact that Kennedy hadn't woken me up all night, and I hoped to god that meant she finally slept through the night. If I felt this bad, I couldn't even imagine how fatigued her little body felt.

I knew that I wouldn't feel fully refreshed without an actual shower, but I didn't want to do anything before checking on Kennedy first.

I stepped out into a quiet hallway, tiptoeing my way to her room only to find her bed empty. I stopped by the bathroom, expecting her to be on the floor by the toilet, but there was no sign of her or Noah in there either.

"Noah? Ken?" I called their names out softly, moving as quickly as I could down the hall until I came to a stop in the living room.

After not eating for two days and barely holding onto a few sips of water, I was already standing on shaky legs. But the sight that met my eyes when I turned the corner filled my heart with such warmth and tenderness that my knees almost buckled from the emotion that washed through me.

Noah was sprawled out on the couch, one leg dangling off the side, an arm draped over his eyes. Kennedy, my strong and sweet girl, was nestled against Noah, her head resting on his chest. I watched them for a moment, tracking the gentle rise and fall of their chests, listening to the soft snores sounding from Kennedy's lips.

My nose burned as tears welled in my eyes and despite the sickness and the exhaustion, I couldn't help but smile.

The sickness, the mess, the exhaustion— they were all part of this beautiful, messy, and imperfect life we were settling into and as much as it seemed to suck, I was thankful in that moment.

Not for the puking. I could do without the puking.

But I was thankful that we'd found somewhere to love and accept all of our shattered and fractured pieces while we found our way to being whole again. I was thankful for Noah and his family. I was thankful for Barb and all the times she swatted my hand away when I tried to pay for a meal.

The tears that streamed down my cheeks were born of exhaustion and happiness, but they were also born of a sweet, beautiful contentment. They were born of gratitude and love.

Kennedy stirred a little against Noah's chest, and his arm moved out of instinct, wrapping tightly around her to keep her from rolling off. There was an ache building behind my breastbone. A good kind of ache that reminded me of what we lost all while promising the best kind of future.

All of this felt too significant for the way I looked and felt, but I took a mental snapshot of the moment anyway.

Then, after telling myself it was okay to rest, I quietly made my way back to my room.

***

Noah's face was far too close to mine given I'd just spent the better part of the last twenty-four hours kneeling in front of my toilet.

I jolted back, yanking the comforter up past my chin.

He let out a soft chuckle and swept his fingers along my cheek with a grin. "Sorry, I said your name a few times. Tried to wake you."

I sighed and ran my hands over my face, laughing as gently as I could. "It's okay."

The mattress shifted under his weight as he sat down next to me, the warmth of his hand radiating through the blanket as he settled it over my thigh. I missed being close to him.

"How are you feeling?"

"Well," I paused, taking a deep breath to test the queasiness in my stomach. "I've said more than five words without puking, so I'm guessing better. I'm still so achy, though. How's Ken?"

His fingers gently massaged my thigh and I sighed, my body turning to putty in his hands. "She's good. No fever. No throwing up. She even ate a good breakfast and lunch."

My heart swelled in my chest, taking up every square inch of vacant space. God, I loved how much he cared about her.

"My parents dropped by with some medicine and some chicken noodle soup and decided to take Nellie back to their place, so Kennedy is hanging out with

Avery and I'm all yours for as long as you need me."

"Thank you," I whispered, his soft smile blurring as my eyes filled with tears. "I know you didn't sign up for this, but I am so grateful. I don't know what I would've done without you here."

"Sign up for what?" His thumb wiped the tear sliding over the bridge of my nose.

"This. The chaos. Taking care of us. Being puked on."

Noah looked down at me and there was a flicker of something in his eyes. Something so gentle and tenderhearted and it moved through my veins like warm honey, slow and sweet.

"This woman I know," he started with a playful roll of his eyes, pulling a small smile from my exhausted lips, "She once told me that caring for someone doesn't mean you tuck tail and run when the going gets tough. You care for the ugly bits, too. I knew what I was doing. I've known every step along the way. And there's not a single thing I would do differently now."

"You mean it?"

"I do. And *because* I mean it," he paused, leaning over to grab something off of the floor. "I need you to drink up." Noah lifted a white plastic bag from the convenience store and dropped a variety of sports drinks onto the bed. "We're gonna shower, then we're gonna eat. You're gonna drink lots of electrolytes, I'm gonna massage your feet, and then we're gonna go back to bed."

"Oh," I said quietly, "Well, Kennedy—"

"Is taken care of. She's watching *Moana* for the third time today. You're still an amazing mom. Now, you're going to let me take care of you." The corner of his mouth curled into a smile, and I folded immediately. My defenses were at an all-time low. Losing the fight to his dimple was inevitable.

"Okay."

He leaned over, his lips sweeping against my forehead. "Good girl."

Somehow, despite the low-grade fever already simmering my blood, those two words had my cheeks burning bright red, and when he straightened, his smile only deepened.

"Drink," he insisted, nudging a drink toward me. "I'm gonna get the shower started."

The fact that he said "we" only sank in when the faucet handle creaked, and water poured from the shower head.

*　*　*

I'd downed half a bottle of something vaguely blueberry-flavored when Noah stepped out of the bathroom.

He stood in the doorway, hip resting against the frame. Noah's arms crossed over his chest, and I realized that at some point while I was passed out, he'd switched from his signature black t-shirt to one that was light, heather gray. His dark-wash jeans were replaced by ones that were *just* a shade lighter. Honestly, the slight shift in color would more than likely be imperceptible to literally anyone else, but it was hard for me *not* to notice every little thing about him.

Given my current state, I kind of hoped he wasn't as observant when it came to me.

"Go get in. I'll be back in a sec." He pushed away from the door frame and snagged my robe from the back of the door, disappearing out of my bedroom.

A minute or so later, I was standing in front of the sink, rinsing the toothpaste from my mouth when he walked back in. The steam that billowed from the shower warmed my skin in a way that felt comforting compared to the heat of the fever I'd been enduring, and I could already feel my muscles relaxing. There was a paper bag clutched in his arms, and I watched him in the mirror as he set it on the counter next to me, fishing inside to pull out a candle, a lighter, something that looked like a foil-wrapped hockey puck, and a small bottle of acetaminophen.

He took a second to set everything up, lighting the candle and setting it on the tray above my toilet. He snagged the foil-wrapped thing and unraveled it, the soft smell of lavender and eucalyptus wafting through the air.

I craned my neck a little to see what it was.

"It's a shower steamer. My mom dropped them off when they came by earlier. She said the lavender is calming and the eucalyptus would help settle your stomach."

"Your mom's a lifesaver," I said with a grateful smile, appreciating the thoughtful gesture.

Noah turned toward the shower and dropped it inside before turning around and gesturing to the wall behind me. "Turn the light off."

I reached for the light switch, plunging the bathroom into a warm, flickering glow as the candle illuminated the small space. The scent of lavender and eucalyptus filled the air, and I had no clue if it was some sort of placebo effect or not, but I swore I was already starting to feel better.

Noah reached up, yanking his shirt over his head and tossing it off to the side. My eyes swept over the dips and curves of his chest, and for the hundredth time since Monday, I thought about how much I fucking hated the stomach flu.

This perfectly sculpted man was standing in front of me, shirtless, and instead of climbing him like a tree, I had to focus on keeping my knees from buckling because my body was weak and exhausted.

His pants came next, sliding down over thick thighs and being kicked to the side, leaving him in nothing but a pair of black boxer briefs.

Slowly, he made his way over to where I stood, his fingers finding the hem of my loose t-shirt. "Is this okay?"

I nodded, lifting my arms as he pulled the shirt over my head. Noah's thumbs hooked into the waistband of my sweats and he slowly eased them down my legs, one of his hands gliding along my calf to steady me as I stepped out of them.

His lips pressed against the stretch marks on my stomach as he stood, and I almost couldn't stand the look of adoration in his eyes. I loved the way he looked at me.

Love.

This wasn't the first time the word had woven itself into my thoughts about Noah. I think at first it was scary, as most new and vulnerable things were, but now it was almost comforting.

Especially after this week.

He'd seen me at my worst, hovering above rock bottom, and that glint in his eyes when he looked down at me remained steadfast and strong. I was terrified about feeling too much too soon, but all of those worries seemed to dissipate when he looked at me like that.

Like the possibility of loving me was the easiest thing in the world.

Noah's lips brushed against my shoulder. "You okay?"

I swallowed, my lips turning up into a small, teasing smile. "No funny business, Kent. I know that I look so utterly irresistible with my throw-up hair and the dark circles around my eyes, but I can't keep up with you right now."

He snorted out a laugh and grabbed my hand, pulling me toward the shower. "I give you my word, Brooks. No funny business."

I stepped into the shower, letting out a loud sigh when the hot water washed over my aching joints. The lavender and the eucalyptus wafted up through the steam and wrapped around me and *god*, this was exactly what I needed.

I faced the shower head and tilted my chin up, letting the gentle pressure of the water distract my body from every other foreign, achy feeling inside.

The shower curtain shifted, and Noah stepped in behind me. I was suddenly *very* aware of just how small this space was.

His chest pressed against my back, his arms winding around my front and settling on my stomach.

My head lolled to the side when his lips pressed against the spot where my shoulder and my throat met. It was impossible not to relax in his arms, my bones resembling something made of rubber.

There was nothing sexual about the way he held me or the way I was pressed against him. It was an embrace filled with care, warmth, and comfort. Three things I didn't even realize had been so obviously missing from my life.

Noah stepped back, his gentle hands gripping my shoulders as he turned me around. "Put your head back."

I closed my eyes and did as he asked, tilting my head into the steady stream of water and letting out a sigh when his fingers sifted into my hair. He worked his hands through my dry, stiff hair, massaging against my scalp until the puke was gone and it began to feel soft and manageable again.

I let out a small sound of disappointment when his hands disappeared, earning a small chuckle from Noah as he pumped some shampoo onto his palm.

He took his time lathering my hair, working his fingers from my scalp down to the ends, and if it weren't for the fact that I was standing, I probably would've passed out again.

Noah tipped my head back into the water once more and continued to knead my hair with his hands, slowly, carefully, intimately, until the suds were gone and washed down the drain. And after he'd done the same thing with my conditioner, his attention moved to my loofah.

His hands roved over every inch of my body in gentle, soothing motions, easing the tension from my muscles. And I could've stayed in this shower all day.

When I initially called him, I thought all I needed was help taking care of Kennedy so *I* could take care of *myself*. And he did that without question. He got up with her when she woke up, he fed her, he put on her favorite movie. He did everything that I would've done without a single ounce of hesitation.

I was so thankful. But I would be lying to myself if I said it didn't feel *amazing* to be taken care of.

To have medicine and food brought to me instead of fighting wave after wave of nausea at the store. To not have to be the one begging for someone, *anyone*, to take care of my daughter until I could stand again.

I, like most women, sacrificed a large part of who I was to motherhood. I was no longer Olivia the person, I was Olivia the mother. It was like I lost the ability to be a person with my own needs, desires, and vulnerabilities.

I knew that Noah loved and cared for my daughter, but he was always going the extra mile to make sure I remembered that I existed outside of her, as well. He reminded me that it was a necessity to have my needs met. It was okay to need someone if I couldn't do it on my own.

When he shuffled me back under the gentle spray of the water, I looked up at him with soft eyes. "Thank you for taking care of me. Of us."

Noah stepped closer, sliding his arms around my waist and tugging me into his chest. "My girls needed me. There's nowhere else I'd rather be."

Chapter 41

Noah

One shower and she was already looking more like herself. I felt guilty about pulling Liv out, and honestly, I would've left her in there all day if I could. She was content even after the water grew cold and goosebumps erupted across her skin. Her shoulders were loose, her head tilted back into the water as it streamed down her face and chest.

But when the first little shiver shook her body, I dried off and slipped out of the bathroom to grab her towel and robe from the dryer.

While Liv took her time getting dressed, I threw on the sweats my mom was sweet enough to drop off earlier and headed to the kitchen to get her some food.

It took Liv and Kennedy getting sick to realize just how much I'd missed the community I'd grown up in. How much I had missed out on over the past few years by rejecting their support.

The second that Barb found out they were sick, she put together a care package with a fuzzy blanket for Kennedy, a hot water bottle, an assortment of herbal teas, and a sleeve of saltine crackers.

My mom made a batch of her homemade chicken noodle soup and ran to some fancy store a few towns over for the candle and shower steamers, adamant that they would make Liv feel better.

Even Colt chipped in, dropping off a book from the library in front of the store, fresh fruit, and some organic ginger lozenges he got at the farmers market to help with any nausea.

Sometimes, there were a lot of disadvantages to living in such a tight-knit community. But times like this made every disadvantage feel so insignificant.

I might've shut out a majority of the community when Addie died, but seeing how just a few people came together to help Liv and Kennedy, reminded me of the few days after the accident. My appetite might've been non-existent, but there was so much food, I didn't need to worry about figuring out something to eat. There was a fundraiser to pay for all of her funeral expenses. While the snow was still falling, my sidewalk was magically shoveled every morning when I woke up.

As annoying as I used to find the somewhat overwhelming love of Rose Hill, I was starting to see just how lucky we really were.

I heard Liv's footsteps approaching as I poured the soup into a pan. She faltered as she entered the kitchen, the countertop she hadn't seen in almost twenty-four hours buried beneath all of her gifts. The steam from the hot shower had given her a rosy glow, and she looked a bit more rejuvenated, although still visibly exhausted.

Her widened eyes swept over the care package, the food, and the assortment of teas. "What's all this?"

"A few people around town heard you two were sick and dropped some stuff off."

She stared at it all for a second, blinking slowly. "For... Us?"

I stirred the soup, trying not to draw any more attention to it. I knew that she appreciated it, but I also knew she felt like she had something to prove and that she (unless her hands were tied) hated asking for favors. "Rose Hill loves you guys. Barb said she was bored when you didn't show up for breakfast or lunch, so she wanted to do whatever she could to get you back." I shot her a smile and rested the ladle on the stove. "They just wanted to help."

Liv looked up at me with watery eyes. "How do I even begin to say thank you?"

Leaning my hip against the counter, I shrugged and crossed my arms. "You just say it. People in this town don't give stipulations when you need help. They just help. No questions asked."

She let out a small laugh, her eyes drifting to the gifts again.

"I'm not used to kindness being anything but transactional. Rose Hill is *very* different than Evergreen in that way."

God, I hated that for her and Kennedy. But I wasn't so surprised given her reaction every time someone offered to do something for her.

Tugging on the hem of her shirt, I pulled her into my chest and pressed my lips to her temple. "Barb and Colt will probably both physically revolt when you try to say thank you. My mom will just tell you to shush. No one expects you to say thank you."

"Well," she started with a sniffle, "that doesn't mean it shouldn't be said."

I buried my smile into her damp hair, my heart swelling with the words I wouldn't let myself say. Not yet, at least. "You're a good person, Olivia Brooks."

She smiled against my skin, her lips gently grazing my bare chest. "No better than anyone else."

"I beg to differ."

* * *

Liv set her half-eaten bowl of soup onto one of the TV trays I'd stolen from Avery and leaned back into the couch. Her hand rubbed a soothing circle over her stomach as she blew out a deep breath and I sat up, ready to help her make a break for the bathroom.

"You okay?"

She smiled softly and closed her eyes. "Yeah, just my stomach reminding me that it has all the control here."

I set my own bowl down, snagged one of the throw pillows from beside me, and moved to her side of the couch, helping her lay down. "Colt swears by those lozenges." I walked into the kitchen to grab the small bag before walking back over to Liv. "I'm pretty sure they're meant to help with morning sickness, but he says they help with hangover nausea." I took one out of the wrapper and handed it to her.

When I sat back down, I tugged her feet into my lap, smoothing my hand over the top of her foot. "Just lie down, try to focus on something else."

My thumb pressed firmly against the heel of her foot and she let out a soft noise that would've turned my blood hot in any other circumstance. I worked my way up the arch of her foot, her muscles feeling tense and knotted beneath my touch.

Liv's eyes fluttered open, her gaze locking with mine. "How's Ken?"

I smiled, maintaining the pressure on her arch, working out the tension. "Avery texted while you were getting dressed. No puking, no fever. My mom sent Ave a few pictures of Nellie feeding the goats, and I guess Kennedy is now trying to figure out how many goats she could reasonably keep in her room without you noticing."

She snorted, her lips pulling into a wide smile as she looked up at the ceiling. "Of course she is." There was a look in her eyes, a flicker of something nostalgic. Then her teeth sank into her bottom lip as she sighed.

"You can talk about him. If you want to, that is. I'll always be here to listen. I think if anyone is going to be understanding of the complexities surrounding the situation, it's me."

I understood the hesitation. It was hard to talk about the person you lost to the person you found in the wake of your grief, especially when the wounds were still so fresh. But it was important to me that she felt like she could talk about such a significant person in her life.

"I know. Trust me, I do." She tilted her head a little to look down at me. "I just— I spiral whenever I think about how much I took away from Kennedy."

My hands paused for a second. "Took away?"

She sighed. "Please don't take this the wrong way, okay? I am so unbelievably happy here, and I know that Kennedy is, too. But sometimes I can't help but feel like moving away was almost a punishment of sorts for Kennedy. I took her away from her family, her friends, the only town she's ever known. A large plot of land where we could own a hundred goats. And chickens. Ducks. Whatever she wanted. Instead, we're in this tiny apartment where I can't even keep a houseplant alive because the natural light is horrible."

Liv's words hung in the air, heavy with the weight of her self-imposed guilt.

I resumed kneading the sole of her foot, taking a second to collect my thoughts since the first thing that came into my mind was begging her to move in with me. She and Kennedy would be the exact thing that house needed to feel like a home again. If that was what they wanted. All of the land and the small creek tucked back into the tree line would be endless entertainment for Ken. We could get some goats, maybe some chickens if Kennedy wanted, there was room. But now certainly didn't feel like the best time to bring all of this up, or how I'd basically already figured it all out.

"Sweetheart, we've talked about this," I murmured, my fingers tracing soothing patterns on her foot. "You didn't take anything away from Kennedy. You gave her a chance at a new beginning, a fresh start. She may have left some things behind, but she also has a happy mother here. And sure, goats are awesome, but something tells me she'd take this version of you over all the goats in the world."

I peeked over at her, watching her process my reassurances.

She took a breath, exhaling slowly. "You're right. I did what I needed to."

I leaned over, brushing a kiss against her cheek. "That's my girl."

We sat in silence for a few minutes, a TV show that I didn't recognize playing in the background. I watched her eyelids as they grew heavy, and when she finally stifled a yawn behind her hand, I patted her leg softly.

"It's so early," she whined. "I shouldn't be tired."

"Well, my foot rubs *are* magical, but unfortunately not that good. You're still sick. You need to sleep."

Liv nodded sleepily, her eyes barely staying open. "Yeah, you're probably right."

I pushed off the couch and extended my hand toward her. "Come on, let's go."

Her hand slid into mine as she stood. "Careful, Kent. I'm gonna get used to this."

"To what?" I asked, playing along.

She grinned playfully, her words filled with affection. "Being taken care of."

God, she had no idea. "I'm planning on it."

Chapter 42

Noah

It took another day for the worst of it to pass. The fever had died down pretty quickly, but the nausea and throwing up did her in.

It had been almost four days since her fever started and almost a full forty-eight hours since the last time she puked, but she was still drained.

Though, not too tired to fight me on how much I was doing around the house. She stood in the doorway leading to the dining room, her arms crossed over her chest and *fuck* she looked so good in my t-shirt.

If it weren't for the no-mouth-kissing stipulation she put into effect after a quick internet search of the stomach flu, I'd kiss that frown right off of her face. She was too worried about getting me sick to risk it.

One more day, according to Liv and the internet.

"You're folding my laundry."

I plopped a folded shirt down onto the table. "Happy to see the fever didn't fry your brain. You were worried for nothing."

The grin I flashed had her rolling her eyes. "Can I at least help?"

"No."

"Noah!" She sighed dramatically and I barked out a laugh, grabbing a pair of leggings from the laundry basket. "Come on, I'm feeling so much better. I haven't thrown up—"

Liv stopped mid-sentence, her eyes wide, and her hands up in the air. "This is my apartment! How am I being bossed around in my own apartment?!"

"It's the good kind of bossing around. The kind that shows you how much I care."

"I *know* how much you care. You held my hair back while I puked and took care of my daughter. You even cleaned my bathroom for me. The least you can do is let me fold my own laundry. Dr. Internet Search told me it's okay to ease myself back into everyday life. Dr. Internet has never let me down before."

I walked over to Liv, framing her face between my hands. She looked up at me with sweet, vulnerable eyes. "I know you don't like it when I use your full name. But Olivia Claire Brooks, sit your ass on the couch and rest. One more day of doing absolutely nothing won't kill you."

"It might."

I rolled my eyes and pushed her cheeks together so her lips puffed out. "It won't."

"I'm getting couch sores," she said with muffled words.

"Doubt it, but I'd be happy to do a little inspection." I dropped my hands from her face and reached to grab the hem of her shirt, Liv swatting my hand away with a laugh.

"Gross."

"Only for you, baby," I winked and her smile grew, though she did her best to hide it. "Go sit. Lay down. Read a book. Watch TV. Whatever you do, just do it in some sort of stationary position."

"You are so unbelievably stubborn."

"I'm failing to see how I'm the stubborn one in this situation." My hands landed on her shoulders and I spun her around, swatting her ass for good measure. "I'll come get you when I'm done."

"Good luck, I'll be one with the couch by then."

I grinned and waited until she was sitting on the couch to turn back around. Not too long ago, my idea of happiness was a six-pack of beer and passing out on my couch when I was *just* drunk enough to forget the pain in my chest, but not so drunk that I was hungover the next day.

Now, my idea of happiness was falling asleep on the couch with Kennedy while watching a princess movie, and folding Liv's laundry while she pretended to sulk on the couch.

Four months.

It only took four months for Liv and Kennedy to sweep into my life and give me a sense of purpose. Four months to change the trajectory of my future and bring me all the way back home.

I couldn't wait to see what the next four months had in store.

* * *

An hour later, I was tucking the last of Liv's clothes into her dresser when the front door swung open. Light, but hurried footsteps sounded through the hallway as Kennedy tore through the apartment in search of her mom.

"Mommy!"

I was assuming whatever noise just traveled from the living room to where I stood in the bedroom was the air punching from Liv's lungs as Kennedy launched herself into her arms.

"Hey, baby!"

I smiled, pushing the drawer back into its place before heading out to the living room.

Avery was pushing through the doorway with an armful of bags and stuffed animals, Kennedy clinging to her mother like a koala. The smile on Liv's face was breathtaking, all signs of fatigue or exhaustion gone.

Just as I reached over to grab something from Avery, Kennedy was squirming in Liv's arms to be put down and rushing over to me. "Noah!"

I bent down to her level and scooped her into my arms. "Hey, kiddo."

Her tiny arms wrapped around my neck, and I held her close, overwhelmed by the realization of just how much I missed having her around. Liv's questions weren't *nearly* as entertaining.

She leaned back in my grasp to meet my eyes. "Did you miss me?"

I scoffed. "What kind of question is that? Of course, I did."

She smiled a wide, toothy grin that hit me right in the chest. "I missed you, too." Ken hugged me tight again. "Thanks for making Mommy feel better."

I looked over her shoulder at Liv, and our eyes locked for a moment. In her gaze, I saw something that made my heart race a little. Maybe it was gratitude, but I think it was something more. I couldn't help but wonder if that look held a deeper meaning, one that she was just as scared of admitting out loud as I was.

"Any time, Ken."

She looked up at me again. "I'm hungry. Avery said you had soup for dinner."

"I sure do. Why don't you and Mom go curl up on the couch and I'll get it started?"

I set her down and she ran over to Liv, snagging her hand and pulling her into the living room without another word.

A bag thunked on the ground next to me.

"I know that look," my sister said quietly.

I glanced over at Avery and then back to my girls, Kennedy's loud laugh piercing through the room. "I'm sure you do."

She leaned against the wall, following my eye line. "You've got a real future with them, Noah. If you want it."

I swallowed as Liv threw her head back and laughed at something Kennedy whispered in her ear. "I do."

* * *

Ken yawned on the couch next to Liv, wiggling to snuggle in closer. Avery left shortly after dinner to grab Nellie, and we'd all retired to the couch for yet another screening of *Moana*.

There was a small, warm smile on Liv's face as she looked down at her daughter, brushing her hair out of her eyes. "Let's get to bed."

Kennedy nodded, yawning one more time, and then looked over at me. "Can Noah tuck me in?"

Her request caught me off guard, but I tried not to show it. I glanced at Liv, who met my gaze with a gentle, appreciative look in her eyes.

"Of course he can."

I rose from the couch and extended my arms out to Kennedy. "Come on, kiddo."

It was probably such a small and insignificant thing to her, but it meant so much to me. I knew that I would never be able to replace her dad, but I hoped that I could be someone worthy of her trust and love. Someone that she could rely on and feel safe with.

I was going to do everything in my power to be the man Liv and Kennedy needed.

Once Kennedy was tucked into her bed, arms piled high with an assortment of stuffed animals, I switched on her night light and the sound machine in the corner.

She let out a little yawn, her eyelids growing heavier by the second. "Love you, Noah."

That tightness in my throat was back, but it was a welcome feeling. One that reminded me just how lucky I was to earn those words and affection from a cute little girl who had been through so much in the last year.

I smoothed her unruly hair down with my hand. "Love you, too, kiddo."

"Night," she whispered.

"Goodnight."

Quietly, I left Kennedy's room, pulling the door gently closed. I was startled when I almost ran into Liv in the hallway.

Her blue eyes were soft but bright, holding the remnants of so many different emotions. The lights in the living room were all switched off, the glow from the TV gone.

There were a lot of things we needed to talk about. A lot of questions, uncertainties, and complexities that need to be unraveled in the days and weeks ahead. But as I stood there, gazing into Liv's eyes, I realized that no matter how complicated it might get, we had one fundamental truth on our side: everything would be fine as long as we figured it out together.

We'd navigate the challenges, celebrate the triumphs, and find our own way in this new chapter of our lives. It wouldn't always be easy, but it would be worth it.

"We've got a lot to figure out," I whispered, my voice barely audible in the quiet of the night.

Liv's smile gave me the answer to everything I'd been questioning earlier. "We do."

"But let's figure it out tomorrow. When Dr. Internet gives you the clear to kiss me."

Her smile somehow grew wider. "Tomorrow."

Chapter 43

Noah

I was never really a fan of waking up early.

Until I was waking up next to her.

The soft rays of morning sunlight filtered in through the blinds, and I watched as they danced across her skin in hues of orange and yellow. Her hair was splayed across the pillow like a golden halo, and the gentle rise and fall of her chest would've lulled me back to sleep if I hadn't been so enamored by the woman lying next to me.

Liv had brought so much beauty into the otherwise empty, dull void that I existed in. She was a field of blooming wildflowers, bringing life and color to an otherwise dreary landscape.

The quiet melody of her alarm broke up the silence of the morning, and she rolled over to switch it off, giving me the perfect opportunity to pull her body to mine. She giggled as I buried my face in her hair, my arm sliding around her stomach. The backs of her thighs were pressed against mine, her back melded to my chest, and I savored the feeling of each soft curve as she sighed into me. Her sweet vanilla scent filled my nostrils as I nuzzled closer, and *god…* I wanted to spend the whole day with her tucked against me.

I kissed her hair, and then the freckle behind her ear, and her head tilted as I moved to her neck, goosebumps erupting across every inch of exposed skin.

Liv's steady breathing turned ragged as I dragged my mouth lower, my lips sweeping down the length of her throat until they landed on her collarbone.

I knew we had to get up soon; I knew that I had to leave before Kennedy was awake, but there were only so many minutes in the day that we had to ourselves and I planned on taking advantage of every single one of them. Despite the nagging sense of responsibility that lingered around the edges of my mind, it was all too easy to lose myself in her soft sighs and the way she arched against me.

Liv sighed my name, her fingers lacing with mine as my lips continued their path over her skin, and this fire burning between us was dangerously close to eviscerating every last ounce of control that existed within me.

My breath began to match hers, choppy and frantic as she pushed back against me. We were teetering on the edge of something we wouldn't be able to come back from and I wasn't sure if I had it in me to stop.

Thankfully, or regretfully, Liv's second alarm of the morning made that decision for me. This one was a shrill ringing, a louder, more high-pitched noise in case we slept through the first one.

It jolted us both from our stupor, my chest heaving with each labored breath as Liv's body melted into the bed. She rolled onto her stomach, groaning into her pillow as she silenced the alarm.

I chuckled and rolled onto my back, spearing my fingers through my hair. That raging inferno between us had once again been tamed, and while it was never gone completely, it was at least contained for the time being.

She looked over at me, disappointment tugging at her brows. Her skin was flushed a deeper shade of pink than usual, and as she rolled onto her side again, my eyes trailed the length of her neck, following that pretty pink color until it disappeared beneath the hem of her tank top.

"Noah," she whined, dragging my name out while burying her face back into the pillow. "It's your turn to put away the bedroom eyes."

"I have no idea what you're talking about." I feigned innocence, but I knew exactly what look she was describing. It was the same one she'd given me countless times as I fought between pulling her body against mine or climbing out of bed.

She snorted into her pillow, her words muffled as she spoke. "I'm weak. You can't look at me like that and then expect me to just go about my day."

"Like what?" I teased.

"Like— Like—" Liv turned to face me, waving her hand loosely in front of my face. "Like you're imagining all these dirty things in your brain."

I let out a low chuckle, rolling toward her and pressing a kiss to her bare shoulder. Dirty didn't even begin to cover it.

Slowly, I moved to the pulse point on her throat, and then to the shell of her ear. "The filthiest."

She groaned again and reached back to grab the comforter, dragging it over her head. "Do you think we should tell her? I'm so tired of being up late and waking up at the ass-crack of dawn just so you can sneak out. Or holding my breath whenever her bed creaks. I honestly don't even think she'd care. She'll probably just shrug her shoulders and ask for a banana or something. *And* you stayed the night when we were sick, she didn't say anything then."

I smiled at her frustration, tugging the comforter down until her pink cheeks were exposed and her bright blue eyes were on mine. "I think that's a question only you have the answer to."

Liv rolled her eyes. "Okay, Yoda. You are far too philosophical for five-thirty in the morning."

"Well, here's something else for you." The way her nose scrunched told me that she knew exactly what I was getting ready to ask. "Have you decided what you're going to do next week?"

She groaned, rubbing her temples with her hands.

Liv had gotten a text from Debra this week asking if she was planning on flying back to Evergreen since Kennedy was out of school for fall break. She'd been tossing the idea around but had yet to land on something solid. I knew that she was going to wait until the absolute last minute to make her decision, and I could understand why. But if she was going to go, the flight needed to be booked.

I propped myself up on my elbow. "You don't have to go."

She sighed.

"Or," I reached over and twirled a strand of hair between my fingers. "You can go. Kennedy can see her grandparents, you can see Gia. And then you come home and we can reenact all of the dirty things I've been picturing in my mind."

Her head rolled against the pillow as she looked at me and arched her brow. "You promised filthy."

"Yes, my apologies. Filthy."

Liv smiled, but it lacked its usual warmth. "I just know it's going to be so weird and awkward. I mean, I haven't talked to my parents since before I moved. Deb and I have been tiptoeing around each other for months. But I also know that Kennedy is more important than me being uncomfortable." She paused and let out another quiet groan. "She misses them." Another pause. "I'm gonna have to go, aren't I?"

I propped myself up on my elbow, my fingers still gently playing with her hair. "You don't *have* to do anything, Liv. But—"

"I hate buts," she whispered.

"*But*, I think you'll feel more negatively about not going."

She sighed again. "I think you're right."

"So you're going?"

"I don't know."

I laughed and pressed my lips against her shoulder again, freezing when a tiny hand knocked on the door.

"Mommy?"

Liv's eyes were the size of saucers as they flitted between me and the door. "Yes, baby?"

"Do I have to wait for Noah to leave or can I come in now?"

Liv's mouth dropped open and I stifled a laugh behind my hand. This kid missed absolutely nothing. I was a little surprised she didn't say something sooner. When she and Liv had been sick, I'd been openly affectionate with Liv the whole time Kennedy was here. Well, as openly affectionate as you could be with someone puking their guts out.

"I think she knows," I whispered, narrowly dodging the playful slap Liv directed at my arm. "You have to answer her. I can hide in the bathroom if you want."

"What good would that do? She already knows you're here," she gritted through clenched teeth. Liv cleared her throat and spoke up. "You can come in."

The doorknob twisted and a tangled mess of blonde hair poked its way through. Kennedy yawned and stepped through, pushing the door shut behind her, her eyelids heavy as she trudged across the room.

She climbed onto the foot of the bed and crawled in between Liv and me, snuggling under the blanket and closing her eyes. Less than thirty seconds later, she was snoring.

I looked over at Liv, her lips turned up into the smallest smile. "Is this okay?"

"Yeah," she whispered back, settling back into bed and pulling the comforter back up to her shoulders. "More than okay, I can go back to sleep."

I shook my head with a laugh and shifted closer, draping my arm around both of them. "I don't think she cares."

Liv grinned and looked over at me. "No, I don't think she does."

Chapter 44

Olivia

I was running out of time to make a decision. If we were flying back to Evergreen, I needed to book our flights. If we were staying, I needed to tell Deb And probably my parents.

But instead of doing that, I did what any rational person would do and procrastinated.

Avery and I left the girls with Noah and took the afternoon to drive to Wilmington, treating ourselves to a trip to Target, pedicures, and a late lunch at a local seafood place.

But all too soon, the day was coming to an end and the distraction was gone. The streetlights rushed by in streaks of warm light as we drove down the interstate, Avery humming to the song playing softly from the radio.

This was why I didn't want to leave. I didn't want this bubble to burst. I wasn't ready for the reverie that I'd been lost in to come to an end.

"You're thinking pretty hard over there."

My fingers tapped against the steering wheel in beat with the song, Avery's eyes burning a hole into the side of my head. I spared her a glance before focusing back on the road. "What do you think I should do?"

She took a deep breath, relaxing back into her seat. "Honestly?"

"Of course."

"I think you should stay."

My eyebrows shot up, my eyes flickering over to hers. "Really?"

"Really. You seem so happy and I would hate for something to jeopardize that."

I sat with her words for a moment, knowing just how true they were.

"You don't think it's selfish?"

"I never said it wasn't. But it's okay to be selfish."

I sighed. "Being selfish is what got me here in the first place. I don't think it can also be the thing that keeps me away, ya know? I eventually have to go back. I have to face everything. Everyone. I can't stay away forever."

"You don't have to stay away forever," Avery said gently. "But you can stay away for now. Learn to be happy again. Being selfish isn't a bad thing. It took me a long time to understand why Noah shut everyone out. I didn't see it at first. The why."

She paused, picking a piece of lint from her jeans while she stared out of the window. "But once I did, I was so mad at myself for missing it before. For being angry that he wouldn't let us help. I know that everyone is taking their own grief out on you, and I know that you feel some sort of obligation to them because, underneath it all, you still love them. But just let yourself be selfish a little bit longer before you chance someone trying to take it away."

Avery's words sank in as I continued to drive down the dimly lit road. I had been carrying a heavy load, trying to balance everyone's expectations and my own grief.

I took a deep breath, the weight of my indecision slowly lifting. "I think I just want to be happy and to keep healing without constantly worrying about everyone else."

Avery nodded in agreement. "So, you should stay. Stay here until you're ready to face everyone there. Stay happy. Stay smiling. You can deal with the rest of it later."

Relief washed over me and I knew my decision had been made. "Thank you, Ave. I honestly don't know what I'd do without you."

She smiled and reached over to squeeze my hand. "Your parents— Deb— they might not understand now, but they will eventually. But until then, just focus on you and that adorable little girl and finally being happy again. Alright?"

I glanced over at her with a smile. "Alright."

***

I could hear the bass thumping from my apartment down the hall, and Avery's grin spread wide across her face. Taylor Swift's "The Man" blasted through the speakers, Kennedy and Nellie's voices screaming along to the lyrics.

One deeper, richer voice sang right along with them.

I looked over at Avery with a smile and couldn't contain the giggle that burst through my lips as I walked faster to the door.

Thankfully the music was too loud for them to hear the jingle of my keys as I fought with the lock to get in.

"Hurry!" Avery whispered with a laugh, bouncing on her toes behind me.

"I'm trying! This stupid lock always sticks!" I threw my shoulder into the door, and it flew open just as Noah and the girls danced their way down the hall, completely oblivious to our presence.

My hand slapped over my mouth to stifle a laugh. Noah's hair was sticking out in a bunch of tiny little ponytails, a variety of butterfly clips, and colorful barrettes decorating the loose strands too short to stay put with an elastic. His cheeks were painted an obscenely bright shade of neon pink, and tiny little gold star stickers were pressed to his temples.

Avery crept forward to take a video as they marched into the living room and I gently eased the door shut, closing my eyes and listening to the musical cadence of Kennedy's laugh and the shameless off-key singing from Noah. My hand pressed against my sternum as if I were trying to hold in this rush of happiness that exploded inside of me. It was a bright, intoxicating feeling like the sun was rising in my chest and breaking through a wall of dense clouds.

This was why I needed to stay. I needed to hold onto this for just a little bit longer.

The song began to fade, and the girls were jumping up and down in the living room, begging for him to start the song over.

"Again, Noah! Again!"

Noah let out a breathy laugh as he struggled to catch his breath. "Okay, okay. One more time before your moms get home because..."

"Eff the patriarchy!" the girls yelled at the same time.

"Exactly!"

"Noah Anderson Kent!" Avery gasped as she rounded the corner, and the laugh I'd been biting back burst through my lips. "I support the message, but *come on!*"

He whipped around as I followed quickly behind his sister and my mouth dropped open as I saw the extent of his makeover.

Noah's eyelids were painted a sparkly purple color, his a shimmering blue. He smiled wide and proud, his hands landing on his hips and only then did I notice the nail polish covering so much more than just the nail.

My god, he looked fucking ridiculous.

And *god*, I was *so* ridiculously in love with him.

I gasped for a breath, bending at the waist when I couldn't hold it in anymore, laughter bubbling up my throat and spilling through my mouth. My lungs burned, my eyes flooded with tears.

Noah walked over, placing his hands on my shoulders as I straightened to look at him. I wheezed out another laugh and wiped a tear from my cheek.

"Laugh all you want, Brooks. But I'm rocking this eye shadow."

"Man," I paused, letting out another obnoxious laugh when he batted his eyelashes. "You really are. I mean, the sparkles really make your eyes pop."

"Right?"

I rolled my eyes at him and looked around his shoulder, and the girls were both grinning from ear to ear. "You guys did a great job, he looks *amazing*."

"Thanks, Mommy!"

Avery snagged their attention and pointed to the floor, instructing them to clean up the beads from the friendship bracelets they were making.

Noah's eyes danced with amusement, the deeper flecks of green actually did stand out more with the purple. My smile felt wild around the edges, brimming with happiness and so much love for the people in this apartment.

These wild, chaotic, *beautiful* emotions were exactly what I'd been searching for this whole time, and I never wanted to lose them.

"How was your day?" he asked, his thumb swiping away the tear that raced down my cheek.

"Perfect," I responded, tilting my head to lean into this palm. "Absolutely perfect. But not nearly as educational as yours. I mean, I got a pedicure. You guys tackled the intricacies of the patriarchy?" I let out a slow whistle. "I should leave you alone with the girls more often."

"I wouldn't say intricacies per se. More of a blanket statement to prove a point."

There was so much love for him building in my chest it almost felt suffocating. Like I needed to get it out before it consumed me whole. Though, something told me it was too late for that.

There was no simple way to love someone like Noah. Someone who protected his heart so heavily after a devastating loss. He would give little glimpses of how much he cared through simple acts and silent support, never letting too much of his vulnerability show. But little by little, I witnessed the transformation, the gradual unraveling of those defenses, and the unveiling of the incredible man he was.

I felt so lucky to be on the receiving end of a love so breathtakingly beautiful and raw.

In an effort to memorialize these beautifully raw emotions, I was about to tell this man, one painted with pink blush and purple eye shadow just how madly in love with him I was.

I could feel it when I looked at him, feel it when he touched me. With every slow curve of his smile and gentle slide of his fingers on my skin, I could feel the love he felt for me in return.

"I—" My phone vibrated in my hands, and I let out a frustrated breath. "Just a sec."

My mom's face graced my phone for the first time since late June, and my stomach dropped to my feet. Something had to be wrong. I hadn't talked to my dad. Or Jackson. If she was calling me, one of them had to be dying or worse, right?

I could feel the blood draining from my face. "I gotta— It's— My mom. I gotta take it."

"Go," he urged, every hint of amusement wiped from his features. "Go."

I stared at the screen for a moment longer, my stomach rolling at the thought that something bad had happened. I couldn't handle another loss. I was just starting to feel human again.

Noah's finger lifted my chin. "You're catastrophizing, sweetheart. Just answer. It's probably nothing."

"Right," I said with a shaky exhale. "It's probably nothing." I smiled at him, but the chest-tightening happiness was washed away and replaced by a sense of unease as I answered the call from my mom.

I rushed into my room and kicked the door shut behind me as I lifted my phone to my ear with a shaky hand. "Mom?"

There was a quiet, shaky breath on the other side and then she cleared her throat and the mask of indifference was in place. "Olivia."

I flinched at the edge of her tone, missing the days when her voice didn't carry so much vitriol toward me.

"Everything okay?"

My mother cleared her throat again. "Fine, yes."

I waited for her to ask about me. Or her grandchild. I waited for her to tell me that something horrible had happened and she would never forgive me for being absent. I waited for something, *anything* that would show me that she missed me.

But none of it came. And when she finally spoke again, there was a brief moment of relief that it wasn't something serious, but it was quickly replaced by a deep, aching sense of dread.

I made my decision to stay in Rose Hill for the week. To stay in this bubble and let the rose-tinted glasses convince me that everything was just fine.

But in a short sixty-second phone call, the bubble had burst, and the glasses were bent in two, the lenses smashed on the floor.

"You wanted updates about the house. Updates that I am providing as the sole real estate agent in Evergreen. There's been an offer put it in. If everything goes to plan, they'd like to close by the end of the month."

I ignored the insinuation that if she didn't have to call me, she wouldn't.

"The— The end of the month? That's in less than two weeks."

"Correct. As you know, there aren't a ton of people coming and going in a town like Evergreen, so I'd suggest jumping on the offer while it's there."

There was a beat of silence. "Okay. We can do all of that over the phone or on a computer?" I hated asking that question. It would do nothing to soothe the bite of her tone.

"The paperwork? Yes. But you'll need to collect your boxes from the bedroom. I counted. There are ten."

Jesus Christ. I didn't realize I'd left so many behind. I knew that I'd left some of Liam's stuff behind, things that I couldn't throw away but didn't have room for or need. My original plan was to give them to Deb. That became a little hard to do when she stopped talking to me, and then I was across the country and the one refusing to engage with her.

I sighed, massaging my forehead with my fingers. "Um— Okay. I'll call Jack and—"

"Jackson won't be able to help you."

"Oh," I responded quietly, giving her a second to expand on why he wouldn't be able to help but she didn't. "Alright."

"I suggest you come get them yourself."

I scoffed. "Mom, I can't just drop everything and—"

"Debra said you were planning on coming to town anyway. It shouldn't be too out of your way to grab your things while you're here."

"I never told Deb I was coming to town. I hadn't— I hadn't made a decision yet." Whether she could hear the lie on my tongue or not, she didn't say.

She let out a long-winded sigh, one that was usually followed up by some kind of speech about how disappointed she was in me. "Listen, Olivia. I just need to know if you're interested in reviewing the offer. It's right at asking price; they'll pay for their own closing costs. The boxes just need to go. Let me know tomorrow by the end of the day what you want to do. But the sooner, the better. You don't want them to walk."

There was another lull. I could hear the girls giggling in the living room, something on the TV playing from my mom's side of things.

I sat down on the edge of the bed, rubbing the heel of the palm against my forehead. I hated that I couldn't be happy about going back to Evergreen. One phone call about facing everything back at home and all of the light, intoxicating happiness I was grappling to control was suffocated once more.

I don't think I'd ever be able to truly be happy here in Rose Hill unless I confronted what was waiting for me back in Wyoming.

"Olivia?"

"Still here," I mumbled, dragging my hand down my face. "We'll be there. Just— I need a few days for flights, and I'll need to—" I snapped my mouth shut, sparing her the details she probably didn't care to hear anyway. "I'll let you know when we're flying in."

"We're terribly busy this week, but I'm sure you could arrange—"

I cut her off with a scoff. "Don't worry about it, Mom. I'll inconvenience someone else with my presence. Thanks for the call."

My thumb slammed down on the screen to end the call, and I tossed the phone somewhere on my bed behind me, burying my face into my hands. I took a deep breath, trying to center myself and clear away the bitter taste left in my mouth. My heart ached from the strained relationship we now had and the realization that it would probably never recover.

I knew I wasn't perfect, but I would never understand the flawed logic behind their judgment. They berated me for leaving but said and did so many things to keep me away.

The door opened and closed with a gentle click, and Noah's socked feet padded across the floor until he was standing in front of me. "Everything okay?"

He squatted down and in any other scenario, I probably would've teased him for the way his knees cracked in the process. His forearms rested on my knees as I lifted my head from my hands, coming face to face with sparkly makeup and tiny stickers.

I sniffled, meeting his gaze through the blurry veil of tears in my eyes. "Your lipstick is smudged."

His mouth tilted into the sweetest smile. "That's embarrassing."

"Happens to the best of us," I responded with a weak shrug.

Noah's eyes swept over my face before he sighed. "You're going back?"

My eyes fell shut and I took a couple of slow breaths. "I'm going back."

He tucked a piece of hair behind my ear. "What do you need from me?"

"A hug." I let out a weak laugh as Noah stood, wasting no time and pulling me into his arms. My body melted into his, fingers curling into his t-shirt. The spicy, warm scent of his cologne flooded my nostrils, and I took a second to commit it to memory.

His lips brushed against the top of my head. "Just promise me one thing," he murmured into my hair.

"What's that?"

"Promise that you'll come back to me." There was something so raw in his voice like he'd torn down every last defense. "That no matter what they say or do, you won't let them get to you. You've come so far, Liv. You are so much stronger than you give yourself credit for. Don't let them pick you apart."

With my heart in my throat, I tilted my head to look up at him, his eyes reflecting the same vulnerability in his voice. "I promise."

His smile was gentle, and I was immediately distracted by the shimmer of his blue lipstick.

"You look ridiculous."

He threw his head back and laughed before planting a sparkly kiss on my forehead. "You're just jealous that you can't pull off blue lipstick as effortlessly as I can."

I smiled at the man I loved, relinquishing some of the smothering tension in my chest. It would be so easy to whisper those three words right here in the privacy of my room. They sat on the tip of my tongue, anxious to be set free. But I tucked them away, knowing that there would be plenty of time for blubbering confessions and heartfelt words when I was finally able to close the chapter that lay ahead.

Chapter 45

Olivia

"I think I don't like flying." Kennedy squirmed in her seat, rubbing her right ear for the hundredth time since we took off and my stomach twisted with guilt.

I'd never had an aversion to flying before, but at this point, I was right there with her. I was exhausted, my head was pounding. Thank god Gia was more than willing to pick us up from the airport, because I don't think I would've been able to endure a forty-five-minute drive with my mom or Deb after such a shitty day.

It was hard enough to say goodbye to Noah at the airport in Wilmington, but then our flight was delayed, and because of that delay, we missed our connecting flight in Chicago. Kennedy was a trooper, but she was at the tail end of her patience for the day and we still had about fifteen minutes until we landed.

I draped my arm around her shoulders and she nestled into my side the best she could. "I know, honey. I'm sorry. It's been a long day, hasn't it?"

Our flight took off around six P.M. from Delaware and now, we were pushing one-thirty in the morning. Driving to Evergreen would add another forty-five minutes. I just wanted to fall into bed and sleep for twelve hours.

Kennedy looked up at me, her eyes drooping with exhaustion. She stifled a yawn behind her hand. "How much longer?"

I tapped the screen on my phone. "About fifteen minutes."

"And when do we get to go home?"

"Aunt Gia is going to pick us up at the airport and then tomorrow—"

"No, Mommy." She cut me off, her brows furrowed. "*Home.* Back with Noah and Avery, and Nellie?"

"Oh." My heart clenched, but there was also a tiny bit of relief that eased some of my nerves about landing in Wyoming. She was happy in Rose Hill. Happy enough that she considered it to be her home. Happy enough that she couldn't wait to go back.

"Um—" I cleared my throat and brushed her hair away from her face. "We go back home on Monday."

"What day is it today?"

"Technically Wednesday."

She huffed. "That's a long time to be away."

"I know, baby. But we're gonna see Gigi and Papa, and Grandma Julie. Grandpa Joe. Aunt Gia. Maybe even Uncle Jackson." I hoped that she couldn't hear the nerves that lingered in my voice.

"How come Noah couldn't come with us?"

The collar of my crew neck was suddenly *very* suffocating. "Well, Noah had to stay back and keep the shop open. And he's going to spend the week with his family."

I could almost see the cogs turning in her brain. "But—" Ken shot me a quizzical look. "Isn't Noah our family?"

My throat tightened and I sucked in a breath as I looked down at my beautiful, insightful daughter. "I think so. What do you think?"

She looked at me with pursed lips and tired eyes. "I think so, too."

"Well, I think we should probably tell him that when we get back."

"You don't think he knows?"

A small smile tugged at my lips. "I think he knows. Maybe we can call him in the morning?"

That seemed to perk her up a little. "Can I tell him about our pizza?"

Kennedy hadn't stopped talking about the deep-dish pizza we had while in Chicago for a few hours. I lost track of the amount of times she asked if Noah would be able to make it for us.

I sure hoped he could because Ken would be devastated otherwise.

"You can tell him all about your pizza."

Seemingly satisfied, she smiled and snuggled a little closer. "I wish he was here."

"Me, too."

* * *

I wasn't expecting the tears when I laid eyes on Gia. It might've been the exhaustion, I had no idea, honestly. But when we turned the corner from baggage claim and she was right there waiting with that anxious look and her bottom lip trapped between her teeth, I couldn't stop the tears from flowing.

She dropped to her knees as Kennedy squirmed out of my grip and took off toward her with a wide smile and bright eyes.

I stood back and let them have their moment, watching as Kennedy's little limbs clung to my best friend so tight her knuckles blanched. Gia peppered kisses all over her cheeks and forehead, whispering how much she missed her in between each kiss.

God, I wish I could convince Gia to move to Rose Hill. She would love it there. And then I wouldn't have to miss her so much.

Her dark brown hair was twisted into a bun on the top of her head, bright blue glasses perched on the bridge of her nose. Gia always had this effortless, natural beauty that I was so jealous of. She could rock the no-makeup look without resembling something on par with a recently embalmed corpse.

Even now at almost two in the morning, there were no hints of dark circles or exhaustion.

She wore a pair of black leggings that hugged the generous curve of her hips and thick thighs, and a cropped zip-up hoodie that cinched at her waist and accentuated her hourglass figure. Even in leggings and a hoodie, she was fucking stunning.

She stood and propped Ken on her hip, extending her arm out in my direction at the same time Kennedy yelled out, "Group hug!"

I stepped into their arms and we stood there, a tiny island of giggles and happy tears amid a sea of tired travelers heading to their next flight.

"I missed you," Gia whispered in a watery voice.

I squeezed her a little tighter, taking in the scent of her coconut and pineapple body spray. I knew I missed her, but I didn't realize just how much until right now. "I missed you, too."

She pulled away and pinched my cheek between her finger and thumb, laughing when I swatted at her hand. "Ready to go?"

"Beyond," I said with an exasperated roll of my eyes.

Gia chuckled and set Kennedy down, snagging the car seat and Ken's suitcase from the floor. "Let's get you kids into a bed."

As we walked out of the airport, the brisk night air hit me, dispelling some of the fatigue from our long journey. I pulled my jacket a little tighter around my body and squeezed Kennedy's hand as we walked through the small parking lot. The city lights twinkled in the distance, and I felt a mixture of emotions swirling inside me. Evergreen was just a short drive away, and I thought I would be eager to see my parents and my brother, but instead, this sense of apprehension gnawed at me.

I couldn't deny the knot of nervousness tightening in my stomach. Coming back to Wyoming meant facing my parents and Deb, the people who had once ruled my life with their expectations and judgments. I wondered how much had changed in their minds since I left, and if they understood my decisions. Based on the latest conversations I had with them, the answer was no.

I installed Kennedy's car seat and got her buckled in while Gia loaded our suitcases into the back of her Jeep. And when I settled into the passenger seat, there was a tug on that string that wove its way around my heart. My phone vibrated in my hand and I looked down to see a text from Noah.

Noah: Land yet?
Me: Just did. Loaded into G's car now and getting ready to head to Evergreen
Noah: Drive safe. Let me know when you're settled.
Me: It's almost 4am, Noah… Why are you still awake?
Noah: Just wanted to make sure you made it okay.
Me: Awww, you were worried about me?
Noah: I always worry about you. You're extremely accident-prone.
Me: I'll let you know when we get to Evergreen :)
Noah: I'll be waiting.

Gia climbed into the car and pressed the ignition, blasting the heat as my phone vibrated once more.

Noah: Miss you two already.

My lips rolled between my teeth to conceal a grin, my stomach fluttering as I read his text three more times.

Me: We miss you, too :)

Gia cleared her throat and looked over at me, her lips tilted into a smirk. She lowered her voice. "Sexy mechanic?"

I nodded, my cheeks flushing as I locked my phone and dropped it into my lap. "He stayed up to make sure we got here okay."

She groaned as she pulled out of the parking lot. "That's so cute. I hate it. I mean, good for you and whatnot, but I hate it."

I laughed, rolling my head against the headrest to look over at her. "Still nothing on the dating front?"

Gia snorted. "Are you kidding me? Drier than the Sahara." She sighed and turned onto the highway. "It doesn't help that I'm holed away all day every day."

"You're on a deadline. That's understandable."

Her lips twisted as she chewed on the inside of her cheek. "If I were writing anything of substance… It would be understandable. Unfortunately for me and my agent, it's all sucky."

"Sucky?" I laughed. "You're an author and the best you can come up with is sucky?"

Her hand slapped against the steering wheel. "You're only proving my point!"

"You're just in your head, babe. This happened with the first one, too. Remember?" When she was writing her first book, she hit a wall about halfway through and struggled for *weeks* to get the rest written out. "Maybe you need to do what you did for the first one when you lost motivation."

She let out a deep sigh, mulling over my suggestion. "You think?"

I shrugged. "I mean, if nothing else is working, why not?"

She drummed on the steering wheel, the hum of the road filling the car for a moment before she finally spoke.

"You might be right." She glanced at me with a faint smile. The last time she struggled like this, Gia rented a cabin somewhere deep into the woods in

Colorado. She was there for almost a month, taking random trips to the closest town near her cabin to comb through old newspapers archived in their tiny library. She sifted through old murder cases, missing persons, literally anything she could find that *might* spark something in her mind.

After two weeks, she stumbled across a few articles about some festival they used to host in another town nearby, and whatever she read did more than just spark an idea. It caught fire and she burned through the rest of her book within a few weeks and had it edited and published within a month.

"Maybe it's time for another adventure," Gia said quietly. I could almost see it play out over her features— the contemplation, the hesitation, the decision, and finally, the resolution. "Okay, no. You're totally right. I need it. I'm gonna look at rentals tonight."

I grinned and nudged her with my elbow. "Somewhere in Delaware?"

Gia's raspy laugh filled the car. "*Maybe* somewhere in Delaware."

"Oh! Can you bring Kevin?"

Gia scoffed. "Of course, I'll bring Kevin!"

"Fucking Kevin," I mumbled under my breath, earning another laugh from Gia. Honestly, I was a little surprised her chihuahua mix hadn't made the drive to the airport with her. She normally didn't go anywhere without that little ankle-biter.

"You love him."

"He's evil," I countered.

"He senses fear. And for some reason, you're terrified of him. So he's a little stand-offish."

"Gia, he's a monster. He has like six teeth and cataracts. I'm not scared of him. He's threatened by our friendship."

She let out a loud laugh. "You realize we're talking about a dog, right?"

I rolled my eyes and looked over at her with a soft smile. "I missed you."

"I missed you, too." She grinned, reaching over and wrapping her hand around mine.

We fell into an easy conversation, the flat suburbia of Cheyenne slowly morphing into rolling hills with lush, green trees. Kennedy fell asleep within the first fifteen minutes of the ride, her exhaustion having finally won over her curiosity and excitement. I couldn't blame her; the day had been long and trying for both of us.

I updated her on Noah and how things were going, conveniently leaving out the fact that I was completely, deeply, undeniably in love with him. The kind of love that you felt in all of the small moments just as profoundly as you did the big ones. The love you felt in the peaceful contentment whenever they were around; the ache and longing that lingered when they weren't.

She would be the one person that I could tell, but it felt like something I should probably keep to myself until Noah knew.

Everything around here looked familiar to me, and it wasn't long before the small town of Evergreen, Wyoming appeared before us. It was as quaint and deceptively charming as I remembered, the street lamps casting a warm glow over the town I used to call home. The hair salon, the library, the diner I used to frequent with Liam. It all passed by in a blur as Gia drove to the outskirts of Evergreen to her house. At one point in time, I would have been excited to come back here, to see my family and revisit my childhood home. But, deep down, I knew that the people in this town, aside from Gia, had a hard time accepting the new version of me.

The one who loved and grieved simultaneously and refused to apologize for the fact that I would no longer be pushed around and walked all over.

When we drove past *that* intersection in town, I kept my gaze fixed forward and Gia reached over to squeeze my hand again. I didn't torture myself with the want to find one little shimmer of a headlight on the ground or see the cross that Deb put there.

We drove past my parent's house, the little lamp in the window illuminating their living room. We drove past the street that would lead us to the home that Liam and I shared. I expected this feeling of nostalgia to carry a little more weight as it settled in my chest. I expected it to hurt. To be a painful reminder of what I'd lost. But it was surprisingly light, a strange feeling that I couldn't quite put into words.

We pulled into Gia's driveway, the relief and fatigue washing over me all at once. Kennedy was still sound asleep in the backseat when Gia turned off the engine. We both sat there for a moment, taking in the familiar surroundings.

Her house sat at the end of a gravel driveway, a small A-frame nestled into a thick patch of pine trees. It was a beautiful, cozy place that held countless memories of our friendship. The green hills and the lush trees surrounding the property only added to its charm.

Gia gave my hand a reassuring squeeze before I climbed out of the car and made my way to the backseat, carefully unbuckling Kennedy from her car seat. She stirred slightly, but thankfully stayed asleep as I lifted her into my arms, her head nestled against my shoulder.

Gia grabbed our suitcases from the trunk, and we made our way into the house, her little spawn of Satan nipping at my feet as I carried Kennedy through the living room and into the small guest bedroom.

Her warmth and eccentricity were reflected in every nook and cranny. The living room featured mismatched, comfy armchairs and a well-loved, overstuffed sofa, with an assortment of cozy throws and pillows in vibrant, mismatched patterns. The walls were adorned with quirky artwork and framed family photos, each with a story to tell.

The walls in the guest room were painted a soothing shade of pale blue, and adorned with an array of eclectic artwork collected over the years. A queen-sized bed right in the middle, dressed in crisp, white linens and a multitude of colorful, mismatched throw pillows. An antique wooden dresser sat against one wall, adorned with vintage knick-knacks and family photos in an assortment of frames.

It was impossible not to feel at home here.

I kicked the door shut behind me, locking Kevin and his six nipping teeth in the living room while I got Kennedy settled. I pulled her shoes off and unzipped her jacket, unsure of how I felt about leaving her in her airport clothes to sleep, but she looked so peaceful. I didn't want to disturb her any more than I needed to.

She curled into the blanket as I pulled it up to her shoulders and placed a kiss on her forehead.

"Mommy?" Kennedy asked with a sleepy voice, peeking up at me through one barely opened eye.

"Yeah?" I sat on the edge of the bed, smoothing her hair away from her face.

"If you talk to Noah, will you tell him I love him and good night?"

I smiled. "Sure, honey."

"Promise?"

"I promise," I whispered. "I'm gonna go get my stuff from Aunt Gia and take a shower, okay? You remember where the bathroom is if you need me?"

She nodded with a yawn.

"Okay. I love you."

"Love you, Mommy."

I kissed her one more time and stood, silently closing the door behind me.

Kevin was already at my feet, growling as I stepped into the living room. "Listen here you little rat, she was my friend first."

He lunged for my feet again and I leaped around him, shooting Gia a glare when she laughed.

"She all good?"

"Asleep before I shut the door."

Gia smiled and leaned against the counter, crossing her arms over her chest. "And you?"

I sighed. "I'm gonna shower and let Noah we got here. And then I'm passing out. I love you, but we'll have to catch up tomorrow."

She waved me off. "I've got some writing to do anyway. I'll catch up with you in the morn—" Gia paused, tilting her head from side to side. "Late afternoon," she corrected. "You still remember where everything is?"

I nodded and walked over, pulling my best friend into a tight hug. "I love you so much. Thank you, G."

Her five-foot-nine frame towered over me, her chin resting on the top of my head. "I love you the most. Go get some sleep." She turned and made her way to her office, whistling for Kevin to follow. And he did. But only after a growl in my direction.

I rolled my eyes and snagged my suitcase, digging through it to find my bag of toiletries before kicking off my shoes and making my way to her bathroom.

I turned on the faucet and let the steam fill the room, shooting a quick text to Noah to let him know we made it.

Me: Safe and sound. Kennedy is asleep, I'm right behind her

My phone vibrated almost instantly.

Noah: Good. Get some sleep. I'll call you tomorrow?

Me: We would love that. Kennedy wants to tell you all about the pizza we had in Chicago

Me: She also asked me to tell you goodnight before she passed out on her pillow

Noah: Tell her goodnight and that I'm looking forward to hearing all about her pizza. Night, sweetheart.

My stomach still fluttered when he called me that.

Me: Goodnight :)

I couldn't help but think that three little words tacked onto the end of that message would somehow make it sound so much better.

Chapter 46

Olivia

We stood on the porch at my parents' house, Kennedy placed in front of me, my hands resting on her shoulders.

I didn't want to be here.

If I could go back in time and give my house keys to literally anyone else, I would. But as the sole real estate agent in the town, I gave them to my mother so she wouldn't have an issue when it came to showing the house. Now, I was using my daughter as a tiny little human buffer between me and my parents.

They might be mad at me, but they would never say anything untoward in front of Kennedy.

I hoped.

The door creaked open and I slowly let my gaze sweep up from the worn and weathered boards that lined the porch to meet my father's blue eyes. There was a flash of surprise across his features, something I hadn't quite anticipated.

"Livie." My nickname fell from his mouth with a whisper.

"Hey, Dad." I shifted on my feet nervously, Kennedy looking up at me with pinched brows.

She might only be four, but she was attentive. She could sense the tension.

I cleared my throat after a lull of silence. "Can we come in? I told Mom we'd be by today."

The confusion on his face deepened before he nodded frantically. "Yes! Yeah, please. Come in. You don't— You shouldn't even have to ask that, Livie. This is— This is your home."

What the fuck? They've been ignoring me for the past five months. Why the hell would unanswered calls and texts lead me to believe I was welcome here?

My father pushed the screen door open and held it for us as we passed through, the familiar scent of cinnamon, clove, and pine soothing some of my nerves as I walked into my childhood home.

Nothing had changed since we left Evergreen. The same beige carpeting covered the floor in the living room, and the same framed photos of Jackson and I adorned the walls. My parents' wedding picture hung above the mantel, mine and Liam's sitting just beneath it. My dad's recliner sat in the corner facing the TV, hockey playing quietly in the background.

My dad hadn't changed much either. His beard was still as gray as ever, the end resting right at the top of his sternum. He was a burly, heavy-set man with a beer gut and a deep voice, his brows permanently furrowed as he surveyed his surroundings.

There were only a few people capable of softening such a solid man, and one of them was getting ready to launch herself into his arms.

"Hi, Grandpa Joe!" Kennedy grinned from ear to ear as the door shut behind us, and my dad bent to scoop her up, holding her tightly against his chest.

"Hi, sweet pea!" He let out a heavy sigh. "God, I've missed you two. When did you get so big? How are you in fifth grade all of a sudden?"

I peeled my eyes away and blinked away the tears and confusion. Kennedy was giggling and happy, and the last thing I wanted to do was take this moment away from her.

"I'm not in fifth grade! I'm in Pre-K!" Kennedy giggled, rolling her eyes. Except she didn't know how to roll her eyes, so it was just her looking from side to side slowly.

My dad laughed, a deep, hearty noise that made my heart swell. "Silly me. I must've forgotten." He set Kennedy on her feet and turned to face me, his eyebrows raised expectantly. "Don't I get a hug from my favorite daughter?"

My lips twitched. "Your *only* daughter."

"C'mere, Livie-Bug." He tugged on my shoulder and pulled me into a suffocating hug. His arms wrapped around my shoulders, my cheek pressing against his chest. It only took a moment for the tension in my muscles to melt away. Because I wasn't this strong, independent woman when my dad hugged me.

I was the little girl who fell off her bike and cried in her father's arms.

I was the teenager who had her heart broken for the first time.

I was the young, naive woman getting ready to walk down the aisle.

I was the broken woman, sobbing into her father's arms as the man she loved was lowered into the ground.

"I missed you, kid."

I fought past the burn in my throat and returned the hug. "I missed you, too."

He pulled away and looked down at me, blue eyes softening the harsh lines of his face. Guess I still had it in me. "Why didn't you tell us you were coming?"

I blinked at my father's question, my confusion intensifying as he waited for an answer. *Why didn't I tell them I was coming?*

Why wouldn't my mother tell him we were coming? Especially since she was the one who called me to discuss coming back to Evergreen in the first place. I struggled to find the right words; my voice laced with bewilderment.

"I... I thought Mom told you. I figured she would've told you. *She* called *me*. She said I had to come this week. Someone wants to buy the house. You guys are supposed to watch Ken today so I can get the rest of our stuff out."

He looked down at Kennedy with a strained smile. "Kenny, why don't you go into the kitchen and grab a cinnamon roll? There's some on the counter from this morning."

She happily skipped into the other room, thankfully oblivious to the tension now blanketing my shoulders.

My father's face reflected a mixture of emotions, his eyebrows knitting together in thought. He let out a slow breath as he seemed to process my words.

"Well, Livie, I hadn't heard a thing from your mother about this," he said, his voice tinged with a hint of frustration. "She hasn't said a word to me about someone wanting to buy the house or about you guys coming by."

My own frustration deepened. It didn't make sense. Why would my mother call me and discuss this entire plan but fail to inform my father? If this was some elaborate scheme to try and get me back to Evergreen, I was going to lose my shit. I struggled to maintain my composure.

"I don't understand. *She* was the one who called *me*, and she was pretty insistent about it," I said, my voice wavering slightly. "This whole visit was her idea. She all but forced my hand. Told me Jackson wasn't here to help. Why wouldn't she tell you?"

My father shook his head, his eyes fixed on the floor as if searching for answers there. He sighed deeply, and I could sense the strain and resignation in his response. "I don't know. Maybe she has her reasons. Things have been... Hard since you guys left. She misses you guys."

Despite the tiny voice in my head telling me to keep my composure, I scoffed in disbelief. "She's not exactly making this easy. I get that it's not her job to. I'm the one who left, I know. But she's not doing anyone any favors by behaving like this."

"Well," he said calmly. "It's not like you've been super responsive, Livie."

There was this kindling of rage deep within me. One that I'd kept in check when it came to my mother, swallowing back every response to her anger and judgmental words. But I could feel it building inside of me, burning brighter with every hard thump of my heart. It burned a path up my neck and slowly stretched across my cheeks. My vision blurred behind a veil of angry tears, and I took a step back, trying to get it under control before I unleashed it on someone undeserving of its wrath.

I took a deep, trembling breath but it did nothing to calm the fire raging inside of me. "I've been reaching out. I've been calling. I've texted. *Neither* of you has responded to a single text or call since I moved to Delaware. I've sent pictures of your granddaughter, pictures of the place we now call home, and *nothing*."

My chest heaved with each labored breath as I fought to keep my emotions under control. "I accepted it— Accepted that you hated me for doing what I needed to do to *live* but I will not sit here and let you make *me* into the villain when I've done nothing but try to make this easier on everyone else."

My father's face contorted, a flash of surprise across his features, and then confusion as he tried to digest my words. The room felt heavy with all of this emotional baggage we had been carrying. He finally spoke, his voice low and filled with regret.

"Livie, I didn't get any texts or calls from you," he said, his voice heavy with sincerity. "I haven't heard from you since you moved in June. Your mother said you weren't returning her calls or texts, and she was worried about you and Kennedy."

The fire within me raged even hotter, but now it was fueled by frustration and disbelief. There were a myriad of possibilities rushing through my mind, each one worse than the last. I reached into my pocket and pulled out my phone, scrolling through the long list of unanswered calls and messages.

"Here, look," I said, thrusting my phone toward him. "I've tried reaching out. I've sent pictures of Kennedy, updates about our life, and not *one* response. Not *one* acknowledgment that you even received my messages."

My father took the phone and studied it for a moment, his expression growing graver with each swipe. The truth was plain for him to see, and a profound sadness took hold of his wrinkled features.

"I don't understand, Livie," he whispered, his voice full of remorse. "I never received these. I've been waiting to hear from you, waiting to know how you and Kennedy were doing."

I'd never seen my father cry. Not once. But his eyes filled with unshed tears. "I've been worried *sick* about you two. I- I thought we both were."

Tears threatened to spill from my eyes at the sound of his voice breaking. "Wh-What?" There was so much confusion and pain radiating between us.

My father's voice quivered as he continued, his eyes never leaving the screen of my phone. "Your mother told me you were distant, that you'd cut off contact, and I believed her. I hadn't received a single call or text from you, Livie. I tried, but I could never get through..." His voice trailed off.

A sinking feeling took hold of me as I connected the dots. My mother's insistence on me returning to Evergreen, her claims that I wasn't responsive, and knowing that she had called me to discuss it all pointed in one direction. One that broke my heart.

"Dad," I whispered, the truth dawning on me, "Give me your phone."

His eyes met mine with hesitant understanding. Like he'd come to the same conclusion that I did but also didn't want to admit it out loud.

"She wouldn't," he stated firmly, reaching into his pocket to grab his phone.

"Livie, she wouldn't do that."

I swallowed my anger and swiped through the apps on his phone until I got to the settings, a sob choking out of me when I clicked on the tab for blocked contacts and my number was typed in bright red letters.

"My— My number. She blocked my number in your phone."

My father's eyes met mine, and in that gaze, we shared the heartbreaking realization that we had both been victims of some cruel game. The tears that had threatened to spill now flowed freely from his eyes.

"Why would she do that?" he asked, his voice shaky.

I shook my head, my own emotions too raw for a quick answer. The extent of my mother's deception, the manipulation of the situation, and the damage it had caused was a revelation too painful to process at that moment.

All those months of feeling abandoned and ignored, the misunderstandings that had driven a wedge between us, were now laid bare as a deliberate and calculated scheme by my own *mother*.

I knew that our relationship had been strained since Liam's passing, but I *never* thought she would stoop that low.

Thrusting his phone back into his hand, I quickly took mine back and dialed her number, pacing the living room until she answered.

"Yes?"

I didn't even *try* to contain the rage in my voice. "Is there even anyone interested in buying the house?" I snapped, lowering my voice when I remembered that Kennedy was just a room away.

There was a moment of stunned silence on her end before she excused herself from whatever conversation she was having. "Are you— Are you at the house? We said two-thirty."

I didn't miss the panicked edge to her voice.

"Answer me," I insisted. "Is there even someone interested in my house?"

"What are you talking about, Olivia?"

"Stop bullshitting me *right* now." My voice carried a lethal punch that was foreign to my ears.

She cleared her throat. "Yes, there is someone interested. The paperwork is on the coffee table if you would like to look."

My eyes slid over to the coffee table and sure enough, there was a manila folder placed carefully in the center. I walked over and flipped it open to see several contracts and a rainbow of highlighted sections for me to initial.

At least she wasn't lying about that.

I looked at my father, who was still standing in shock in the entryway, his eyes glued to his phone. "How could you?" My voice shook with anger and grief, horrified that she was capable of something so hurtful.

"I don't know what you're insinuating."

"Oh, save it," I responded with a sardonic laugh. "What was the endgame here, Mom? What were you trying to accomplish?"

There was another pregnant pause before she cleared her throat again. "Why don't we discuss this when I get home?"

"Where are the keys?"

"Oliv—"

"Keys, Mom. Where are the keys?"

She sighed, but there was shuffling on her end as she gathered her things. "They're on the hooks by the door. Why don't you just—"

"Goodbye." I hung up the phone and shoved it into my pocket, turning to face my father.

He looked up at me with sad eyes. "I'm so sorry, Livie. I should've known. I should've—"

"No, Dad." I wiped the tears from my cheeks and walked over to where he stood, wrapping my arms around his waist. My words were muffled by his shirt. "It's not your fault."

"I just— I don't even have the words." His strong arms wrapped around my shoulders.

"Me either," I said with a sigh. I needed to leave. Now. Before all of these emotions inside of me reached a boiling point. "Are you— Is it okay if I leave Kennedy here? Sounds like Mom was coming home. I just wanna get Liam's stuff out of the house."

"Of course, she can stay here. Take your time. We'll be here." He pulled away, sparing a glance to where Kennedy sat at the kitchen counter. "I won't say anything to your mother until you get home. Promise."

"Thank you," I whispered. "It won't take too long, I promise."

He kissed the top of my head and clapped a hand on my shoulder. "I love you, kiddo. Always."

"I love you, too, Dad." I gave him a watery smile and snagged the keys from the hook on the door, walking back out to Gia's Jeep. Yet another reason to be best friends with an introverted night owl.

It was just past noon, and she was still asleep with no plans to leave her house for the day, so she left me a note and told me to take her jeep if I needed to.

Thankfully, that meant I didn't have to wait for my mother to take me over to the house.

As I left my childhood home and drove to my old house, a mixture of anger and sorrow swirled inside me. I couldn't believe my mother would go to such lengths to manipulate the situation. Part of me wanted to figure out where the hell it all went wrong and why she would do this. Not so much for my sake, but for my father. And Kennedy. But another part of me wanted to be selfish and change my flight so I could leave first thing in the morning and leave all of this behind.

I turned onto the street that would lead me to our old house, trying to calm the anger burning inside me. There were already so many horrible memories that tainted this house in my eyes, all of them starting the night that the police officer stood on my porch.

I wasn't going to allow my mother's manipulations and betrayal to deter me from confronting the past and finding closure. I wouldn't let this day become something else I hated about this house.

My heart grew heavy with the weight of my memories. Our home stood with its weathered wooden exterior, nestled in the embrace of tall, ancient trees. The lawn was a little overgrown, but with winter coming and someone putting an offer in, Jackson probably didn't see the point of mowing again.

I parked Gia's Jeep and took a deep breath before stepping out. I fought the urge to scream into the trees and let the quiet settle the rage inside of me.

The familiar creak of the porch echoed in my ears as I approached the front door. The porch swing swayed gently in the breeze, a silent reminder of the moments we'd shared curled together as a family.

I toyed with the keys for a minute before my thumb slid along the familiar serrated edge of the one I needed.

I inserted the key into the front door, and the sound of the lock turning felt unusually loud in the stillness of the house. With a deep breath, I pushed the door, the hinges groaning in protest as I eased it open.

When I stepped inside and shut the door behind me, the emptiness enveloped me in a cold chill. The echoes of my footsteps reverberated through the vacant room. The familiar scent of our home, a blend of memories and comfort, lingered in the air, but it had faded over time.

A surge of emotion gripped my throat in a tight fist, and on this blank canvas that used to be our home, I could see the ghost of every memory playing out in front of me.

The day we moved in... How grateful we were to Deb and Todd for lending us money for the down payment. Even if they hated that we weren't married yet. Though, Liam was quick to rectify that. Our first Christmas together, our first anniversary... Finding out I was pregnant with Kennedy.

Apart from our wedding, every big moment that we shared happened under this roof.

I started toward the living room, slowly retracing the steps of our shared life. I missed so many things about this place. The vaulted ceilings, the brick fireplace in the corner, the original hardwood floors. A peephole on the fucking front door.

A lone tear trickled down my cheek as I remembered just how happy we felt in this space.

I could see Liam chasing Kennedy around the couch. I could hear him whistling his way through the house as he gathered his stuff for work.

Turning to the kitchen, another tear fell as I thought back on how many mornings I'd spent sitting at the island with Kennedy perched on my knees, Liam moving happily around the stove while he cooked us breakfast.

I climbed the creaking stairs, passing the walls that used to be lined with framed photographs. Now, just a shadow of the frame was smudged onto the wall. Each picture told the story of our lives, from our wedding day to Kennedy's first steps. The pictures were gone now, hung on a different wall across the country. Soon, the evidence that they once existed here would be painted over and become just another piece of us erased from what used to be.

The door to our room was shut at the end of the hallway and I hesitated at the top of the stairs, standing on wobbly legs as the weight of the day threatened to bring me to my knees.

This was a horrible mistake.

I shouldn't have come here. I should've waited until I was calmer, until I had someone to help me and distract me from the silence.

The front door swung open and my hand rested over my pounding heart as I raced down the stairs.

I skidded to a stop when I turned the corner.

Chapter 47

Olivia

"Mom?" Almost instantly, the rage I'd been so focused on shoving down was back, burning hotter and brighter than it was before because *how dare she?*

How dare she intrude on this moment?

How dare she give me *one* more bad memory of the house I only wanted to cherish in my mind?

"Olivia," she panted. Her short, blonde bob was frizzy and out of place, her white blouse untucked from her pencil skirt.

I thought for just one second that she was here to apologize. But then she opened her mouth and I saw red.

"How could you tell your father? There was— I had a plan. I had everything figured out and you showed up early! You were—"

"Don't you *dare* put this on me! For *months*, I've been trying to reach out to you. *Both* of you. I sent texts, made calls, and not one response. You blocked my number from Dad's phone, and you think you had some kind of *plan?* This isn't about you, it's about Kennedy, and it's about Dad! It's about making your daughter feel more alone during the worst year and a half of her life than she needed to! *How could you?*"

My voice shook with anger, my eyes locked onto hers, unyielding. She recoiled from my intensity, but she refused to back down.

"How could *I?!*" She scoffed and threw her purse onto the kitchen counter. "You did this, Olivia. You moved across the country for no goddamn reason.

You tore our family apart. *You forced my hand!"*

"It wasn't for no reason, Mom, and you know that," I snapped, jutting my finger out in her direction. "I should've known that you would find some way to make this about you. It was never about you! I needed space. I needed— I needed *out!* No one here was going to help me so I had to help myself and moving to Rose Hill has been the best thing for me."

"You have people here! You have a whole family that you tossed aside for what? Some podunk town in *Delaware?"* She threw her hands up and scoffed again. "You ran away from the people who care about you. What were we supposed to do, Olivia?"

"*Help!*" I screamed, my words tearing through my throat like sandpaper and echoing through the empty house. "Help me! You were supposed to *help me, Mom.* I—" I paused, my fingers trembling as I clenched them at my sides. "I told you I wanted to kill myself and you told me to *buck up.* I needed *help.* I *asked* for it. And you told me to *buck up!*"

She released a shaky breath, her lips quivering. "You have a daughter."

"*So do you!*" I had never raised my voice like this before. It had never cracked and shook with such raw, visceral emotion. "I am a *person.* I am *your daughter.*" I choked out a sob, slapping my hand over my mouth as tears poured down my face. "I *needed* you. I was *drowning.* And you couldn't even throw me a lifeline!"

Her mascara left streaks of black down her face as she cried, her red lipstick smudged as her fingers gently rested over her mouth. "I was—" She shook her head, failing to come up with an excuse this time. "I didn't know." The defiant facade slowly began to crack. "I didn't know how to help you."

"Clearly," I snapped back. "And I might've been able to forgive you if you would've just said that, but instead you invalidated everything I was feeling and made me feel like it was my fault for *mourning my husband's death.* So you can be mad at me for leaving, you can take it out on me all you want, but I found something in that 'podunk town' that no one here cared to offer. I am *living* again."

I paused to take a deep breath, wiping away the tears that cascaded down my cheeks. "You don't get to take it out on my daughter. And you don't get to make my father feel like I didn't care enough to reach out."

Her eyes were glazed over, fingers trembling as she wiped her own tears. "I— Livie I didn't— I had a plan." She looked defeated, the weight of her actions heavy on her shoulders.

"What exactly was this plan?" I asked, refusing to hide the venom that still laced my voice.

"I— I was—" Her voice broke and the tears fell faster. In this moment, I hated that her cheeks flushed like mine. "I was hoping that it would get you to come back. I thought that maybe if you thought we were mad or if you thought we didn't want to talk to you, you'd get—" Shame deepened the pink on her face. "Lonely. I was hoping you'd get lonely and come back to us."

The truth of her intentions hit me like a sucker punch to the gut. My anger was still there, but beneath it was a deep sense of betrayal and hurt. The realization that my own mother had orchestrated some of my lowest moments, thinking it would manipulate me into returning, was a bitter pill to swallow.

I stared at her, my voice quieter but still firm. "You wanted to make me feel *lonely*? To manipulate me into coming back? Mom I— My husband died. The father of my child. *Dead*. I left because I couldn't bear to drive by the broken glass on the side of the road anymore. I left because I could hear people whispering about how I should've moved on by now."

She took a step toward me, but I backed away from her touch.

"I couldn't breathe in this town knowing my husband was buried less than two miles away from our *home*. And the only thing you could focus on was making me feel *lonely?*"

"Livie." My nickname was a broken plea as it left her lips. "God, I'm so sorry. I'm so sorry."

"Don't." I shook my head. "I don't need your apologies." I froze, taking a sharp breath. "What have you said to Debra?"

The muscles in her throat worked as she swallowed.

"Be. Honest. What did you tell Debra to make her hate me so much?"

"I—" Her eyes squeezed shut, more tears tracking down her face. "She's upset that you left— that you took Kennedy. So I lied. God, Livie. I told her awful things. Things that you never said about her. And then I told her I didn't know why you weren't talking to her. She and your dad don't ever talk or see each other. I figured it would be okay. That you would come back and everyone would apologize, and we'd be okay. I was the one—" Her voice trailed off with a whimper.

"What?"

"I was the one who sent you that text. From her phone."

"What text?" I gritted out through clenched teeth. I knew *exactly* which text she was talking about, I just needed her to admit.

"I knew you wouldn't respond. So I sent it while she was in the bathroom and deleted it after. I was the one who— who said you were unfit to be a mother and that you would never be forgiven for moving."

I staggered back a step, her words punching the air from my lungs. "I need you to leave. Get out. So I can clear out my things and go home."

God, *of course*, Deb hated me.

"*This* is your home. Evergreen is your home."

"No," I responded. "Not anymore. You made sure of that."

Her face twisted with anguish. "What can I do? How do I fix this?"

The laugh that I let out was void of any humor. "That's for you to figure out, Mom. I can't even begin to wrap my head around forgiving you. You should've seen the hurt on Dad's face. The *tears. You* fucked up. *You* fix it."

I sniffed, wiping my nose with my sleeve. "But for now, I need you to leave. Kennedy is at your house. *Do not* make a scene in front of her. Dad promised to save it for later."

She stood, stunned in silence in the middle of my vacant house.

"Now, Mom. Go."

Without further protest, she gathered her belongings from the island and rushed out of the house. I waited until I heard the crunch of her tires against the gravel to collapse onto the stairs, sob after sob wracking through my chest and leaving my throat raw.

I just wanted to go home. I wanted to tell Noah that I loved him. I wanted him to hold me while he whispered in my ear that everything was going to be alright. Losing Liam was an extraordinary pain that I would never wish on anybody, but this... This level of betrayal and hurt tore through me in the most devastating way.

My chest ached for the strained relationships that my mother caused, for the hatred and the lies.

I cried into my hands, wishing that Noah was there to hold me together while I fell apart.

The last thing I wanted was for him to worry, especially being so many miles away, but I dug my phone out of my pocket and called him anyway.

The phone rang several times, each second feeling like an eternity. I knew he was probably busy at the shop, or entertaining Nellie since she would be out of school, too. He was probably stressed and the last thing he needed was my family drama, but before I could hang up, his deep voice filled my ear and my shoulders sank with relief.

"Hey, sweetheart."

"Hi," I choked out, sucking in a couple of choppy breaths as I fought to regain my composure.

There was a clanging noise on the other end, something slammed shut, and then his words rushed out. "What's wrong? What happened? Are you okay?"

"No," I sobbed, my shoulders shaking with each cry. "Why did I come back? Why did I do this to myself?"

"Liv, baby. I need you to take a deep breath, okay? Come on. In through your nose, out through your mouth. Deep breaths."

I followed his instructions, taking deep, measured breaths with him to calm the storm inside of me. After a few moments, my sobs began to subside, and I regained some control over my emotions.

He gave me a second to take a few more careful breaths before he spoke up again. "Better?" he asked gently.

A breath shuddered out of me and I sniffled, wiping away the lingering tears on my face. "Yeah," I answered softly, my voice hoarse. "Better."

"Good." There was a pause, nothing but the steady sound of his breathing coming through the phone. "What happened? What's going on?"

"You sure you're not busy? I don't wanna be a bother."

He chuckled softly, the sound itself soothing some of the ache inside. "You could call me in the middle of the night, and I'd drop everything to be there for you. You're not a bother, and you never will be. What's going on, Liv?"

I took a deep breath and the words rushed out of me so fast, I wasn't sure if he heard half of them. I told him every chaotic, infuriating detail, and explained her manipulations, lies, and misguided attempts to handle the situation. I told him about the text from Deb and how it was actually my mother who sent it. Most of my words were slurred and choked out between sobs, but I think he got the gist.

Noah listened in silence, letting me vent and express my feelings without interruption. When I had finished, he spoke in a tone filled with understanding and concern. "I— God, Liv. I am so sorry. I don't even know what to say." He let out a shocked laugh. "Jesus Christ. What the hell was she thinking? I mean, clearly, she wasn't. But *fuck*."

I sighed, the weight on my chest lifting marginally. "I just— I don't understand. Who could— Who could do something so horrible to their *child*?" My eyes brimmed with new tears. "To their grandchild?"

Noah's voice was a mixture of anger and sympathy. "I can't even wrap my head around it. I'm so sorry."

I massaged my temple with my free hand, my brain pounding against my skull. "Thank you for listening to that. I'm sure most of it made zero sense."

"It made sense," he said softly. "What can I do? What do you need?"

Another sigh pushed through my lips. "You. Just— You. I wish you were here."

Noah's response was immediate, and I could hear the longing in his voice. "Me, too."

A comfortable lull fell over the conversation, both of us content with the sound of our breaths crackling through the phone. I knew that I loved Noah before I got on the plane to come back to Evergreen, but I could feel it so prevalent in my bones now. He was the lifeline that Evergreen failed to throw me, the one person who understood me like no one else.

I wasn't the same person that left this house in June. But Noah proved to me time and time again that I didn't need to be. There were so many differences between *that* person and the person I became in Rose Hill.

The woman that Liam loved was all smooth edges and perfect smiles. She had the privilege of knowing a life without heartbreak.

All of the pieces of me that were bruised and broken, and scattered on the ground like shattered glass, Noah picked up and handled with gentle hands and soft lips. Slowly, he mended the pain and wounds that were left bleeding when I moved my life across the country. Like pieces of stained glass, the fragments of me that I thought were dead and buried were soldered into something new.

Someone who could stand her ground and speak her truths.

"I miss you," I murmured after a second. "*We* miss you. I don't think Kennedy has stopped talking about you for a minute."

Noah huffed out a laugh and I imagined him running his fingers through his hair, leaving behind a smudge of oil on his forehead. "I miss you guys, too. It's so..."

"Peaceful?" I teased.

"I was gonna say quiet. But not in a good way. I couldn't sleep. I thought about breaking into your apartment and stealing the sound machine."

God, I loved him so much.

I snorted out a laugh. "I gave Avery my key, no need to break any doors. But I couldn't sleep either. Mostly because Kennedy spent the better half of last night kicking me in the gut. But you might have something to do with it, too."

His laughter floated through the phone again, and I let out a small sigh as it washed over me. "Only a few more days and we'll be sleeping soundly again."

"*Thank god.* I'm ready to get out of here."

Noah's voice held a hint of concern as he asked, "You feeling better?"

"I am. Thank you. Sorry if I interrupted something."

"Stop apologizing for needing me, Liv."

I smiled to myself. "Right."

There was another lull, one that begged to be filled with a sappy love confession from miles apart, but I forced something else out instead. "Well, if I ever have any hope of getting back to you, I should probably start moving boxes."

"You sure you're okay?"

"I don't know. I will be— I am. I'm... Something."

"I'll take it," he replied with a gentle voice. "Don't forget to call me tonight, I gotta hear about this pizza."

"Even if I did forget, Kennedy would probably remind me before I even got the chance to kick my shoes off."

I could practically hear the grin in his voice. "Good."

"Bye, Noah."

"Bye, sweetheart."

A long, heavy sigh escaped me as I hung up, feeling lighter and more supported than I had in a while. I wiped the drying tears from my cheeks and stood, turning to head up the stairs.

I didn't come into this thinking I would want to rush out of here, but the quicker I got everything sorted in Evergreen, the sooner we could go back to Rose Hill.

Despite the headache and the exhaustion that weighed my eyelids down, the thought of going home gave me the push I needed to open the door at the end of the hall and face the remnants of my past.

Chapter 48

Olivia

I took a cautious step into the room, the hardwood creaking under my feet. Our room used to be a place of so much warmth and happiness, so many memories and so much love... But now, it was cold and empty. The only signs of life were the boxes stacked in the center, all of them labeled with 'Liam's Stuff.' Dust motes danced in the afternoon sunlight, casting a bittersweet glow over the emptiness.

Each step I took echoed through the room as I approached the boxes, and my heart stuttered a nervous rhythm. I left all of this stuff behind because I couldn't bear to go through it. I couldn't stand the thought of sorting through his things and deciding which of them needed to be thrown out. I knew I couldn't take it all with us when we moved, so I left some of it behind and told myself it was something I could deal with after I had some time to heal.

I gently ran my fingers over the cardboard, swiping at the layer of dust that formed on the top. Slowly, I unfolded the flaps, the scent of Liam's cologne wafting into the air as soon as I cracked the box open.

Clothes, carefully folded and waiting, filled the box. There were his favorite worn jeans, soft from years of wear, and the T-shirts he'd insist on wearing even though they'd seen better days. Each piece was a memory, a moment of laughter, a stolen kiss, a shared secret. My trembling fingers picked up a shirt, and I held it to my chest, inhaling his scent deeply, as if trying to capture him within it.

The tears welled in my eyes, blurring my vision as I folded the shirt back and gently set it back inside. I fingered through the rest of the clothes, deciding that this box could be taken to Deb's. If there wasn't anything that she wanted to keep, I could take it to the donation bin before we left town.

I'd already kept all of the shirts and sweatshirts that reminded me of him the most, though they hadn't smelled like him in ages.

I slid the box toward the door and moved onto another one, uncovering his sketchbooks, some pictures, and movie stubs from the drive-in. I shuffled it all to the side, my fingers brushing against a smaller cardboard box toward the bottom.

Gently, I pulled out an old shoe box, a wide grin spreading across my lips. How could I have forgotten about *these*? I lifted the lid, careful not to disturb the hundreds of little slivers of paper inside.

Every fortune from the inside of every fortune cookie since our very first date sat inside this box. Some of them were so old that the print was almost completely worn off, some of them creased or ripped from being shoved into his pocket for safekeeping until we got home.

My smile grew as I sifted through them, memories of countless shared dinners and Liam's mocking voice telling me to just wait and see, flooded my mind.

I choked on a sob as I pulled one out, Liam's almost illegible handwriting scribbled onto the backs of several of them.

"Your life will be peaceful and happy." *What if it already is?*

"Attitude is a little thing that makes a big difference." *And her name is Kennedy Brooks.*

"You have a secret admirer." *It's not a secret. She told me she loved me.*

"Your current relationship will last a lifetime." *God, I hope so.*

"Good news is on the way!" *It's already here. She said yes.*

I took a shaky breath, and as I continued to browse through the fortunes, the tears in my eyes began to subside, replaced by a warmth that filled my heart. I wanted to keep these. I needed to. I needed Kennedy to see just how much we loved each other. These memories that we shared would stay locked in my mind for the rest of my life, but she was so young. As she grew older, she would forget so much about her father and I wanted her to be able to have something tangible outside of the pictures that decorated our home. I wiped my cheeks and placed everything back into the larger box, knowing they would be shipped home to me.

I continued to go through the rest of the boxes, laughing and crying at the memories that accompanied each item. The more I sorted through them, the clearer it became that most of Liam's belongings could be sent to Deb's. The books, the gadgets, even his vinyl record collection could find a new home with someone who would appreciate them. The memories would stay with me forever, but I didn't need all these physical reminders to just sit and collect dust.

Once I had determined what was going to stay here in Wyoming and what was going to go back to Delaware, I loaded everything into Gia's Jeep and did one last sweep of the house.

We'd planned to spend forever in this home and in a bunch of little ways, we kind of were.

My fingers traced the notches in the door frame of Kennedy's old room, each one a little higher than the last as we documented her growing up. I smiled at the chips in the drywall and little indents in the hardwood, knowing that while we didn't get to live the life that we had dreamed of, it was nothing short of beautiful.

I walked over to the closet in our room, reaching inside to switch the light off when something caught my eye.

One of Liam's old jackets hung toward the back of the walk-in. His favorite fleece-lined denim jacket. He'd gotten it for a Halloween costume one year and despite my pleas to wear *anything* else when it was cold out, he'd slowly incorporated it into every outfit he wore during the winter.

I took it from the hanger and draped it over my arm, flipping the light switch on my way out.

I used to hate this jacket. But now it carried a memory, a feeling that was so intrinsically Liam, I knew I would never be able to let it go.

A slow creak sounded through the house as it settled, almost as if it were finally ready to let go of us. It breathed out a sigh of relief, just as I did, knowing that even though Liam was gone, and I was turning the page to a new chapter in my life, the love and the memories we created would always linger with or without us.

With one last look around, I descended the stairs and made my way to the front door. My thumb slid over the serrated edge of the key a few more times before I pulled the door shut and slipped it into the deadbolt. I walked to Gia's Jeep, Liam's jacket in hand, and got in. It was time to leave this place behind and embrace the start of something new.

* * *

"Do you think we can call him yet?" Kennedy panted as she ran over to me, her cheeks pink from the cold. Kevin trotted happily behind her, then glared at me from beneath the cataracts when he realized she'd stopped in front of me.

Gia snickered as she kindled the bonfire, meeting my eyes with a playful smirk.

Kennedy had been asking about Noah since I picked her up from my parent's house hours before. I'd been making excuse after excuse, trying to prevent yet another disruption to his day, but Kennedy was starting to catch on. This was the fifth time in twenty minutes she had skipped over to ask me what time it was and if Noah could talk.

I sighed, digging into my pocket for my phone. It was past seven; he should definitely be home from the shop. "Sure, I think it would be okay."

He picked up after the second ring. "Hey, Liv." There was a rumbling in the background, Nellie's loud singing filtering through the phone.

"Hey, you busy?"

"No, just— Uh— Heading to Wilmington. Avery needed something from the store. I offered to drive."

There was a muffled noise and the sound of a smack, Avery whispering something to him in a harsh tone that I couldn't pick up. "A-Are you sure? We can call back before bedtime."

"No, I'm sure. Put her on."

Kennedy's eyes widened with excitement as I held the phone out for her. "Noah!" she screamed into his ear and took off around the yard, Kevin following quickly behind her. She launched into a very detailed, yet somehow incredibly inaccurate description of the pizza we had in Chicago. I made a mental note to tell Noah that there weren't Skittles or Peanut Butter M&M's mixed into the pizza sauce.

A warm smile bloomed across my face as I watched my daughter talk with Noah. Her arm lifted above her head in excitement as she told him about the fire and all the s'mores we were going to make, and I could picture Noah's animated expressions in my mind as he listened to her.

I loved how much he loved her.

I sat on the steps leading up to Gia's house, the cold, November air crisp and biting at my skin. Kennedy's laughter filled the night air, Kevin howling and barking after her as they traipsed through crunchy leaves on the ground.

I was still so unbearably mad at my mother— So mad that I couldn't even go into my parent's house when I picked Kennedy up. But the day had been weirdly cleansing. I wasn't the villain everyone was making me out to be and that in itself lifted a huge weight from my shoulders.

Gia made her way over, plopping down onto the stairs next to me. I kept my eyes on Kennedy but could feel Gia's stare as she watched me with keen eyes. She lifted her beer and took a long pull, leaning back and resting on her elbows. "You love him?"

I mimicked her posture, then leaned my head on her shoulder. "Completely."

Chapter 49

Olivia

I took a long sip of coffee, the chill in my bones dissipating as the warmth spread through my body. Kennedy was still fast asleep, her tiny limbs tangled in the thick blankets. I'd planned to sleep in, but the weight of the previous day lingered in my thoughts all night and I tossed and turned for hours.

The second the sun started peeking through the curtains, I slid out of bed and started a pot of coffee.

Gia's office door eased open, her feet dragging against the floor as she walked toward me. I watched her over the brim of my mug as she started her electric kettle and grabbed two packets of sleepy-time tea from the cabinet.

She let out a sigh and shuffled over to the table, plopping down onto the wooden chair across from me. "I'm a one-hit wonder."

"Bullshit."

"Tell that to my empty document."

"What do you do in there all night if you're not writing?"

Gia groaned and lowered her head to the table. "Research. Watch dog videos on the internet. Stare blankly into the void."

I hummed my response and took another sip from my mug. "Anything I can do?"

She shrugged. "Find me a new brain?"

"I'll get right on it." I stood and padded my way over to the sink to rinse my mug before setting it in the dishwasher.

"You sure about leaving so soon?" Her voice was muffled by the wooden table.

I'd gotten the confirmation email earlier that our flights had successfully been changed from Monday to Friday. The decision to move our return flights up had obviously been a last-minute one, but with all the necessary arrangements and goodbyes completed in Evergreen, I felt an urgency to go back to Rose Hill. To go home. I needed time to heal from the wounds the people in this town inflicted.

We had a few more stops to make, but after that, we would be ready to go.

I rested my hip against the counter and crossed my arms over my chest. "I mean, I'm sad. I don't wanna take Ken away from my dad or Liam's parents, but I know she also misses home. It just all sucks. I'm tired of being sad and angry."

"I get it," she replied softly. "But it's okay to feel sad about making the right decision."

"I know. And we'll come back once I figure out how the hell to forgive my mother for what she did. But right now... I just need space."

"That is more than understandable. I wish you would let me egg her car or something."

I barked out a laugh, shaking my head at my best friend. "First of all, I think knowing how disappointed and hurt my Dad is, is punishment enough for now. And secondly, if someone egged her car the day after our fight, she would *immediately* know it was you."

Gia sat up and scoffed. "Bold of you to assume that I wouldn't key my name into her car so she *knew* it was me."

I rolled my eyes with a smile. "Direct that energy into writing a book."

"Thanks, Mom," she deadpanned.

Pushing away from the counter, I snagged the kettle and poured her a cup of hot water. "Stop being so hard on yourself." I walked the mug over to where she sat and put two teabags on the table. "Your next book is going to be just as amazing as the first. You're just thinking too hard."

Her lips tilted into a small but appreciative smile. "Thank you."

"You're welcome," I replied. "Now, you drink your tea and go to bed. I, on the other hand, am going to take a shower and start my day."

Gia steeped her tea with tired eyes. "Wake me if you need anything."

"Night, G."

I headed toward the bathroom while Gia stood to let Kevin out before they both retired to her room for the day.

The hot steam from the shower filled the bathroom, and I stepped under the warm water as it cascaded from the shower head. A deep, involuntary sigh escaped my lips as the soothing embrace of the hot water began to relax my muscles and wash away the lingering tension from a night of restless sleep.

I wasn't exactly sure what to expect when we came back. But this trip to Evergreen had been a heavy mixture of so much pain and so many exposed lies, and I was just so ready to get back to Rose Hill and Noah.

I wanted to see the look on his face when I told him I loved him, and I wanted to feel his arms around me while he told me everything was going to be okay. I'd done the best I could here, battling a constant storm of emotions. He was the only person who made them fade away. The only person who could clear my mind and give me peace.

I didn't want to be in Evergreen and reminisce about the life that I had. I wanted to be back in Rose Hill and live the life I built from the ashes.

* * *

I think I was more nervous about pulling up to Deb and Todd's house than I was about my parents. I was bracing for a fight, putting on whatever armor hadn't been obliterated by my mother, and preparing for the worst.

My relationship with Deb had never been more strained. All I wanted was for her and Todd to spend a few hours with Kennedy before we left. It shouldn't feel like such a far-fetched expectation to spend those few hours without fighting and throwing around insults.

We pulled into the driveway, and Kennedy squealed, kicking her feet excitedly. I hoped they wouldn't do anything to rip this excitement away from her.

"Ready?" I asked, meeting her gaze in the review mirror.

"Yes! Let's go!"

I laughed, climbed out of the Jeep, and rounded the hood to the passenger side. My hands trembled slightly as I unbuckled her harness, but thankfully, she was too distracted to notice.

Within half a second of her feet landing on the pavement, she was sprinting toward the house.

Their house hadn't changed at all since our departure from Evergreen. It was still the picture-perfect definition of small-town charm. A modest garden that was starting to wither from the cold, pinwheels stuck into the dirt, a white picket fence that closed everything in.

Kennedy shoved her way through the gate and ran to the door, her finger pressing down on the doorbell several times.

"Oh, Ken! No, don't do that!"

The front door swung open, and I expected the look on Deb's face to be one of shock, but my steps faltered at the soft, emotional look she wore instead. Her eyes brimmed with tears as she bent down to scoop Kennedy into her arms, holding her tight as she swayed back and forth.

"My sweet, sweet girl. How are you?"

"Good, Gigi! We had pizza in Chicago with candy and chocolate! It was so good, you *have* to try it!"

Deb gave me an amused look over Ken's shoulder, and I let out a nervous laugh.

"Deep dish," I corrected. "There wasn't any candy, but it *was* good."

She smiled, her eyes lingering on me for a moment before she set Kennedy on her feet. "Why don't you go inside and surprise Papa? He's in the den watching TV."

Needing no further prompting, Kennedy took off inside the house, and I was left on the porch with Deb. I wasn't sure what to say, and the tension was palpable as we stood there, neither of us breaking the silence.

I cleared my throat and started to speak, but Deb took me by surprise and stepped toward me, wrapping her arms around me in a tight hug. My body froze, my muscles locked and tense, unsure of how to respond.

Deb's voice was thick with emotion. "I'm so sorry, Olivia. Your mom— Your mom came by earlier to talk and— and I'll never be able to take back some of the hateful things that I said to you, but I am *so* sorry. I'm sorry I believed her."

I sucked in a breath, blinking back tears as they flooded my eyes. "She came to talk to you?"

Deb pulled away, keeping her hands on my biceps. "She did. She told me about everything. About the text. And I'm so sorry that you've spent so long thinking those cruel things about yourself. I know that I said some hateful things, and there is no excuse for that, but you are a *great* mother."

My face twisted up as I fought the urge to cry, Deb blurred by a sheen of tears. My throat tightened, and I had no clue what to say back.

"I'm not asking for your forgiveness. I know that'll take time. I didn't grieve in the best way, and I'm so sorry I took it out on you. I— Olivia— I'm just so sorry." Her voice trembled as she spoke, her words hanging heavy in the air.

I struggled to find my voice amid the whirlwind of emotions that had consumed me for so long. I'd spent so many months beating myself up for the way she spoke to me. Knowing that it was partly due to the lies my mother spread made me want to instantly forgive and forget, but on the other hand, I couldn't ignore the hurtful words that had been thrown at me. It wasn't something that could be fixed with a simple apology, no matter how heartfelt.

A few tears slid down my cheeks, and I wiped them away, hoping Kennedy would stay inside with Todd. "Thank you, Deb. I— I know that you've been hurting, and I'm so sorry for the lies that my mother has been feeding you. I swear, I just wanted to live again. I needed to live. For Kennedy. But also for myself. I just couldn't do that here."

Her lips quivered as she battled with her own tears. "I know. I'm so sorry it took me so long to see that." Deb's hands slid down my arms as she took my hands in hers. "From the bottom of my heart, all I want is for you to be happy. Here, or in Delaware. Liam would want—" She choked on a sob and cleared her throat. "Liam would want that for you, too."

"Thank you," I whispered.

She smiled softly and gave my hands a squeeze. "So, take whatever time you need. I'm here when you're ready. All I want is a chance to make things right."

We stood there for a moment longer, sharing an unspoken understanding that this was just the beginning of a long journey toward reconciliation. Deb's willingness to acknowledge her mistakes was a start, but the wounds were still so fresh. I just needed more time.

"I— Um— I have some stuff of Liam's in the back." I hooked my thumb over my shoulder. "I figured you could go through and keep whatever you wanted, and I would take the rest to the donation bin."

"Well, come on. I'll help you carry everything in."

Kennedy's laughter echoed from inside the house, and I couldn't help but hope that, with time, we might find a way to rebuild what had been broken.

Chapter 50

Olivia

A few hours later, Deb and I went through the last of Liam's things, bonding over shared memories and warm, happy tears. As I suspected, she ended up keeping almost everything aside from some shoes and a few pairs of pants and socks.

Todd helped me load the boxes I was taking to donate back into Gia's Jeep and pulled me into a tight hug, his own apology similar to Deb's. It was clear that they both genuinely regretted the harsh words exchanged and it gave me hope for the future.

It gave me hope that it wouldn't always be this strained and that coming back to Evergreen could be something that I looked forward to instead of something that I kept pushing off. Hope that I could get my parents or Deb and Todd to fly over and see just how happy we were.

Hope that when I finally told them about Noah, there would be nothing but happy thoughts and well-wishes.

I stood at the kitchen counter with Deb, watching Kennedy and Todd kick a soccer ball through the backyard. She loaded the last plate from lunch into the dishwasher and dried her hands on the towel that hung from the oven door. "How long are you guys staying?"

I cleared my throat and turned to face her. "Just one more night. We leave for Cheyenne at noon tomorrow."

Deb looked thoughtful for a moment, then met my gaze with a warm smile.

"Thank you for letting us spend time with her. I can't say that I would've done the same thing if I were you."

My gaze slid back over to Kennedy as she played in the yard. "It's not about me or my hurt feelings. It's about her. Everything I've done for the past year and a half has been for her. I know it might seem selfish, but moving was the best thing I could've done for her."

I smiled when Ken threw her head back and laughed, then turned to face Deb again. "Because I'm *alive* again. I'm happy. I can breathe and work through my grief in a healthy way. Maybe I could've done that here if— if my mother would've just listened to me. But she didn't and I did the best thing that I could at the time."

Deb reached over and placed her hand over mine. "I know. For what it's worth, I am very proud of you."

"Thank you," I whispered, swallowing back another wave of emotion.

I cleared my throat and glanced outside again. "I actually have a few things to do. Can she hang around with you for a couple of hours?"

"Of course," she answered quickly. "No rush. She can stay as long as you need her to."

"I won't be too long. I'll just poke my head out and let her know I'm leaving."

Kennedy kicked a goal right as I slid the backdoor open, her cheers and screams echoing through the yard. "I told you, Papa! Ha!"

Todd groaned and threw his head back. "How do you beat me *every single time?*" He winked at me while she took another victory lap.

"Hey, Ken?" I called out, waiting for her to look over. "I'm gonna run into town for a few things. Are you okay to stay here with Gigi and Papa?"

"Yes, Mommy!" She ran over and gave me a quick hug before sprinting back into the yard. "Bye!"

I waved at Todd, then headed back inside to grab my things. As I passed by Deb, I gave her a grateful smile. "Thanks again. I'll be quick, promise."

She nodded and waved me off. "Anytime. No need to be quick, we'll take all the time we can get."

***

There was really only one place I wanted to go before the sun went down, but since I was driving through town anyway, I decided to swing by the donation bin to drop off the rest of Liam's stuff. And because you couldn't do anything in a town this small without running into several people that you knew, I got sucked into twenty different conversations about where we were and how we were doing.

Knowing that whatever came out of my mouth would likely find its way to the Evergreen gossip mill, I kept my responses mostly vague and non-committal. But despite the surface-level conversations, it felt somewhat reassuring to know that we weren't forgotten, that the town still cared in its own way, and perhaps, someday, the stories that circulated about us would be more about our healing journey and less about the painful past and the lies that followed.

I made a quick stop by the post office to ship the rest of Liam's stuff to Rose Hill and then made my way to the florist down the street.

Posy Parlor was a small shop tucked between the grocery store and the laundromat, owned by the sweetest, gentlest soul named Emily. When her mom opened it in the seventies, no one thought it would survive in such a small town. But year after year, she stuck around. Emily's daughter, Lila, had plans to take it over whenever she decided to retire.

It used to be one of my favorite places in town.

The bell above the door chimed gently, announcing my presence, and a friendly, familiar face greeted me from behind the counter. Emily. She smiled warmly, stepping around the counter with her arms open wide.

"Olivia, dear," she said, her voice filled with genuine concern. "It's been so long. How have you been? How's Kennedy?"

Her warm smile and open arms drew me in, and I couldn't resist embracing her in a tight, heartfelt hug.

"Emily," I breathed, my voice quivering with emotion, "God, it's been a roller coaster, but we're doing really well. Kennedy is growing up way too fast, unfortunately. Thank you for asking."

She pulled away, squeezing my arms as she stepped back. "It's so good to see you. What brings you in today?" She rounded the counter and took a seat on the stool behind the register.

"I think I'm gonna head to the cemetery. I wanted to grab—"

"A dozen red carnations?"

I smiled. "Yes, a dozen red carnations. You have a good memory."

Emily chuckled softly. "You used to visit the cemetery so often; I remember you always chose red carnations. It's a beautiful way to remember him."

For every special occasion, every moment that held some kind of significance to us, Liam always bought me a bouquet of red carnations. It started as a joke; he'd gotten them for me on our first date, thinking they were red roses, and then it just kind of... Stuck.

"I think so, too," I replied quietly.

Emily got to work, preparing a stunning bouquet of a dozen deep red carnations. Her hands moved with the skill of someone who had spent a lifetime arranging flowers, but she moved a little slower these days.

"How's Lila?"

She smiled and shook her head. "Love drunk and soon to be married, I suppose. She met some kid from a few towns over in July or August. Got engaged in October, wanna tie the knot before the end of the year."

"Wow," I breathed. "That's... A lot."

She chuckled and wrapped the flowers in kraft paper. "When you know, you know. I met her daddy in February, got married in May. What's meant to be will be." Emily handed the carefully crafted bouquet over to me. "Besides, you should see her smile. Even if it doesn't work out in the end, her being so happy for the time being can't be a crime."

I pulled my card out of my wallet, and she swatted my hand away.

"On the house, dear. Tell that boy I miss him when you get there."

"I will," I promised. "Thank you, Em. It was good to see you."

"Likewise."

I walked back to Gia's Jeep, the bouquet of red carnations cradled carefully in my arms. As I drove through town, the nostalgia of Evergreen tugged at my heart, reminding me of all the pain and growth I had experienced here.

I drove past the diner, the grocery store, and the park we used to take Kennedy.

But the memories that played through my mind now, the same ones that drove me out of Evergreen to begin with, were no longer laced with an overwhelming sadness. They brought a smile to my face and a warmth to my chest that I hadn't felt since before Liam died. I thought that this town would forever remind me of the most unimaginable pain, but time away, healing on my own, and catching my breath, brought back everything I loved about it.

When I finally pulled into the cemetery, I sat on the road beside his gravesite for a few minutes, staring at where I knew his headstone rested. I'd been in such a different place the last time I walked this path in June. I was barely hanging on, drowning in my grief.

Every time I sat at his grave, I was clinging on to what I had left of him. I was fighting tooth and nail to overcome this heart-stopping pain that lived inside me, searching for something— *anything* to take away the weight on my chest.

It was almost surreal to be here now with such a light feeling in my chest.

Taking a deep breath, I opened the car door and stepped out, the bouquet of red carnations in hand. I stopped around back and grabbed a blanket and Liam's old jacket, the cool breeze rustling through the trees and sending a shiver down my back.

I approached Liam's resting place and knelt down, gently placing the bouquet beside his headstone. The vibrant red of the carnations was a stark contrast to the dying grass and the weathered stone marker. I traced my fingers over his name, feeling a bittersweet mixture of love and loss.

I laid the blanket on the cold ground and sat, pulling my knees to my chest. There was a lot that I had to say to him, but I took a moment to simply breathe, feeling the gentle breeze on my face and listening to the whispers of the leaves in the trees overhead.

The setting sun cast a warm glow over the cemetery, bright reds and oranges blending in the sky, ducking in and out of the clouds. I cleared my throat and rested my chin on my knees.

"I know it's been a while." There was another soft breeze that tugged at my hair, and I smiled softly, telling myself it was his way of letting me know he was here. "Emily said Lila's getting married. Can you believe that? Sometimes I forget that she's not twelve anymore."

I laughed softly and sniffled, my eyes flooding with tears. "God, I miss you." I wiped my cheeks as a few spilled over the edge. "I don't— I don't really know what I want to say. I don't really know what's left to say that I haven't said before. But things just feel... *Different*. I— I never thought I'd be happy again, Li."

My tears were falling faster, spilling over faster than I could wipe them away, so I just let them fall. "Is this wrong? Should I even be telling you this?" I let out a watery laugh. "I never thought that I'd have to exist in a world without you. I never thought I'd have to navigate... love again. You were supposed to be my forever person."

Another breeze swept through the cemetery, and a shiver raced down my spine. I reached over to slide his jacket on, pulling it tight to my body.

"I— I fell in love again. And you know the weirdest part? I think you would love him." I laughed again and wiped my cheeks. "God, he's so great. I wish you could see him with Ken. He— Well, his name is Noah. His wife died a few years ago. And I guess we were just two broken people who figured out how to make each other feel whole again.

"Sometimes, I wonder how it's possible to love two people in such different ways," I mused, my heart heavy with the complexity of my emotions. "But please know that I will never stop loving you, Liam. I'll cherish the beautiful moments we had and the amazing little human that we created. I won't ever let her forget you. I promise."

I traced my finger over his name once more. "I wish there was a way for you to tell me I was doing the right thing. I think that deep down, I *know* you'd want us to be happy. To be loved and cared for. You'd want this... Right?"

I adjusted his jacket around my shoulders and held my breath like I would be able to hear his answer in the wind that rustled the leaves. The sun dipped a little lower into the horizon, another chill sweeping through the air. I shoved my hands into the pockets of his jacket, my brows pinching together as something crinkled against my fingers.

A laugh burst through my lips when I pulled it out, a perfectly wrapped fortune cookie in the palm of my hand. My pulse fluttered as I stared down at the unexpected but somehow completely perfect surprise. With trembling fingers, I gently cracked it open, revealing the tiny slip of paper within. As I unfolded the fragile message, tears flooded my eyes once again, the small red writing becoming a blur as I read.

Something beautiful is on the horizon.

A sob wracked through my chest as the words on the fortune cookie's message came back into focus, and I realized the depth of the sign I had received. Maybe some people would think it was a load of shit, but I knew exactly what it was. Liam's silent answer was clear, a poignant reassurance that everything I stumbled onto in Rose Hill was exactly what he wanted for us. As the sun painted the sky with hues of red and gold, I clung to the hope and promise carried by those simple words.

I tucked the fortune back into the pocket of Liam's jacket for safekeeping and wiped my cheeks with the sleeves. The sun sank lower, casting long shadows over the cemetery, and this sense of closure that I was longing for washed over me.

"Thank you," I whispered, brushing my hand over his headstone again before pushing to my feet.

Leaves crunched behind me, and I jumped, turning quickly and stumbling a few steps back as my mouth parted in surprise.

"Wha—What the hell? You— You're— You're here. How— Why are you here?"

Noah's smile was soft and sweet, the dimple in his cheek popping as he laughed at my blubbering confusion. "You said you needed me." He took a couple of careful steps in my direction, his hands shoved into the pockets of his coat. His hair was brushed out of his face, moving softly with the breeze.

I blinked at him, speechless for a moment, feeling overwhelmed by the emotion of the day and the unexpected sight of him here. Finally, my voice quivered as I managed to say, "Noah, you didn't have to come all the way out here. I mean— The cost of a ticket and the shop being closed. You didn't have to do that for me."

He closed the distance between us, his large, warm hands cupping my face. "I'm here because I want to be. Because I can't imagine my life without you in it. Because I would fly across the world and close the shop permanently for you. Not because you asked me to or because you want me to, but because you mean the world to me, more than I ever thought possible." There was a flicker in his eyes, something that looked a lot like nerves as his brows pulled together. "I love you, Liv."

The butterflies in my stomach swooped into my chest, and my eyes filled with tears once again, but this time they carried nothing but pure, unbridled happiness. My fingers curled into his jacket as I pulled him closer. "You love me?"

Noah's thumbs swiped at the tears flowing down my cheeks. "So fucking much, sweetheart." He paused, his Adam's apple bobbing as he swallowed. "How could I not? Every breath in my lungs, every beat of my heart... It belongs to you. I will, forever and always, be *exactly* where you need me to be."

In hindsight, I probably should've said something back. I should've said everything that I'd been bottling up for the past month about how much I loved him and his black t-shirts and tight jeans or how that love grew even stronger with blue lipstick and butterfly clips and the many beautiful moments he shared with Kennedy. I probably should've said something. But I stood on my tiptoes, and my lips crashed against his in a kiss that melted every last worry that existed inside of me. *Because he loved me.*

He loved me despite all the rough edges and missing pieces of who I used to be.

Noah's fingers threaded into my hair, and I could feel his smile against my mouth and the nervous tension that melted from his body.

Reluctantly, he pulled away, our breath mingling in the space between us in tiny little puffs of air. "Does that mean what I think it does?"

A surprised laugh burst out of me because, honestly, how could he not know? "I love you. In ways that I didn't even realize were possible. Like the stupid kind of love that makes me wanna carve our names into a tree and dedicate a song to you on the radio. I love the way you love Kennedy and how you know exactly what I need when I don't know how to say it.

"I love that you cook for us and take care of us. I love how well you rock purple eye shadow, and I love that you call me Liv and that you love Taylor Swift. Honestly, I think I could keep going, but I hope you get the gist. I am so hopelessly in love with you, Noah Kent."

His smile somehow widened, and my thumb brushed against the dimple on his cheek. "Good, that's good. Otherwise, this would've been really fucking embarrassing."

I threw my head back and laughed, tears slowly trailing down my temples. When I met Noah's gaze again, the look on his face stole the breath from my lungs. His smile was wide, hazel eyes dancing with so much love that my heart squeezed in my chest. My eyes swept over every inch of his face, memorizing every small detail of this moment.

His thumb brushed against the apple of my cheek, and I still couldn't believe he was here in Evergreen.

"Wait, how did you know I was gonna be here?"

Noah's face flushed. "Avery found Gia on Instagram, and Gia has your location. They're best friends now, by the way."

I laughed and shook my head. "Of course."

His lips pressed against the top of my head. "Do you need another few minutes?"

I looked over my shoulder at the red carnations on the grass. "We can go. I think I said what I needed to say."

He cleared his throat. "Do you— Uh— You wanna go back to the car? I think I'll— I'll say something. If that's okay with you?"

"Of course," I breathed, my throat thick with emotion. "I'll be at the car."

I turned and made my way to Gia's Jeep, resting against the hood as Noah kneeled at Liam's headstone.

The low murmur of his voice carried with the wind as he spoke, and I couldn't make out most of what he said, but I knew that whatever he whispered made me love him even more.

I stayed by the car, the soft breeze playing with the edges of my hair as I watched Noah speak to Liam. There was a quiet beauty in the moment, the past and the present coexisting, and the future taking shape.

After some time, Noah stood and brushed his hand over the headstone just as I did. He turned and walked back towards the car. His eyes were glassy with tears.

He reached out and slid his arm around my shoulders, pulling me close. "I love you, Liv," he whispered into my hair.

I nestled into his chest, winding my arms around his waist. "I love you, too."

Grief was tricky. It was messy and fucked up, and it hurt like hell. The healing process was a lot like watching a pot of water come to a boil. The longer you stare, the longer it takes. The more I expected to just wake up and be fine, the longer it took to do just that.

But time doesn't heal all wounds. That was a load of shit. Giving yourself grace and letting yourself process, heals all wounds. Accepting this new reality instead of living in the what-ifs and leaning on the people you love, heals all wounds.

So yes, it was messy and fucked up, and it hurt like hell, all of those things were true. But it was beautiful and bittersweet, and it made me stronger. Liam would always be a part of me, and I never wanted that to change, but Noah patched up the hole in my chest, finally allowing me to breathe.

I wasn't treading water anymore; I was no longer fighting for a peace I was convinced would never come. The waters were still, my heart was full, and I was happy.

Epilogue

Olivia

One year later

Coming back home after leaving Noah and Kennedy alone for a day always put me on edge. It gave me that same sinking feeling I got when Kennedy was two and I left her alone for a *little* too long and the house got a *little* too quiet. The kind of feeling that started with a want to fold a load of laundry and ended with cleaning permanent marker scribbles off of the wall.

I could almost never anticipate the outcome.

Noah had every ounce of my trust and I knew he would take care of her, but he also had a problem with telling her no.

For the most part, it was adorable. It usually just meant extra sugar or a few small gifts here and there. The real issue was Kennedy *knowing* that Noah was at her mercy. My last solo trip to Wilmington ended with a fuzzy little hamster by the name of Bridget now residing in our apartment.

So when I pushed open my front door and was greeted by absolute silence, I knew something was off.

"Hello?" I called out, gently kicking the door shut behind me. I placed my keys on the hooks like I usually did and toed my shoes off, waiting for Kennedy to run in and greet me like she usually did. But I was met with silence.

A suspicious silence.

I took a step and then paused when there was a soft crunch under my socked foot. I sighed and looked down, knowing better than to give them the benefit of the doubt. A tiny piece of straw clung to the cotton as I lifted my right foot.

Straw. Why the *hell* was there *straw* in my apartment?

"Hello?" I called out again, tucking the piece of straw into my pocket and taking another step into the apartment.

Noah slid around the corner, his hands behind his back, and a sheepish grin pulling at his lips. "Have I ever told you how beautiful you are? Just out of curiosity, you meant it when you said you loved me this morning, right?"

"What did you do?"

"Nothing *too* out of pocket. I just *really* need to know you love me before we meander any further into the apartment."

"No one uses a word like 'meander' in a sentence unless they did something they weren't supposed to."

His chest expanded as he sucked in a deep breath, his hands landing on his hips when he exhaled. "I don't think that's true."

"Noah," I deadpanned.

He smiled sweetly and walked over, pressing a lingering kiss to my lips. "I missed you. I love you. And I love Kennedy. And most importantly, you love both of us with your *whole* heart. And... I have a plan."

"What is in my living room?" I asked, trying to peer over his shoulder. Kennedy was still suspiciously quiet. "It's not another hamster, is it?"

Noah pursed his lips and shook his head. "It is *definitely not* a hamster."

My eyes narrowed at the weird emphasis on his words and I stepped around him to head into the living room.

"Just— I need you to know I have a plan!" His words rushed out as I turned the corner and skidded to a stop in the doorway.

Kennedy sat in the middle of a makeshift playpen, surrounded by piles of straw and what looked like puppy pee pads. She aimed her toothless grin in my direction as she raised a bottle to the mouth of a little baby goat. "Hi, Mommy!"

What the fuck?

I whipped around and met Noah's nervous expression with wide eyes. "There's a *goat* in my living room."

"I have a plan," he offered weakly, scrunching his nose.

He was trying to gauge just how upset I was and truthfully, I wanted to be mad. I wanted to be pissed. There was a goat in my living room, after all. But *dammit* when they both looked at me with those wide doe eyes, it was damn near impossible.

"Okay," I sighed, scratching my eyebrow with my thumb. "What's the plan? How the hell did we end up with a goat?"

Noah's eyes widened briefly and he gave Kennedy a low thumbs-up that I immediately smacked away. Kennedy giggled from the playpen and I rolled my eyes.

"Hey, no. None of that," I scolded. "We're not celebrating quite yet. If there's a plan, you better tell me before I come up with one neither of you is going to like. Spill." I crossed my arms over my chest and quirked my brow.

"Well, while you were gone, I took Ken to the petting zoo a few towns over. We got to feed the goats. I talked a little with the owner. They're actually shutting down in a month. A lot of the goats had been relocated or had homes in mind. Most of them... Except for that little lady right there."

My gaze slid over to Kennedy, her hand stroking over the goat's head as she smiled. I melted at the look of contentment on her face. God dammit. His plan better be a good one.

"Kennedy asked if we could take her to my parent's barn. I said yes because how the hell am I expected to tell her no?"

"It's actually very easy. You just look at her and say the word."

"Not possible, I'm afraid. That's how we ended up with a hamster."

"Trust me, Noah. I am well aware of that fact." Despite the small part of me that was adamant I remained at least a little upset, I smiled. "What's your plan?"

He took a deep breath and while the nerves stayed, they seemed to shift in meaning. "We keep her," Noah declared, his eyes locking onto mine. "I know it's impulsive, and I should have consulted you first, but Kennedy's so attached to her already. And, Liv, they're both just so damn cute. I *couldn't* say no."

I sighed, my resolve weakening as I looked at the pair of them. Kennedy was giggling, blissfully unaware of the domestic chaos she'd brought into our lives. The little goat continued to suck on the bottle of milk held out in front of her, seemingly content in her newfound home.

"Goats don't exactly thrive in apartments," I noted, shifting my eyes back to

Noah.

He swallowed, wringing his hands together. "That's part two of the plan. What if we... build a house? I know you don't want to live in my house and I understand why. So... I sold it. Or... am selling it. There's a plot of land a few miles away from my parents. We could create our own little beautiful destination in Delaware."

I blinked, caught a little off guard. We'd talked about this before and it made sense. We spent basically every waking moment together, but I wasn't sure how I felt about living in the home he shared with Addie. There were just so many precious memories of the two of them together, and even though he insisted I wouldn't, I didn't want to overstep.

That resulted in a lot of sleepovers here at the apartment, but we were quickly figuring out it was just too small to be sustainable. I knew we were staying in Rose Hill, but the real estate business wasn't exactly booming, so that left us with few options to move forward.

"You want to build a house with me?"

Noah's smile melted into something impossibly sweet. "And so much more. I want to build a *life* with you, Liv."

He squeezed my hand and I blinked back the tears forming in my eyes.

"I think in order to do that, we need somewhere fresh; somewhere new that's just... us. Somewhere Ken can have a hundred goats and you can have a dog... Or five. Somewhere we can settle and finally be a family."

I took a shaky breath as he pulled me into his chest, his lips brushing against the top of my head. "You're making it really hard to be upset about the goat in my living room."

Noah chuckled and wrapped his arms around my shoulders. "What do you think, sweetheart? Does that sound like something you want?"

My chin rested on his sternum as I looked up at him with a grin. "I love it. I want it. All of it."

The End.

Acknowledgments

I want to start by thanking my wonderful husband, Nick. We've both made a ton of sacrifices to make this book happen and I am forever grateful for everything you've done to make this dream of mine come true. I will never be able to tell you just how much I love you. Thank you for designing the cover and thank you for editing. Thank you for constantly doing everything in your power to ease my mental load and giving me grace while we tried to figure out how to balance making all of this come to life. I am so incredibly thankful for your love and support.

Thank you to our families for sacrificing some of their weekends to babysit so I could meet my self-imposed deadlines and sleep in on the days I stayed awake until three in the morning.

To The Real Housewives of St. Louis (Maddie, Maizee, and Steph), I love you guys so much. Thank you for listening to my rants and being the best support system a girl could ask for. There are a lot of things that I'm grateful for when it comes to you guys, but I can't tell you how much that night in Hermann meant to me. I'm not one to put myself on the line and seeing your faces when I told you I was writing a book made every nerve worth it. Thank you for giving up what little free time you have to give me advice and notes because I constantly let imposter syndrome get the best of me. Thank you for being the best friends and the best aunties!

To my Canadian soul-sister, Megan, thank you for constantly supporting all of my crazy ideas and being the best sounding board when I need to figure shit out. Thank you for believing in me and yelling at me when I fail to recognize my worth. Thank you for always supporting my work and being the best cheerleader.

To everyone who has loved and supported me on this journey, thank you!

It's been a crazy two years but I'm so incredibly grateful and I can't wait to see what else is in store.

Manufactured by Amazon.ca
Acheson, AB